CRYSTAL
GLOBE

The Haves and Have-Nots of the
New World Order

Marvin Cetron • Owen Davies

ST. MARTIN'S PRESS • NEW YORK

Design by Anne Scatto

Library of Congress Cataloging-in-Publication Data

Cetron, Marvin J.
   Crystal globe: the haves and have-nots of the new world order /
order /
Marvin Cetron and Owen Davies.
      p. cm.
   Includes index.
   ISBN 0-312-06325-3
   1. International economic relations. 2. Twenty-first century—
Forecasts. I. Davies, Owen. II. Title.
HF1359.C43   1991
337'.09'049—dc20   91-19065
                                                               CIP

First Edition: September 1991
10 9 8 7 6 5 4 3 2 1

*This book, like all we do, is dedicated to our wives,
without whose tireless support and precious companionship
little would be possible and even less
would be worth doing.*

CONTENTS

The Four-Part World
of the Year 2000

"The world will be a more peaceful and prosperous place
. . . because the rules by which it is governed have changed.
In the coming years it will no longer be ruled to suit the
needs of ideological and military competition, but instead,
to promote international trade and the well-being of the
trading nations."

In the late 1940s, the treaties that ended World War II set the
stage for a new kind of conflict, a confrontation between impla-
cably hostile superpowers. This battle for global supremacy was
fought in the main by proxy, often in the guise of homegrown
revolution, but there was never any doubt that the real contest
was between the irreconcilable ideologies of the United States
and the Soviet Union. Virtually the entire industrialized world
belonged to one camp or the other, and many of the developing
lands as well. Nations on the outside seldom wielded much influence in international affairs, and few of them reaped the benefits of superpower patronage.

In an odd way, this division served the world far better than
we usually acknowledge. Under the threat of atomic war, the
West achieved an approximate unity of purpose as it rebuilt the
economies destroyed by the Second World War. The defeated
nations of Japan and (West) Germany found places among the
leaders of the "free world." And if the East bloc territories failed
to prosper, Soviet domination at least suppressed the murderous
rivalries between Czechs and Slovenes, Serbs and Croatians, Armenians and Azerbaijanis—hatreds that centuries of intermittent

war had failed to quell. It was an inefficient and sometimes dangerous way to run a world, but for more than four decades it provided the only political structure capable of doing the job since the decline of the *Pax Britannica* early in this century. The forty-five years from the end of the Second World War through 1990 were the longest period of peace among the world's major powers in modern history.

The cold war between West and East is now over, both in the official rhetoric of Washington and Moscow and in the realities of political and economic control. In economic terms, the Soviet Union has unquestionably lost; the inefficiencies of central planning, combined with the inevitably bloated and sluggish bureaucracy, have reduced the country to near starvation. Soviet political power has suffered as well; former Soviet client Saddam Hussein recently went so far as to declare that the world now has only one superpower, the United States. Yet this does not mean that America won the cold war, as its leaders once fantasized. The United States does not rule the hearts and minds of an admiring world any more than the Soviet *politburo* still rules the governments of Hungary, Poland, the late East Germany—or even those of its own republics. The political and military structure that gave order to the world for some forty years has been swept away, and no new arrangement has yet arisen to replace it. What new power will fill this vacuum is the primary topic of this book and one of the questions that most tantalize political and economic forecasters, newspeople, and everyday citizens around the world. There are many other economic and political concerns that will dominate the remainder of the 1990s. Among them are:

• *Glasnost* was born in the mid-1980s as Mikhail Gorbachev's attempt to modernize the Soviet economy, left in the doldrums from years of Brezhnevite stagnation and degradation; ironically, while it seemed poised to destroy the nation, *glasnost* helped stave off the August 19, 1991 coup attempt—the proliferation of photocopiers, fax machines, and personal computers with modems made it impossible for the putsch to shut down communications. All of the USSR's fifteen component republics have declared their sovereignty, and many of them have suffered rebellions of their own. The coup appears to have been in large part a response to this instability by Party hard-liners who feared their own loss of power. It may yet prove to be the mistake that ends the dominance of Soviet reactionaries. But what happens if the Party—the only force that has managed to hold the nation together, despite an extraordinary variety of ethnic hatreds—at last falls? Will the Soviet Union dissolve into chaos, as it did in 1917 and 1918? Will the Red Army panic and impose its own harsh order? Or—on the surface it hardly seems possible—will Mikhail Gorbachev or his political heirs find some way to recast Moscow's empire into a voluntary confederation in the Canadian mold?"

• In the Middle East, it appeared briefly in 1990 that tensions might finally be about to ease. The bloody Iran-Iraq war had finally ended in 1988. Yasir Arafat, on behalf of his Palestinian Liberation Organization, had renounced terrorism, and though his sincerity might be doubted, the simple statement seemed a positive development. Even Lebanon's chaos appeared to be winding down. Then Saddam Hussein invaded Kuwait in August of 1990. Four months later, the world went to war against Iraq, and we all know how that turned out. Will the United Nations manage to dismantle Iraq's chemical, biological, and nuclear weapons programs? Will Saddam yet be deposed?" Will Kuwait build a more democratic constitutional monarchy under the al-Sabah dynasty? Will America's new prestige finally bring an end to the long years of war and terrorism in the region?

• As 1990 began, it seemed that South Africa would finally awake from the long nightmare of *apartheid*. Nelson Mandela was released from prison. The African National Congress (ANC) had been legalized. Talks between the government and black leaders were finally in the planning. But in a few short months, that long-awaited progress seems to have evaporated. By mid 1991, Winnie Mandela was convicted of charges of kidnapping and assault; followers of the Zulu Inkatha movement, funded by the government, and abetted by the police, had declared war on the ANC; and no fewer than seventy-eight right-wing organizations had arisen to block any rapprochement with the nation's black majority, including more than thirty paramilitary and terrorist groups. Will President de Klerk find some way to calm the situation, or will South Africa explode into civil war? Not even the periodic attempts of the Soviet right to bring back the "good old days" when their power was unquestioned can seriously impede the political evolution now taking place. It was born in the policies of Mikhail Gorbachev and made permanent by the withdrawal of Soviet troops from Eastern Europe and by the formation of the coalition that fought the Gulf War.

Despite all these uncertainties, and thousands of others like them, the outlines of a new, more flexible world order are already clear. The world will be a more peaceful and prosperous place in the 1990s than it has been in the decades since World War II because the premises by which it is governed have changed. In the coming years it will no longer be ruled to suit the needs of ideological and military competition, but instead, to promote international trade and the well-being of the trading nations. Major military conflicts will be all but unthinkable because they are contrary to the mutual interests of the trading nations. War will not suddenly disappear, but it will no longer be sponsored by the superpowers and resolved only at their convenience. Instead, conflicts will stem from local antagonisms and the ambitions of Third World rulers, and peace will be restored by the joint effort of the entire world community, by boycott and blockade whenever possible, with the might of the United States and the Soviet Union held in reserve until it is clear that bloodless measures have failed. This fundamental change will be the guiding theme of the 1990s, much as the defeat of Nazism was the great work of the 1940s.

Politically this will be an interesting era, for nations will increasingly band together, however briefly, even with traditional enemies, to further their short-term interests. We can already see the beginnings of this trend in the 1990–91 crisis in the Middle East. Irag and Iran officially ended their eight-year war only in September 1990, more than a million of their citizens dead. In the Gulf War, Iran largely adhered to United Nations policy. Yet its sympathies clearly lay with its former enemy; the Ayatollah Ali Khamenei even called for a holy war against the forces mobilized against Irag in the Persian Gulf. As the Persian Gulf crisis developed, diplomacy was reborn as it existed before NATO and the Warsaw Pact were forged, as it was in nineteenth-century Europe, during and after the age of Metternich, a constant maneuvering for national advantage in a network of shifting alliances.

No single nation will have the power to dominate this new global order. World leaders will not be military powers; these will be replaced by three powerful regional economic blocs now coming to dominate international commerce. Each group will be heavily influenced by its largest members, but from now on nations will act primarily by consensus in all matters of common interest.

The most powerful of these blocs will be the European Community (EC), which will begin to lower its internal trade barriers in 1992 and hopes to complete the job late in this decade. By the turn of the century, the European nations will have built a loose confederation with a level of effective unity not previously seen outside the states of the United States.

The second major economic bloc will be the Pacific Rim—Japan, Taiwan, Singapore, Hong Kong and Macao (while they remain British and Portuguese colonies), Korea (both North and South, possibly as a single nation), Australia, New Zealand, and mainland China. Early in this period Japan will continue to dominate its neighbors. Later, as its hidden economic and social weaknesses make themselves felt, this giant will lose much of its influence in the region and in the world. Mainland China, which will then include Hong Kong, Macao, and—by voluntary reunion—Taiwan, will slowly abandon its hard-line communism and adopt capitalist ways; in doing so, it will gain much of the leadership that Japan will lose. By the year 2000, the People's Republic will have far more in common with today's Taiwan and Hong Kong than with its present-day self.

The third major bloc will be the North American alliance—made up primarily of the United States and Canada. Economically, they will be united by the free-trade agreement signed in 1988, and the process of economic unification that will continue in stages through 1998. There is every chance that Canada will also be absorbed politically within the next ten years by its giant southern neighbor, save for the intensely independent province of Quebec. If Mexico can bring its economy under control it too will join this economic confederation, though not a political union; this process already seems well under way. And President Bush's "Enterprise for the Americas" proposal may enlist the rest of Latin America into the structure, offering those nations a chance at the prosperity they have never been able to achieve on their own.

Vast regions of the earth will be left out of this interlocking arrangement, save on occasions when they can serve the interests of the major powers. The Middle East will retain much of its wealth and poorly regulated influence, thanks to the continued importance of oil. Africa, the Indian subcontinent, and Southeast Asia will remain much as they are now, little more than stockpiles of raw material, doomed, largely by their own leaders, to poverty and exploitation by the industrialized nations. Yet even they should benefit from the new global structure. In a more peaceful and prosperous world, the developed nations will have a better opportunity to help their less fortunate neighbors deal with economic and social problems, to whatever extent local politics allows it. Progress will come slowly in the Third World, but it will move more quickly under the new commercial priorities than it did under ideological and military domination.

All this is clear, even inevitable. The proverbial old walls are coming down, and more useful structures are replacing them. But international change must be accomplished by national governments; it can go only as fast and far as local pressures allow. We do not yet know how severely national politics—the game of partisan backbiting that subordinates long-term benefits to the interests of transient campaign advantage—will interfere with the global transformation now taking place. So far the evidence is not wholly encouraging, but neither is it entirely gloomy.

When the European Community (EC) announced its pending unification, many economists feared that it would surround itself with almost impenetrable trade barriers, making it impossible for others to benefit from the change. Such a move would have prompted the North American and Pacific Rim nations to erect barriers of their own, touching off an all-out trade war. So far, that has not happened. Instead, in electronics, aerospace, chemicals, and pharmaceuticals—four high-tech markets crucial to both American and Japanese interests—the EC has adopted product standards based closely on those of the United States. This will make it dramatically easier for the rest of the world to do business with Europe.

As recently as mid-1990, Europe's restraint seemed to offer the hope that eliminating trade barriers within the great economic regions might presage the removal of barriers between them. In that case, the developed world's economic growth could well surpass the rate of exponential gain registered by the United States in the 1950s—and this time, everyone would share in it, not just those American corporations whose overseas competitors were bombed out of existence during the Second World War. Recently, however, overwhelming political pressure within the United States and the European Community has halted progress toward that goal.

What may have been the turning point—from singular national competition toward economic alliances of regional blocs—came at the so-called Uruguay Round of the General Agreement on Tariffs and Trade (GATT). Since 1947, the one hundred member nations of the GATT have been bound not to discriminate against other nations in international trade. Most have done so anyway. The EC bans imports of U.S. beef and pork on the pretext that American ranchers dose their animals with growth-promoting hormones; the real purpose of this so-called health measure is to protect inefficient European farmers against outside competition. France once ruled that Japanese VCRs must enter the country through a single inland "port," where there was only one customs official to process the necessary paperwork. For its part, the United States has negotiated "voluntary" agreements to restrict imports of Japanese automobiles and erected a broad range of obstacles to foreign companies in banking, insurance, and other service industries. Yet modern trade restrictions have been far less destructive than in the days when America's Smoot-Hawley Tariff Act of 1929 stifled international trade and worsened the world into the Great Depression. Tariffs on manufactured goods fell from an average of 40 percent in 1945 to only 5 percent in the 1980s. As a result, between 1950 and 1975, the volume of trade grew by some 500 percent, twice as fast as the output of goods and services.

GATT originally dealt only with trade in manufactured goods. A major purpose of the Uruguay Round was to extend its liberalizing influence into such areas as agriculture, foreign investment, services, and the protection of intellectual property, such as video recordings and computer software. These are all necessary components of any trade agreement comprehensive enough to rule out economic warfare between Europe, America, and the Pacific Rim. But more than four years after it began, in September 1986, none of these issues has been resolved, and the Uruguay Round is near its final collapse. Europe's farmers, and particularly those of France, are too powerful for their governments to sign any agreement that would open their markets to competition. So are America's banks, stock brokerage firms, insurance companies, and other financial services industries. So are Japan's rice farmers and small merchants, as the United States has often found. There is little evidence that these obstacles will soon be overcome.

Yet this does not mean that the peace and prosperity we forecast will evaporate as so many other hopes have done in recent years. Superpower militarism of the kind practiced by Stalin and Hitler is mostly a thing of the past, and the European, American, and Pacific trading blocs are large enough to grow strong on their own. It does mean that we will not immediately gain all the benefits of unobstructed world trade. When the twenty-first century arrives, more work will remain to be done.

In the pages that follow, we will examine many of the issues to be resolved in the coming decade and map out the world that will emerge from today's ferment. If the new global community is not perfect, it will at least be a much better system to live under than the cold war world we have endured since Yalta and the end of the war in 1945.

PART ONE

EUROPE

INTRODUCTION

Twice in this century, the distribution of world power has changed dramatically. World War I swept away the great empires of the 1800s, leaving little more than chaos in their place. World War II impressed upon that disorder a new, bipolar structure in which the totalitarian countries of the East vied with the self-described free world for domination of powerless developing nations. In each case, the forces that realigned the planet were unleashed in Europe.

In the late 1980s, there began yet a third remarkable change in the distribution of world power; for the result, we have accepted President Bush's term, "the new world order." This time, the basic contest was not limited to Europe, but instead stretched from the Soviet Union in Asia to the United States in the New World. Yet the rivalry was at its most intense, and the stakes were highest, on the Continent. And when the cold war finally thawed, it was Europe that changed first and most dramatically. It is in Europe that the new world order will be refined during the 1990s.

The nations of the European Community decided the structure of the new world economy when they adopted their ambitious plan to unify their economies. Japan's modern version of the Greater East-Asia Co-Prosperity Sphere and the North American free-trade zone are a direct response to the fear that Europe may wall itself in behind a barrier of tariffs and trade restrictions, and thus deprive the other trading nations of markets they desperately need. Europe's decisions on these issues will set the rules by which the new trading blocs will deal with one another.

However, the political precedents now being set in Eastern

Europe may be even more important than the economic choices of the West. The Soviet Union is watching closely to see whether its former client states can make the difficult transition from totalitarian communism to democratic capitalism without erupting into civil war or collapsing in ruin. The results will help to determine whether Soviet hard-liners or reformers win their current struggle to control the future of the USSR. And that, in turn, will decide whether the superpowers make a lasting peace or return to the *realpolitik* of the postwar years.

In Part I we begin our study of the new world order by looking at the changes of the Old World. Once more, this time peacefully and unexpectedly, Europe is redefining our world.

··

Role Model for the Post-Postwar World

"By 2015, the three-hundred-mile trip from London to Paris will take less than three hours. It will be possible to board a morning train in London and get off in Lisbon, Hanover, Amsterdam, or Marseilles later that day."

··

At the beginning of the 1980s, Europe's economy was foundering. Industrial productivity was low and economic growth was slow to nonexistent; interest rates were high, unemployment even higher. And Fortress Europe, as it was sometimes known was still the center of the cold war, divided by Winston Churchill's iron curtain and fortified on both sides against possible invasion. Yet less than ten years from now, around 2000, the Continent could enjoy the largest, most vibrant regional economy in the world.

The European Community's plan to accomplish this monumental economic transformation began several years before the Soviet Union set free its European vassal states. Today, the changes first wrought in Europe in the late 1980s have already evolved into a political and economic system that will govern the entire Continent for many years to come. The nature of that government is still being debated intensely, and much of the original vision, of a free and united European confederation, may be diluted or lost as concept is turned into reality. Yet the EC has already set an example that the rest of the world is poised to follow.

Like the United States and the Soviet Union, the nations of Western Europe are putting aside political barriers and national antagonisms that have lasted for decades, and in some cases centuries. According to plan, in 1992 the thirty-two-year-old Common Market will at last begin to live up to its name. By then, the twelve nations of the European Community will abandon their mutual tariffs and trade quotas, and adopt common product standards. A year later, Belgium, France, Germany, Italy, Luxembourg, and the Netherlands are scheduled to open their borders to free travel by citizens of the other nations; and Britain, Portugal, and Spain are likely to ratify the plan before 1991 is over. The result will be a monolithic economy like no other in the world, at least 340 million people doing business at a rate of $4 trillion per year.

That is only the beginning. Before the end of the century, the EC hopes to establish Continent-wide citizenship rules, build common foreign and defense policies, unify their monetary policies, and even issue its own international money, the "hard ECU," or European currency unit. (As it stands, the ECU is little more than an accounting device, used by Europe's central banks to balance the books in foreign exchange.) By 2000, Italians, Spaniards, and Germans may all be Europeans in the same way that Vermonters, Texans, and Californians are all Americans.

Since 1986, when the EC officially adopted the goal of Continental union, progress has been remarkably rapid. By the end of 1990, the Eurocommunity had proposed no fewer than 279 changes designed to eliminate trade barriers; 183 had been adopted. There are no longer any restrictions on capital flow between EC nations. Customs barriers are scheduled to fall in 1993. All the member states, with the exception of the United Kingdom, have agreed to form a European central bank in 1994, and Britain is expected to join the plan now that Margaret Thatcher has been replaced by Prime Minister John Major, who seems relatively sympathetic toward the European union.

Even more impressive, the European Community is knitting itself together physically, not just in theory. The English Channel tunnel is only one link in a network of bridges, tunnels, and high-speed railroads that will cost some $100 billion. By 2015, the three-hundred-mile trip from London to Paris will take less than three hours. It will be possible to board a morning train in London and get off in Lisbon, Hanover, Amsterdam, or Marseilles later that day. (Now, if only one could board a train in Scarsdale and be sure of getting off in New York City the same day. . . .) The trip from Madrid to Seville alone now takes seven hours; by 1992, when this leg of the new rail line is scheduled for completion, it will require only three. There is no way to estimate at this point exactly how strongly this new freedom of travel will stimulate the European economy, but port cities from New York and Chicago to Rotterdam, Marseilles, and Hong Kong have been built on similar foundations.

Yet Greater Europe faces some problems that will hamper it in taking advantage of its size. One problem is practicality: It is a lot easier to rewrite product standards, and even to build new rail lines, than it is to change the electrical outlets and associated infrastructure of a continent. Until that is accomplished, European TV makers will still have to stock and pay for more than a dozen different kinds of plugs, power supplies adapted for three different voltages, and receivers tailored to no fewer than seven transmission systems. Outside of the chemical and pharmaceutical industries, most manufacturers will continue to face similar obstacles. The EC has managed to replace its patchwork of incompatible mobile telephone systems with a single network, but that was only the easiest of many such problems.

Another hurdle is economic. It costs money to make the changes implied by unification; modifying national electrical systems is just one of many such problems. Privatization of government-owned companies is nearly as great a challenge in the EC as it is in Eastern Europe. Between 20 percent and 40 percent of the Common Market economics have been nationalized; returning these firms to private hands will take a substantial investment. This task alone may require more capital formation than is available for investment on the Continent. It will cost even more to bring the backward factories of Eastern Europe up to Western standards, and the European Community will be expected to shoulder much of that burden. We will look at that problem in Chapter 4.

A particularly insidious problem is bureaucratic. For several years, EC regulators have been poring over the vast array of product standards, work rules, and liability practices in effect in the nations of Europe, setting regulations to be followed by the entire community. Like bureaucrats everywhere, they will inevitably select the most stultifying restrictions they can find; this problem has already been confirmed by some of the decisions coming out of EC headquarters in Brussels. The combination of short workweeks, long vacations, strong unions, comprehensive health benefits, and many other requirements that limit productivity while raising the cost of doing business will give Europe a competitive disadvantage in the world's export markets.

But, inevitably, the most important and difficult challenges are political. Some of the proposed changes have stirred powerful, sometimes violent opposition among people who have benefited from the status quo, such as the farmers who have profitted from hefty subsidies. The transition may also be slowed by the unexpected need to integrate the nations of Eastern Europe into the rest of the Continent. And hidden behind the seemingly nuts-and-bolts proposals for unification are some profound philosophical questions that must be answered before Britain and some other nations will be comfortable with the new union. There is little doubt that Europe will soon be united; what form it will take is still unclear.

Ten years from now, at least four major issues will have been resolved:

One relatively easy question is how much of Europe will find its way into the consolidated trading bloc. Though the 1992 plan was intended to unite only the nations of the European Community, it is already clear that the EC is just part of the alliance now coming into being.

To the European Community, add the European Free Trade Association (EFTA), a miniature EC for nations that do not belong to the original. Its six wealthy members—Austria, Finland, Iceland, Norway, Sweden, and Switzerland—do business unrestrictedly with the Common Market countries but have no political ties with them. Austria, which until the cold war was clearly over shunned the EC in order to preserve its political neutrality, has already applied for Community membership, and seems likely to be granted it. In 1996, give or take a year, Switzerland, Norway, and perhaps Finland will probably enter the European

Community as well, expanding the core bloc to more than 400 million people.

Factor in as well, the former Soviet satellites in Eastern Europe that are quickly achieving associate-member status in the Continental partnership; Hungary, Poland, Yugoslavia, and even the Soviet Union reportedly asked about joining the EFTA as early as Autumn of 1989. At least Poland and Hungary, the most westernized of the former Soviet satellites in Eastern Europe, will receive apprentice-member status by the mid-1990s. Czechoslovakia may be admitted directly to the EFTA or EC. The attempted Soviet coup of August 1991 may well bring membership years closer for all the Eastern European nations, as the EC countries try to promote economic and political stability in the former Soviet satellites, and in the Soviet Union itself.

By the turn of the century, the European bloc will include some twenty-three nations with 520 million people and a gross domestic product of roughly $5 trillion. Even the Soviet Union itself may become an associate member of the EC, if it manages to convert its economy to private enterprise—a difficult forecast to make as this is written; this would swell the European market to nearly 800 million people! America's GNP, in contrast, is $4 trillion, Japan's only $2 trillion; their combined population is less than 375 million.

It is less certain just how free Europe's markets will really be. As the deadline for removing trade barriers draws near, the powerful cartels that run some of the Continent's major industries have remembered that "open market" is another way of saying "competition." Suddenly the idea seems less appealing than when it was no more than a far-off dream. Both within the European Community and in foreign trade, the anticipated free market of 1992 will retain some familiar barriers after all.

EC trade policy has long been at its worst in agriculture, where tiny, inefficient farms are protected by a huge, costly network of trade restrictions, tariffs, and government subsidies. Wheat, for example, trades elsewhere at a price of about $80 per ton; in Europe, thanks to price supports and antiquated production methods, the price is $230. Yet EC farmers export about one-sixth of the grain sold in the world market. The reason is an "export refund" of $150 per ton, a government handout that costs Third World farmers, whose products cost less to grow and deliver, export sales worth perhaps $5 billion per year. European farmers are understandably hostile to the idea of open markets; when American negotiators at the recent GATT talks demanded that Europe lower its tariffs and price supports, French farmers responded with street riots, and even burned alive a truck load of two hundred unsubsidized British sheep. EC negotiators rejected lower tariffs and price supports and refused even to discuss export refunds. They even demanded new tariffs on imported farm products now exempt from them. Since then, EC Agriculture Commissioner Ray MacSharry has been working to reform the European subsidy program, but there is no sign that any major changes will soon be made. So much for a free market.

The auto industry is another example. European carmakers have used a variety of government-sponsored or government-tolerated restrictions to wring the greatest possible profit from Continental consumers. One restriction is national quotas: France allows Japanese makers just 3 percent of its auto market, Italy only 1 percent. Another is the block exemption that prohibits retailers from buying cars in countries where prices are relatively low—Ireland, perhaps, or Denmark—and reselling them in France, Spain, or Italy, where prices can be 60 percent higher. Even individuals who want to import a single car for their own use must cope with a variety of regulations with little purpose other than to make the process inconvenient and costly.

The EC once promised to do away with national quotas and other such barriers to free trade. As this is written, it is considering a move to tighten the block exemption, making it still more difficult to trade cars across national borders. The Brussels Eurocrats have already agreed to retain quotas until 1998. After that, they would be replaced by so-called voluntary restraint agreements that will serve the same function. The new system would be even more restrictive than the old, because these restraints will limit sales, not only of imported automobiles, but also of cars built under Japanese brand names in European factories. Making these trade barriers voluntary, if only in name, neatly sidesteps the fact that they are illegal under both EC policy and the General Agreement on Tariffs and Trade.

The EC is making similar concessions in air transport. Airlines have always been one of Europe's most heavily regulated industries, and the rules are tailored to minimize competition and maximize corporate profits. Until 1987 only two national airlines were allowed on each route; prices were fixed, and the two airlines divided the permitted number of seats between them. Under current rules, newly licensed airlines—but not those existing prior to 1987—may fly any routes they wish and may discount the official prices by as much as 70 percent—if the destination country allows the proposed reduction. So far, none has.

Officially, this anticompetitive system will come to an end in 1993. Governments will lose the power to veto price cuts, opening the way to price wars like those that have reshaped U.S. aviation. Proposed regulations would force EC member nations to license anyone wishing to enter the industry, provided they have the money, skill, and equipment to run a safe, reliable airline. Yet in practice, not much will change. The licensing initiative has been tabled, and no new airlines will be allowed to fly the unfriendly skies of Europe until the Brussels bureaucrats can write uniform licensing regulations—no earlier than mid-1992. The existing flag airlines have grandfather rights to the takeoff and landing slots at Europe's busy airports, meaning that new competitors may be unable to get in or out of Orly, Heathrow, Frankfurt, or the Continent's other crucial transportation hubs. And the EC has ruled that existing airlines may continue to fix their prices jointly, rather than compete in anything that resembles an open market.

None of these developments offers much hope that Europe will build a truly free market in the next ten years.

To anyone familiar with the European Community's philosophy and structure, that comes as no surprise. At present, there is nothing at all democratic about it. The freely elected European Parliament is little more than a symbol; the real power lies with the fourteen thousand hired bureaucrats of the European Commission and with the European Court, whose verdicts on EC policy can overrule national governments on issues formerly considered matters of sovereignty. And these Eurocrats have little love for the decentralized, free-market approach dear to Britain's former prime minister, Margaret Thatcher.

Both the European Community and its unification plan were crafted largely by Jacques Delors, president of its governing council. President Delors is one of the few influential Europeans who, after the failure of socialism in Eastern Europe, still declares himself a socialist. His model for the future Europe is not America, where state governments retain powers that Washington may not touch, but something like the Soviet Union of old, where nominally independent states were ruled by *dictat* from Moscow. The free-market approach is not his way of doing things. It was the conflict between his vision and Mrs. Thatcher's, and not traditional British insularity, that inspired the United Kingdom's go-slow approach to unification. Resolving it will be one of the most difficult and important issues of the 1990s.

To date, this battle has been fought on the territory of monetary and financial policy. Unifying national fiscal and monetary practices throughout the EC has long been one of Jacques Delors's prime objectives. In the long run, the Delors plan will strip the national central banks of their power to set national monetary policy and replace them with a single European bank modeled on the U.S. Federal Reserve Board. Like most of his other goals, Delors means to impose this system from Brussels down. In 1988 the European Court ruled that Britain must extend its value-added tax to cover industries previously immune. It was the first time any outside body had tried to force taxes on the House of Commons since King Charles I decreed his ship tax in the seventeenth century, a mistake that cost him both his crown and the head that wore it.

Despite this, it seems increasingly likely that Britain will eventually accept the Delors plan for European monetary union. In October 1990, Britain took a small step toward union by agreeing to join the EC's "Exchange Rate Mechanism," fixing the exchange rate between the pound and the deutschemark, though only under such stringent conditions that skeptics doubt the change will ever go into effect. A month later, eleven of the EC's twelve national leaders set January 1, 1994, as the day when a European central bank will open for business and agreed in principle to replace national currencies by the hard ECU later in the decade. Britain refused, but Prime Minister John Major offered a market-oriented alternative: issue the hard ECU as a thirteenth currency. Over time, the marketplace would probably adopt it in preference to the national monies now in use.

In fact, that process has already begun. France, Italy, Spain, and several other EC members have begun to issue government bonds in offerings of up to $2 billion denominated in "soft" ECUs. Fiat has announced a joint venture to manufacture 300,000 automobiles per year in the Soviet Union, conducting all business in ECUs. And executives at Philips, the Dutch manufacturing giant, estimate that doing business in ECUs could save the company $300 million per year. With that kind of incentive, the days of the British pound, deutschemark, lira, and franc are numbered.

Whether the transition is made by centralized authority or the free-market approach, the EC's monetary policy will probably look about the same a decade from now. But if the Delors plan wins out, the precedent will eventually give Brussels at least as much power over Europe's national governments as Washington enjoys over American states. For nations such as France, Germany, and Italy, where democracy has never achieved a long, stable tradition, that idea is relatively easy to accept. Britain, whose Magna Carta dates back to 1215, could hold out against it for many years. Rather than face such a stalemate, we believe the European Community will loosen its centralist policies and adopt a free-market version of monetary union. At the turn of the century, the Bank of England may still reign over the British pound, but the ECU will dominate international commerce.

As Europe works to unite its economy, a similar process is taking place in the arena of foreign policy. Diplomatically and militarily, the new Europe presents a bewildering network of overlapping alliances whose roles have been shifting almost daily since Mikhail Gorbachev loosened his country's grip on Eastern Europe.

The North Atlantic Treaty Organization (NATO), the sixteen-nation military alliance whose forces were designed to repel a Soviet invasion of Western Europe, has clearly lost its original purpose, the comp by Kremlin hard-liners in August 1991 not withstanding. Yet NATO seems unwilling to fade away, in part because the United States sees its power in the organization as its strongest source of influence in the EC and is unwilling to give up that leverage.

The relatively little-known Western European Union (WEU) is a sort of discussion group for security issues, composed of nine of the twelve EC nations: Belgium, France, Germany, Great Britain, Italy, Luxembourg, the Netherlands, Portugal, and

Spain. Its powers are limited, its duties ill-defined. It too seems to have lost its purpose with the decline of East-West hostilities. Italy has suggested transforming the WEU into a strictly European edition of NATO, but so far the proposal has won little backing from the other EC member states.

The Warsaw Pact, NATO's East-bloc counterpart, all but lost its existence when the German Democratic Republic was incorporated into West Germany; East Germany supplied virtually all of the bloc's effective troops outside the Soviet army. It was not long before the Pact dissolved itself legally as well as in fact. Even before that, Hungary, officially a Pact member, declared that it would like to join NATO. The Soviet Union raised little objection to the loss of its former bulwark against the West. Instead, it threw its support to another organization:

The Conference on Security and Cooperation in Europe (CSCE) includes all members of both NATO and the Warsaw Pact—33 European nations, plus the United States and Canada. It was the CSCE whose 1975 summit meeting produced the famed Helsinki Accord, which endorsed the existing European boundaries in trade for Soviet concessions on human rights. Though the CSCE has no troops—until recently it had no permanent organizational structure at all, not even a mailing address—both Soviet and EC supporters have nominated it as the logical defender of the united Europe, replacing both NATO and the Warsaw Pact. A summit meeting late in 1990 moved a step closer to that goal by giving the organization its own legislature (though no power to enforce its resolutions), a secretariat in Prague, and a Conflict Prevention Center in Vienna. Whether this small, powerless organization, more debating society than security structure, can grow into the pivotal role now being offered it remains to be seen.

Some such mechanism is clearly needed. In a continent as unified, politically and economically, as the new Europe aspires to be, there seems little use for national armies. (The Falklands War was one exception, but such conflicts are increasingly rare.) In fact, the whole notion of nation against nation at war has changed, a cataclysmic social revolution in its own right. Henceforth, Europe's battles will be fought on other continents as part of international efforts modeled on the Persian Gulf crisis of 1990 and 1991. The CSCE will probably command them, if only because it is easier to adapt the tools in hand to new purposes than it is to forge new ones.

We believe that NATO, too, is destined to play a much broader part in world affairs. If the CSCE provides the international umbrella for European military commitments, by the turn of the century NATO will supply the troops. In ten years, it will be visibly evolving into a general-purpose European army, the Continent's answer to its global military obligations.

As Europe enters its next millennium, unification of the Continent's economy and diverse foreign policies will give it a level of prosperity and world influence equaled in recent history only by the America of the 1950s. This is true whether Europe structures itself as a democracy of nations or as a centrally directed federation, and whether it deals freely with its partners or continues to surround itself with trade barriers. We will see in later chapters how the United States and Pacific Rim nations are responding to this new and overwhelming competition.

One *Deutschland—*
Über Alles?

"If the average East German worker, aided by western methods, is capable of producing just $30,000 per year in goods and services—close to a minimum estimate—unification could add almost $300 billion per year to the German economy. . . . Unification will clearly pay for itself in a very short period."

In a very real sense, the history of Europe in the twentieth century has been the history of one nation. Germany fought and lost two wars that reshaped the Continent. In the Cold War that followed, Germany was the potential flash point that could trigger a third world war, the garrison for the shock troops of both superpowers' armies, and the battleground where the bombs of both sides would fall. And in the reconstruction after World War II, West Germany began as the most thoroughly destroyed economy in Europe and ended as the most successful, a leader of the Common Market and one of the most powerful trading nations in the world. Germany will remain the center of European history well into the next century.

The reason, of course, is reunification. On August 30, 1990, the German Democratic Republic's only freely elected government in that nation's forty-five-year history effectively voted itself out of existence. On October 3, 1990, both East and West Germany disappeared from the map of Europe and were replaced by a single country not much different from the one that twice came close to ruling the Continent. Once more, this time peacefully, Germany has reshaped Europe.

The new Germany faces many difficult challenges, all of which must be solved in the 1990s if it is to reshape itself into a single nation with a strong economy and a stable position in world affairs. It must rebuild or replace all the factories and infrastructure in the East, where technology still seems frozen circa 1935. It must find some way to give former East Germans a Western lifestyle, though their income has long been only one-fourth that of their cousins across the border, and industrial productivity in the east runs at only 40 percent of western levels. It must find some way to pay the bills for both these demands, and many others as well; the costs of unification may well total more than $500 billion over ten years. And it must somehow build a new national identity, one that fits the international role expected of so powerful a nation.

The economic problems alone will be a difficult challenge. Because factories in the east are so antiquated, their products cannot compete with western merchandise. Production there fell by more than half in 1990, as factories closed or cut their hours. Of the eight thousand companies, with nearly six million employees, formerly operated by East German state conglomerates, at least one-third will go bankrupt, while the rest will survive only with heroic modernization; an estimated 90 percent would have shut down even before unification if not for emergency loans from the Bonn government. (On election night, in December 1990, Chancellor Helmut Kohl said that Berlin will remain only a symbolic capital and that most of the real German government will stay in Bonn—since then his position has flip-flopped.)

As expected, unemployment has soared. According to East Berlin's official figures, there was no unemployment at all among East Germany's 8.5 million workers until the country adopted the deutschemark. Six months later it had risen to more than 14 percent and is not expected to top out below 25 to 30 percent; a few economists say it could even reach 50 percent. Close to two million more workers have been forced to work part-time. Under the benevolent terms of unification, East German workers whose jobs have been destroyed by competition from the West will receive up to 90 percent of their former salaries. Add in other transfer payments, and the Bonn government will have to supply the East with subsidies totaling one-fourth of the region's annual gross product. In contrast, the postwar Marshall Plan, credited with driving Germany's reconstruction, never amounted to even 4 percent of the nation's GNP.

Coping with unemployment will also strain relations with several of Germany's neighbors. In the past, many of West Germany's less desirable jobs have gone to "guest workers"—or *Gästarbeiter*—imported primarily from Yugoslavia, Italy, Turkey, and Greece. These semipermanent immigrants made up 11 percent of the West German workforce and sent hundreds of millions of deutschemarks back to their home countries each year. By 1993, nearly all of the guest workers will have been returned to their native lands, their jobs taken by former East Germans. This will be a hardship for the people and countries affected, but in the long run this economic loss may be short-lived. Before the decade is over, German economic growth could cause a labor shortage and make it necessary to invite the foreign workers back.

Rebuilding the East's infrastructure will demand enormous public-works spending. During the 1990s it will cost at least $160 billion to bring roads, sewers, airports, and the like up to Western standards. Another $35 billion will go to modernize the telephone system.

Pollution in the East is an even uglier problem. It's worse than Pittsburgh in those post–World War II days when the steel mills belched unprocessed soot and sulfur into the air. Massive electrical plants burn high-sulfur brown coal ripped from open pits surrounding the generators. Buildings in the East, most of them virtually unmaintained since the Communist takeover, are insulated with carcinogenic asbestos, long banned in the West. And EC planners estimate that just halving the level of pollution in the Elbe will cost $17 billion. In all, the cost of installing pollution controls and repairing environmental damage will come to at least $140 billion.

East German consumers did not fare well under Communist leadership, one more problem the new Germany must address. Only 9 percent of households in the former East Germany have telephones. Scarcely more than half of the households own cars, compared with 98 percent of those in the West—until unification came most of them were the pitiful, spartan Trabants, many of them propelled, if it can be dignified as propulsion, by two-cycle engines that no Western manufacturer would mount on a chain saw. Apartments, owned by the state, rent at 1940's prices, and their condition shows that even with East bloc wage scales, no one could afford to maintain them. By one estimate, Germany's new eastern states will need half a million new homes every year through the decade of the 1990s.

Western competition actually lowered East German consumer prices by about 5 percent during 1990. Luxury items like color televisions and coffee, taken for granted in the West, but once scarce in the East, dropped to one-fifth, or even one-tenth, of their price two years earlier. Even with access to western products, living standards in the East will not equal those in the West until at least 1995.

But the biggest challenge will be modernizing East German industry. As a result, Germany is working hard to attract private investment to the East. Government programs will pay up to one-third of the capital required for a start-up or takeover in the East, and generous loan programs add to the region's appeal.

With that incentive, Western companies are rushing to take advantage of the new market in the East. Even before East Germans cast their final vote for unification, Volkswagen had broken ground for a new factory at Mosel; by 1995, it will be turning out the Volks Polo model at a rate of nearly seven hundred per day. Two days after the vote, General Motors moved the first Opel Vectra off its 20,000-per-year assembly line in Eisenach. According to a survey conducted in September 1990, nearly half of the companies in West Germany expect to have invested in the East before 1991 is over.

The most successful of those efforts will probably be the new factories. Most would-be investors who have looked at factories in the East have backed away in horror.

The sorry state of the East German chemical industry reveals just how difficult a chore it will be to modernize what is left of German manufacturing after four decades of Communist rule. The second largest industry in the German Democratic Republic, chemical manufacturing once employed 335,000 workers and provided 9 percent of the nation's gross domestic product. Since the chemical industry was once considered the pillar of East German manufacturing, and that was the best in all of Eastern Europe, the conventional wisdom held that it should be easy to integrate it into the Western economy. It has not turned out that way.

Take Synthesewerk Schwarzheide, a polyurethane maker with annual sales of close to $370 million. West Germany's BASF did, but only after the government agreed to some stiff terms. BASF got its new subsidiary for free, demanded and received ownership before September 1990, just a few weeks after negotiations began, and it is protected against any liability for Synthesewerk's past pollution. BASF argues that it required such favorable terms because the East German chemical industry is so backward compared with its Western competitors. Worker productivity amounts to less than half that of Western plants. Most of the formerly East German chemical factories are small and decrepit and, based on pre-1930s technology, they are some of the worst polluters in Europe. The clean-up bill will be enormous. In all, it would be easier for chemical producers simply to close the plants in the East and raise the output of their existing factories to make up the difference.

And this is the best of East Germany's industries. No one has yet dared to guess how difficult it will be to modernize the rest of the economy built under Communist rule. Many steel factories are in the same condition, and the copper and potash industries are even worse.

Germany once hoped to recoup a significant portion of the cost of modernizing the East by selling off the eight thousand companies formerly owned by the Communist government—assets that Treuhandanstalt, the holding company running the sell-off, estimate are worth $400 billion. But the Synthesewerk Schwarzheide sale was one of privatization's rare triumphs. By the end of 1990, Treuhandanstalt managed to sell fewer than 250 companies, raising scarcely $700 million in the process. Just scraping up working capital to keep the rest operating, cost some $20 billion in loan guarantees.

Even when the assets on the block are relatively attractive, it has proved difficult to get hard cash for them. One of the few profitable companies Treuhandanstalt had to offer was Planeta A.G., one of the world's most successful manufacturers of large-format offset presses. Planeta yielded about $350 million in sales in 1990. Yet after six months of trying, it was sold to Koenig & Bauer A.G., a West German printing firm. The buyer put no money down; instead, it agreed to keep two-thirds of Planeta's 5,500 employees, raising their pay from the five dollars an hour that East Germany considered adequate, to the twenty-two dollars expected in the West, and to feed $30 million in working capital into their new acquisition. In the largest buyout to date, a consortium of West German firms paid bargain rates for three-fourths of the East's three largest energy producers and the controlling interest of eleven smaller firms. Again, the price itself was low, but the buyers agreed to upgrade the powerplants at a cost of $20 billion. With the best companies' properties difficult to sell and average-to-poor ones all but impossible, Germany has had to cut dramatically the profits it expects from the sales. The consensus now is that it will have a hard time netting even $10 billion from the transactions.

That disappointment has helped to breathe new life into privatization in the West. In the 1980s, the West German government raised $6.8 billion by selling off its interest in such companies as Volkswagen; Salzgitter, a steel and engineering firm; and Veba, an energy company. Even after that, the Bundesbank estimates that the government holds well over $250 billion in financial assets, much of which could be sold to private buyers. High on the list are the controlling interest in Lufthansa and sole ownership of Deutsche Telekom, a telecommunications giant with profits of over $2.3 billion per year. Because Deutsche Telekom is owned by the federal post office, it will take an act of parliament before it can be sold to private investors. With merchandise like that to offer, Germany could yet pay the bills for unification.

If any of Europe's nations can afford such costs, it is Germany. By a wide margin, the reunited Germany is the largest and strongest economy in Europe. With a population of nearly 78 million, it is more than one-third larger than France, Italy, or the United Kingdom. At roughly $1.4 billion, its gross national product is proportionally even larger—nearly twice that of Britain. And because of its strict monetary controls, Germany has the lowest inflation rate and highest balance of trade in Europe. Under the EC plan for European monetary union, the deutschemark has become the currency standard for the Continent.

Even for Germany's normally robust economy, the 1980s

were a boom time. Employment in the West is at an all-time high; more than two million new jobs have been created since the expansion began in 1982. Industry worked at 90 percent of capacity in 1990, the highest level in twenty years. In 1989 West Germany's budget deficit was less than one percent of the GNP, and its trade surplus came to more than $90 billion; in the first half of 1990, its surplus was about $50 billion, far larger than Japan's. Better yet, for a nation in dire need of investment capital, Germans save more of their disposable income than anyone but the Japanese, about 13 percent; an estimated $675 billion in private investment will be required by the year 2000. Reducing the combined German armies from nearly 600,000 men to 370,000 will also save money for more useful purposes.

Yet the German budget is already showing the strain. In 1989 the budget deficit was only $20 billion. By the end of 1990 it had already reached $70 billion and was expected to pass $100 billion in 1991. Traditionally low interest rates were nearing double digits. As a result, export sales had dropped by more than 7 percent under year-earlier figures, while imports from other EC nations were up nearly 11 percent. To pay its bills, Germany is considering its first budget cuts and major new taxes in years. Civil servants may lose some of their regular pay raises. Long-planned corporate tax cuts have had to wait.

In the long run, unification will be worth the pain, in economic terms alone. In one move, Germany will expand its workforce and internal market by 25 percent. A year before unification, the waiting list for a Trabant, a car so primitive that the poorest American would rather walk than drive one, was sixteen years long. By late 1990 over half a million vastly better, used Volkswagens and Mercedes had been snapped up and driven east. Simply manning enough gas stations to keep them all moving will create a vast new job market.

Even after forty-five years of Communist rule, the entrepreneurial spirit remains strong. In 1990, nearly two hundred thousand small and medium-sized businesses were born in the former East Germany. Half or more were restaurants, video rental shops, and similar mom-and-pop concerns, while another 20 percent were professional corporations operated by doctors, lawyers, and dentists. The remainder were the kind of manufacturing and service businesses likely to generate new jobs.

All this will give the German economy an enormous boost. If the average East German worker, aided by Western methods, is capable of producing just $30,000 per year in goods and services—close to a minimum estimate—unification could add almost $300 billion per year to the German economy. Deutsche Bank estimates that by mid-1991, the economy in the East will be growing by a phenomenal 7 to 10 percent per year, bringing growth in the unified Germany to around 4 percent. Unification will clearly pay for itself in a very short period.

There is another side to unification, and it has both economic and political consequences for the new Germany: its relations with neighboring countries. Germany is quickly finding itself at the center of a network that spreads throughout Europe, and beyond. Its ties to its former enemies in the Soviet Union have grown with surprising speed.

Arranging to rid Germany of Soviet troops was probably the hardest part of negotiating unification. Actually carrying it out also will not be easy. The $8 billion Germany agreed to pay the Soviet Union over four years simply helps to defray the cost of shipping home some 360,000 Soviet troops and 220,000 of their dependents. The task will require ten thousand trains of fifty cars each and will take more than two and one-half years, and the Soviet government will have to build some forty thousand new apartments just to house the officers and their families. In the meantime, Germany has been paying one-third of the soldiers' wages in deutschemarks in order to offset the rise in living costs caused by monetary unification.

This bond to the Soviet Union, though undesired, has turned out to be only a first step in the growth of Germany's ties to Eastern Europe. How this development will proceed is one of the major questions about Germany's future foreign policy quite apart from the worries raised by the August 1991 coup.

In the years before World War I, Germany was Russia's largest trading partner; nearly half of Russian imports came from Germany, and almost a third of its exports went there. Though the proportions are now much smaller, postunification Germany is already the Soviet Union's largest trading partner. Both nations would clearly like to see that trade grow. When Germany agreed to subsidize the removal of Soviet troops from its soil, it demanded and won for German construction firms the right to build the new apartments for Soviet military families returning to their homeland, a contract worth an estimated $4 billion. Bonn also assured the USSR that Soviet contracts with formerly East German firms will be met; East Germany had been selling the Soviet Union one-fourth of its machinery imports and nearly half of its imported machine tools, receiving payment in oil and natural gas. And at Christmastime 1990, Germany began shipping to hungry Soviets the 350,000 tons of groceries formerly kept in bunkers beneath West Berlin as a defense against any future Soviet blockade. The donation will go a long way toward sealing the new friendship between Germany and its former enemies in Moscow.

Despite the vast expense of redeveloping the new eastern states, Germany will also play a major role in developing the former Soviet bloc nations. Many German manufacturers see in Eastern Europe the chance to find skilled workers at bargain-basement prices, but there are even stronger reasons for Germany to help its eastern neighbors. In recent years, Bonn has developed close ties with Hungary and Czechoslovakia—Hungary, because in 1989 it opened its border with Austria, allowing East Germans to flee the Honecker regime and triggering the process that ended with a single Germany, and Czechoslovakia, because President Vaclav Havel was an early supporter of unification.

At the same time, Germany's ties to the United States are weakening. America's most important source of influence over Germany was the military forces stationed there to act as a front-line defense against Soviet aggression. The need for that American force has disappeared, and so have many of the troops themselves. The U.S. has already taken more than one hundred thousand troops from the NATO countries for deployment in Saudi Arabia. Most of them came from Germany, and there is little chance they will return; Washington sees the Persian Gulf crisis as a "socially acceptable" opportunity to cut its military expenses in Europe, and in a poll shortly before the two Germanys were reunited, some 70 percent of West Germans favored removing all foreign troops from their country.

This change, too, will cost the German economy. Before the withdrawal, the United States spent about $170 billion per year to maintain its troops in the NATO countries. If only half of that was spent in Germany, it would cost the nation about $50 billion to $70 billion each year—enough to slow German economic growth slightly. But in return, Germany will gain slightly more freedom, both in its dealings with the Soviets and Eastern Europe and in helping to form EC trade policy.

With these financial ties will come enormous political influence as well. The Soviet Union has already proposed that the new Germany become a permanent member of the United Nations Security Council, a distinction neither of the separate Germanys held. The United States, too, has been pressing Germany to begin taking a greater role in international politics.

Recognition of Germany's new potency is one major factor driving the fast pace of European unification. Though France and Germany have built, in the last twenty years, an effective partnership to lead Europe, and Germany accounts for some 40 percent of French trade, there is no real love or trust between the two traditional enemies. And if German power within the EC rises, French power must decline. The French, and many of their neighbors, reason that the only way to keep Germany under control is to weld it securely into the structure of a new European Community. This goal has come to seem more urgent since German unification has brought new ties with Eastern Europe and the Soviet Union, whose interests may not always coincide with those of Paris and Brussels. To a large extent, German leaders agree with their former enemies. The memory of Nazi atrocities is so strong that the thought of a powerful, independent Germany is one that few Germans can face.

Whether Germany should accept any larger role in world affairs is still widely debated in Germany itself. Just before the Germanys were united, a survey found that fewer than one-third of those in the West endorsed rewriting the constitution to allow sending troops to help deal with international crises such as Iraq's invasion of Kuwait. Their Eastern cousins, their attention focused on their own economic problems, appear even less likely to support foreign military involvements. Nonetheless, few German constitutional scholars think a constitutional amendment is actually needed, and the Bonn government seems to agree. In the first week of 1990, it sent eighteen fighter planes and their crews and support personnel to Turkey, to help defend the country's border with Iraq in case the Kuwait crisis turned into a shooting war—the first foreign deployment of German troops in postwar history.

In the long run, Germany will be forced to assume many such duties. It can, and will, try to weld itself so tightly into the European Community that it acts almost exclusively by consensus. The call for "a European Germany, not a German Europe" is heard often throughout the land, an incantation meant to ward off any repetition of past mistakes; it is a sentiment with which the rest of Europe heartily concurs. Yet, in any good circus, the elephants lead the parade. Whether Europe becomes a loose confederation or a highly centralized superstate, Germany's size and power guarantee it a leading role in the Community, whether it wants that responsibility or not.

C H A P T E R 3

....

From Totalitarianism to Democracy—in Many Hard Steps

"Most East Europeans find the idea of democracy intensely exciting, but few of them understand it well."

....

As the nations of the European Community voluntarily trade some of their sovereignty for the benefits of economic and political cooperation, the nations of Eastern Europe are rebuilding a degree of self-government not available to them since before World War II. This has turned out to be a clumsy, uncertain process for people only the oldest of whom ever lived with national independence, much less democracy.

It is not just the individuals of Eastern Europe who have little experience of freedom, but the nations. Most of the newly independent countries built some form of parliamentary government in the nineteenth century, but only Hungary and Poland have substantial records of self-rule. Poland, the victim of endless partitions throughout history, lost its autonomy late in the eighteenth century, reestablished itself as a sovereign republic in 1919, and returned to foreign tyranny under the Nazis only twenty years later. Hungary was dominated by others from the early fourteenth century until it became junior partner in the Austro-Hungarian Empire in 1867; under the Empire's laws, only 6 percent of the population were allowed to vote. Neither

Czechoslovakia nor Yugoslavia existed before World War I. Their constituent lands had been passed back and forth between competing monarchies for centuries; so had Albania, Bulgaria, and Romania. After such a history, most East Europeans find the idea of democracy intensely exciting, but few of them understand it well.

Poland, where Solidarity and Lech Walesa broke the Communist monopoly on power in Eastern Europe, still leads the region's move toward democracy and a free-market economy. If Poland can make the transition from communism to a Western-style society, its example will prove to its neighbors that the conversion is possible; even in the Soviet Union, one clear success will immeasurably strengthen the pro-democracy movement. If Poland falls into anarchy or dictatorship, totalitarians throughout the Communist and formerly Communist world will find all the evidence they need that Western governmental forms are not for them.

Czechoslovakia provides another test case crucial to the democratic future of Eastern Europe. In this land, the tradition of self-rule was strong for decades before the yearning for freedom was crushed by the Nazis and chained by the Allied leaders at Yalta. The famed Prague spring of 1968, when Alexander Dubcek tried to build a "socialism with a human face," was not simply a revolt against fossilized Stalinism, but a return to Czechoslovakia's own past. If memories of a glorious history can sustain Czechoslovakia through the difficult transition from totalitarian communism to democratic capitalism, it will offer hope to other struggling nations. If even the birthplace of East European democracy fails, others will doubt their own chances of success.

One less-than-optimistic Polish aphorism likens a free society to an aquarium, and a Communist society to fish soup. We know from experience that an aquarium can become fish soup. The question now, they say, is whether anyone can turn fish soup back into an aquarium.

To succeed on an economic level, Poland and its neighbors must solve three difficult problems. One, ironically, is to wrest day-to-day power back from the people who won their nations' freedom and invest it in democratic political institutions; unless that is accomplished, "people power" leads only to the chaos of the Philippines. The second is to control the ethnic animosities that have plagued the region throughout its history. The third is to restore capitalism where virtually the entire economy has been owned and operated by the government for decades; we will hold that topic for the next chapter. So far, none of these efforts is going well.

On November 25, 1990, Polish citizens voted for a new president in their first free election in more than four decades. If there was any surprise about the outcome it was that Lech Walesa had not taken public office a year earlier, when he all but gave the post of premier to his ally, now turned rival, Tadeusz Mazowiecki. Some of the issues over which the election was fought must have come, if not as a surprise, then at least as a disappointment to proponents of American-style democracy. So must the ugliness with which that battle was sometimes waged.

The Polish election turned on two major arguments; with variations, they are subjects of heated debate throughout Eastern Europe. One is the straightforward search for scapegoats. Throughout the region, governments are throwing Communist-era bureaucrats and business managers out of office, even when there is no one qualified to replace them. Several have arrested, or have attempted to arrest, former national leaders under charges of looting the national economy and other forms of malfeasance. Under Mazowiecki, Poland refused to follow suit, and that restraint both frustrated many citizens and gave Lech Walesa a campaign issue. "Mazowiecki is a wonderful man," one typical comment held, "but he is too soft on the Communists." Czechoslovakia's Vaclav Havel has inspired many similar statements.

Since the election, this urge to punish the defeated has surfaced in an unexpected way. Immediately after the run-off vote, Stanislaw Tyminski, the third major candidate, was ordered to remain in the country to face possible prosecution for maligning the government during the campaign. In Poland and its neighboring countries, there are still lessons to be learned about democracy.

The other argument concerns the trade-off between economic reform and social pain: How quickly should the government privatize state-owned enterprise? How high should it let unemployment rise in order to build an economy that can compete in Western markets? How much of its economy should be sold to foreign investors—if buyers can be found—in order to gain their help in modernizing? In Poland's election, the choice between the candidates was clear. Premier Mazowiecki had enacted strict monetary controls to halt runaway inflation, but in general he favored gradual reform to avoid even worse recession and unemployment. Lech Walesa argued for immediate change at whatever price the task required.

In Poland, however, more than economic policy was at stake. The major candidates turned the election into a referendum on who would hold the greater power in government, the president or the Sejm, Poland's legislature. Mazowiecki, deeply committed to consensus-building and the rule of law, upheld a strict constitutional government in which laws would originate with the Sejm. Walesa argued that economic reform could never move quickly enough if it depended on building agreement among bickering legislators; therefore he would shortcut the parliamentary process by giving the president broad powers to rule by decree. For many skeptics, President Walesa's success with this platform represents a chilling step into the authoritarian past. It is a defeat as well for the idea that the power of government should rest with institutions, not with men, and it will impede the growth of representative democracy in Poland.

There is worse to come. Though Walesa undoubtedly means well, it has been clear from the first that he could not hope to deliver on his campaign promises. He simply offered the impossible—jobs for workers, welfare money for peasants, government start-up capital for would-be entrepreneurs—all in a country deep in recession and headed deeper still. In doing so he divided the constituency that brought him to prominence, and he must now disappoint those who supported him. Lech Walesa still wields enormous influence among his people; in May 1990 he was able single-handedly to head off a nation-wide rail strike. If he had thrown his support behind Mazowiecki's cautious approach to reform, he could have defused the social tensions that will build as the economy continues to deteriorate. As it stands, he will become their focus. Long before his term in office expires, we may well see anti-Walesa riots among his former constituents. His failure could destroy his presidency and undermine the idea of a democratic renaissance in Eastern Europe.

In some ways the style of Walesa's campaign was even more disturbing than its substance and probable result, for it played to the worst elements of Poland's national character. Faced with unexpectedly strong support for his opponents, Walesa searched for a subject to give his campaign the appeal that mere issues lacked. He found it in anti-Semitism. "A gang of Jews," he declared in one televised speech, had "got hold of the trough and is bent on destroying us." He later modified this accusation. It had, he said, been directed only to a selfish minority of Jews, not "against the Jewish people as a whole." In another statement, he said that he had been referring only to certain Jews in government.

This is a strange claim to come from a would-be statesman in Poland. Before World War II, some 3.5 million Jews lived there, including 500,000 in the Warsaw ghetto. Today, only nine thousand remain. All the Jews who attend Warsaw's lone synagogue would fit comfortably in a one-room geriatric clinic. None of them holds government office.

Unfortunately, Walesa's outburst is more than a minor lapse. Anti-Semitism has a long and ugly history in Poland. This country may not have invented the pogrom, but like pre-Soviet Russia, it refined it to a high level of perfection. Communism repressed anti-Semitism, as it did many other forms of nationalism, ethnocentrism, and xenophobia not compatible with comradeship; but before World War II, price hikes, recession, and other hardships were almost automatically blamed on "the Jews." Now that communism has passed, suspicion and hatred of Jews, what few of them are available to receive those emotions, is sure to return.

Anti-Semitism is just one of the rivalries endemic to most of the region. America built its system of government on the idea that people must enjoy the same rights, no matter what their ethnic or religious background. This concept is alien to Eastern Europe, where tribalism, albeit Slavic in nature, is as intense as anything found in Africa. Throughout the region, ethnic hatreds have flared repeatedly, held in check only by the universally repressive Communist regimes. The world remembers the assassination of Austrian archduke Francis Ferdinand, on June 28, 1914, by a Serbian nationalist at Sarajevo (now part of Yugoslavia) as the event that precipitated World War I, but it was merely the climactic incident in forty years of intermittent war in the Balkans. Today, almost a century later, not one battle has been forgotten or forgiven. The people of these lands will find it difficult to develop the mutual respect that freedom demands.

Ethnic strife is at its worst in Yugoslavia, a nation that may well cease to exist in years to come. Yugoslavia was cobbled together at the end of World War I as "The Kingdom of Serbs, Croats, and Slovenes," three peoples whose common factors include related languages and centuries of mutual hatred. Its six semiautonomous republics are the leftovers of the Ottoman and Austro-Hungarian Empires. They include five major ethnic groups, three primary religions, three official languages, dozens of dialects, and even two different alphabets. There is little chance that Yugoslavia would have survived this long if it had not been held together, first by Nazi occupation, and then by rigid Communist discipline and the charismatic leadership of Marshal Josip Tito, who died in 1980.

After more than seventy years as a single nation, Yugoslavia's republics are still divided on roughly the same ethnic and religious lines as they were a century ago. Though there has been some movement between the regions, Slovenia, the richest area of the country, is still populated largely by Slovenes, Croatia by Croats. Both groups are primarily Roman Catholic and use the Roman alphabet. Predictably, Serbia, is home to ethnic Serbians, Macedonia to Macedonians, and Montenegro to Montenegrans. All three groups belong to the Orthodox Eastern Church and use the Cyrillic alphabet. Bosnia-Herzegovina is the most heterogeneous of the republics, with many Yugoslavs of undeclared nationality, and over two million Muslims.

With its complex stew of ethnic feuds, Yugoslavia might be expected to disintegrate at almost any excuse, or for no comprehensible reason at all. And, in fact, virtually every ethnic and religious group has its quota of nationalist demagogues calling for independence. Yet its current troubles hinge on only two factors:

Four republics—Slovenia, Croatia, and Bosnia-Herzegovina in the northwest and Macedonia in the south—have elected nationalist, strongly anti-Communist governments. Slovenia and Croatia have demanded nearly total autonomy for all of the Yugoslav republics, each of which would have its own money, army, and diplomatic service. Both Slovenia and Croatia have voted to secede if the change were not made by mid-1990—Slovenia by a landslide of 88 percent.

Serbia and Montenegro have returned hard-line Communists—now called Socialists—to power. Serbia has also voted for full autonomy, but its version is considerably different from that envisioned by Slovenia and Croatia. Serbian leader Slobodan Milosevic wants to maintain most of the nation's current federal structure but to place it under effective Serbian control. He has fanned Serbian hostility toward Croats and Slovenes in order to boost his own popularity. He has refused to discuss the possibility of a confederation, and in late 1990 he introduced illegal tariffs against goods from Slovenia and Croatia. Yugoslav defense minister General Veljko Kadijevic, a Serb, has threatened to use the army to keep the nation together. But the divisive "Balkanization process" that pitted all of the nationalities of Eastern Europe against each other may be upon us again, re-creating a pattern of internecine rivalry that once triggered a world war.

If Yugoslavia manages to avoid a civil war, it will be waiting only for its Fort Sumter to begin a bloody dissolution. One potential flashpoint is Kosovo, a small, desperately poor, semiautonomous province in Serbia. Ninety percent of its 1.8 million inhabitants are ethnic Albanians. Yet many Serbs consider the region their historic homeland. All of Kosovo's policemen are Serbs. Serbian authorities have abolished the provincial parliament and arrested more than one hundred of its members for treason, fired over two thousand Albanian government employees, and violently repressed ethnic Albanian citizens for more than two years. Over one hundred Albanians have been killed in street demonstrations. In the republic's first multi-party elections, held in December 1990, Albanians boycotted the polls.

Croatia has its own Kosovo in the Serbian enclave of Knin. Milosevic accuses Croatia of "fascist genocide" against the six hundred thousand ethnic Serbs in the republic, and Serbia is pouring weapons to its ethnic brethren in Knin. The conflict almost erupted into open war when federal troops were sent in to disarm Croatian police reservists who were accused of planning an insurrection.

Serbia's Milosevic fanned the flames by declaring that "all Serbians must have the right to live in one state." Onlookers in neighboring states interpreted this to mean that in the event of a national break-up, he would attempt to annex the Serbian districts of both Croatia and Bosnia-Herzegovina. Unfortunately, that would also bring about six million non-Serbs under Serbian rule, about evenly divided between Croats, Albanians, and Muslims.

To complicate matters even further, six of Yugoslavia's seven neighbors harbor long-standing territorial claims against it. If the country disintegrates, Albania could seize possession of Kosovo, a possibility that grows with each year that passes. With the highest birth rate in Europe, Albanians will be the largest ethnic group in the Balkans by 2010. Both Greece and Bulgaria claim Macedonia, and either or both could move to annex that territory.

Yugoslavia's chances for survival seem much less than 50 percent. Slovenia has already begun amending its constitution to eliminate all references to Yugoslavia and expects to declare its sovereignty even before this book appears. Croatia is not far behind. There is at least a chance that Yugoslavia can avoid a violent revolution. Yugoslavia and its component states all need capital and credit, and even the bellicose Serbia would be reluctant to begin violence that would put an end to Western financing. A third Balkan War, eight decades after the first two, cannot be ruled out.

By contrast, Czechoslovakia is positively stable. Its "velvet revolution" against the Communists was probably the easiest transition of 1989; playwright-President Vaclav Havel may be the most universally loved national leader in Europe, East or West. Some ethnic antagonisms, formerly repressed, have flared since the Communist regime fell. The Czech and Slovak populations speak different languages and have little historical cause for affection, and pressure for an independent Slovak nation has grown rapidly. In an attempt to defuse it, the nation has been officially renamed the Czech and Slovak Federal Republic. It seems unlikely that this cosmetic change will satisfy dissident Slovaks, and the nation may well restructure itself as a loose confederation; yet there seems minimal prospect of violence of the kind that faces Yugoslavia.

Despite the republic's ethnic tensions its greatest challenge is still economic reform. (More on that in Chapter 4.) Vaclav Havel's approval ratings have begun to fall, as stringent austerity measures reduce the Czech standard of living. There is a good chance that, "more in sorrow than in anger," voters will turn him out of office in the 1992 national elections. However, democratic institutions are well enough established so that there is no risk of a return to totalitarian rule.

The same cannot yet be said of Hungary. Voter turnouts in 1990 made one of the problems clear: After four decades under Communist rule, no one really believes that elections will change "the system." In their first six national votes, no more than 65 percent of Hungarian citizens went to the polls; in one referendum, only 13 percent bothered to vote.

Ironically, political alienation is worse in Hungary than in many of the other newly democratic nations because so much of the government's power was administered at the local level. To date, nearly all of the country's elections have focused on the national leadership, a political level so distant that few ordinary citizens expect it to touch their lives.

Yet they are unlikely to respond better to local elections. Long experience has taught ordinary Hungarians that the purpose of local government is not to help people, but to interfere and coerce. Thus, well-meaning citizens who might otherwise serve their communities have no more incentive to run for office than to vote for the Party hacks left over from the years of Communist rule. Virtually all of the 300,000 or so local council members, bosses, police captains, chief judges, and mid-level bureaucrats who took office under the Communist patronage system are still in place. In recent local elections, the majority ran unopposed. It will be several years before Hungary builds up the level of political awareness needed for voters to take control of the local governments. And until that is accomplished, they will have relatively little interest in national issues.

In contrast to Czechoslovakia and Hungary, Bulgaria has far fewer democratic traditions. Yet in Bulgaria, almost everyone is fascinated by the national government, but the reasons have less to do with politics than with entertainment. Government has become the Bulgarian equivalent of a long-running soap opera.

A year after the Communist regime of Todor Zhivkov fell, attempts at democracy had left the nation with no effective government at all. Elections in June 1990 divided the nation's parliament between the Bulgarian Socialist party—Zhivkov's Communist party, renamed to fit the new environment—and the reform Union of Democratic Forces, and wrangling between the two had paralyzed the legislature. When Socialist President Petar Mladinov was forced to step down and UDF leader Zhelyu Zhelev took his place, the change had little effect.

It is difficult to see what will break Bulgaria's legislative deadlock. President Zhelev has the power to require new parliamentary elections; but as this is written, he has yet to use it. There is a chance that a new vote will give the UDF enough of a majority to enact economic change. There is also a possibility that the two parties will forge a coalition to break the impasse, as some Socialist leaders have urged. Until then, farmers will continue to hoard their crops, hoping for reforms that would allow them to sell their produce at market prices, the cities will go without food, and factories will lack the oil they need to operate. This stalemate could continue for many months to come.

Romania is little better off. Under the neo-Stalinist rule of Nicolai and Elena Ceausescu and their extended family, Bucharest sucked what little wealth was available from the countryside and squandered it on heavy industries that were obsolete before they went into operation. As the economy declined, both maintenence and new investment disappeared, and the economy collapsed even faster and more completely. By the time Romanian Army turncoats executed the Ceausescus, the nation was one of the poorest and most malnourished in Europe, the government had been purged of competent administrators (Romania's paranoid dictator feared that the capable people might contest his leadership), and whatever spirit the citizens once possessed had been crushed almost beyond redemption. That Romania suddenly exploded into a successful revolution in December 1990 says more about the fragility of tyrants than about the power of the people.

It now seems that the revolution may have been less successful than onlookers first imagined. In May 1990, Ion Iliescu's National Salvation Front came to power in a landslide election that many onlookers suspected had been rigged, but resistance to it is limited almost exclusively to urban intellectuals. The Iliescu government still includes most of the same Communist bureaucrats who worked for the Ceausescu regime. "Most of the current regime aren't even reform communists," one French diplomat observed. "They had simply fallen out with Ceausescu."

There seems little chance that Romania will build a working democracy in the near future. Unlike some of its East European neighbors, it has no significant memories of self-rule or personal freedom to fall back on. Political discourse remains at the level found in most failing totalitarian regimes. When angry Romanians took to the streets of Bucharest to protest government policy, they were met by troops and club-wielding miners imported from rural communist strongholds. Smaller-scale repression is a daily routine. Rather than face continued repression, seventy-six Romanian tourists in Britain sought political asylum late in 1990; another 150 arrived by cargo jet from the Middle East. At the year's end, demonstrators in Timisoara celebrated the first anniversary of Ceausescu's ouster with cries of "The only solution is a second revolution."

As 1991 began, rumors held that the army would soon overthrow President Iliescu and invite expatriate King Michael to return as head of a constitutional monarchy. At present, the situation is too fluid to allow firm predictions. However, as dissent grows and the political situation becomes ever more chaotic, the hereditary ruler will gain favor as a symbol of stability. We will not be surprised if King Michael returns to power.

Albania seems poised to follow Bulgaria's unpromising lead. In a bid to preempt growing opposition, President Ramiz Alia has called for snap elections, which will take place while this volume is in press. There seems little chance that the new Albanian Democratic party and Christian Democratic party will be able to get organized, pick candidates, and campaign effectively in the forty days allowed them—particularly as the Communists have denied them access to state-run media. These tactics all but guarantee the ruling Communists a majority in the coming general election. In that case, further unrest is unavoidable. The Party may try to retain power, citing its biased vote as a popular mandate. If so, a violent revolution appears inevitable. However, the Party seems more likely to step down when the opposition becomes too strong. One way or the other, the current government is on its way out, and a period of chaos is destined to follow.

How quickly these nations achieve stability depends as much on the West as on local factors. Ethnic strife was relatively quiet under the Communist regimes, not only because it was ruthlessly repressed, but because factional differences seem less important when the competing groups are all subordinated to some higher authority. The Conference on Security and Cooperation in Europe has already offered to mediate Yugoslavia's ethnic differences, and been rebuffed, but the European Community may have more influence. The nations of Eastern Europe are nowhere near being qualified for EC membership; they lack the economic and political stability expected of the Western nations. But they do need whatever help the EC can provide—not just investment capital, but free markets for farm products and whatever manufactured goods they can produce. That help will come with a price: The formerly Communist lands will have to earn whatever help they receive by enacting free-market reforms and building functional democratic institutions.

In addition, a new network of international associations has begun to spring up to deal with regional issues. There has already been one attempt to build closer ties between Hungary, Poland, and the Czech and Slovak Federal Republic. And the so-called "Pentagonal Initiative" between Austria, Hungary, Italy, Yugoslavia, and the Czech and Slovak Federal Republic, and soon possibly Poland, promises to build cooperation in such areas as the environment and transportation. These efforts, too, can be used as test cases in which the nations of Eastern Europe demonstrate their ability to cooperate with their neighbors. The attempted Soviet military coup of August 1991 will galvanize further cooperation. As they develop into working partnerships, they will strengthen the framework supporting the fragile democracies born in 1989.

CHAPTER 4

Instant Capitalism

"To the extent that Eastern Europe prospers in the 1990s, it will do so because the West will provide the money and training needed to repair crippled ex-socialist economies."

Economically, the 1990s will be a difficult decade for Eastern Europe. Throughout the formerly Socialist nations, it has proved far easier to win political liberty, than to build free markets on the rubble left by more than forty years of centralized production and distribution.

All the problems that exist in East Germany are found throughout the region, and in many cases they are far more severe. Factories capable of manufacturing products that meet Western standards are a tiny minority, even in the best of the Eastern economies. Two generations of training in the Socialist doctrine "you pretend to pay me, and I pretend to work" have damaged whatever work ethic once existed in many of the former Soviet satellites. Public infrastructures failed, by and large, long ago. And in many East European nations, education is not up to even the lax American standard. Despite the initial optimism that greeted the collapse of socialism, this is not a recipe for good times ahead—and these nations have no big brother in Bonn to help them survive the change.

A few of these handicaps are already healing themselves. In the most Westernized countries—Hungary, Czechoslovakia, and Poland—the entrepreneurial tradition has not been forgotten.

Hungary has allowed people to operate small retail and service businesses since 1968. Ninety percent of Poland's farms have never been nationalized. And the black market has thrived wherever capitalism has been officially forbidden. After hearing for decades that no one should earn more than his neighbor, many in the East still regard businessmen as profiteers and exploiters, but that has not stopped many of their neighbors from setting up small stores and factories. These concerns are already the fastest growing sector of the Eastern economies. By the end of the decade, they will be driving economic growth and new employment at a pace not seen in the West since the end of the Second World War.

Other problems have proved less tractable. These are the structural distortions left by four decades under an economic system that subordinated economic reality to Socialist ideology. East bloc industries are not merely inefficient, they were designed for a world that, at best, has not existed in decades, and may never have existed outside the fantasies of central planners. Socialist doctrine, formed in the age of Karl Marx more than a century ago, romanticized heavy industry, which it considered the real source of all economic growth. So throughout the formerly socialist world, industry has focused disproportionately on such fields as iron and steel, mining, bulk chemicals, heavy machinery, and the like. Service industries and consumer goods have been neglected almost completely. And Socialist countries liked their companies *big*. In East Germany, three-fourths of industrial workers have labored in companies with more than one thousand employees. Among Poland's eight-thousand-odd state-owned enterprises, fewer than one in ten employ less than one hundred people. The average is more than eleven hundred, with nearly four hundred workers per individual plant. (In the West, the average is only sixty-six workers per plant.) Few of these industries can survive in open competition. As they close, they are throwing vast numbers of people out of work, causing riots and protests in numerous countries.

The situation is even worse, because the dissolution of Comecon, the Warsaw Pact's answer to the European Community, has deprived many of these crippled giants of their only markets. Until 1989, the East bloc countries traded almost exclusively among themselves; few other nations would accept the dated and poorly made goods turned out by the East's 1930s-vintage factories. Three-fourths of Czechoslovakia's foreign trade, for example, was with the Soviet Union and East Germany. But in 1990, trade among the Eastern countries declined by nearly one-fifth and continues to plummet. East Germany, once the largest Comecon market outside the Soviet Union itself, cancelled more than three-fourths of its scheduled imports from its former Communist neighbors. The Soviet Union also has cancelled many of its orders, leaving factories in Hungary, Czechoslovakia, Poland, and their neighbors with little to do.

That is not the only blow the Soviets have dealt these frail economies. Before the peaceable revolutions, trade between the East-bloc nations was transacted in a unit called the "transferrable ruble." As money, it did not exist; it was just an accounting device to help keep track of barter. But early in 1990, the Soviet Union began to demand dollars or deutschemarks for the products it sells to its former vassal states. In return, it now pays hard currency for most of the goods it buys from them. But Western money is scarce in Eastern Europe, and the transitional nations have found it increasingly difficult to pay for the goods they need. According to one estimate, the demand for hard currencies will cost Bulgaria between $2 billion and $3 billion per year in trade, or one-fifth of its gross domestic product.

By far the most important Comecon trade was in Soviet oil and gas, which powered much of the industry in Eastern Europe. Meeting energy needs has become difficult, because the USSR has eliminated the subsidies under which it sold oil to its client states. On January 1, 1991, the cost of oil in Eastern Europe leaped from about $7.50 per barrel to the full market price. It will cost the region between $6 billion and $10 billion to pay for its oil in 1991. With oil at twenty-five dollars per barrel, Bulgaria would have to spend all of its anticipated hard-currency revenues in 1991 on energy, and perhaps more. Poland's fuel bill amounts to about 90 percent of its hard-currency income.

The Soviets have also cut the amount of oil and gas they are willing to deliver to the region at any price. For more than a year now, lack of power has forced factories in the former iron curtain lands to close for months at a time. The situation is particularly acute in Poland, which bought nearly ninety million barrels of Soviet oil in 1989; in 1991, the Soviets have committed to delivering only 31.5 million barrels. In the Persian Gulf crisis, Poland, Bulgaria, Hungary, and Yugoslavia have lost an additional several billion dollars' worth of oil owed them by Iraq.

In the long run, this energy shortage may even work to Eastern Europe's benefit, for it will force them to upgrade the energy efficiency of their factories, which are among the most fuel-hungry in the world. American energy consultants are already whistle-stopping Poland and Hungary, promoting the use of energy-saving electric motors, waste heat recycling, and other conservation techniques. However, it will be at least five years before such efforts even begin to cut the region's gas bill. It will take another ten years to reduce fuel consumption per unit of GNP to something approaching Western levels.

There are no such silver linings to obsolete industry and unemployment. To heal these wounds, the former Warsaw Pact nations must somehow take the economy out of the government's hands and turn it over to private owners, and they must find some way to pay the enormous cost of modernizing whatever industries they can save and scrapping the rest. Neither has proved easy.

Privatization is an enormous task. At their peak, the Polish and Hungarian governments owned an estimated 90 percent of their nations' industry; in Bulgaria, it was close to 100 percent. Selling small stores and similar businesses has proved easy. Poland had privatized half of its 130,000 state-owned shops by the end of 1990, and at this point virtually all such enterprises are in private hands. Czechoslovakia has managed to return many of the seventy thousand shops nationalized in 1950 to their original owners or their heirs, and is in the process of selling off several hundred thousand more. But even after two years of effort, the task of privatizing large industrial combines has barely begun.

To some extent, this is the result of simple inefficiency. For example, when Hungary's Ganz Electric Works went on the block early in 1990, no fewer than five major European and American companies eagerly bid for part or whole ownership. By the time the government agency in charge of privatization got around to the transaction, all but one of the bids had been withdrawn, and the remaining offer was unacceptably small.

Yet there are more fundamental problems than bureaucratic delay. One is the same fear that many Americans feel when thinking of Japan: no one in the East wants to see their nation's entire economy sold off to bargain-hunting foreigners. Nor do they want it to wind up concentrated in a few hands; both good economics and a sense of fairness dictate that the benefits of ownership be spread as evenly as possible. And virtually everyone understands that the first thing any private businessman would wish to do is end the enormous overstaffing typical of Eastern businesses. That means more unemployment.

The Eastern countries have tried a variety of ways to deal with these concerns. Czechoslovakia has adopted a variety of privatization methods, including a plan to distribute vouchers that citizens can trade for stock in companies formerly owned by the state. In Hungary, a similar scheme remains stalled, but seems likely to be enacted before long. Poland limits foreign investors to buying no more than 10 percent ownership in large companies, with special permission required for larger stakes. Another 20 percent of each company's stock is offered to the firm's workers at half the market value, while the rest goes on sale to Polish citizens. They eagerly snapped up the first few companies marketed under this plan, but sales have lagged in recent months, and it seems clear that native interest in stock ownership will run out long before the supply of companies to be sold. So will the supply of Polish capital with which to buy shares.

And that is the problem with trying to avoid the sale of national assets to foreign investors: None of the former East bloc nations has any way to fund its own modernization; Czechoslovakia owes $3.4 billion in foreign debt, Bulgaria owes nearly $10 billion, Hungary $21 billion, and Poland $40 billion. Only Romania has a positive net hard currency balance, and that will not last long. All of these countries are reluctant to finance expansion by going deeper into debt, and Western banks show understandably little interest in lending to them. Poland has been forced to reschedule its debt payments, while Bulgaria has simply stopped making them. To the extent that Eastern Europe prospers in the 1990s, it will do so because the West will provide the money and training needed to repair crippled ex-Socialist economies.

One source of funds is the European Bank for Reconstruction and Development. Headquartered in London, it will provide investment advice and development capital to the depressed, formerly Communist nations of Eastern and Central Europe. As of

January 1991, forty-one nations had pledged nearly $14 billion to the effort. Britain added $195 million to a Know-How Fund to supply technical and management advice to Poland, Czechoslovakia, Hungary, and the Soviet Union. Such efforts are a beginning, but not nearly enough. According to the investment banking firm of Smith Barney Harris Upham & Co., the damaged economies of Eastern Europe will need between $10 billion and $15 billion per year, just to survive in competition with the West. Forecasters at Morgan Stanley & Co. say that "an adequate social safety net" for the region will cost between $270 billion and $370 billion by 1995.

Thus, the only hope for that kind of money is private investment from the West. So far, there have been relatively few successes in attracting it. GE purchased Hungary's Tungsram lamp works for $150 million, and Schwinn put $2 million into a small bicycle factory there. Volkswagen is pumping an estimated $5.3 billion into Czechoslovakia's state-owned Skoda Works, an automaker that was one of Europe's leading manufacturers until the Nazis commandeered it in the 1930s. And Virginia building contractor John Kowalczyk plans to spend $100 million to convert Warsaw's forty-two-story Palace of Culture and Science into a business center and shopping mall. But most East European assets have proved a hard sell. A year ago, the Polish government hoped to have 15 percent of the economy in private hands by the end of 1991. That target now seems much too optimistic.

Faced with these conflicting priorities—the economic and political dangers of foreign ownership vs. the desperate need for capital—Europe's formerly Socialist nations have divided themselves into two camps. Some have found it possible to accept considerable short-term pain in order to achieve long-term prosperity; others have tried to avoid it and have thereby guaranteed themselves long-term pain and far less gain.

In making that decision, or by failing to make it, for better or worse, these nations have helped to decide how Western investors will deal with them. Where countries have made a clean break with the past, economies should be relatively strong. If factories are relatively modern (by East bloc standards) and workers are relatively sophisticated, Western firms will pursue joint ventures with locally owned companies. But where nations long for a "third path" that somehow provides both the efficiency of a capitalist market economy and the welfare guarantees of socialism, economies will remain weak. All these countries will find it difficult to attract joint ventures, so they will encourage a policy developed by Ireland. Their plea will be, "Open a factory, and hire our people." Again, Western companies will take advantage of the opportunity.

Two nations clearly fit into the first group. Czechoslovakia and Hungary have decided to end central planning, establish free markets, and privatize state-owned companies as quickly as they can manage. In both nations, progress has been difficult; yet it will gain momentum rapidly by 1995. Five years later, the worst will clearly be over.

Czechoslovakia waited until the beginning of 1991 to free prices, end most subsidies, and begin privatizing its state-owned companies, but the delay has done little to ease the pain of change. Consumer prices have risen by more than one-third, and unemployment has spiked since the turn of the year. Before the process is over, free-market reform is expected to bankrupt one-third of Czech industry, sending unemployment to levels never seen in the West, even during the Great Depression.

Yet, of all the East European nations (save for the former East Germany), Czechoslovakia is best positioned for rapid improvement. Though factories are inefficient and labor productivity poor by Western standards, they are among the best the East has to offer. Volkswagen's joint venture with Skoda Works should prove to be only the first of many. By 2000, it will be the most prosperous of the former Socialist lands. We will be surprised if it is not the first to be accepted into the European Community.

Of the Westernized nations, Hungary has found reform the most trying. When the government tried to raise gasoline prices by 65 percent, bringing them closer to 1990's free-market levels, angry truckers and cab drivers blocked roads, and the increase was halved. The GNP is shrinking, while according to government figures inflation is running at nearly 50 percent; in reality it remains near triple-digit levels. One-third of the population lives below the poverty line, and living standards are still falling.

Progress will remain much slower in Hungary than in Czechoslovakia, where people are less ambivalent about capitalism. Privatization is being phased-in over four years, and for the moment free enterprise is limited to small business. We expect this to change before the planned four years is up. Once Hungary commits itself to capitalism, Western investors will regain their interest in joint ventures. Economic recovery will then move far more rapidly.

In sharp contrast, Romania and Bulgaria have condemned themselves to a kind of Third World limbo. When Romania cut government subsidies late in 1990, consumer prices doubled—and that was the good news. For nearly a year, it has been almost impossible to buy consumer goods, and gas lines are up to three miles long. Industrial production is off by nearly one-third, exports by almost half. Bulgaria is in even worse condition. For more than a year, the country has been bankrupt, electricity and gasoline have been rationed, and consumer goods have been so scarce that women must prove to a physician that they are menstruating, before they can buy sanitary napkins. Food has returned to the cities now that farmers are allowed to sell their produce at market prices, but few Bulgarians can afford more than a subsistence diet. In each nation, efforts to cut government payments and end price controls have been met by strikes and street demonstrations. This instability has already discouraged Western investment and will continue to do so for at least three more years. During that period, Romania and Bulgaria will subsist largely on handouts from the European Community. But by 1995, citizens of these lands will have learned from bitter experience that the only way to survive in a capitalist world economy is to take whatever work is available. This supply of low-cost labor will lure companies from America, Japan, and the European Community, and the process of "Irelandization" will begin.

Between these two extremes lie Poland and Yugoslavia.

Poland's economic reform campaign started well, but foundered soon after its first successes. Late in 1989, the Polish inflation rate had reached 40 percent, and store shelves were bare. Then the Mazowiecki government cut both the budget and government subsidies, tightened credit, and made the zloty convertible with Western currencies. A year later, inflation was minimal, and store shelves were filled with Western consumer goods. This progress was bought at a stiff price, however: Real wages had fallen by 40 percent, industrial production was down by nearly one-third, and unemployment had risen to over one million and was expected to double before the worst is over. Poland is still trying to figure out how to dig itself out of the recession, and the declining popularity of both Tadeuz Mazowiecki and Lech Walesa suggests that the voters' patience is wearing thin.

Yet Poles clearly understand that they have little choice. If they want Western prosperity, they must pay in pain for the excesses of the past forty-five years. Social unrest may build, but it will not shake Poland's commitment to free-market capitalism. And in the end, this determination will pay off. Five years from now, Poland will have turned the corner. It will enter the next century with the third-strongest economy in the East, just behind those of Czechoslovakia and Hungary.

In Yugoslavia, economic reform is at a standstill, put on hold by the ethnic conflict that has dominated national attention for more than a year. Even if Yugoslavia survives as a single nation, the move to capitalism will be regionalized. Slovenia and Croatia are two of the most heavily industrial areas in Eastern Europe. Like Czechoslovakia, as soon as their political situation stabilizes, they will attract foreign investors for a wide variety of joint ventures. Serbia and Bosnia-Herzegovina are less industrialized, but should be able to lure at least some joint ventures if they throw off their Communist governments—as they are likely to do when they see Slovenia and Croatia beginning to prosper. Macedonia and the Kosovo district of Serbia are the least industrialized regions of all. What they have to offer is manpower, so Irelandization will be their route to a modern economy. By 1998, even the poorest sections of Yugoslavia will have begun the climb to prosperity.

The easiest way to anticipate the future of Eastern Europe is to recall the early days of postwar Japan. Japan's economy had been destroyed by years of war; Eastern Europe's has been destroyed by decades of Communist mismanagement. Japan had some advantages that the socialism has not provided. Its people were eager to master Western economic methods, and dedicated enough to work long hours for little pay; socialism left behind an ingrained suspicion of capitalism and fading memories of a work ethic forty years dead. Japan also benefitted from America's Marshall Plan; little such aid is available today.

It took Japan twenty years to recover from the Second World War, and twenty years more to build its current industrial might.

Nothing the West can do will bring Eastern European living standards up to those of the United States, Japan, the Nordic countries, and the Western section of Germany in less than a generation. Whether the citizens of Eastern Europe will be satisfied with the pace of progress is not yet certain.

Despite the remaining questions, the prognosis for Eastern Europe is fairly optimistic. Though economic and social progress will at first be slower than many Poles and Czechs, Hungarians and Yugoslavs hoped during the peaceful revolutions of 1989, it will come, and it will improve daily life in these emerging democracies. The aid being marshalled by the European Community—not only money, but highly favorable trade agreements—will provide further encouragement. The EC will be motivated to help head off possible rightist coups, such as the August 1991 temporary take-over in the U.S.S.R. We believe that in most of the region this will be enough to maintain political and social order as economic repairs gain momentum. And that will ensure that life in Eastern Europe does improve significantly in the years to come.

C H A P T E R 5

....

Soviet Confederation: A Canada with 15 Quebecs

"To buy a Japanese television on the black market, the average Soviet citizen would have to save his entire income for five years. A used foreign car costs at least twenty years' average salary."

....

In the 1990s, as always, the great question is what role the Soviet Union will play. In the last few years, its place in world affairs has rapidly dwindled as Mikhail Gorbachev turned its attention inward. He tried, apparently with growing desperation, to solve the problems of a faltering command economy and a country held together only by force of arms. There is little sign of success. Though some of the most dramatic changes in that nation's history have taken place during his tenure, Gorbachev achieved remarkable failures as well:

• *Perestroika,* Gorbachev's vaunted restructuring program, was supposed to revitalize the Soviet economy in only two or three years. It has not happened. According to many estimates, the gross domestic product fell by nearly 10 percent in 1988 and has continued its decline since then. Unemployment has tripled, to more than 6 percent. Foreign debt has grown from about $22 billion in 1985 to $50 billion in 1990, according to official government figures. The national budget deficit ballooned to an estimated $200 billion in 1989, about 13.5 percent of the gross national product. (The feared U.S. deficit amounted to only 3 percent of the American GNP that year.) And because the government has tried to pay its debt by printing more rubles, no one is really sure of the current inflation rate. Estimates range from the World Bank's conservative 8 percent, up to 50 percent per year. The only certainty is that the rate is growing quickly.

• *Glasnost,* or "openness," the second plank in Gorbachev's reform platform, was collapsing rapidly even before the coup of August 19, 1991. Freedom of the press, which the Soviet premier once said was indispensable to the new U.S.S.R., had gone to the wall. The censors had returned to *Tass, Pravda, Izvestia,* and Soviet telvision, and the media increasingly hewed to the Party line. Political dissent, which was encouraged only a year earlier, was vilified by government functionaries from Gorbachev on down. Behind this abrupt reversal of policy was the Communist Party's right wing, which never abandoned its belief that Joe Stalin really knew how to run a country. More recently, the pendulum swung again toward *glasnost,* where the cycle might at last ended, had the proposed new Union Treaty been signed. The hard-liners of the Red Army and the KGB, who have more guns than the reformers do, temporarily interrupted that progress, as they threatened a bloody crackdown.

• Close to one-third of the Soviet people live below the official poverty line, and their ranks are growing rapidly. At the official rate of $.56 to the ruble, the average citizen earns only $1,920 U.S. dollars per year; at the black market exchange rate of $.04 to the ruble—the only one that means anything to ordinary citizens—it is closer to $140 per year. To buy a Japanese television on the black market, the average Soviet citizen would have to save his entire income for five years. A used foreign car costs at least twenty years' average salary.

• Although the USSR harvested a record 230 million tons of wheat in 1990, it was forced to import another forty million tons—and even with that, bread seldom reached the empty store shelves. Soviet farmers keep more than one-eighth of their wheat for use as seed the following year; American farmers manage with only 4 percent. Much of the remaining Soviet grain is spilled from open trucks bouncing along unpaved roads. More rots while waiting for the trucks to arrive, or is eaten by birds, while piled outside inadequate storage facilities. More than one-fourth of Soviet grain is lost before it reaches the market.

That almost qualifies as a success, by the standards of Soviet agriculture. Only one-fourth of the potatoes grown ever reach the market. Farmers keep many of them for local markets, where they sell for triple the official price.

• In 1985, the Communist party promised to give every Soviet family its own house or apartment by the turn of the century. President Gorbachev urged the creation of a modern housing market, complete with new banks to finance construction, and joint ventures with foreign companies to do the actual building. The goal: to double the number of new homes built each year and provide forty million new housing units by the year 2000. None of this has happened, nor will it. Most of the people who survived the 1988 earthquake in Armenia are still living in shanty towns. Soviet soldiers returning from duty in Czechoslovakia and Hungary have been housed in tents, because there is nowhere else to put them. Something like three million people were homeless in the USSR by the end of 1990, and the number is growing rapidly.

• The few bright spots in the Soviet economy are its too-rare attempts at private enterprise. Those in agriculture are the oldest and most successful. For some years, farmers have been allowed to grow and sell their own crops on tiny private plots within the country's giant collective farms. They work only two percent of the land under cultivation, yet produce one-fourth of the nation's fruit and vegetables.

Outside the farms, private enterprise is not so healthy. Despite encouragement from Moscow, few of the Soviet Union's 164 million workers are employed in the private cooperatives that pass for capitalism under the reforms enacted to date. Estimates ranged from 500,000 to perhaps three million at the peak, in 1989. Whichever was correct, the number is declining. In part, this is because local bureaucrats, most of whom still are hard-line Communists, have surrounded would-be entrepreneurs with so much red tape that few can cope with it. High taxes have also stifled small businesses. Private enterprises must send Moscow 45 percent of their net revenues and two-thirds of whatever profits they manage to save. But the real obstacle is that after decades of Marxist training many Soviet citizens despise the few who get ahead through their own initiative. The philosophy that equates success with exploitation remains strong, even as the Party that championed it loses its following.

By comparison, the black market employs an estimated 10 percent of the workforce. It adds $150 billion a year to the national economy, according to Gosplan, the official economic-planning ministry.

• Soviet oil exports have been falling, though the USSR has the fourth-largest crude reserves in the world. From 144 million tons in 1988, exports declined to less than 100 million tons in 1990. Since then, they have dried up almost completely. One reason is that civil unrest in Azerbaijan, where most of the 1950s-style drilling and pumping equipment is manufactured, has cut into factory output. In the second half of 1990, another problem intervened: the United Nations embargo against trade with Iraq. It seems that much of the oil the Soviets had been "exporting" for scarce foreign exchange, came from Iraq, which traded it for such necessities as Scud missiles and MiG fighters. Soviet technology and distribution networks are too inefficient to meet even their own petroleum needs.

Moved in part by disappointment with the failing economy and in part by ethnic hatreds that have always simmered just below the surface of Soviet society, virtually everyone but the Communist party has opted to disassemble the USSR into its component parts. Most republics have declared their independence. All of the fifteen republican legislatures have declared their sovereignty. So have many of the "autonomous" regions within the republics, and even a few cities. In Moldavia, ethnic Russians have declared their sovereignty. The 150,000 ethnic Turkish Gagauz were blocked from doing so only when an armed mob of ethnic Romanians interrupted their plebiscite. The Armenian parliament has even voted to set up its own army, and the Russian Republic has threatened to do so.

The process has gone the farthest in Boris Yeltsin's giant Russian Republic, which includes nearly half of the Soviet population and three-fourths of its land mass. No fewer than nine of its sixteen autonomous ethnic regions have declared that their laws supersede those of the republican government. Yeltsin apparently approves. He has urged them to take on as much power as they can wield effectively, leaving as little as possible to central authority. It is a policy he has pursued vigorously with Moscow.

The centerpiece of Yeltsin's program is the 500-day economic miracle originally proposed for the Soviet Union itself. The plan, devised by economist and former Gorbachev adviser, Stanislav Shatalin, calls for a systematic transition to free-market capitalism, to be carried out with blinding speed. From a standing start in fall 1990, it was to have been completed by April 1992.

In early 1991, there was no evidence that Gorbachev would ever enact meaningful economic reforms. He clearly had lost whatever enthusiasm he had, even for the limited changes he advocated only months ago. His first act, with the dictatorial powers granted by the Soviet legislature in 1990, was to put reform on hold for a year. Only some budget cuts have actually gone into effect, and those mostly because Moscow can no longer afford such luxuries as a foreign-aid program. Gorbachev actually raised military spending; in 1991, the Defense Ministry received fully 37 percent of the national budget.

In contrast, Yeltsin bought the Shatalin plan, whole. So did the Russian Parliament, by a vote of 213 to 2. The Russian republic and the central government, have been on collision courses ever since. In November 1990, the Russian Parliament passed a law claiming ownership of all government property within its territory, save only that belonging to the army or the KGB. It plans to disband unprofitable collective farms or break them into private plots, privatize nearly all businesses, and scrap most wage and price controls and production quotas. Unlike the Soviet government, the republic has specifically endorsed the concept of private property.

Soon after the republic adopted its economic reform package, it voted to cut its tax payments to Moscow by 85 percent. It is difficult to say which vexed the Kremlin more.

These and other insults have brought the Soviet president growing criticism from the KGB, the army, and other pillars of the Communist right. Some of Gorbachev's actions most appreciated in the West added to the neo-Stalinist pressure. His unilateral demobilization of 500,000 soldiers humiliated an army already smarting from its defeat in Afghanistan. The haste with which Germany reunified itself, and the rest of Eastern Europe overthrew their Communist governments, both horrified and frightened the Party's old guard. Gorbachev's support for the movement of American troops into the Persian Gulf added yet another strain. Fifty-three hard-liners finally sent him an open letter. It read:

> Dear Mikhail Sergeyevich!
> Our Mother Russia, the greatest treasure created by the entire people's potential over a thousand years of history, our Motherland is under a threat. The structures of the state and of public life are falling apart, dooming the people to famine and chaos. We are addressing you with a demand to stop the chaos, to prevent a collapse of the country using all the levers of power and authority which are in your hands.
> We suggest that immediate action should be taken against separatism, subversive antistate activity, provocations, and national discords. If constitutional measures prove ineffective, we suggest that a state of emergency and presidential rule should be introduced in the zones of large conflicts.

It was followed by a charge in the Congress of People's Deputies that Gorbachev had lost the "moral right to lead the country" and a vote of no confidence that was approved by nearly one-fourth of the Congress's members.

Facing this growing pressure for decisive action, Gorbachev answered many challenges to Moscow's rule in time-honored Party fashion: first with bluster, then with direct threats, and finally with guns. For more than a year, Moscow and the republics played an odd and inconclusive little game: The republics declared their control over some facet of society formerly governed from Moscow. Gorbachev then ruled their declaration void, and the republics passed another law declaring that his nullification was itself void. In the end, the republics usually wound up doing as they pleased. Occasionally, Gorbachev found more effective ways to respond. When the Russian Republic tried to set up its own banking system late in 1990, he declared the bank computing centers to be Soviet government property. Yeltsin could have his banks, but they would have to keep their accounts by hand. The two reached a compromise of sorts: Yeltsin will do without a separate banking system until Moscow reaches some final accommodation with its separatist movements; the Kremlin will then reconsider.

The stakes got higher later in the year. In a speech Gorbachev authorized, KGB head Vladimir Kryuchkov harangued TV audiences, threatening a crackdown by KGB troops if would-be separatists did not start to toe the Moscow line. In Lithuania, Red Army troops, in early 1991, fired on peaceful demonstrators. Although the crackdown on the Baltics later eased, the army harshly quashed small insurrections in Georgia and Moldavia.

Another of Gorbachev's ploys was to call for a new "voluntary" confederation designed to supply the Soviet Union with the legitimacy it so clearly lacks. The draft Union Treaty, which may yet replace the one signed under duress in 1922, defines a new governmental structure that at least gives the appearance of sharing power with the republics. In theory, at least, the document is a paragon of democracy. Under the new system, the president and the new vice president would be elected directly by the populace; they would have to win more than half the vote both throughout the country and in a majority of the republics. The plan also gives republics the right to choose their own form of government; guarantees basic human rights; including "use of native languages, unhindered access to information, freedom of religion"; and offers republics "the free choice of forms of property and economic management." Read optimistically, that could install at the regional level both democratic rule and the right to private property as the Russian Republic eagerly assumed.

The key to the plan is the new Council of the Federation, which until recently has been only a forum for the republican presidents to voice their dissatisfaction with Moscow. Under the new system, it appears to become the nation's ultimate ruling body. It would include the Soviet president; the new vice president; the republican presidents, if they are willing to join (at least six have said they will not); and the heads of the autonomous regions within the republics. That is close to 40 members, enough to turn the Council into an ineffectual debating society firmly led by the Soviet president.

In that case, it could leave the Soviet president with even more power than he now possesses. Moscow retains authority over such matters as defense, military organization, foreign policy and trade, and the currency. The draft treaty speaks somewhat vaguely about respecting property and declares that each republic is "a sovereign state and enjoys full authority over its territory," save for those powers needed to administer the central government's prerogatives. It never defines just what those powers might be, and the judge appears to be the Soviet president. The end result is a further concentration of authority in the president. Many onlookers assume that this is the real purpose behind the simulated liberalization.

The scheme won very little enthusiasm among the republics. Lithuanian president Vytautas Landsbergis rejected Gorbachev's proposed union, complaining that it failed to recognize Lithuanian independence. "In the Baltic countries," he declared, "one can exercise the powers given by the Soviet Parliament to the president only with the help of brute military force. The Baltic countries will defend themselves." In Georgia, a nationalist group known as the Round Table garnered 54 percent of the votes in recent elections for the republic's parliament; its major campaign promise was not to sign Gorbachev's new treaty. In all, six of the republics declared that they would boycott the plebescite meant to ratify the continued union of the USSR. The Russian Republic added a question to the plebiscite asking whether its citizens believed their president should be elected by popular vote rather than by members of the Parliament. A positive response gave Yeltsin even greater stature.

Unlike their local governments, many Soviet citizens might approve the new Union Treaty. Many were sick of the chaos and would have accepted nearly anything that promised a return to stability. Some were even more completely fed up. At the end of 1990, a poll found that 22 percent said they would even welcome a military coup, if only it would restore order.

They temporarily received half their wish. On August 19, 1991 Mikhail Gorbachev vanished amid official claims that he had been suffering from medical problems. In his place was an eight-man "emergency committee" composed of Party hardliners, among them the head of the KGB, the defense minister, interior minister, and Gorbachev's own vice president. Tanks rolled through the streets of Moscow, most of the radio and TV stations broadcast somber music punctuated by official commanda, and the army proclaimed itself in control of Lithuania, Leningrad, and other centers of liberalism. Gennady Yenayev, Gorbachev's "acting" replacement, claimed that the crackdown was necessary to eliminate the growing criminal gangs, "liquidate" the armed bands that operate freely in the outlying republics, and restore food to a starving country. In all, it was a familiar scene, repeated often in the Soviet Union and its satellites in the years following World War II.

The timing of the coup was crucial. Moscow's right wing saw August 19 as the last day on which they could reassert their dominance with even a flimsy veil of constitutionality. On the follwing day, Gorbachev would have signed the new Union Treaty, passing on much of the central government's power to the individual republics and forever stripping the Party hierarchy of their legitimacy.

It was a desperation move, and clearly not well thought out. Gorbachev's approval ratings have been so low—in one recent poll, only seven percent of Soviet citizens felt he had been doing a good job of running the country—that the plotters must have expected to win public support for ousting him. It never materialized.

The take-over's execution was just as inept. For a coup to succeed, the new government must take immediate control of the media, and the military and must be willing to impose its rule by force. The "emergency committee" never met any of those requirements. At least some pro-Gorbachev radio and television remained on the air in most of the country, and the Voice of America was never jammed; Soviet citizens could find relatively unbiased reporting throughout the coup. And when the time came to use the army to quell dissent, the committee members could not bring themselves to act. It would have been relatively easy to bring troops from, say, the Soviet Union's Moslem regions and order them to put down unrest in Moscow and Leningrad, just as Beijing imported Mongolian troops to deal with the Tienanmen Square demonstrations. But the plotters may have remembered that Romania's Nicolai Ceausescu faced the firing squad because he had ordered his troops to fire on his own people.

With a powerful enough show of force, the coup's leaders might have whipped their recalcitrant citizens back into line. A round of purges like those of the 1930s could have eliminated Boris Yeltsin and his fellow radicals in a few weeks or months; a "night of the long knives," like that in which Hitler murdered followers he considered untrustworthy, would have done the job even faster. Party hard-liners must have been considering such measures at least since 1990. They remember with almost instinctive dread the chaos that followed the October Revolution of 1917, when the Russian people last slipped out of Moscow's control and only the mobs ruled. In their rigid, authoritarian world-views, almost any threat to the Party's dominance is a giant step toward anarchy. As they proved on August 19, they are determined never to let it happen again.

Yet these are tools the Party can no longer afford to use. During the winter of 1990-91, Moscow has fed its people largely through Western generosity. Germany sent it the 350,000 tons of grain, canned fruit, and other foodstuffs once stockpiled to keep West Berlin alive if the U.S.S.R. resumed its 1948-49 blockade; it was a gift worth nearly $1.7 billion. The European Community provided aid worth another $1 billion. Japan sent medical supplies and other essentials. The United States, the EC, and Japan have committed some $2 billion in economic aid during 1991 and early 1992. The coup interrupted that flow of generosity within hours; any serious crackdown on dissenters would have ensured that Western aid resumes only when the Party has been overthrown. It was a price the "emergency committee" was not willing to pay.

All this brings up an intriguing possibility, one that has left some Washington intelligence officials scratching their heads. In this view, the entire coup was staged, if not by Gorbachev himself, then at least with the complicity of his advisors. Though the hard-liners would have been sincere in their determination to take power, Gorbachev's aides could have encouraged them with two goals in mind. One is to discredit the hard-liners and win Gorbachev the freedom to carry out democratic reforms. The other is to show the West just what it risks in refusing the economic aid he requested at the last meeting of the G7 economic ministers. The risk was that, with Gorbachev out of power, his successors would decide not to invite him back. The rewards could be far greater. Gorbachev wants $20-30 billion in Western aid over the next year; maintaining American troops in Europe will cost five times that. The threat of a right-wing coup in Moscow could be all that is needed to convince Washington, Brussels, and Tokyo that $20-30 billion is a small price to pay in order to stabilize the Gorbachev regime. It could also convince the European Community to hasten its long-term plans to give the Soviet Union associate membership, in hopes that forging closer economic ties with the West will stabilize the fragile Soviet political situation. In fact, there is every chance that Gorbachev will now receive both rewards.

They have not been won without a price, however. By surviving a rightist coup, Gorbachev has at last won some of the political legitimacy enjoyed by Boris Yeltsin, who took office in a popular election, rather than through Party politics. But he has retained his position only with Yeltsin's determined assistance. Gorbachev now owes an enormous debt to his one-time rival, and Yeltsin has emerged as a man who can stand up to the Party hard-liners. This could permanently change the balance of power between the two men and give Yeltsin far more influence in national affairs.

We in the West may never know whether the coup was a real attempt to seize power or a clever and desperate stratagem. But just three days after the coup, *Tass* pronounced the coup over, its leaders were arrested, and the army withdrew its tanks and armored cars from Moscow, Leningrad, and the Baltics. It all happened so quickly that some onlookers are now convinced that both the West and the right-wing extremists have been had.

In the long run, an even more influential pocket of liberalism will form around former Foreign Minister Eduard Shevardnadze; His credentials as a liberal leader are impeccable. Mikhail Gorbachev admits that he first considered attempting to reform the Soviet system during a conversation with Shevardnadze as they strolled along the shore of the Black Sea. He resigned from a position of power voluntarily, as a matter of principle. Since his resignation and warning that a new age of Soviet dictatorship was at hand, there have been rumors that Shevardnadze would emigrate to the West and become either a consultant on foreign policy or a college professor. In fact, like his father before him, he will become a teacher, just as he was before Gorbachev elevated him to the national government. He will inevitably gather a following among students with a future in politics. No matter what today's hard-line Communists wish, it is Shevardnadze's followers who will form the nucleus of the liberal government that will rule ten and twenty years from now.

So the cycle of progress and retreat will continue, driven not by Moscow and the Party but by the republics and the liberals, both in and out of office. Gorbachev, or his successors, will assert their power from time to time, in response to right-wing pressure, but the fundamental changes have already been made. They cannot be reversed.

The Union of Soviet Socialist Republics is no longer a union. What remains will be a smaller nation, its central government much less powerful. Lithuania will regain its independence, thanks in part to the recent plebiscite in which 90 percent of its people voted overwhelmingly to secede from the Soviet Union. In their own voting, Latvia and Estonia came remarkably close to equaling that unanimity, though one-third of the people in Latvia and 30 percent of those in Lithuania are ethnic Russians, many of them retired army officers. In these nations too, secession votes handily topped the two-thirds majority required under Gorbachev's restrictive rules; even significant minorities of the ethnic Russians opted to leave the union. In the end, all of the Baltics will go free. Other republics will content themselves with a more liberal government in Moscow and effective control over their own territories. The combination of Gorbachev's power and Yeltsin's enormous popular mandate—if the two men can continue to work together—will create a force for stable change that not even the Party can resist. The post-coup communist party will never regain its previous stature and will remain alive only as a splinter group.

The confederation that will still unite the republics is already under construction without any help from Moscow. Yeltsin's Russian Republic has signed economic cooperation agreements with eight of its neighbors and is negotiating similar treaties with the rest. The five Central Asian republics have signed an economic pact of their own. These economic treaties will be the real structure of the Soviet Union, not the Communist right's forlorn attempt to recapture the past. They will form a much less rigid nation than the pre-Gorbachev USSR. It will be much more capable of rebuilding the Soviet economy to fit a capitalist reality. It will also be less inclined, even than Gorbachev himself, to meddle destructively in world affairs.

PART TWO

NORTH AMERICA

INTRODUCTION

In the mid-1980s, the United States was still one of the two pillars of the postwar order. Its conflict with the Soviet Union had heated and cooled repeatedly over the decades. Early in the Reagan years, the vision of Cowboy America shone brightly, the nation riding tall in the saddle, proud but essentially cut off from its peers. In that context, it seemed that the mutual antagonism between the world's superpowers might never end.

Of all the surprises since then, few have been more remarkable than the transformation in the United States. North America did not start the trend toward economic and political integration, but it is embracing the process almost as warmly as Europe itself. It did not end the cold war—that accomplishment is to Mikhail Gorbachev's lasting credit—but it has seized the opportunity eagerly. During and after the Persian Gulf War, the Bush administration has done everything it could to encourage the development of the new world order, in which power is shared whenever possible and tensions are dissipated rather than exploited. This change of heart is one of the most promising developments of the 1990s.

For the remainder of the decade, the United States will devote more and more of its attention to its own hemisphere; this too is a sharp departure with the past. A North American economic union similar to that now forming in Europe has become one major facet of U.S. foreign policy. The essential unity of this region will become even more clear as the 1990s unfold and the economic ties between Canada, Mexico, and the giant neighbor between them grow ever stronger.

This economic union will accomplish what America alone has

not been able to do: it will rescue the United States and its neighbors from their growing inability to compete with the faster, better integrated competition from the Pacific Rim and, increasingly, from Europe.

As we will see in the coming chapters, the rich of North America are destined to become wealthier still.

C H A P T E R 6

The Rich Grow Richer

"America is not an economic weakling, but a sickly giant now beginning a convalescence that will take much less time than most people believe. By the middle of this decade, it will be healing visibly. At the turn of the century, it will again be a firm cornerstone for the economy of a continent."

In large part, the future of North America is the future of the United States. For Canada, Mexico, and even Cuba, the single most powerful influence shaping their economic and political futures is their proximity to the U.S. The essential unity of this region will become even more clear as the 1990s unfold. The ties between Mexico and its neighbors to the North grow ever stronger, and the once-powerful link between Cuba and the United States will be rebuilt.

Economically, the relationships between Canada, Mexico, and the United States are crucial to all three. U.S.-Canadian trade in 1988 amounted to over $147 billion—more than between any other two countries. Sixty-nine percent of Canada's imports come from America; 74 percent of Canadian exports go to the U.S. And though trade between Mexico and the U.S. is smaller in absolute terms—about $21 billion in 1987—it represents 65 percent of Mexico's exports and 60 percent of its imports. Trade between the United States and both its neighbors is growing rapidly and can only accelerate in the 1990s.

The Canadian Parliament all but assured this continent's prosperity by a single vote on December 31, 1988. That act ratified the historic free-trade agreement with the United States, the first elements of which took effect the following day. Under this pact, U.S. manufacturers will gain free access both to Canada's markets and its vast reserves of natural resources—oil, natural gas, lumber, and even fresh water for the increasingly parched American West. Canada, in turn, will gain free access to the enormous markets and investment opportunities of the United States. It is a fair exchange that will stimulate the economies of both nations.

Changes elsewhere may work to the American bloc's benefit as well. One great fear growing from the consolidation of Europe was that the EC would build almost impenetrable trade barriers around their unified market, making it difficult for others to benefit from the economic unification of Europe. That has not happened. Instead, in electronics, aerospace, chemicals, and pharmaceuticals—four high-tech markets crucial to American interests—the Common Market has adopted product standards based closely on those of the United States. This will make it dramatically easier for North America to do business with the Common Market. Beech and Cessna, for example, may have to alter their airplanes to meet the strict German noise standards being adopted throughout Europe, but this will require only minor modifications, not wholesale redesign. The result must inevitably be greater prosperity for all.

More immediate benefits are already flowing from the conclusion of the Gulf War. Kuwait has formally declared that it will pass out the contracts for the mammoth task of rebuilding its shattered industry and infrastructure to the nations that freed it from Saddam Hussein's Iraq, in proportion to the magnitude of their commitment to the war; Saudi Arabia seems to be following the same rule. At least two-thirds of that money will go to the United States. It will cost $1.5 billion to get Kuwait's water, power, and telephone systems working again, and even then the repairs will be far from complete. Just putting out the fires in Kuwait's oil wells and controlling the flow of petroleum will cost at least $2 billion. In all, Kuwait's construction bill could total $100 billion. Even in an economy as large as that of the United States, an additional $70 billion—not counting money from

Saudi Arabia and the rest of the region—will have a major impact.

As the 1990s opened, the United States seemed, at best, a frail reed to support the economy of a continent, and perhaps a hemisphere. Despite the publicized Gramm-Rudman-Hollings "balanced-budget" law passed in 1985, spending cuts and higher taxes have brought the Federal budget deficit under $150 billion—just barely—only once since the 1983 fiscal year, in 1986; in 1992, it is expected to reach $300 billion, its all-time peak. The nation's merchandise balance-of-trade deficit, though dropping, was still nearly $130 billion in 1989. Its rate of worker productivity growth, the engine that lifts a nation's standard of living, was one of the lowest among the major industrial powers. And in a world whose workers require ever more basic education, technological "savvy," and specialized skill, America's schools are the least successful in the Western world. All this puts the United States at a competitive disadvantage that, it appears, can only grow in the years to come. It is difficult not to assume that a continent whose economy is keyed to such a land is doomed to growing backwardness and poverty.

In fact, the United States is well on its way to solving the problems it has made for itself. By the turn of the twenty-first century, its twin deficits will be under control, more of its students will graduate from high school, and those who do will be better equipped for a productive life in a technological world. America will be, not less competitive, but far more so. Its neighbors will benefit almost as much as the United States itself.

We have already presented our reasons for believing that America is due for a dramatic revival. The details filled two previous books (*American Renaissance: Our Life at the Turn of the 21st Century* and *Educational Renaissance: Our Schools at the Turn of the Twenty-First Century*). In part, they are a statement of faith, based on history. Almost invariably, when something has been desperately necessary, from America's entry into World War II to its departure from Vietnam, the United States has gotten the job done. Americans meet their challenges with foot-dragging reluctance and act only at the last possible moment, but they do meet them. We believe that for the tasks of repairing America's economy and school system, the last, triumphant moment is nearly at hand.

We have already seen indirect evidence of this in the remarkable performance of American troops in the Persian Gulf War. That conflict was fought under difficult conditions, against numerically superior opposition, with weapons that require a high degree of technological sophistication if they are to be used successfully. It was all but over within hours after the land battle began. The troops who wrought that miracle were not, for the most part, college graduates, and it is a good guess that few of them attended rigorous private schools. Instead, they were the same high school graduates and dropouts who, in Vietnam a generation earlier, fought so badly with less demanding weapons. It made a difference that the American military of the 1990s is composed of volunteers, not draftees, and that more of them today have completed high school. It helped, too, that they were incomparably better led. But these factors alone do not explain the thorough competence of individual soldiers with demanding tasks to perform. That must reflect much better preparation before today's recruits enter the military, and it can only mean that America's schools are doing a better job today than they did twenty years ago. In the years to come, the U.S. economy will benefit from that schooling just as the U.S. military has done.

There are more direct arguments as well. One is the relative simplicity of reducing the federal budget deficit to a manageable level. By early 1991, time and the growth of the American economy had already done half the job with relatively little aid from Washington. At its peak in the boom year of 1986, just over $221 billion, the deficit amounted to one-nineteenth of the gross national product. By 1990, it had been reduced by about $70 billion—less than half of the cut required by the Gramm-Rudman-Hollings law—but equaled only one thirty-fifth of the GNP. When the figures are totalled for 1991, a year of mild recession, even the worst-case estimates put the deficit at no more than 1986 proportions. Once the recession has passed and tax receipts have recovered, the deficit should fall rapidly with little help from the government's reluctant budget-cutters.

Another painless factor that may reduce the deficit will be decreased military spending. Though tensions between the United States and the USSR have risen with Moscow's crackdown on separatist movements in the Soviet republics, and with the right-wing coup in August 1991, the return of democracy to Eastern

Europe has permanently reduced the need for American troops in the NATO countries. The majority of troops moved from Europe to the Persian Gulf during the Kuwait crisis will never return to the Continent. The war with Iraq has cost the U.S. an estimated $70.5 billion. America's allies have pledged to defray $53.5 billion of this cost. (About 60 percent had been repaid by early April 1991.) The Gulf War, however, is a one-time expense. Once it has been absorbed, this dramatic reduction in overseas defense commitments will save the United States about $140 billion per year. Perhaps half of that will go to fund increased government programs, particularly in education and health care. The rest will reduce the federal deficit by as much as all the budget cuts enacted between 1986 and 1990 combined.

If that is not enough to bring the deficit under control, there are any number of other opportunities. Admittedly, most of them are politically difficult at best.

Raising the excise taxes on gasoline, alcohol, and tobacco would add about $30 billion per year to the federal Treasury, even if the increases no more than offset the effects of inflation since the last adjustments.

Much of the money spent on farm price supports goes to pad the earnings of huge corporate agribusinesses that would be profitable without subsidies. Limiting payments to farmers who actually need them would save something on the order of $10 billion per year.

Virtually all of the huge dams, canals, and other pork-barrel projects built by the Bureau of Reclamation and the Corps of Engineers in recent years have been no more than disguised hand-outs for local businessmen. We have not dissected out of the national budget exactly how much these projects cost, but any funding stripped from them will be money well saved.

Not counting what would be saved by eliminating pork-barrel spending, we are now roughly $110 billion closer to balancing the Federal budget—and that is without tackling the politically difficult big-money changes. Former Commerce Secretary Peter G. Peterson estimates that limiting cost-of-living adjustments for Social Security to 60 percent of the inflation rate would save $150 billion per year by the turn of the century. Raising the retirement age for Social Security from sixty-five to sixty-six would save another $18 billion a year. Raise it to age seventy, and the savings total $90 billion per year. (This is not unreasonable. When the Social Security Act was passed in 1935, average life expectancy at birth in the United States was only sixty years; today it is more than seventy-five.) Further savings can be found in the bloated pension programs for government employees and the military.

Finally, savings beget savings. The smaller the deficit, the less Washington must borrow in order to pay the interest on its previous debt, and the less it must offer lenders in order to borrow their money. Reducing interest rates by just two percent would save more than $60 billion per year.

With enough political will, the United States could save enough from its budget to cover almost any conceivable deficit. We do not expect American legislators to display the kind of courage required to cut benefits to retirees. Even enacting a means test to eliminate Social Security payments for the wealthy is beyond their capacity. Yet, thanks largely to the political changes in Europe, no great display of courage or imagination is required. Under the circumstances, a nearly balanced budget seems nearly inevitable by the end of the decade.

Once that is accomplished, other improvements become possible. The American balance-of-trade deficit has been, in large part, a result of the budget deficit. When Washington borrows abroad to pay for its spending at home, the extra interest it is forced to pay, raises demand for the dollar on the world's financial markets. This lifts the dollar's value compared with other currencies, and that in turn makes American products comparatively expensive on the export market, while reducing the cost of imports in the United States. Before the recession of 1990, falling interest rates had helped to reduce the U.S. balance-of-trade deficit from nearly $170 billion in 1986 to just under $110 billion in 1989. As the Federal budget deficit falls in the mid-1990s, American interest rates will decline as well, and the trade deficit will follow.

Worker productivity is one problem that seems unaffected by either deficit, but there are connections. Productivity has grown slowly in the United States in recent years, for two reasons. In part, productivity growth has lagged because capital that should have been used to fund new investment has gone instead to pay for government spending. In part, it has been slow because the service industries have been the fastest growing sector of the American labor market, and productivity there is generally lower than in manufacturing. In the late 1980s, American labor productivity remained almost flat, compared with an average increase of 4 percent per year in Japan.

This, too, will change in the 1990s. In many industries, and especially in manufacturing, the most powerful force that improves productivity is new technology. Acquiring it means a capital investment, and that becomes easier to make when interest rates are low. After a long delay, new forms of automation, such as expert systems, are beginning to raise productivity in the labor-intensive service industries as well; any improvement in this large sector will have a marked affect on overall productivity. In addition, American manufacturers appear at last to have learned the importance of export markets. Before the current recession, U.S. labor productivity had begun to rise again, in large part because the relatively low price of the dollar on foreign exchange markets had spurred exports in the highly productive manufacturing sector. That trend will reappear once interest rates drop and the dollar declines again.

America's schools are the most difficult problem the United States now faces, and their situation is far too complex to permit a capsule summary. An extraordinary variety of factors has undermined the U.S. educational system in recent decades. Schools have been forced to compete for scarce funding with other governmental priorities and have often lagged behind. In many areas, a huge influx of non-English-speaking immigrants has raised the demand for multilingual teachers, who are in short supply. Textbooks have been so watered down that it is sometimes difficult to tell what subject they were intended to teach. Nearly one-fourth of all American students drop out of high school; in some inner-city districts the figure is more than one-half. (In comparison, some 94 percent of Japanese students and 94 percent of German students finish high school.) Teaching itself has been handicapped by spurious educational theories, endemic politicking, untalented recruits, professional organizations more interested in work rules than in student achievement, poor support from parents, and all the structural ills of cancerous bureaucracy. If any problem could afflict American schools in theory, it probably does so in fact.

To date, the reformers have made little visible progress in fixing the ills of American education. SAT scores have stopped their precipitous decline, but they have yet to approach their levels in years past. Dropout rates generally have not improved. It would be easy to conclude that nothing has been accomplished.

Yet we believe that America's schools have already turned the corner. In more than a year of preparing *Educational Renaissance: Our Schools at the Turn of the Twenty-First Century,* Forecasting International surveyed several hundred school reform efforts throughout the United States and examined dozens of them in detail. Throughout the nation, in decaying inner cities and in rural farm communities, we found a vast, highly diversified transformation taking place. Some districts were using computerized education to give disadvantaged youngsters a leg up on learning. Others were recruiting teachers with real-world experience from industry. One school district had cut its dropout rate from more than one-third to less than half of one percent. Still others had so improved their academic performance that the worst of dead-end city schools are suddenly giving educations on a par with the best private institutions. As their innovations are passed from district to district, adapted for local conditions, and applied to new situations, their benefits will be visible to all. We believe that American school reform has reached its "critical mass" and will soon explode throughout the nation.

The United States has a long way to go to cure all the problems that have dogged it for decades. It will be twenty more years before the children now in grammar school turn educational reform into business competitiveness. But other changes will act much more rapidly, and the structure now being repaired is fundamentally sound. America is not an economic weakling, but a sickly giant now beginning a convalescence that will take much less time than most people believe. By the middle of this decade, it will be visibly healing. At the turn of the century, it will again be a firm cornerstone for the economy of a continent.

Canada is well matched as a partner for the United States, and it has long been a very active one. In 1988, over $147 billion-worth of merchandise crossed the 5,335-mile border between the two countries, more than between any other two nations of the world. Overall, Canada ranks seventh in the world in its volume of foreign trade. The two nations are closely linked by direct investment as well as by trade. Canadian companies own $32 billion worth of corporate shares, real estate, and other holdings in the United States, well over half of Canada's investment abroad. Seagram's, one of Canada's largest multinational corporations, had nearly three-fourths of its assets in the United States by 1987, and the share has grown since then. Northern Telecom alone owns more than $4 billion in assets south of the border. U.S. companies, in turn, have sunk $67 billion into Canadian assets, much of it in the natural-resource industries.

Like its neighbor to the south, Canada suffers from serious financial problems. With a GNP less than one-tenth that of the United States, it is even more heavily addicted to debt. According to the influential Business Council on National Issues, in Ottawa, combined federal and provincial government debt, late in 1990, totalled 70 percent of the country's GNP, a figure exceeded only by Italy. Canada's budget deficit totalled $30 billion, its national debt exceeded $380 billion, and both figures were headed higher. Inflation was running at 6 percent, unemployment at 9 percent, and the prime interest rate was pegged at 13 percent—and Canada's recession, the first produced by local factors rather than by a downturn in the United States, has produced a serious case of "stagflation." Rather than reduce its spending to cut its mounting debt, the Mulroney government has imposed a 7 percent value-added tax on virtually all goods and services in the country.

All this has had a predictable effect on Canada's export trade. With interest rates so high, the Canadian dollar has risen to nearly ninety U.S. cents on foreign exchange markets. According to the Canadian Pulp and Paper Association, whose members earn 80 percent of their revenue from foreign markets, every one-cent increase in the value of the Canadian dollar costs its industry alone $100 million per year in export sales. By the end of 1990, that pushed the nation's current account to a $9 billion deficit. As a result, net foreign debt (both federal and provincial) rose from $137 billion in 1983 to an estimated $380 billion at the end of 1990.

Like the United States, Canada must pay off its foreign debt by selling more goods abroad. Once it controls its budget deficit, either by cutting government programs or by raising taxes, interest rates will come down, exports will begin to grow again, and the problem will solve itself. Even without the free-trade agreement, we would expect Canada to be solvent again by the end of the decade.

With the free-trade agreement, far more is possible for both nations. The first restriction eliminated under the pact was Canada's 3.9 percent tariff on computers and some related goods, which ended in 1989. Other barriers will be phased out gradually. Tariffs on telecommunications equipment are slated to disappear in 1994; those on precision instruments and scientific devices will remain in place until 1999. With each trade barrier eliminated, we expect trade between the neighboring countries to take a noticeable leap.

Although the agreement has had little effect to date, the U.S.-Canada Automotive Agreement of 1965 offers a good idea of the changes to come. That accord provided for free commerce between the two nations in a single industry, cars, trucks, and auto parts. Two-way trade in this field amounted to only $175 million in 1964; by 1988, it had grown to $51.5 billion—nearly one-third of all trade between the two nations.

As trade between the United States and Canada grows, other barriers between them will vanish as well. Canadian companies such as Seagram's and Campeau (if it survives its current cash-flow problems)—firms that derive most of their revenue from trade with the United States—will find that there is little reason to maintain their headquarters in Canada, while there are major benefits to be gained by moving closer to their market. Many of them will relocate to Chicago, Seattle, Boston, and Washington.

U.S. companies will be moving as well, and not just to establish branch offices in Ottawa and Montreal. By the end of the 1990s, North America will have two great financial centers—and neither of them will be New York. In the north, Quebec has already built a thriving financial industry. Montreal's stock exchange is the third most active on the continent, its largest banks are comparable to their U.S. counterparts and are less exposed to the dangers of Third World debt. As of 1989, the province of Quebec did nearly $41 billion worth of foreign trade, 15 percent of the Canadian total, and most of that was with the United States. As the free-trade agreement promotes ever greater business across the border, Montreal's financial institutions can only grow as well.

The other financial center will be Washington, D.C. By 2000, and probably well before, it will be home to both the New York Stock Exchange and the American Stock Exchange and to many of the major corporations now headquartered in New York City. For many years, the regulators in Washington have been by far the most powerful influence on American financial institutions. That power can only grow in the years to come. Both major stock exchanges have often contemplated leaving New York, with its high taxes and decaying infrastructure, and many corporations have already made their moves. Within ten years, the exchanges and many more companies will follow. They will not move to New Jersey, as the exchanges have occasionally threatened, or to the Sun Belt. They will move where the power is, where they already support legions of lobbyists, attorneys, and influence-peddlers. Washington is the only place it makes sense for them to be.

The U.S.-Canada Free-Trade Agreement is an important step in uniting these two nations, but it is only the first step. During the 1990s, a growing network of investment and trade will link the two nations ever more inseparably. As the U.S. and Canada grow more dependent on each other, the few real differences between them will shrink. English-speaking Canadians will come to feel more a part of the nation with which they deal so closely, rather than one that contains Montreal, while French Canadians will view with growing alarm the perceived displacement of their culture by creeping Americanism. For both, the historical bonds that have kept their nation together—never the strongest—will dwindle under the immediate impact of these more pressing concerns. It will not be long before these changing personal allegiances transform the political face of North America, as we will see in the next chapter.

C H A P T E R 7

....

55 United States, and Quebec

"In a national poll taken before the outbreak of war in the Persian Gulf, 59 percent of Canadians asked said they would sooner be led by George Bush than Brian Mulroney."

....

Ironically, the U.S.-Canada Free-Trade Agreement could be obsolete even before the final barriers between Canada and the United States are scheduled to fall. We expect that by 2000, or soon thereafter, Canada will cease to exist as an independent dominion. It will be replaced by the nation of Quebec and four new states of the United States. Ontario will form one state, more or less in its present form. The Atlantic provinces, Nova Scotia, Newfoundland, and Prince Edward Island, will join to create a second. And two more states will be cobbled together from the western provinces: Manitoba, Saskatchewan, Alberta, British Columbia, and the Northwest Territories.

The reason is the failure of the Meech Lake Accord, a proposed supplement to the Canadian constitution that would have granted Quebec status as a "distinct society" within the Canadian confederation. Quebec is bound by the national constitution, but has refused to ratify it until the province receives both guarantees of its special status and a variety of practical powers not granted to other provinces. They were set out in the Meech Lake Accord, which had to be approved by the provincial legislatures no later than the summer of 1990. Both Manitoba and Newfoundland rejected the measure, a decision that eventually will spur more than six million French-speaking Canadian citizens to seek independence.

That separation has seemed inevitable, almost since Canada's founding. As a concept—one nation with two cultures, two languages, and even two legal systems—Canada most closely resembles Yugoslavia or Czechoslovakia, countries that would not have survived even fifty years without the Nazi and Soviet armies to keep them united. Given that Canada has managed to survive in its current form for more than 120 years, it is surprisingly difficult to find any common factors that bind it together.

Canada was born as New France, a colony that once took in about two-thirds of North America. The British captured it in 1759 and, following standard colonial practice, retained the native regime as their representatives. The Quebec Act of 1774 guaranteed French Canadians their own language, laws based on the Code of Napoleon, and the Catholic religion, which then was banned in Britain itself. When American revolutionaries tried to "liberate" Quebec, and then again in the War of 1812, French residents helped the British army turn them back. Today's Quebecois know that Canada would be part of the United States if their ancestors had not moved to defend the English-dominated country; it is one reason they feel entitled to special privileges.

During the American Revolution and the years that followed, thousands of English speakers loyal to the Crown fled to the still-British territory north of the St. Lawrence River. Lord Dorchester, the colony's British governor, settled them in what was then called Upper Canada, now the province of Ontario. Upper and Lower Canada each had their own parliamentary government and acted more or less as separate colonies.

So they remained for some twenty years. But in 1837, democratic rebellions broke out in both Upper and Lower Canada. In response, in 1840, the more-or-less independent colonies were united under a central government, but retained their separate-but-equal legislatures.

As long as Canada's two halves were approximately equal in population and power, the system worked well. But in 1867 the British North America Act formed the Dominion of Canada. The new structure included, not only Quebec and Ontario, but the Atlantic provinces: Nova Scotia, New Brunswick, and Prince

Edward Island. British Columbia, Alberta, Manitoba, and Saskatchewan were added to the nation as soon as railway links could be completed. (Newfoundland was ruled from London until its citizens voted to join Canada, by referendum in 1949.) Suddenly French Canada was vastly outnumbered by English, both in land mass and in population.

It was not overpowered, however. With populations far larger than those of the other provinces, Quebec and Ontario dominate both the elective lower house of Parliament and the appointive, largely symbolic Senate. They are also far richer than the rest of the country. As far as many citizens of the western and Atlantic provinces are concerned, Quebec and Ontario run Canada, and largely for their own benefit. The dominant provinces tend to feel that they have supported the rest of the country at their own expense. There are elements of truth on both sides.

Newfoundland is one of the poorest areas in Canada. Unemployment in the province is nearly 19 percent overall and more than 27 percent on the Atlantic coast. Average earned income in Newfoundland is less than half that in Ontario. In unemployment payments, welfare, and other subsidies, Newfoundlanders receive more than $6,800 per capita from the central government. Their nearest neighbors, Quebecois are on average, Canada's wealthiest citizens.

Labrador has even more cause to resent its French-speaking neighbors. One of Quebec's most profitable industries is the sale of hydroelectric power to New York and the New England states. It buys the power cheaply in Labrador and sells it at a markup of several hundred percent. Labrador would like to sell its power directly, but a transmission line from Labrador to the United States must pass through Quebec. Quebec's provincial government has refused to grant a right-of-way.

Quebec, meanwhile, has its own concerns. French Canadians can look back at a time—admittedly more than two hundred years ago—when their forebears dominated much of the continent west of the Appalachians. They ranged south as far as New Orleans, west to the Pacific. Today only six million or so are left. Many of the French religious beliefs, moral precepts, and traditions regarding the extended family have been leached away by contact with others. The birthrate among French-speaking Quebecois has dropped to 1.4 children per couple, well below replacement level. Few French speakers are immigrating to take up the slack, and most of them come, not from France, but from Vietnam, Haiti, Algeria, and Senegal. French Canadians see their way of life dying out.

Their attempts to protect it have done little to endear them to Anglophones. In 1977, Quebec passed a provincial law restricting the use of English in the workplace, commerce, and schools. A later bill required that all outdoor signs appear only in French; in Quebec, Colonel Sanders sells *Poulet frite dans la manière de Kentucky.* Some 250,000 English-speaking children in Quebec have been placed in experimental "immersion classes" in which all subjects except English itself are taught in French. Such measures have angered the eight hundred thousand or so Quebecois or in this case the Quebeckers, who are English-language natives. They have also convinced many in other provinces that Quebec has little interest in whatever shared history and character makes them all Canadian.

As these and other irritants have set the French- and English-speaking Canadians against each other, English-Canadian nationalism has waned. The process began with the Mulroney government's tightfisted economic agenda. Lacking any better way to define their national identity, many Canadians have focused on the contrast between Canada and the United States. There is a strong air of European socialism in Canada's universal medical insurance, generous unemployment plan, and publicly funded broadcasting, and this government involvement in the welfare of its citizens gives many Canadians a sense that in this way, at least, their land is superior to their larger, wealthier neighbor to the south. But that distinction is quickly disappearing. Plagued by a huge national debt, Mulroney has been trimming social programs and privatizing government-owned corporations. With the exception of Quebec, the Canada he has produced looks more like the United States every day, even to its own citizens.

The U.S.-Canada Free-Trade Agreement dealt another blow to the nebulous vision of Canadian identity. The major argument against the accord was that it would erode the nation's sovereignty by giving the United States too much economic leverage to dictate Canada's policies. When the agreement passed, largely with the help of prosperous Quebecois who anticipated even greater wealth from a North American free market, many English-speaking Canadians appeared to have given up. Maintenance of a distinct national identity in the face of an American business invasion seems a lost cause to them.

The agreement also removed the last concern that tempered the eagerness for independence of some French-speaking Canadians. The prospect of secession last arose in 1980, when 60 percent of the Quebecois voted in a referendum to stay within the confederation. Not even the most ardent separatists then really believed that Quebec's economy would be viable as an independent nation. Yet even then, economic concerns proved a frail restraint. Just two years later, citizens of Quebec refused to sign the new Canadian constitution because it failed to guarantee them the rights later written into the Meech Lake Accord.

And attitudes have changed dramatically since then. By 1989, shortly before the accord was voted down, a majority of Quebecois surveyed in a provincial poll, said they favored secession if the measure failed. The credit or blame for this change goes to Quebec's economy, which has grown into the second strongest manufacturing and financial power in the nation. Today, Quebec has a population of 6.7 million people and a GNP of some $130 billion (in U.S. dollars). As a nation, Quebec would be roughly as populous and prosperous as Switzerland, and about three times as large. Its foreign trade is already some $40 billion per year, most of it with the New England states to the south. It should grow dramatically in the coming decade, whether Quebec remains part of Canada or declares itself an independent nation; few Quebecois expect any difficulty in negotiating their own free-trade agreement with the United States. In all, there is no longer any economic reason for Quebec to remain part of Canada.

Already several years have passed since the Meech Lake Accord was allowed to die. There were a few heated exchanges in the Canadian Parliament at first, a few calls for immediate secession, but the furor abated almost immediately. This has been a time of contemplation. Quebec Premier Robert Bourassa, a long-time Federalist who worked hard for the Meech Lake Accord, has hinted that he would like to see Canada become a loose federation, much like the one planned for the European Community after 1992, but he has called the idea of full political autonomy "logically and practically feasible."

In fact, there are no fewer than six courses for Canada to choose from in the 1990s. Which one the nation eventually follows will depend on how much or little independence Quebec requires:

Canada may retain its existing federal system more or less unchanged. Given the overwhelming support for the Meech Lake Accord among Quebecois, this will probably be the most difficult of the alternatives to sustain.

It can transfer some of the central government's power to the province. Quebec would want at least some taxing authority and control over many of the programs now administered from Ottawa. In essence, this is what the Meech Lake Accord tried to do. How it could be accomplished now, after failing to win national acceptance, is unclear.

Canada could divide itself into four or five semiautonomous regions, reserving for the central government only such functions as defense, monetary policy, and the like. Quebec and Ontario would obviously be two of the regions. The Atlantic provinces and the Prairie provinces would band together in their own areas. British Columbia could join with Alberta and Manitoba, or it might form a region of its own. In some crucial ways, this is essentially the status quo. Quebec and Ontario would remain the richest, most populous, and most influential regions of Canada, while the Atlantic and western provinces would still be poor, underpopulated, and largely dependent on Ottawa and Montreal for their economic survival—a condition that Quebec and Ontario resent almost as much as their beneficiaries do. It is difficult to see why the poorer provinces would accept such an arrangement.

Several more variations would divide the country into just two parts: Quebec—about one-fourth of the national population—and everyone else. The two unequal units would operate somewhere along the spectrum between federation and loose confederation. The more closely they remain united, the more difficult it will be to arrange equitable representation in the central government. Among liberal Quebecois, the idea of a loose confederation has considerable support. But in a confederation, Quebec would hold the power to veto national policies supported by the English-speaking majority. It is a privilege that the other twenty million Canadians are not likely to grant.

That leaves secession. As the period of shocked diplomacy following the Meech Lake debacle wears on, more and more Quebecois are lining up behind the independence movement. By 1996 or so, the political pressure will have built up enough to require yet another referendum. And this time, secession will win. For Quebec, it truly is "logically and practically feasible." The province will declare itself a sovereign nation before the end of the decade.

When Quebec goes off on its own, it will take with it nearly one-fourth of Canada's GNP. Without its tax base, the rest of Canada will find it difficult to maintain welfare programs, and even roads, in the poor provinces. Can Canada survive as a single nation? Should it even try?

Like Quebec, the Atlantic and western provinces have long-standing arguments with the central government. For a century, until the signing of the free-trade agreement, Canada used a network of tariffs and other trade barriers to protect industrialized Ontario and Quebec from American competition. In doing so, it denied the Atlantic and Western provinces the benefits of cheaper imports. In 1980, the National Energy Program "Canadianized" windfall profits of Western oil producers; some $50 billion (Canadian) was pillaged from Manitoba, Saskatchewan, Alberta, British Columbia, and the Northwest Territories and deposited in Ontario. And recently, the Mulroney government has decided to cut the government budget by closing down many of the rail lines that opened the west to development. All these actions, and many like them, have convinced many people in the outlying provinces that Ottawa does not have their interests at heart.

Quebec's secession will destroy that idiosyncratic, multicultural concept on which Canada is built. It will also deprive the country of tax revenues that pay for many of the benefits now given to the poorer provinces by the Federal government. Without those factors to bind them, the English-speaking parts of Canada will find they have almost nothing in common but an odd historical association. Ontario is a prosperous industrial center. The Atlantic provinces are poor, largely dependent on fishing for their livelihood, and Quebec's secession will cut them off from the main body of Canada. The western provinces are thinly populated, with strong mining and lumber industries. Not only do the provinces resemble each other, they resemble the nearest region of the United States. Nova Scotia and Newfoundland clearly have more in common with Maine than with Ontario, which might well be part of New York, Ohio, or Illinois. The western provinces are almost indistinguishable from Wyoming, the Dakotas, Montana, or Alaska. As parts of the United States, they might band together with their neighboring states and achieve more influence in Washington than they can hope to have in Ottawa.

This idea has already occurred to many Canadians. Nova Scotia's provincial premier has already said that he believed his people would be better off as part of the United States. And in a national poll taken before the outbreak of war in the Persian Gulf, 59 percent of the Canadians asked, said they would sooner be led by George Bush than Brian Mulroney.

These attitudes can only grow when Quebec declares its sovereignty. Forecasting International believes there is now a 60 percent chance that English-speaking Canada will opt to join the United States within the next ten years.

C H A P T E R 8

....

Economics Across the Rio Grande

"Mexico is not merely a source of cheap labor for American manufacturers. As a relatively stable nation open to foreign investment, it could become a vast new market."

....

Eastern Europe is not the only place attempting the difficult transition from central planning to free markets. A similar miracle is taking place in Mexico. By 2000, at their current pace of progress, Mexico should enjoy one of the most vibrant national economies in the world. If, in addition, the United States and Canada (or the United States, Canada, and Quebec) allow their southern neighbor to join their free-trade area, the unified North American economy will have a population of roughly 370 million and a GNP of $6 trillion—larger than that of the expanded European Community and three times as large as that of Japan.

For Mexico, almost any viable economy will be a dramatic change from the recent past. Over the years, it has made just about every mistake available to a developing country.

In the early 1970s, it seemed that Mexico's fortune would float on the nation's oil, as Venezuela's has done; Mexico has the eighth-largest reserves in the world. For nearly ten years, oil was a source of much needed foreign trade, and this unaccustomed prosperity encouraged the Mexican government to spend far more than it could afford on social programs. Then the price of oil fell, the economy sank into recession, and by the mid-1980s the national debt grew to more than $100 billion. For a time,

Mexico was the world's second-largest debtor nation, behind only Brazil.

Throughout most of the 1980s, Mexican free enterprise seemed headed for a permanent siesta. For more than fifty years, Mexican governments had been nationalizing major industries, beginning with petroleum in the 1930s. In 1982, the country nationalized sixty private banks. By 1988, the government owned about 30 percent of the country's corporate assets. Most of the rest was in the hands of a few well-connected families. Only about 5 percent of corporate assets traded on the Mexican stock exchange. Private investment in Mexico almost came to a halt. No one knows how much Mexican capital fled the country to more hospitable business environments. Estimates range between $50 billion and $80 billion.

The nation's odd tax and regulatory system discouraged whatever commerce might otherwise have grown up outside this anticompetitive structure. Large corporations were saddled with nightmarish paperwork and income taxes of 35 to 60 percent. "Small businessmen" were exempted from complex record-keeping and were allowed instead to pay their taxes bimonthly to state government inspectors. In practice, that often meant paying no taxes at all; a small bribe would satisfy most inspectors just as well. They were also exempt from collecting value-added taxes—but that prevented them from wholesaling their products to larger companies, which were stuck with the VAT, and required receipts to prove that it had been paid on their raw materials and purchased parts. Small companies were also forbidden to issue stock, cutting off a source of needed development capital. Rather than cope with the restrictions that hobbled larger enterprises, most small businesses were happy to remain small. The system stifled economic growth and cost the Mexican government tax revenues it could hardly do without.

And because the Mexican government was so strapped for cash, it could do little to improve or maintain the nation's infrastructure. Bridges rotted. Paved roads decayed into dirt tracks. Where traffic outgrew local capacity, as the crossing from Juárez to El Paso did long ago, nothing could be done to speed the flow of vehicles. Municipal water was impossible to drink, where it was available at all. And Telmex, or Teléfonos de Mexico, ran what may have been the most antiquated, unreliable telephone system in a major trading nation.

If that were not enough, Mexico actively discouraged whatever foreign investors might otherwise have been brave enough to enter such an unpromising economy. Outsiders were allowed only minority interests in Mexican concerns, and most such investments required government approval.

By the mid-1980s, Mexico was showing all the evils of inept central planning. In 1986, the nation's budget deficit peaked at sixteen percent of the gross domestic product. Inflation seldom sank below 60 percent per year; at times, it hit 200 percent. Real income sank by more than 60 percent from 1982 to 1988; fully half of the Mexican population lives far enough below the poverty line to suffer at least minor malnutrition. The official growth rate of 7 percent per year was in danger of extinction, though that neglects a major sector of the economy: According to one estimate, fully one-fourth of business in Mexico was done off the books.

The one bright spot was the *maquiladoras,* factories that import parts from abroad for assembly and sale. Because the government exempts such factories from many of its most burdensome restrictions—so long as at least half of the products are exported—American corporations, and a few of their Japanese and European competitors, have found Mexican assembly plants a welcome alternative to facilities in Korea or Thailand. The average factory worker in Mexico earns only $1.63 per hour (plus lunch), compared with nearly fifteen dollars in the United States—even the most skilled vocational school graduates earn only one-third as much as their American counterparts—and it costs little more to ship materials to customers in the United States than it would if the factories were located in Texas. Such savings have proved a powerful attraction. As of 1988, Mexico was home to some 1,500 *maquiladoras,* most of them owned by U.S. corporations and located just south of the American border. They employed some 350,000 workers and contributed $1.6 billion in foreign reserves. Only two years later, there were 2,200 such factories employing 560,000, and their annual output had grown to $2.3 billion. *Maquiladora* profits have been growing by 20 percent per year for more than five years. There is no sign that the trend will slow during the 1990s.

One more source of Mexico's new economic strength is President Carlos Salinas de Gortari, a Harvard Ph.D. in political economics and government. He put his theoretical knowledge to work soon after taking office.

A wage and price freeze brought inflation under control. These days, it is running around 20 percent per year—still high by the standards of the industrialized countries, but livable.

Salinas also negotiated with Mexico's creditors. Mexico had never missed a payment on its international loans, but with its economy in trouble, the possible threat worried bankers in the United States and Europe. They were quick to offer help when asked for it. In the end, they cut $3.7 billion per year from the annual payments due on the nation's $108 billion or so foreign debt. It was less than Salinas would have liked, but enough to keep the payments flowing.

The new president pushed hard to reduce the nation's dependence on petroleum. Since Salinas took office, non-oil exports have quadrupled. Mexico now has major export industries producing automobiles and auto parts, aircraft components, televisions, computer chips, and even satellite parts.

Salinas then cut the top marginal tax rate to 35 percent. This was only the most recent in a series of reductions from the 60 percent peak of 1986. And that 35 percent is higher than it seems, because it applies to incomes of only seven thousand dollars per year, a level at which even Americans are untaxed. But it is an improvement, and there is probably more to come.

Small businesses no longer enjoy special tax privileges. The government inspectors have been cut out of the payment process, so tax revenues actually reach Mexico City. More important, small companies and large ones must now keep the same, somewhat simplified records, and they all collect the same VAT. Thus, small companies no longer suffer a penalty for trying to grow. Though these regulatory changes are still new, already there are signs that a wave of mergers, takeovers, and hard competition is forming at the bottom end of Mexico's corporate scale.

Salinas has also welcomed foreign investors. Outsiders may now buy 100 percent of almost any business that interests them, and in most areas investments of up to $100 million are exempt from government approval.

Though some tariffs remain in effect, most other barriers to trade are gone, including domestic-content quotas for electronics and automobiles.

To refurbish the national infrastructure, Salinas turned to private industry. The new $20 million bridge from Juárez to El Paso was built by Grupo Gutsa, one of Mexico's largest construction firms, using its own capital. The company hopes to recover its investment, and earn a profit of at least 25 percent per year, by collecting tolls. After sixty-six months, ownership of the bridge will revert to the government. Similar deals have been made for construction of 625 miles of roads, including one from Monterrey to the U.S. border and another from Mexico City to Acapulco.

And the Salinas government has been selling off most state-owned industries, nearly eight hundred companies so far. Among the assets sold to date are the largest copper mine in the country; the two national airlines, Aeromexico and Mexicana; steel mills; and the three thousand supermarkets and food processing plants formerly owned by Conasupo. The most dramatic success so far has been the $1.76 billion sale of Telmex to a consortium including Mexico's Grupo Carso, Southwestern Bell, and France Telecom. The buyers are expected to spend some $9 billion modernizing the monopoly's creaky telephone system.

Many of these were difficult sales, and they brought with them a practical cost to Mexico. Under government control, payrolls ran out of control. The government's petroleum monopoly, Pemex, is only half the size of Exxon but employs twice as many workers, 220,000 in all. Where private owners have bought state holdings, firings have quickly followed. In all, the Salinas government's policies have cost Mexican workers an estimated 1.5 million jobs. Somehow, Salinas has managed to control the resulting labor unrest. (Imprisoning corrupt labor leaders may have helped, though this administration has punished dishonest businessmen just as diligently.) Yet many state-owned companies remain up for sale, either because no one has been willing to meet the government's price or because no one has bid at all.

The tourist industry has received special attention: The Salinas government is offering developers low-interest loans for new resort construction. Between 1985 and 1987, tourism jumped by

30 percent. Five million foreign vacationers per year now spend about $2.6 billion in Mexico. The plan is to double those numbers in the next five years.

All these changes have helped to spur Mexico's once-stagnant economy, but they have not been enough to satisfy government planners. Foreign investment in Mexico rose from $3 billion in 1988 to $3.5 billion in 1989, but Mexican officials had hoped to attract $5 billion. Early in 1990, Salinas toured Eastern Europe to examine his competition and returned with two dramatic proposals:

First he offered to privatize the banks, a move that banking officials had ruled out only weeks earlier. The change required a constitutional amendment, which the legislature duly passed. The first eighteen banks were put up for sale almost immediately, but as this is written, only a minority of banks have been returned to private hands. Foreign investors are allowed to buy up to 30 percent ownership, an opportunity that seems more attractive to European banks than to their American colleagues.

The second idea seemed even more dramatic: Salinas proposed to set up a free-trade agreement with the United States, much like the one the U.S. and Canada signed in 1988. Negotiations began late in 1990 and will probably take two or three years to complete.

In fact, there is a bit less to both these proposals than meets the eye. Private investors already control nearly one-third of bank shares through special bonds called Certificates of Patrimony. And many of the most profitable financial transactions once handled by banks have moved to stock brokerages, many of them owned by ex-bankers whose property was nationalized in 1982.

In the short run, at least, extending the U.S.-Canada Free-Trade Agreement to include Mexico also, could have less direct benefit than might be expected. Mexican tariffs on American goods average only 11 percent, while U.S. tariffs on Mexican goods are only 4 percent. In addition, each country does have some special restrictions against specific products. The United States limits imports of Mexican vegetables during the U.S. harvest seasons and maintains tight curbs on Mexican textiles and steel. For its part, Mexico requires special import licenses on about 20 percent of products, including cars. And to date, Mexico has refused to open its oil fields to foreign exploration and investment, a politically risky move that would require a constitutional amendment. With the exception of the petroleum industry, however, tariffs and other barriers have done far less to restrict trade between the two nations than the tax and investment policies already changed by the Salinas government.

In the longer term, however, a free-trade agreement with Mexico could spur economic growth and development in both countries. An agreement among Mexico, the U.S., and Canada would form the world's largest market to date, of 370 million consumers and annual production of over $6 trillion. It could even become the foundation of a hemispheric arrangement.

The United States hopes to reduce tariffs to zero, over a decade. Significant changes have already taken place regarding tariffs. At the end of 1987, Mexico cut tariffs on imports from all countries from 40 percent to a maximum of 20 percent—far more stringent than the overall 50 percent ceiling that Mexico accepted in the GATT framework it agreed to in September 1986.

The U.S. also wants to reduce the nontariff barriers on goods and services, eliminate restrictions on investment, and protect intellectual property rights, such as software copyrights. As noted above, some of these objectives may be more difficult to achieve; yet, here too, there has been dramatic progress. Mexico has reduced the number of items subject to import licensing—now equal to 8 percent (by value) of American exports, most of which are in the agricultural sector. The United States accounts for 65 percent of all investment in Mexico and seeks further liberalization of the investment process that has affected categories valued under $100 million. In January 1990, the U.S. removed Mexico from the "priority watch list" of the "special 301" provisions of the 1988 Omnibus Trade Bill, which permit economic reprisal against nations discriminating against American products. Mexico's exoneration reflects its willingness to extend the terms of patents to twenty years.

One other benefit of privatizing banks and dropping trade barriers may be largely symbolic. As statements of Mexico's new stability and the Salinas government's commitment to private enterprise, they could help to attract back to Mexico some of the native capital shipped to other countries in the last twenty years.

The knowledge that the trade border will remain open would also reassure potential foreign investors that their money will be safe in Mexico. And that is the real key to modernizing the nation's economy.

To American executives, and to the Bush administration's free-trade idealogues, the idea of a Mexican free-trade agreement seems reasonable, on the face of it. Mexico is already America's third-largest trading partner, behind only Canada and Japan. The United States exported some $25 billion in goods to Mexico in 1989, and imported another $27 billion-worth, fully two-thirds of Mexico's exports. American companies have supplied nearly two-thirds of the $26.6 billion in outside capital invested in Mexico. Trade between the two nations could grow almost explosively once businessmen on both sides of the Rio Grande are certain their investments will be secure, and that would bring greater prosperity for both nations.

Mexico is not merely a source of cheap labor for American manufacturers. As a relatively stable nation open to foreign investment, it could become a vast new market. Mexico's population—about 86 billion—is young, literate, and growing rapidly. In 1985, forty percent of all Mexicans had yet to reach their fourteenth birthdays. The World Bank estimates that the Mexican population will reach 105 million by the year 2000 and could top 140 million only twenty-five years later. As Mexico modernizes its economy, those millions will constitute a prime market for automobiles, consumer electronics, appliances, and all the trappings of modern life. Labor-intensive products will be assembled in Mexico, but the profits will be shipped home to the United States. President Salinas's economic reforms have already given a taste of the benefits to come—if Washington passes the FTA. They have added significantly to the size and income of Mexico's middle class. As much as 15 percent of their increased income is spent on U.S. goods and services. And every additional $1 billion in real net exports to Mexico creates about 25,000 new jobs in the U.S.

Free trade offers Mexican concerns a major benefit as well. Mexico's interest rates run 20 percent over the inflation rate. By comparison, American financing is relatively inexpensive. A world-scale Mexican firm with a capital-intensive business to build can save handsomely by locating it in the United States and funding it with American loans. Many of them are likely to do so.

Major corporations in both countries are already scurrying to establish themselves across the border. Ford has sunk nearly $1 billion into a factory at Hermosillo, where it builds Mercury Tracers for the U.S. market. Kodak turns out camera parts in Monterrey. IBM, Wang, Hewlett-Packard, and many of their suppliers have set up a Silicon Cañon at Guadalajara. The migration north is proving just as attractive for Mexican firms. Vitro, the largest glassmaker in Mexico, paid $920 million for Tampa, Florida's, Anchor Glass Container Corp. Cementos Mexicanos has been buying up companies in Texas and California as part of an $800 million expansion. These deals are certain to be just the first of many.

Yet, establishing a true free-trade area could be a wrenching experience for both nations. Competing in the world market will not be easy for Mexico's large corporations, many of them family-owned conglomerates, which have been protected by high trade barriers for forty years. Sales have depended on government contacts, not on quality, price, or reliable delivery. Marketing is a skill that Mexican companies are still trying to learn. Many could find it difficult or impossible to survive outside competition.

In the United States, opposition to the free-trade proposal sprang up quickly. Labor leaders and Rust Belt congressmen have focused, not on markets, but on the Mexican workforce. At prices of less than two dollars per hour, this vast supply of manpower has American blue-collar workers scared. The 1980s saw a major transfer of jobs from the industrial Midwest, where manufacturing still provides nearly one-third of the jobs, to the South and West, where wage rates and taxes are lower and unions have far less power. In the 1990s, they fear, even more jobs could flee to Mexico. The unions also note that a free-trade agreement will require painful restructuring in many industries, force down American wages, introduce new competition, and hit some regions harder than others. (For instance, Texas will benefit at Michigan's expense.) Farmers, too, could suffer as low-cost Mexican laborers grow ever more produce for American consumers. "Agro-*maquilas*" have become the fastest growing segment of the *maquiladora* industry. Between 1989 and 1990, the number of agro-*maquilas* "assembling" mature plants from imported seeds and cuttings more than doubled to over forty, and the wholesale value of their produce grew from less than $20 million to more than $100 million. If these lobbies do not kill the free-trade agreement, they could so riddle it with exceptions and special cases that it becomes meaningless.

In addition, the governments still must resolve two major differences before any agreement can be signed. The U.S. does not want to open its borders; as far as Washington is concerned, the FTA is meant to strengthen the Mexican economy so as to stem illegal immigration—not to legalize the border crossings. The other problem is Mexico's refusal to open its undercapitalized oil industry to U.S. investment. The U.S. is particularly keen to invest in the oil industry in order to reduce its dependence on Middle Eastern oil supplies. This is also one industry in which the United States can compensate for the Mexican advantage in labor-intensive industries, such as automobiles, textiles, and toys; the U.S. will be the stronger of the two in capital-intensive areas. Salinas says oil will not be on the negotiating table.

Unfortunately, Mexico offers at least two fundamentally unrelated weapons that protectionists could use to undermine the free-trade proposal. One is its weak drug enforcement program. An estimated 300 metric tons of cocaine, and perhaps as much as 350 tons, flows through Mexico to U.S. markets every year. Americans also suspect that high Mexican officials helped to cover up the 1985 killing of Enrique Camarena, an agent of the U.S. Drug Enforcement Administration. Yet the Salinas government has gone a long way toward smoothing the often-acrimonious relationship between U.S. and Mexican drug enforcers. Mexico has arrested a number of prominent figures in the narcotics underworld, including several corrupt Mexican officials, and it has stepped up its program to intercept drug-smuggling aircraft. Such efforts have won President Salinas high praise from American officials and may have removed one obstacle to the closer relations required by a free-trade agreement.

The other problem, far more difficult to solve, is Mexico's antiquated political system. In Mexico, an old joke holds that "Mexicans enjoy full democracy 364 days of the year; they only lack this form of government on election day." Like every Mexican president since the 1920s, Salinas belongs to the Institutional

Revolutionary Party, the PRI, and was hand-picked by his predecessor, Miguel de la Madrid Hurtado. The PRI has retained its power, over the decades, through rigged elections, intimidation, and even political assassination. In the 1988 election that narrowly put Salinas in power, his main opponent charged that the ballots had been deliberately miscounted. A year later, PRI victories in the states of Michoacán and Guerrero provoked riots and charges of ballot rigging. This is ready ammunition for anyone wishing to smear Salinas and his free-trade plan.

Yet Salinas appears to be serious about electoral reform. In July 1989, with his support, the governorship of Baja California Norte and legislative and municipal posts in five of the country's thirty-one states went to the right-of-center National Action party (PAN). In future, primary elections will precede final ballots, a change that could strengthen both the PAN and the left-wing Democratic National Front. And Salinas has given the task of nominating his successor to a party council, rather than making the choice himself. The 1991 legislative elections should give at least a preliminary view of how well campaign reform is working.

President Salinas does not have long to modernize his nation's economic and political life. The Mexican constitution limits him to a single six-year term in office, and there is a lot left to be done before Mexico can achieve full membership in the North American trading bloc. As noted above, Mexico's roads and telephone system are barely adequate for a rural agrarian society; a major trading nation will need much better. Though 87 percent of his people qualify as literate, by the tolerant elementary school standards used to measure such things, relatively few are equipped for life in a technological society; the educational system requires an extensive upgrade. With a population now approaching twenty million, Mexico City ranks as the largest and most polluted municipality in the world; cleaning up its air and water are among the nation's most urgent challenges. There is little hope that whoever follows Salinas will be as well qualified to meet such problems.

Yet, six years with the right leader may well prove to be enough. By 1994, American investment in Mexico will be a powerful force for development, and Mexican firms in the

United States will be providing jobs to replace those migrating south of the Rio Grande. Even if American protectionists derail a formal free-trade agreement, Salinas has made nearly all of the necessary changes without help from Washington. In doing so, he has guaranteed both nations a prosperous future.

··

Cuba Rejoins the West

"Castro has announced that no new women's clothes will be made for five years, a sure sign that popular revolution may be imminent."

··

As 1990 closed, an air of expectancy hovered over the Cuban community in Miami. In a single year, tyrants had fallen throughout the world. In Europe, Romania's Ceausescu was dead; East Germany's Erich Honecker, his nation a memory, faced possible imprisonment; even Albania's hard-line President Ramiz Alia showed signs of losing his grip on power. Closer to home, Panama's Manuel Noriega had been deposed and clapped into an American prison, while Nicaragua's Daniel Ortega had been *voted* out of office. With the tide of history so clearly running in democracy's favor, could it be long before Fidel Castro at last fell from power?

The anti-Castro forces could still be waiting as the next century opens. Thanks largely to the same liberalization of Soviet policy that freed Eastern Europe, Cuba is in such economic and political trouble that some change seems inevitable. Yet it is difficult to see what, other than old age, could end the sixty-five-year-old *Jefe Máximo*'s reign.

By Third World standards, Cuba has done relatively well since Castro took power in the early days of 1959. The state guarantees all Cubans a job, housing, and enough food to live on. If housing is a little primitive and rations a bit short, Cubans can find people living in far greater poverty throughout the hemisphere. And the island's medical care is among the best in the region. At 16 per thousand, the infant mortality rate is one of the lowest in Latin America or the Caribbean—half that of Argentina, and one-fourth that of many neighboring countries. Life expectancy is seventy-two years for men, seventy-four for women, again, among the top in the area. Even minor cosmetic surgery is available without charge.

Yet over the years, Cuba's standard of living has slipped almost continuously. The island's population has risen to over ten million, three million more than when Castro took power. Yet the gross domestic product has not grown significantly since the end of the Batista regime in 1958; it actually shrank by nearly one percent per year between 1986 and 1989. During the same period, labor productivity fell by an estimated 2.5 percent. Cuba's budget deficit more than quadrupled, and its foreign trade deficit soared to over $2 billion per year. For several years, the government has had to ration thirty-five basic commodities, including meat, milk, rice, and soap.

It would have been far worse without massive foreign aid from the Soviet Union. The Soviet foreign aid budget is more than five times greater per capita than that of the United States, and one-fourth of it has gone to Cuba. It is hard to get reliable figures on just what that amounts to. Military aid comes to about $1.2 billion per year. Barter goods for Cuba tie up 15 percent of the Soviet merchant fleet, in part because the island's harbors will not accommodate larger ships. The Soviet Union says its trade subsidies and other aid to Cuba are worth $3 billion per year; American sources put the figure at roughly twice that. At that rate, Soviet aid accounts for about one-fifth of Cuban GDP.

In all, the Soviet Union reports that Cuba owes them 15 billion rubles, or about $25 billion at the official exchange rate. The Soviets' second-largest debtor, Vietnam, owes less than half as much.

Cuba remains exquisitely dependent on Soviet aid. Its reserves of foodstuffs and other supplies are extremely low. In 1989, a single Soviet grain ship arrived three weeks late. The delay forced the government to raise the price of bread in Havana and caused rationing elsewhere. To feed its pigs and chickens, Cuba had to buy twenty thousand tons of wheat on the open market, using precious hard currency. The price of eggs doubled.

On the face of it, Castro can still count on Soviet aid to keep his nation afloat. A one-year trade agreement signed in 1990 reportedly increased Soviet trade and technical assistance by nearly 9 percent over the previous year. But other changes have been far more important, and they have hurt Cuba badly.

Much of what the Soviets once counted as trade with Cuba was in reality an outright gift. That ended on January 1, 1991. In the past, the Soviet voluntarily bought Cuban sugar at prices three to five times higher than the world average. They are now paying strict market prices. The changes will cost Cuba about $2 billion in barter every year. And barter itself is on the way out. The Soviets now demand hard currency for their merchandise, and the Cuban hard currency reserve is estimated at only $50 million—scarcely enough to pay for three weeks of essential supplies.

The most damaging cuts involve oil. Soviet oil has provided for 90 percent of Cuba's needs. In 1989, Cuba took thirteen million tons of Soviet oil, or 250,000 barrels per day. A year later, according to Cuban officials, oil shipments had fallen dramatically. This has cost Cuba more than heat and light. Soviet economists estimate that Cuba once earned up to 40 percent of its foreign exchange revenue by reexporting Soviet oil. Profit on this trade dropped from $621 million in 1985 to $189 million in 1989. At this point, it has probably disappeared entirely.

The former Soviet colonies in Eastern Europe have reduced their trade with Cuba even more sharply. Cuba needs spare parts for the five thousand Hungarian buses that provide public transportation in Havana. It needs Czech tires for cane-cutting machines, Czech and (East) German parts for power plants, parts for sugar centrifuges. It is not getting them, because the East European nations, too, are demanding payment in hard currency. Czechoslovakia has even stopped representing Cuba in Washington.

Indirectly, Cuba has been able to trade with the United States, despite the thirty-year American embargo. In 1975, Congress amended the ban to permit foreign subsidiaries of U.S. companies to sell their products to Cuba under certain conditions. The subsidiaries must be able to prove to the satisfaction of the U.S. government that they enjoy the freedom of making their own management decisions. (Read: IBM need not apply.) Even then, these subsidiaries may not sell U.S. manufactured goods to Cuba. U.S. subsidiaries located mainly in the United Kingdom, Switzerland, Canada, France, and Spain, and the members of the Organization of American States have taken advantage of this exception to the "Trading With the Enemy Act." Total trade with Cuba (both imports and exports) by U.S. foreign subsidiaries in 1990 amounted to nearly $325 million, according to the U.S. Department of Treasury's Office of Foreign Assets Control. By the end of 1989, a total of 233 U.S. subsidiaries had made applications to this office. Sales to Cuba by U.S. subsidiaries accounted for a little more than half of this total. In 1991, Senator Connie Mack of Florida still seemed determined to end this trade. He had included an amendment to the 1990 Export Act that would have outlawed this provision had the bill not been vetoed for other reasons. Doubtless, Mack will try again.

According to one estimate, Cuba will produce one-fifth less of the basic necessities in 1991 than in 1990, thanks largely to shortages of fuel and spare parts. And that is the best they can hope for.

Losing the subsidized trade has inspired draconian austerity measures. New restrictions added more than 180 items to Cuban ration books, including twenty-eight kinds of food. Canned meat and fruit are being rationed. So are fish, pasta, cream cheese—even ketchup. (Cuban agriculture has collapsed so completely that farm officials have taken to breeding a variety of cane-field rat for food.)

It has always been difficult to get refrigerators, televisions, and many kinds of large and small appliances; it is now almost impossible. Air conditioner sales have stopped entirely; people who had been scheduled to receive air conditioners will be allowed to buy Chinese-made fans instead. Electric irons are available only for newlyweds. Castro has announced that no new women's clothes will be made for five years, a sure sign that popular revolution may be imminent. Even medical supplies are being rationed, and new investment in Cuba's showplace health-care system has been frozen.

Fuel restrictions are even more painful. Gasoline allowances have been cut by 30 to 50 percent for both personal and official cars. Homes have been required to cut their use of electricity by

10 percent; slackers will have their power cut by 30 percent. The Che Guevara nickel factory, a major source of export sales, was shut down in autumn 1990 for lack of fuel. Other factories have been closed as well. Cuba is replacing trucks with horse carts, tractors with oxen. And there is talk of cutting the workweek from five days to three.

The severest measures are reminiscent of China's Cultural Revolution of the 1960s. The government is sending twenty thousand Havana office workers to the countryside for "voluntary" three-week periods to help with harvests. Many of them have been permanently laid off from their city jobs—even half the Communist party staff has been fired—and many suspect that permanent "ruralization" will come next.

There is little chance that the Soviet Union will cut Cuba off completely; the Castro regime has been far too useful over the years. When the Soviets wanted to provide training and arms for Marxist guerillas or to send troops to prop up friendly regimes in Angola and Ethiopia, it was Cuba that did the dirty work. And Cuba has been a convenient base for its submarines and reconnaissance planes. These are services that Soviet hard-liners still appreciate. And the Soviet Union still needs Cuban sugar, citrus, and nickel.

But technology has improved, and Soviet policy has changed even more dramatically. Both have undercut Cuba's role in Soviet affairs. Spy satellites and other technology have all but replaced spy planes and made Cuban bases less important. Even more significantly, President Gorbachev's decision to concentrate on domestic problems and settle his nation's differences with the West have made it far more useful to save money than to project Soviet power through his Cuban proxy. Gorbachev has forbidden Castro to supply rebels in El Salvador with weapons provided as part of Soviet military aid. Cuba is still shipping them arms, presumably from other sources. Not long ago, it would have been a useful service. Today, it is an embarrassment. If Cuba is going to cure its economic ills, it will have to find the solution outside the former Soviet bloc.

It is scrambling to do so, but with limited success. Cuba cannot get Western credit since it was forced to suspend payments in 1986 on a $6.8 billion hard-currency debt. (Because of this, 85 to 90 percent of Cuba's trade in 1989 was with the Comecon nations, up from 74 percent in 1980.) Cuban officials have been hoping to reduce their debts to Japan, Spain, and other Western alliance countries, but their prospects appear slim. Ecuador, Mexico, and Venezuela have all refused requests to sell oil to Cuba at better-than-market prices.

In theory, Cuba could get more hard currency by demanding it for exports of sugar, citrus, nickel, and tobacco. But fully three-fourths of Cuban export revenues come from sugar, and there is no shortage of that on the world market. It gives them little leverage for negotiation.

All this leaves Cuba with relatively few trading partners. Castro has signed trade agreements with Albania, China, and North Korea—none of them among the world's major industrial powers. Business between Cuba and China doubled in 1988, but rose by only 9 percent the following year; it now totals around $420 million per year. One of Cuba's largest single orders was for hundreds of thousands of Chinese bicycles to replace the failing Hungarian buses. Its largest marketing success was the sale of between $80 million and $100 million worth of meningitis vaccine to Brazil, for which the Castro government is said to have received hard currency. Cuba is now trying to expand its medical exports to include AIDS test kits and similar items too sophisticated for most of its neighbors to produce on their own. But no matter how successful these efforts are, there is no hope at all that they will make up for more than a tiny fraction of the trade lost in Eastern Europe and the Soviet Union.

Cuba's only native source of hard currency is tourism, which the government claims now brings in about $150 million per year. It is working hard to develop this industry—even experimenting with capitalist methods. The government has set up several joint ventures with European firms to build and renovate hotels. Spanish investors in a joint venture have completed luxury Sol Palmeras Hotel on Veradero Beach, near Havana. Two more projects are under way. Unlike other Cuban enterprises, these resorts will be allowed to fire their employees and to reward good workers with productivity bonuses of up to 30 percent of their salaries.

Yet, Fidel clearly sees in tourism at least as much threat as promise. Tourists, after all, are outsiders. Even those from the Soviet Union no longer adhere to Cuba's strict "one-for-all, and precious little for anyone" brand of communism. Ideological contamination is a risk that Castro has never been able to tolerate. As a result, Cubans are barred from tourist hotels and nightclubs. It is a kind of apartheid that many of them resent.

There is another threat as well. Castro experimented with limited capitalism in the early 1970s and found that it produced spectacular gains in farm productivity. Yet, he returned to strict central planning in 1986. Capitalism, he complained, had created a bourgeois class that exploited the people by charging outrageous prices for food and services. He was probably more concerned that people earning their own money are less dependent on the government and thus are less easily controlled by it.

Experiments with limited political reform seemed equally threatening. In the late 1980s, Fidel released some long-term political prisoners, allowed formation of two small human rights groups, and made tentative peace with the Catholic church. Cuba even joined the United States in negotiations over the fifteen-year civil war in Angola and agreed to pull its troops out of that battered land. As late as 1990, the Roman Catholic church was allowed to stage religious parades in seventy towns in honor of national saint, La Virgen de la Caridad del Cobre. It was the first time nonofficial public gatherings had been authorized in years.

It seems that Castro hoped his new policies would encourage the U.S. to relax its embargo. When it became clear that the trade ban would remain in force, he clamped down again. But by the time the Catholic church held its celebrations, Fidel had changed his mind and blasted the church with a scathing speech.

So far, Cubans have been remarkably patient with both hardship and repression. Few appear to blame the *Jefe Máximo* himself for shortages. This could reflect simple fear of punishment, but it seems more likely that Castro's revolutionary prestige remains largely intact. Unlike the East European leaders who were overthrown in 1990, Castro has never been accused of material corruption. Neither has he been embarrassed by his wife, as were Ceausescu or Honecker, whose wives held public office. His long-time mistress was Celia Sánchez, a popular revolutionary who was widely mourned when she died of cancer in 1980; their relationship was never questioned. And unlike the former East European leaders, Fidel had not replaced his nation's heroes; he actually led the revolution against the hated dictator, Fulgencio Batista.

That may not be true for much longer. There is evidence that disaffection is growing in Cuba, especially among young people, who have no memory of the revolution and now make up more than half the population. Petty crime and alcoholism are on the rise. In one widely reported incident in 1989, Castro appeared on a movie screen, and the theater audience started singing the words to a popular song: *"¡El es loco!"* (He's crazy!) Twenty-seven prominent artists, diplomats, musicians, and scientists defected in 1990. Twenty-two more dissidents took shelter in the Spanish and Italian embassies, which were blockaded by police. In protest, Spain ended its token $2.5 million in yearly aid.

There are also clear signs of unrest within the Cuban government itself. In July 1989, Castro staged a Stalinesque show trial in which General Arnaldo Ochoa Sánchez, was accused of treason and drug trafficking. Ochoa was a popular war hero and second-in-command of the Cuban army, and Fidel acknowledged the existence of wide public support for clemency. Yet Castro ordered Ochoa executed. Though there have been rumors that other high officials really had been smuggling drugs, and Ochoa was picked as the scapegoat, it was widely assumed that his real crime was either to advocate political reforms or to plan an anti-Castro coup.

Castro followed the Ochoa trial by purging some two hundred people from the government and state security apparatus. Colonel Antonio de la Guardia, of the Interior Ministry, was also executed for drug trafficking; he is believed to have run a department that specialized in smuggling goods into Cuba to get around the U.S. embargo. José Abrantes Fernández, head of internal security and intelligence, was sentenced to twenty years in prison.

Since then, trusted military men have been put in charge of many nominally civilian functions. General Abelardo Colomé Ibarra took over the Interior Ministry and replaced many civilian employees with army personnel. General Juan Escolona became president of the National Assembly of People's Power. General Sexto Batista Santana took over the Committees for the Defense of the Revolution, a pseudo-civic organization that makes sure children get vaccinated, recruits volunteers for night guard duty, and watches for suspicious characters. Its real function is to report disloyalty to the regime.

The committees have been busy of late, for Castro has once more cracked down on civilian dissent. No one is quite sure, but there are estimated to be at least fifteen dissident groups in Cuba. None is led by a figure with the stature of a Lech Walesa or a Vaclav Havel, and their ranks have been decimated by recent arrests. Jorge Quintana, a mathematics student at the University of Havana, wrote the Union of Communist Youth accusing Castro of Stalinism; he and three fellow dissidents were arrested. Human-rights activist Elizardo Sánchez was jailed in the summer of 1989 for saying that General Ochoa had been psychologically tortured after his arrest and drugged during his trial. A so-called "anticorruption" drive has jailed hundreds of alleged speculators; most were probably arrested for political reasons. And a journalist was fired from the official newspaper, *Juventud Rebelde* for saying on a Havana radio program that the publication did not represent the view of Cuban young people.

As all this was taking place, Fidel lost virtually all of his outside political support. Conservative presidents were elected in Honduras, Costa Rica, and El Salvador. The downfall of Panama's Manuel Noriega and Nicaragua's Daniel Ortega cost Castro his only real allies remaining in the region.

The Soviet Union's political support has declined as sharply as its economic aid. In May 1990, Mikhail Gorbachev even sent officials to Miami to talk with Cuban émigrés. One of them was Jorge Mas Canosa, chairman of the Cuban-American National Foundation, a conservative lobbying group with close ties to Washington. Canosa pledged that the government that succeeds Castro will honor Soviet interests in Cuba, including paying $25 billion in debt.

And in March 1990, a meeting of the United Nations Commission on Human Rights voted to ask the Cuban government to comply with its pledge not to detain, repress, or otherwise mistreat Cuban human rights activists. In the past, Cuba's East European allies would have helped veto such a measure. Instead, Poland and Czechoslovakia cosponsored the proposal, and Hungary and Bulgaria voted for it. Castro responded by arresting nine members of the Pro-Human Rights Party, which he said was a "counterrevolutionary organization."

In the past, Castro has been able to use emigration, both legal and illegal, as a kind of safety valve for social pressure. In 1989, some four thousand Cubans legally emigrated to the United States. A year later, some four hundred made their way past Caribbean sharks to Florida on vehicles ranging from wooden rafts to rubber tires. Cuba even made an industry of selling visas to Cubans who wanted to leave for Panama; it pulled in an estimated $70 million between 1985 and Noriega's overthrow in 1990. There are roughly one million Cubans in America, a tenth of the entire Cuban population.

When Castro's reign is at last over, those émigrés will form a resource that may give Cuba a powerful advantage over other nations trying to repair their crippled economies. The people who fled the Castro revolution in the early 1960s represented the island's wealthy, old-guard families. Nearly one-third of the men in this generation are self-employed. Many are rich. And many of them look upon their homeland as West Germans once viewed East Germany, as a brother nation to be given all possible help in building new lives once their repression ends. The Miami-based, Cuban-American National Foundation already has an emergency plan to ship food, medicine, and industrial supplies to begin the rebuilding process once Castro leaves power.

Today it is clear that emigration and repression will not be enough to block change permanently. "Castro's Cuba may have more in common politically with postcolonial one-party states such as Burma, North Korea, Vietnam, and China than it did with the former Communist regimes of Eastern Europe," *Newsweek* writer Charles Lane pointed out recently in *The New Republic*. "Those countries have either suppressed or avoided the wave of democracy sweeping the world." But Cuba has been more prosperous than those lands. Its people are used to high-quality health care and far better living standards than Vietnam or Burma (since renamed Myanmar) have ever enjoyed. Cubans know what they are missing.

Fidel has been trying to reinforce his flagging popular support by stirring up a new wave of Cuban nationalism. Throughout most of his rule, he cited the Communist governments of Eastern Europe as brothers-in-arms in the struggle against capitalism. Now he distinguishes between those failed regimes, which were forced on their nations by Soviet might, and his own homegrown revolution. Socialism, he claims, is the only thing that has allowed Cuba to survive as a nation. The United States lent that argument credibility when its invasion of Panama brought back horrified memories of the Bay of Pigs.

Yet there are signs that Castro has recognized that he must change his ways. Raul Castro has promised a wide variety of democratic reforms, including direct election of the National Assembly and looser immigration controls. Cuba will even permit avowed Christians to hold government office. And for first time in more than thirty years, English is being taught in some elementary schools, and the authorities plan eventually to provide classes for all Cuban students. Electoral reform could be no more than a gesture to relieve the feeling of repression without changing its substance. Teaching English seems a clear sign that Castro hopes at last to reconcile his conflict with America.

The United States is the only country in the world with both the economic power to help feed Cuba's people and enough interest in the island to bother doing so. Fidel Castro clearly knows this. In the 1990s, he will do whatever is necessary to enlist its aid.

In recent months, Castro's prerevolutionary slogan, "History will absolve me!" has changed to the grim "Socialism or death!" In fact, it will probably be "socialism until death." But it will not be the same kind of hard-line socialism that Castro has practiced to date. And with Fidel only in his mid-sixties, it could well last into the next century.

PART THREE

THE PACIFIC RIM

INTRODUCTION

For nearly ten years now, Western writers have looked at the rapidly growing Japanese economy and proclaimed that, as the twentieth century was supposed to be the "American century," the twenty-first would be the century of the Pacific. That now turns out to be very close to correct, though the reality will be considerably different from the one that would-be forecasters envisioned.

In the Pacific Rim, the governing theme of the 1990s will be the healing of long-standing divisions. Japan, following its policy of co-opting its competitors, has already begun this trend by investing in its neighbors' economies. North and South Korea have started talks that, although still fragile, may by the turn of the century reunite the two countries—an event that until recently seemed even less likely than the reunification of the Germanies did only a few years ago. Mainland China will reopen its doors to the West. In part, it will do so by allowing Hong Kong to remain a vibrant center of Asian capitalism when Britain's lease runs out in 1997. In part, also, it will rescind the restrictions placed on internal capitalism as part of the crackdown on the democratic movement of 1989. In the long run, this process will construct a network of trading agreements that will slowly come to resemble the European Community. Well before the end of this decade, the resulting growth of trade, both within the Pacific Rim nations and with other trading blocs, will be obvious to all.

Yet this one region, which straddles the developed and developing worlds, is unlikely to wield political power commensurate with its wealth. Japan, perpetually unwilling to accept foreign entanglements since its disastrous role in World War II and facing a period of unaccustomed economic reverses, will remain turned

118 · THE PACIÍC RIM

inward. China, the only other candidate for world political status, will be too occupied with strengthening its economy and modernizing its government to give any more attention to world affairs than it must. This willingness to stand aside from global politics will make it easy for the Pacific Rim to maintain good relations with the other trading blocs.

C H A P T E R   1 0

••

Powerhouse of the 21st Century

"The Pacific Rim is already an economic Goliath."

••

As recently as the 1970s, commerce in the Pacific was focused in only two locales: the growing manufacturing and trading economy of Japan and the frenzied trading and banking center of Hong Kong. South Korea and Taiwan were struggling to begin their economic revolutions, and such nations as Malaysia and Thailand were sleepy Asian farmland. And international trade meant breaking into the American consumer market. Today, many neighboring economies—neighboring on the vast scale of the Pacific—are growing as fast as Japan ever did, and they are devoting much of their attention toward each other. In the next ten years, the industrialized and industrializing nations of Asia will knit themselves into a regional economic network on the scale of North America and Europe. They will become the powerhouse of twenty-first century trade.

The Pacific Rim is already an economic Goliath. The world's six largest banks are based in Asia. Six of the world's ten largest ports are found there. Steel consumption, a good measure of economic activity even in this silicon-chip era, is higher in Asia than in the United States or Europe. By 1992, the demand for semiconductors in the region will exceed that of Europe. The combined GNP of the west Asian nations already equals that of Europe and is three-fourths as large as that of North America. It should equal or surpass North America's GNP by the turn of the century. And this is a wealthier market than many Westerners know. McKinsey & Co., a U.S. management consulting firm, estimates that as of 1988 fully 72 million people in the region lived in households with incomes of $10,000 or more, and that did not include Japan. The number could grow to 110 million by the turn of the century.

There is certainly room for further expansion. No fewer than 1.7 billion people live in the trading nations of the formative Asian bloc, including 1.1 billion Chinese. One-third of them live in the economic heart of the region: Japan; the "Four Tigers" of South Korea, Taiwan, Hong Kong, and Singapore; the "ASEAN Four"—Indonesia, Malaysia, the Philippines, and Thailand, the four largest members of the Association of Southeast Asian Nations; and the coastal provinces of China, Fujian and Guangdong. And this is a young population, just reaching its years of peak productivity. Five out of every six people there were born after the end of World War II. According to the United Nations, their numbers will grow by 400 million in the next decade. Tokyo's Nomura Research Institute estimates that the region's gross product will grow at 7 percent per year through the rest of the century.

Trade and investment between the nations of western Asia is expanding even more quickly than between Asia and the West. Japan's second-largest trading partner is South Korea; South Korea's is Japan. Japanese investment in Hong Kong, Korea, Singapore, and Taiwan grew by an average of 50 percent per year in the 1980s; in the ASEAN Four, it doubled annually. Taiwan and Hong Kong are also investing heavily in neighboring economies. Taiwan's investments in Asia grew from only $60 million in 1986 to $3.2 billion in 1990; like Japan, it has focused much of that money on the ASEAN Four. And these figures do not include technology transfer from Japan to the rest of the Rim, an exchange worth an estimated $1 billion during the 1980s. Intra-Asian exports today make up more than 40 percent of the total trade of the Pacific Rim nations. In ten years, according to Nomura, it will be 55 percent.

To some extent, the new riches this trade represents were a gift from the United States. Back in the mid-1980s, the American greenback was the strongest currency in the world; Japan's mighty yen traded at 240 to the dollar. U.S. export industries nearly died as a result. So, in September 1985, the United States negotiated the Plaza Accord, which aimed to lower the dollar's value on foreign-exchange markets. It almost succeeded better than anyone wished. Soon thereafter, the dollar was worth 130 yen, and as of early 1991, it has traded near that level ever since. American exports soon recovered, but the change drove the cost of Japanese products through the roof. Japan responded in the only way it could, by shipping its labor-intensive manufacturing to South Korea, Taiwan, and Singapore, where pay scales were a lot lower. Over the next three years, the new investment caused a boom in those nations. Wages, land values, and the price of the Singapore and Taiwan dollars and the Korean won all shot up, and companies in all four nations again went shopping for cheap labor. They found it in the ASEAN Four.

At the same time, political changes were sweeping the target nations. For years, Indonesia's metastasized bureaucracy and inconvertible rupiah had made those islands a difficult place to do business; in the early 1980s, President Suharto swept most of the obstacles away. Malaysia had been, at best, ambivalent about foreign investment; after trying and failing to spur the economy through state-run heavy industry, it is eagerly seeking help from private enterprise wherever it can be found. And in the Philippines, President Marcos's regime had been synonymous with corruption and growing instability; in 1986, the first reasonably free elections in more than fifteen years gave at least the hope of improvement. Throughout the region, governments deregulated and privatized their economies, and shed their tariffs and other trade barriers. Corporations in the more developed Pacific Rim nations seized the opportunity. In half a decade, industrialization spread through most of western Asia.

Predictably, the Japanese not only started this wave, they have ridden it the most aggressively. In 1989, Japan invested $12.5 billion in its neighbors, six times as much as in 1985 and more than three times as much as the United States. Government aid to the region added another $4.4 billion. Matsushita assembles air conditioners in Thailand and televisions in Thailand, Indonesia, Malaysia, and the Philippines. Nippon Electric is investing $260 million in joint ventures that will produce integrated circuits and telephone switching equipment in China. In Tiexi, Manchuria, Bridgestone builds rubber fenders to protect Chinese docks. And

Toyota has one of the most complex production networks yet developed: The film builds diesel engines in Thailand and ships them to Malaysia. It makes transmissions in the Philippines and exports them to Malaysia and Indonesia. Steering linkages are built in Malaysia for use in Indonesia, the Philippines, and Thailand. And electrical equipment originates in Thailand and travels to Malaysia and the Philippines. Toyota factories in all these countries assemble finished cars for sale in the local market. By selling hard and relying on native workers, Japanese manufacturers have captured 50 percent of the car market in the ASEAN Four. By 1995, the market will reach 700,000 cars per year.

Despite Japan's reputation for government manipulation of trade, very little of this has been accomplished with assistance or guidance from the Ministry of International Trade and Industry. Tokyo did give China $3.7 billion in construction loans that helped Japanese companies enter the mainland building market and promoted sales of steel and heavy equipment; yet its aid in the region is seldom targeted that directly. Almost exclusively, the spread of Japanese factories, joint ventures, and investment through Asia has been motivated by the pure capitalist drive to cut production costs and open new markets.

This trend has a long way to go. In 1989, less than 4 percent of Japanese manufacturing was done in overseas plants, compared with 18 percent for the United States. That will rise to almost 7 percent by 1995, more than 10 percent by 2000, and will continue growing for many years to come.

Taiwan's expansion through Asia has similar roots, and at least two that are unique within the region. As of late 1990, Taiwan had the largest supply of foreign reserves in the world—$66 billion, not counting gold. (Japan, in second place, then had $63 billion.) Japanese investment flowed in as well. Taiwanese per capita income rose from $3,000 in 1983 to $5,000 in 1987, to $8,000 in 1990. This new wealth had nowhere to go. Until the mid-1980s, foreign exchange controls kept it bottled up on the island, superheating the local stock and real estate markets.

As that was happening, Taiwan spawned the most powerful environmental movement in the East. Protest groups have blocked construction of a Du Pont chemical factory, a $7 billion petrochemical plant, and the fourth of the twenty nuclear power plants the government had planned to build by 2000. In 1988, when a mob shut down Taiwan's largest petrochemical plant for five days, causing heavy damage, the government fined the plant's owners $45 million for polluting local fishing waters. For the island's health and welfare, this development is probably overdue. At least one-fifth of the island's farmland is now poisoned by industrial waste. But for business, it is just one more expense that drives up manufacturing costs and makes Taiwanese products less competitive on the world market.

Taiwanese manufacturers have fought back by moving into products that offer a higher profit margin. Roughly a dozen companies there now sell one-fourth of the world's personal computers.

Taipei added the final element in 1986, when it began to relax its exchange regulations. Suddenly, capital flowed away from Taiwan, and the flood has continued ever since. Corporations there have invested more than $2 billion in the Philippines. Another $2 billion has gone to Southeast Asia. And more than $1 billion has funded investments theoretically banned by Taiwanese law, in Fujian province in mainland China. As we will see in Chapter 12, investment in the mainland is destined to grow dramatically.

South Korea, spurred by sagging business, has moved rapidly to follow in Japan's footsteps. In 1989, the Korean won rose by 30 percent on foreign exchange markets, eating into export sales. A year later, the yen sagged, making Japanese products more competitive. Labor unrest and wage hikes also battered the economy. There were more than 7,200 labor disputes in South Korea between 1987 and 1989. In March 1989, fourteen thousand policemen stormed the Hyundai shipyard to put down a strike that had lasted nearly four months. The continuing conflict drove average manufacturing wages up by 15 percent in 1987, another 25 percent in 1988, and more than 20 percent in the first half of 1989. The price of Korean autos shot up, and exports plummeted by nearly two-thirds in the first half of 1989. Export sales of Korean footwear, home appliances, and VCRs dropped as well.

All this hurt South Korea badly. Exports account for nearly 35 percent of the nation's GNP and 28 percent of jobs. They grew at a compound rate of 26 percent per year from 1986 through 1988. In 1989, that plummeted to only 2.8 percent, and in the first quarter of 1990, exports actually dropped. In 1988,

South Korea's trade balance with the United States totaled $9 billion. In the first six months of 1989, it dropped by 40 percent from the first half of the previous year. That August, Korea imported more than it exported for the first time in nearly five years. GNP growth dropped from a peak of 12 percent to just over half that.

All this is likely to prove only a temporary setback; Korea's trade picture is looking better already. Government intervention has helped to halt the slide; so has the unions' recognition that they pushed too hard. The price of the won is off slightly. Wage hikes are still running well above Seoul's single-digit target, but they are coming down. And there were only one-fifth as many strikes in 1990 as there were the year before.

More important, South Korea has met adversity the same way Japan did five years earlier: Companies there are moving into more profitable activities at home and shipping their labor-intensive businesses to lands where hourly wages of more than three dollars an hour are still a distant dream. And in doing so, they are opening new markets for their products. South Korean businesses are investing heavily in Indonesia, Thailand, and the Philippines. Samsung, Korea's largest *chaebol* (a family-dominated conglomerate), is negotiating with Nissan and Toyota to form an auto-making joint venture. Ssangyong Group's cement-making joint venture in Singapore won the construction contract for the enormous new Raffles City complex, a job that will bring the company $400 million. Daewoo has even built a clothing factory in unstable, insular Burma and plans to expand there into televisions and home appliances. And the Korean government has expanded the definition of "Pacific Rim" by donating several billion dollars worth of trade credits to the Soviet Union. A South Korean paper plant in Siberia is reportedly in the planning stage. Trade between the two nations is now about $4 billion per year, up from less than $600 million in 1989, and is expected to triple by about 1995. Best of all, this is one of the few places where the Japanese have yet to compete.

Korea does suffer some weaknesses that its neighbors do not. Korean industries are only just starting to move beyond their original focus on cheap labor. Automakers still dependent on technology from Japan. Chip manufacturers must buy their photolithography equipment and supplies from abroad. And almost

5 percent of Korean products have defects, according to the Trade and Industry Ministry—almost four times as many as in Japan. These problems have not kept South Korea from growing rapidly, but they will make it difficult to sustain the rate of expansion it enjoyed in the 1980s.

However, Korea also possesses a resource that to date only West Germany has been able to use: the chance of reunification with a repressed and economically backward section of the country separated from it by politics. On the face of it, there is little promise in current relations between the two Koreas. Animosities in this region can last for centuries, and it was only 1983 when emissaries of North Korean leader Kim Il Sung bombed a South Korean delegation in Rangoon, and 1987 when terrorists working for the North bombed a South Korean passenger jet, killing 115. The atmosphere between the two has not improved greatly since then. In March 1990, South Korea discovered that the North had cut yet another possible invasion route beneath the demilitarized zone separating them; it was the fourth tunnel uncovered so far. When the Koreas agreed to open their border briefly in August 1990 so that relatives trapped on opposite sides could meet for the first time in more than four decades, North Korea reneged. When their prime ministers met in Seoul a month later, the North began negotiations by demanding that South Korea eject the 38,000 American troops stationed there; it was not taken as a sign of good faith. North Korea's personality-cult communism maintains its hold on the country much as Bulgaria's did, by keeping its people in strict isolation. Why would it open the gates to South Korea and the loss of its own power?

In the long run, it no longer has any choice. North Korea is on the verge of starving. Its old patrons, mainland China and the Soviet Union, have both tired of the region's instability, and neither has the patience or money to continue supporting bankrupt clients. Both have slashed their shipments of grain, oil, and raw materials to North Korea, and neither is buying as much of its exports as they once did. The Soviets may relent slightly during periods when their hardliners gain control, but there is no prospect of any great or enduring change. Soviet economists estimate that North Korea's GNP shrank by 5 percent in 1990. There is worse to come now that the Soviet Union is demanding hard currency and fair market prices for its goods—unless the North accepts change.

The South, too, has practical cause to wish for reunification, in addition to its long emotional and political commitment. In 1988, South Korea authorized trade with the North, so long as it is handled through intermediaries such as Japan. Since then, Daewoo, Samsung, and Ssangyong have been buying modest amounts of iron ore, zinc, and other commodities from the North. There are chrome, copper, and tungsten to be had as well. According to one conservative estimate, free trade between the two Koreas would probably top $1 billion in the first year and $10 billion after five or six years, most of it in natural resources from the North. But the real prize is labor. North Korea has a population of twenty-one million people, half of them still living as subsistence farmers. Workers in North Korea earn perhaps forty-five dollars per month, just one-twelfth of an average salary in the South. When that potential labor source is developed, it will trigger an economic boom in both halves of the divided nation.

It will be both difficult and expensive to reunite the Koreas, Kim Il Sung's fear of peninsular *perestroika* aside, the process will cost at least $170 billion over ten years, $100 million more than the two would save by slashing their exorbitant defense budgets. But reunification is inevitable. Kim, if he survives, will be eighty-eight in the year 2000. Sometime in the next ten years, he will almost surely retire or die. The border between the Koreas will not long outlast him.

Like its larger clients, Singapore is moving its money to other lands, for obvious reasons. When Sir Thomas Stamford Raffles founded the city in 1819, Singapore was just a swampy island surrounded by sixty or so smaller islets; there were no natural resources, save the world's largest natural deep-water harbor. Today, Singapore is one of the most densely populated and industrialized places on earth. It packs 2.7 million extraordinarily productive people into an area of only 224 square miles, a space smaller than Manhattan. A single commercial center, the Jurong Industrial Estate, covers nearly one-tenth of the main island. Since Singapore became independent in 1965, its GNP has grown at an average of 8 percent per year, to roughly $27 billion, and the pace shows little evidence of slowing significantly in the 1990s.

Room for expansion is understandably at a premium, and the demand for labor has driven wages to $400 per month. So Singapore, too, has begun to relocate its labor-intensive industries to less densely populated, and much less expensive, regions in neighboring Malaysia and Indonesia. On the Indonesia island of Batam, just 12.5 miles away, factory workers earn only $110 per month. Singaporean investors have just completed an industrial park there to assemble high-tech electronic components built in Singapore itself. Bintan, a neighboring island, and the state of Johor, in southern Malaysia, have also attracted development money from their affluent and crowded neighbor.

The Four Tigers started their growth cycle with foreign capital. They lured investors with cheap labor, government subsidies, and tax incentives. And they had few competitors in the cheap-labor market. As we have seen, this scenario is now being played out in the ASEAN Four.

Indonesia is probably the "hottest" of these fast-growing nations, and not only because of Singapore's proximity. Wages there average less than forty dollars per month, the lowest pay scale left in the region, and the nation's 13,700 islands are blessed with abundant oil, natural gas, bauxite, copper, nickel, and tin. As a result, some $8 billion in foreign investment arrived in Indonesia between January 1989 and June 1990, fully one-fourth of it from Japan. Almost every major company in Japan has committed itself to factories and joint ventures in Indonesia; Asahi, Daihatsu, Komatsu, Matsushita Electric, Mitsui, and Toyota all have major dealings there. The textile industry alone has grown from $150 million in 1983 to $3 billion in 1990.

Business seems destined to flow toward Indonesia at a fast pace throughout the 1990s. With 188 million people, more than 40 percent of whom have yet to reach their twenties, Indonesia has 2.3 million new workers every year. Unemployment is a constant problem, and the country needs real economic growth of at least 5 percent annually just to create enough jobs for them all. It will be well into the next century before the supply of labor becomes so tight that prices rise significantly. As wages in the other ASEAN nations move upward, Indonesia's appeal can only grow.

Malaysia's economy once rose and fell with the tide of prices for palm oil and natural rubber, of which it was the world's largest supplier. Those days passed in the 1980s, when the government finally sought to draw electronics firms to Kuala Lumpur and the surrounding area. Japanese companies alone responded with investments of over $225 million. Assembling and testing integrated circuits brings well over $500 million per year to Malaysia, and the industry is still growing rapidly. In the state of Penang, the nation's chief producing region, foreign-owned factories provide more than 40,000 jobs. Wages have only started to rise, but already companies in Malaysia reportedly are considering investments in Vietnam, where industry is all but unknown and the pay scale is lower still.

Thailand is in a similar position. Most of its 55 million citizens are subsistence farmers, and salaries of scarcely $120 per month are more than enough to draw them to city factories. Here, too, overseas electronics firms have established chip-assembly plants, and exports of finished products are fast expanding. A $1 billion petrochemical plant just built by the government to use the nation's plentiful natural gas should spur development of a local plastics industry in the 1990s.

Though both nations have been growing rapidly, each must solve important problems if it hopes to continue expanding into the twenty-first century. One is educational. Where Singapore has no compulsory education, fully 85 percent of its school-age citizens attend classes. In contrast, fewer than half of Malaysia's young people attend high school, and six out of seven Thais drop out of school before age fourteen. In Thailand, infrastructure also presents an obstacle. Roads are scarce, ports inadequate, and both electricity and telephones are running short. The Thai government is working to solve its infrastructural problems, but has done relatively little to upgrade its workforce. For now, at least, it gives Malaysia a competitive advantage in attracting new business.

The Philippines suffers even worse problems in its drive to modernize. Both Japan and Taiwan have invested heavily in Corazon Aquino's "people power" revolution; Taiwan has put some $2 billion into the Philippines since 1987. This support may not last much longer. Aquino has been unable to bring about meaningful land reform, and virtually all of the development profits have gone to the same elite who owned the country under Ferdinand Marcos. Roads are poor, schools poor to nonexistent, and few basic services reach the people. As this is written, the government has withstood two major coup attempts and several minor ones since 1986. More will surprise no one. This instability is likely to repel even the most nerveless potential investors. President Aquino's announcement that she will not run for office in the 1992 elections only increases the air of uncertainty that hangs over Manila.

It seems that in the 1990s, politics can only make the Philippine economy even less stable. The 1987 constitution bars any extension of the current military-bases agreement under which the United States maintains Clark Air Base, Subic Bay Naval Base, and four lesser installations. It runs out in September 1991, and Aquino has called for an "orderly withdrawal" of American soldiers and sailors from the Philippines. This is the nearest thing to economic suicide. The bases provide jobs for 80,000 Filipinos, a payroll second only to that of Aquino's government, and generate $1 billion per year in U.S. aid and expenditures. Each year, the American armed forces—fifteen thousand soldiers, twenty thousand civilian workers, and their families—spend $530 million in the country. It now seems likely that this influx of needed cash will soon come to an end.

With Indonesia, Malaysia, and Thailand all offering eager workers, natural resources, and far greater stability, it is difficult to find any compelling reason for offshore companies to continue investing in the Philippines. These islands may already have seen all the prosperity that the 1990s will bring them.

One more region has been virtually untouched by the wave of Pacific development: Australia and New Zealand.

Many Westerners instinctively think of Australia as a distant but modern industrial power. In fact, it might almost be the richest of the Third World nations. With a per capita income in excess of $15,000 per year, it is priced far out of the cheap-labor market, and it lacks the kind of high-value-added industry that would allow it either to compete against Japan and South Korea in the world market or to supply them with the few manufactured products they cannot yet produce on their own. Thus, it relies almost exclusively on mining and other natural resources for its export income. For years, government policy stifled banking, taxed industry heavily, blocked outside investment, and inhibited trade in manufactured goods. Australian coal fuels the steel mills of Japan, South Korea, and Taiwan, but nearly one-third of the country's high-tech exports go to New Zealand and Papua New Guinea, while most of the rest are shipped to the United States and the British Commonwealth.

New Zealand is slightly ahead of its larger neighbor in modernizing its economy. In the late 1980s, it scrapped its limits on foreign exchange and abandoned extensive wage and price controls. Most government-owned corporations were privatized as well. The new government, elected in 1990, has announced that it intends to preserve these reforms. But New Zealand's export trade depends almost exclusively on meat and dairy products. It is not well positioned to carve out a role in the burgeoning Asian economy.

In a minor attempt to end their economic isolation, the two nations recently entered into one trade pact—with each other. This "Closer Economic Relationship" was the South Pacific equivalent of the European Community's 1992 plan, creating a single market of 19 million consumers. By promoting trade and reducing the effects of protectionism, it may foster more substantial improvements later in the decade. But before Australia and New Zealand can truly join the modern trading world, they must decide which of the three major blocs they wish to join. Their location places them firmly in the Pacific Rim, but their hearts and economies have more in common with the United States and the British Commonwealth. They will find it difficult to resolve this conflict.

The unification of the Pacific Rim is much less advanced than the evolution of Europe, or even than that of the North American trading bloc. As we have seen, it has been carried out, to date, almost exclusively via contracts and trade between corporations, rather than by treaties between governments. Even the Association of Southeast Asian Nations has made no effort to promote trade between its six members.

The growing interdependence of this bloc is no less real for its informal nature. Trade among the Pacific Rim nations is growing twice as fast as Asia's trade with North America and four times as fast as their trade with the European Community. One-third of the Pacific Rim's international trade occurred within the region in 1986, more than 40 percent in 1989. And by 2000, about 55 percent of their trade will be intra-Asian. In 1986, nearly half of Taiwan's exports went to the United States; only four years later, the fraction had dropped to about one-third. South Korea sold 40 percent of its exports to the U.S. in 1986, Japan nearly as much; by 1990, America accounted for just over 30 percent of their export trade. By 1990, the East Asian nations as a group were exporting more to each other than to North America.

To a great extent, this growing reliance on one another insulates the Pacific Rim from the risks of doing business with the European Community and the North American bloc. With savings rates as high as 35 percent, the countries of Pacific Asia can finance their own growth, even if trade sanctions in the other blocs hinder their trade outside the region. The Pacific itself provides the fastest-growing markets for a wide variety of Rim products. Asia now buys more telecommunications equipment per year than any other region. And the car market in Southeast Asia has grown by 20 to 30 percent per year since the mid-1980s; according to Deutsche Bank, the market will triple in the 1990s, to seven million cars. A major recession in the United States or Europe would still hit the Pacific Rim economies hard, but not nearly as hard as would have been the case a decade ago.

In the long run, internal problems could slow or halt the growth of individual Pacific Rim nations. Indonesia's President Suharto, who has ruled the country since 1967, is now in his early seventies; there is no obvious successor to step in when he retires or dies, and that invites political turmoil that could damage the national economy. And a number of the region's countries are largely Muslim states or have large Muslim minorities. Their puritanical populations may resist development of the kind of consumer market that drives Western economies. Yet, these are concerns for the distant future. A devastating war in the region seems highly unlikely, and it is about the only catastrophe that could slow the growth of the Pacific Rim economies before the end of the decade.

C H A P T E R 11

Â·

The Rising Sun Sets

"As the 1990s began, Japan was the most vibrant economic force in the world. When the decade ends, it will not even be among the top ten."

After reading the world's business news for a few hours, it becomes hard not to view Japan as a force of nature, its continuing ascendency a matter of physical or genetic law. In only forty years, these enigmatic islands have climbed from the bombed-out ruins of World War II to become the richest, most industrialized nation in the world. Their trade balance is the strongest, their people the wealthiest, their economy the fastest growing of any comparable nation. Of the twenty-five largest corporations in *Fortune*'s "Pacific Rim 150," all but three are Japanese. And when Japan's gross national product grew in 1990 at something over 4 percent, rather than its traditional 6 to 7 percent, economists the world over considered it the closest thing to a recession—though their growth rate was still nearly twice that of the United States. For America and the European Community, Nippon represents a competitor with the power to destroy national economies, or to buy them.

For the Third World, and particularly along the Pacific Rim, it offers hope of investment and aid that could bring prosperity where unemployment and hunger now reign. In the 1990s, both hopes and fears will give way to a much less overwhelming vision.

Behind its impressive facade, the Trading Empire of the Rising Sun hides problems that soon will shoot down its soaring prosperity. Among them are a rapidly aging labor force, a new generation of employees with little interest in working the long hours their parents endured, record low fertility, growing antagonism among their trading partners, and a sharp tightening of the credit that has always driven Japanese corporate expansion. In any other nation, the effects of these pressures would already have grown obvious. As the 1990s began, Japan was the most vibrant economic force in the world. When the decade ends, it will not even be among the top ten.

Japan's worst and most immediate problem is the continuing growth of the so-called "silver generation." The retirement age in Japan was set at fifty-five for many years. Companies employing about 70 percent of the Japanese full-time labor force have since raised it to sixty or more, and some workers stay on the job even after their official retirement. Yet, by 1990, more than one-fifth of the Japanese people working in 1985 had already retired on pensions equal to 80 percent of their salaries. By 2000, 16 percent of the population will be over age sixty-five, compared with 7 percent in the United States today. By 2010, the number will reach nearly one in four. No nation in history has ever had to support so large a proportion of retirees.

And Japan has just set a world record for longevity: life expectancy for Japanese men is now nearly seventy-six; for women it is almost eighty-two. While this is good for the individual, it represents a continuing demand on the nation's resources that even Japan will be hard pressed to meet. A savings rate of over 15 percent during their working lives has made elderly Japanese more able to care for themselves than their American counterparts, but they still have begun to drain their country's pension funds. The aging in Japan already require $1.1 trillion worth of goods and services annually, and approximately one hundred new retirement complexes must be built each year. The cost of supporting the aged will soon begin to push up the price of Japanese goods, reducing the country's export sales. And as now-elderly Japanese stop investing their money and begin spending it to cushion their retirement, corporations will find it more difficult to fund modernization and expansion. By the end of the decade, these problems will be clear for all to see.

The new generation of workers will not match the rising demand for social services with the growing output required to pay for it. For one thing, there are too few of them. Not long ago, finding a good job was one of life's most difficult tasks for all but the best Japanese students. In 1990, the average male college senior received offers from more than four companies. The number of job openings for college graduates is growing more than three times as fast as the number of qualified people to fill them. Over all, there were one-third more job openings than applicants at the beginning of 1990.

There is little prospect that this trend will soon be reversed. Japan's birth rate is now the lowest in the world. It takes a fertility rate of 2.1 children per woman, simply to maintain a nation's population. As of 1989, Japanese women were producing, on average, only 1.57 children in their lifetimes. The cost of housing and education has simply priced young adults out of the "parent market." More than one in three Japanese wives in their peak childbearing years say their apartments are too cramped and their incomes too small to give a child an adequate upbringing. Nearly as many did not want to face Japan's enormous social pressure to give children a top-quality education. In one recent survey, more than 70 percent of married couples in France and the United Kingdom said they expected to enjoy raising children; so did half the couples in the United States. Only one Japanese couple in five agreed.

Until recently, a statistical anomaly disguised the significance of these trends. When tallying its labor force, Japan, traditionally, has not counted women. Employment was considered full when all men had jobs, no matter how many women were out of work. Yet there are few jobs Japanese women could not handle. Nearly all are high school graduates, and more than one-third have a degree from a two- or four-year college. Thus, it seemed that Japan need only recruit still more women to fill the positions left vacant by the shortage of male applicants.

It isn't so. As of 1990, more women than men had entered the labor market for fourteen straight years. Women now make up nearly half the Japanese work force. Today, one Japanese woman out of two works. Two-thirds of them either retain their jobs after marriage or return to work when their children reach school age.

The only thing new in this is that so many women are now being counted. The truth is that the majority of Japanese women have always worked, particularly among the less affluent. Much of the small manufacturing in Japan is done as piecework. The man of the house officially holds the job, but the entire family pitches in at home to earn a living. There are far fewer women available to take new jobs than the official statistics imply. They will not maintain Japan's growth on their own.

The only way to compensate for a labor shortage is to make the available workers get more done. Unfortunately, the recruits now available are likely to accomplish far less than the postwar labor force. In part, this is a matter of government policy. Rengo, Japan's largest organization of trade unions, reports that total working hours in Japan averaged 2,088 per year in 1989, about 400 hours longer than in the United States and Western Europe. In an effort to placate American trade officials, the labor ministry aims to reduce average working hours to 1,800 in fiscal 1992. It has also raised to twenty, the number of annual paid days off, and asked employers to urge their workers to take all of the time allotted to them. These adjustments, too, will eat into Japan's rate of growth.

Yet the most important changes are personal. Young Japanese today are both more self-centered and less interested in hard work even than the so-called "me" generation in the United States. The attitudes of Japanese born in the sixties and seventies are so different from those of their parents that this age group has come to be called *shinjinrui,* "the new race." It is a label they seem to wear proudly.

A host of surveys have defined *shinjinrui* values, and they have dismayed most social planners. Dentsu, the largest advertising agency in the world, asked people in Tokyo, New York, and Los Angeles about their attitudes toward life and work. The results will surprise anyone who considers Americans overly materialistic. More than three-fourths of young Tokyo residents said that their purpose in life was to achieve wealth and comfort; less than 60 percent of their cousins in New York agreed, and only 55 percent of those in Los Angeles. And where the great majority of young Americans still believed in hard work and honesty, fewer than one Japanese in four expressed any great admiration for such old-fashioned virtues. Sixty percent said that they do not "pay off" in Japanese society.

Many other studies in recent years have yielded similar results. In one, the prime minister's office found that scarcely more than one-third of Japanese aged 20 to 25 considered social concerns ahead of individual fulfillment—and they placed their own jobs in the first category, not the second. The Life Insurance Culture Center, in Tokyo, found that only 10 percent of young people considered work a major priority, while just two in every hundred were concerned with contributing to society. Half said their greatest interests were individual activities, such as hobbies, exercise, or spending time with friends. In their parents' generation, work and society are still the primary values.

This change has already upset the Japanese labor market. One symptom is the rise of job-hopping. People under 30 are two to three times more willing to change employers than those over 40. Only one student in six plans to find a job and remain with the company through retirement. More ominous yet are the "freetors," young people who deliberately take only part-time work, trading the security and pay of a full-time job for extra freedom. One government estimate says that freetors will make up nearly one-third of the Japanese labor force by the year 2000.

If that were not enough, even the over-40 generation has begun to suffer from what the Japanese Ministry of International Trade and Industry calls the "paradox of prosperity." While the country as a whole is very wealthy, most individual Japanese are not. Polls indicate that more than half of these highest-paid people in the world say that they do not feel affluent. Even those with incomes double the national average complain that they are frustrated with their standard of living, and especially with their tiny apartments, tedious commutes, and long days at the office. This, too, will cut into the phenomenal productivity on which Japan's growth was based.

Japanese consumer frustration can be seen in the growth of leisure spending and the decline of savings. Not long ago, Japanese families save nearly one-fourth of their income. This has shrunk to 15 percent and seems destined to slide further. By comparison, leisure spending has been on the rise. It now accounts for some 30 percent of total consumer spending, up from one-fourth in 1984. Money saved can be used to buy stocks and bonds, promoting further economic growth. Money spent on sports and travel is simply gone.

This revolution in values is also changing public policy in significant ways. Rice farmers have always been a potent symbol of Japan's unique national character, much loved in a nation long divorced from its agrarian past. They have also been a powerful force in the ruling Liberal Democratic party. As a result, the Tokyo government subsidizes its rice farmers at a rate of more than $1,200 per ton, and Japanese consumers have willingly paid five to six times more for their rice than would have been necessary in an open market. When the Tokyo government proposed cutting the rice subsidy in the mid-1980s, the nation's largest coalition of consumer groups staged massive street rallies, demanding that rice farmers never be exposed to foreign competition. But agrarian nostalgia is a waning force for many Japanese. By 1990, three nationwide surveys found that two-thirds of the citizens polled favored at least some lowering of trade barriers in the rice market. Prime Minister Toshiki Kaifu has already conceded the merit of opening perhaps 5 percent of Japan's rice market to imports. This has recently become official policy. It seems a small concession, but the introduction of competition will reduce the price of Japan's rice to world market levels. This small experience will genuinely free markets is likely to set off a consumer movement that will erode corporate profits for many years to come.

Added dangers grow from the soaring cost of real estate. In 1986, a Tokyo apartment of 788 square feet cost $192,000. Today, the average Tokyo home of 675 square feet—only 25 by 27 feet—costs $432,000. In 1978, 32 percent of Japanese planned to buy homes; a decade later, only 19 percent still expected someday to own their own homes. The price of commercial property is equally out of control. At their peak in 1989, a $1,000 bill bought a piece of land in downtown Tokyo roughly the size of the bill itself, and the grounds of the Imperial Palace—a large compound, but not overwhelming—were worth more than all the property in Florida.

In 1990, however, Tokyo stock prices crashed and took land values down with them. For years, canny Japanese bought stocks, borrowed against their winnings in that market to buy land, and then borrowed against the growing value of their property to buy more stocks. With the Nikkei average down nearly 50 percent in one year and apparently headed lower, this pleasant little game has collapsed, and many of the players are scrambling to cover their losses. Many of them are doing it by selling their real estate. In the Tokyo suburbs, residential land is now worth about 20 percent less than at its peak. In Kyoto, the price of condominiums is reportedly half what it was only a year or two ago. Not even New York has suffered such declines.

Oddly, one more factor that will depress land prices is the coming competition in the rice market. One reason real estate is so expensive in Tokyo and other major cities is that much of it remains locked in vest-pocket rice farms that have been passed on in the same families for generations. They survive on government rice subsidies and favorable tax laws. When the price of their crops falls to world levels, they will no longer be able to survive as farmers, and their land will finally enter the market.

In the United States, a major decline in real estate values has all but destroyed the nation's savings-and-loan industry and weakened many commercial banks. Japan is at least as vulnerable. The Japan Center for Economic Research estimates that a 30 percent decline in average real estate prices would cut nearly 3 percent from GNP growth, almost 4 percent from growth in consumer spending, and bankrupt firms owing more than $27 billion to Japan's banks and other lenders. Several large real estate developers have already defaulted on their loans. In any real crash, the losses would send shock waves through the world economy.

Tightening bank profits have added to one more problem that has already begun to slow Japan's economic growth. Through most of the late 1980s, the high cost of the yen on foreign exchange markets reduced Japan's export trade. In order to maintain the capital investment needed for further growth, the Bank of Japan eased the money supply and cut its discount rate—the price charged on loans to other banks—to only 2.5 percent. At the same time, the price of oil and other imports dropped sharply, so Japan was spared the inflation that would normally accompany such rapid growth. As stock prices skyrocketed, corporations also found they could issue convertible bonds in Europe at interest rates as low as 1.5 percent. Converting the borrowed money back to yen gave more than that in profit on the foreign exchange market. In effect, the loans were free. For five straight years, capital spending rose at a compound rate of more than 10 percent per year.

It was an artificial heaven, and it could not last. Import prices began to rise, bringing inflation back into the picture. Then the cost of oil jumped from less than 11 dollars a barrel to more than eighteen, in little more than a year—and that was before the Kuwait crisis. The Bank of Japan suddenly reigned in the money supply and jammed the discount rate up to 6 percent. Since 1989, the cost of capital has tripled, and for many businesses, loans are becoming more difficult to obtain at any price.

On the surface, it seemed at first that Japan's major corporations were in good shape to weather even so powerful a financial storm. Many of them appeared to be sitting on huge reserves of cash. There was less to their excess funds than met the eye, because the Japanese giants often hide their borrowing in the accounts of subsidiaries. On average, Japanese firms have borrowed 80 percent of their net worth; among small concerns the proportion is even higher. Suddenly all but the strongest companies are having trouble funding their plans. This problem will grow throughout the 1990s.

One other danger is worth mention because it seems inevitable, though when it will strike is impossible to predict. Seismologically speaking, the Japanese islands are one of the most active regions in the world. Minor temblors are common, and destructive earthquakes are far from rare. In 1923, one of the largest earthquakes ever recorded, leveled half of Tokyo, killing 150,000. Since then, the city has required that tall buildings be designed to resist quake damage. There is little doubt, however, that a shock on the scale of 1923's would again reduce much of the city to rubble. When it happens, more than buildings will collapse. Japan's economy will be destroyed, and the economies of all those nations that depend on it, including the United States. This is one sure route to another global depression.

We are not counting on an act of seismic violence to destroy Japan's economy. Some of the trends we have examined in this chapter will have powerful effects, others are less important. But a pattern emerges from them all, and it will quickly change Japan's position in the world. With more jobs than people to fill them, more social expenses in the future than in the past, and more need for growth than money to fund it, Japan's corporations must run faster every day just to avoid losing ground. For the first time since World War II, they are facing more problems and more difficult problems than they can solve. On all sides, Nippon will be losing its industrial might throughout the 1990s. We see little chance that it will survive the decade with its wealth intact.

....

CHAPTER 12

Reuniting The Chinas

*"If Taiwan does not find some way to mend its differences
with the mainland, it will find itself increasingly isolated."*

....

Germany is again a single nation. By the turn of the century, and probably sooner, there will be only one Korea. Can it be long before the Chinas also heal their divisions? We doubt it.

To hear the governments of both Taiwan and mainland China tell it, in fact, there is no need to reunite them. Hong Kong, of course, will remain a British colony only until 1997, and Macao will revert to the mainland's control in 1999, but even today the People's Republic of China and the "Republic of China"—Taiwan—are one country indivisible. On this, Deng Xiaoping and Taiwanese president Lee Teng-hui agree. In Taiwan, the government still considers the island to be part of mainland China; merely advocating independence from the rest of China is illegal. The island's twenty million people seem equally tied to their ancestral homelands. In a Gallup poll, only 16 percent of the anonymous participants said they supported the idea of declaring Taiwan independent; fully 63 percent rejected it. However, the two Chinas strongly disagree over which government has the legitimate claim to both pieces of the country, the Communist regime in Beijing or the "one-party democracy" in Taipei.

In reality, the common heritage that both sides feel still binds them is little more than a memory, albeit a powerful one. The two Chinas have far less in common than they did 40 years ago:

Economically, they are separated, almost literally, by centuries. On the mainland, the Chinese people have remained stuck in the agrarian poverty of millenia, their lives not much different under Communist rule than it was under the Ch'ing Dynasty, three hundred years ago. On the mainland, nearly 70 percent are farmers. Eighteen percent more, work in industry and commerce. Many of the remainder work directly for the government. Contrast that with the modern capitalist society of Taiwan. More than 40 percent of Taiwanese workers are employed in service businesses. Another 40 percent work in industry and commerce. No more than 17 percent work the island's farms, and the number diminishes each day.

Taiwan has foreign exchange reserves of $66 billion, not counting gold. That is $3 billion more than Japan and more than four times the mainland's reserves.

The mainland's per capita GNP is only $330; Taiwan's is $6,200. Per capita income is even more disparate. In the People's Republic, it amounts to only $258. The average Taiwanese earns $8,000 per year, more than thirty times as much. On Taiwan, there is one telephone for every three people. On the mainland, there is one telephone for every 134.

With twenty million people, Taiwan packs 1.5 million passenger cars into less than fourteen thousand square miles; the island's roads are ten times as crowded as those of Los Angeles. The mainland has more than 1.1 billion people and a land area exceeding 3.7 million square miles, but only 1.1 million cars.

Eighty-five percent of Taiwan's people were born there. Their only link to the mainland is through the memories of their parents.

Politically, of course, the difference is even greater. For nearly four decades after the triumph of Mao Zedong in 1949, Chiang Kai-shek's Kuomintang ruled, essentially by decree; its chief claim to legitimacy was its uninterrupted existence since it won a majority in the first national assembly of the Chinese republic in 1913. But since the late 1980s, Taiwan has become increasingly democratic. In less than five years, the government has ended martial law, guaranteed freedom of the press, allowed the formation of labor unions and new political parties, and even permitted its citizens to visit the mainland. (By 1990, more than one million had done so.) The Democratic Progressive party, which came into being only in 1987, is already a major force in national politics. And when a ninety-five-year-old legislator died in September 1990, the mighty Kuomintang finally lost its majority in parliament. Almost eighty years after Sun Yat-sen offered popular rule to the Chinese people, his heirs have reluctantly granted it to Taiwan.

On the mainland, democracy was the fleeting hope of a tiny minority of students and intellectuals. It died in Tiananmen Square. No Westerner can more than guess how many people have been imprisoned or killed for their roles in the ill-fated protests of late May and early June 1989; in 1991, the trials were still in progress. But the government itself bragged about one phase of the continuing crackdown. In the autumn of 1990, Beijing and the nearby port of Quinhuangdao played host to the Eleventh Asian Games, a mini-Olympics of the East. Some seventy thousand security police were mobilized to deal with the largely imaginary threat of protesters and the real problem of petty criminals who might have preyed on the 100,000 tourists attending the event. In May and June, a law-and-order campaign paved the way for the festivities. The government later announced that the clean-up had solved some 350,000 criminal cases, including 62,000 "major" crimes. Amnesty International reported that more than five hundred people had been executed by order of China's kangaroo courts.

When the Soviet Union quashed the 1956 rebellion in Hungary, it was more than twenty years before democracy again stirred there. When it put down the "Prague spring" of 1968, it was twelve years before the trade-union movement began to agitate for popular rule, nine years more before their efforts brought down the Communist government. There is no reason to hope that democracy will bloom in Beijing with less delay.

Economically, however, the changes are profound and continuing. In the early 1980s, Beijing began to experiment with limited capitalism, hoping that where a command economy had been unable to bring prosperity, Western methods would. The test caused both an economic boom in regions where free-market enterprises flourished and a schism between provinces. In Guangdong, the province bordering Hong Kong, capitalism was at its most active. Per capita income there, quickly grew to double that of the country at large. A class of prosperous entrepreneurs and farmers arose whose income often topped $3,000 per year, ten times the average for city workers. The government's first priority in the period after Tiananmen was to make sure the stream of capitalist investment resumed as quickly as possible. Eighteen months after the massacre, it was signing contracts at a rate of nearly $8 billion per year, more than at the previous peak in early 1989. It has even allowed a private company in Hong Kong to begin building a 162-mile road from the colony to Canton at a cost of $1 billion. The firm expects to make its investment back, and a healthy profit as well, by charging tolls to travelers on the route.

The growing prosperity of Guangdong and other coastal provinces where exports flourished has created conflicts that only more capitalism can cure. Silk, tobacco, wool, and other commodities flowed out of Hunan, Sichuan, and the other inland territories, to be made into cloth and cigarettes and exported through Hong Kong, Shanghai, and Canton. Relatively little money flowed back. In reprisal, the provinces surrounding Guangdong erected roadblocks, charging tolls to the supply trucks going toward the coastal factories. Often, they simply would not let the trucks through. Shortages of raw materials forced capitalist enterprises in Shanghai to cut back their workweeks, while those in producing regions had all the materials they could use. The post-Tiananmen crackdown has done little to control this anarchy.

This combination of political repression and economic freedom presents an interesting contrast with the Soviet Union, where until recently, political freedom has grown rapidly and economic change has proved almost impossible. According to Lucian W. Pye, Ford Professor of Political Science at the Massachusetts Institute of Technology, it probably grows from the traditional Chinese culture, which four decades of communism have done little to change.

In a practical sense, governmental forms seem to mean less in China than they do elsewhere. Writing in the journal *Foreign Affairs,* Pye points out that Chinese civilization long ago developed a unique pattern of relations between the central authority and those whom it purported to govern. Even in the days of the emperors, the worst of whom ruled in a style that closely resembled that of the Communist party today, the central government was a distant force. It offered a display of grandeur, which gave people a source of pride and dignity that their primitive lives would otherwise have lacked. But their lives remained communal and inward-looking. They asked nothing of the government and gave it very little in return. When the emperor gave a command, his subjects bowed obediently and went on about their business. Superiors were careful not to check too carefully how well their subordinates obeyed orders, and all were satisfied. So long as no one openly questioned the emperor's authority, the peasants in Kiangsu or Sichuan could live without interference from anyone more remote than the local warlord. But as Pye observes, "Should central authorities be embarrassed, however, they can act with mad fury." Tiananmen was neither an isolated incident nor a uniquely Communist atrocity.

This odd and enduring social structure explains why China finds it so difficult to open its political system as it has its economy. "This distinctively Chinese relationship between the state and society was sustained by a shared belief in a moral order, the upholding of which gave the government legitimacy, and the existence of which gave the people security and peace," Pye observes. Under dynastic rule, the emperor claimed a moral superiority, and his officials held their posts by virtue of their skill in matters of doctrine. Under the Communist party, only the ideology has changed, and that, far less than Mao liked to claim. But in a democracy, the right to rule no longer grows from the ruler's virtue. It springs from the will of the governed and remains with the ruler only so long as he can convince his citizens that he is doing more to promote their well-being than his political competitors can. To the extent that China becomes democratized, its rulers become responsible for improving the lives of their people. They cannot hope to succeed without capitalist aid.

Yet they cannot afford to keep capitalism out, and thus avoid its democratizing influence. In part, this is because the Communists long ago set themselves the task of bringing China into the modern world. It was the need to better the lot of their people that justified their revolution in the first place. Whatever pressure can be exerted from the grass roots also demands practical improvement. Even in so isolated a society as that of the People's Republic, people know their lives are far less comfortable than in the nations of the West. For the foreseeable future, China will punctuate its growing economic freedom by incidents of abrupt, often vicious political repression. But that economic freedom will continue to grow, and in the long run, greater political freedom will become unavoidable.

As this evolution gradually narrows the practical gap between the two Chinas, Taiwan is also facing changes that will make it more open to a rapprochement with the mainland. One is its growing need for new sources of cheap labor, examined in Chapter 10. Even with investment in the mainland banned by law, Taiwanese companies had sunk more than $1 billion into factories and joint ventures in the PRC by 1990. This commitment can only grow in the years to come.

Taiwan also faced a series of diplomatic reverses in 1990. In just a few weeks, Indonesia, Saudi Arabia, and Singapore all broke their ties with the island's government and opened relations with the mainland. South Korea maintains diplomatic relations with Taiwan, but it will probably abandon its longtime ally as part of its own reunification with North Korea; it has already established a series of trade offices in the People's Republic. Twenty-seven nations still recognize Taiwan, but only South Korea and South Africa are economically significant, and the trend is clear. If Taiwan does not find some way to mend its differences with the mainland, it will find itself increasingly isolated.

One last factor has also begun to aid this process. Time is finally removing the last of the excessively durable generation whose mutual antagonisms divided their people. Chiang Kai-shek died in 1975, Mao Zedong in 1976. Deng Xiaoping, officially retired, but clearly still in command, was born in 1904. He and his contemporaries will pass quickly from the scene. And Taiwanese courts have ordered the nonagenarian elite of the Kuomintang to retire in 1991. The fossilized hatreds of half a century are losing their power.

Deng Xiaoping has long offered Taiwan a formula for reunion: "one country, two systems." While Chiang's contemporaries still held power, there was no chance at all that Taiwan would accept the offer. Taiwan is still understandably skeptical of the idea that the People's Republic would leave its capitalist economy and growing democracy intact for long after the two Chinas were reunited. But Taiwan's sixty-three-year-old, island-born President Lee Teng-hui has recently done away with the cabinet's mainland committee, which administered the government's empty claim to run all of China, and established a National Reunification Committee, which he chairs himself. This can only be seen as a step toward reconciliation.

How quickly the process continues will depend on the two test cases taking effect late in this decade. Under a 1984 treaty, the mainland Chinese government promised that Hong Kong's lifestyle and freewheeling capitalism will remain undisturbed for at least fifty years after the British leave, in 1997. Macao, which reverts to mainland rule two years later, has received the same guarantee. More recently, the mainland government has begun to grumble, menacingly about the growing democratic movement in Hong Kong; the people of the British colony can forget their dreams of free elections once Beijing takes over, it warns. Yet we believe the People's Republic has no choice but to honor its promises. Hong Kong, and to a lesser extent Macao, provide windows to the industrialized world, through which billions of dollars in foreign exchange pass each year. Imposition of a Communist economy and government would close them instantly.

So far, the 5.5 million residents of Hong Kong do not seem convinced. Cathay Pacific, Hong Kong's prestigious airline, gives clear evidence of the impact this "brain drain" is already having on the colony. In 1990, the firm lost one hundred of its mechanics to Quantas, in Australia. So many of the company's computer programmers have fled that it now exports much of its work to an office in Sydney. Some seven hundred managers are considered critical to Cathay's operations; on average, seventy of them emigrate each year. According to one estimate, the company has had to raise its pay scales by 30 percent, to retain its key workers.

This is far from an isolated example. In 1989 alone, well over sixty-thousand emigrated to less troubling parts of the world; Canada and Australia together have received one thousand per week since 1988. Vancouver, in fact, has grown into something of an outpost of Asian civilization. The number fleeing would probably have been higher still, if the United Kingdom had not refused to grant a haven to its 3.3 million subjects in the colony. And the exodus is being led by the affluent executives and professionals that Hong Kong depends on for its prosperity.

In the closing years of the twentieth century, mainland China will continue working to heal the self-inflicted wounds of the Tiananmen Square massacre. When Beijing regains possession of Hong Kong and Macao, it will do its best to encyst them so as to prevent the ideological contamination of the mainland, but it will leave their economic and political systems intact. The economic links between Taiwan and the mainland will continue to grow, and the examples of the British and Portuguese colonies will reassure its government that the People's Republic can be trusted to keep its reluctant bargain with the devils of capitalism and democracy. In the end, it too will begin to negotiate for reunion with the mainland. Its technological sophistication, managerial expertise, and ready capital will prove too much for Beijing to resist. Some time early in the next century, and perhaps by the year 2000, the two Chinas will make a deal that both can live with. In name, at least, the two will reunite. And China's tiny capitalist democracies will begin the long process of bringing the mainland into the twenty-first century.

PART FOUR

THE HAVE-NOTS

INTRODUCTION

In leaving the Pacific Rim, we move out of the world's "have" nations, the ones where most people can count on having enough food to eat, a roof over their heads, schooling, adequate health care, and, in the majority, a say in their own destinies. People in the "have-not" lands seldom enjoy any of these luxuries. Hobbes might almost have been thinking of Africa or Southeast Asia when he observed that life in the state of nature is nasty, brutish, and short.

The have-nots of the new world order form two groups: those possessing natural resources valuable to the developed world, and those in which the only resource is the people themselves, of whom there are too many. In the past, countries in either group could at least hope to improve their standards of living, given enough talent, determination, and hard work; Japan raised itself from the rubble of World War II to become the world's second most prosperous nation—in only forty years, despite an almost total lack of resources. However, Japan could build on a relatively well-educated population, and it had little Third World competition for trade with the wealthier lands of the West. To-day, virtually all of the less-developed countries are struggling to attract foreign business. Only those will succeed who offer unique assets, such as oil or proximity to an industrialized nation in need of cheap labor. The remainder will find themselves condemned to growing poverty, as their populations expand faster than their economies.

Politically, the 1990s will be a difficult time for the have-nots of the new world order. Where people are sufficiently poor, civil unrest and international conflict are sure to follow. In the twenty-first century, as in the twentieth, stability will elude many of the developing lands.

In Part 4, we examine the have-not countries, both with and without natural resources. As bright as the future will be for the people of the great trading blocks, it will be equally dark throughout much of the Third World. It will not improve until the industrialized trading nations solve their own economic and political difficulties and can afford to turn their attention outward.

THE HAVE-NOTS:

The Middle East

....

Rebuilding After the Desert War

*"If Egypt, Iraq, Syria, and Jordan hope to improve the lives
of their people, they will do it largely with Western money.
Any future Palestinian state will find itself equally dependent
on Western good will."*

....

The disparate peoples of the Middle East like to describe themselves, at least to outsiders, as one people—brother Arabs, united
in Islam. This is at best a polite fiction. Like the Balkans, and
sub-Saharan Africa, the Middle East we know today is an artificial construct impressed upon the native populations by European powers to suit their own purposes. The nations of the
Middle East were created or remodeled by the League of Nation's soon after World War I. Many still claim the territory of
their neighbors, and all still resent Western interference in their
affairs. The world has seen, of late, just how fragile their claimed
unity can be. Repairing the damage left by this lesson in the limits of brotherhood will be one of the great challenges of the
1990s. Yet it is worth whatever effort is required. If the job is
done well, the region could be a far more peaceful place in the
twenty-first century than it has been in the twentieth.

What remains of Kuwait and Iraq is an indisputable mess. The
airplanes of the U.S.-led Coalition forces dropped more tons of
bombs on Iraq and occupied Kuwait almost every day of the
Six-Week War than the Allies dropped in the mammoth D-day
invasion. Granted, the bombs fell over a much broader area—the

Normandy beachhead was smaller than many airports—but because they were guided to their targets, they were far more likely to hit them. More than Iraq's tanks and airplanes is gone. Throughout Iraq, bridges, communications systems, power plants, and factories have been destroyed or severely damaged. In Kuwait, Iraqi ground forces pillaged as thoroughly as they could in the months available to them. They looted hospitals of their equipment, plundered factories, burned public buildings, set on fire more than one-third of Kuwait's oil wells, and damaged nearly all the rest—including the zoo. Crude petroleum still clogs the waters of the Persian Gulf. Rebuilding after the Gulf War is one of the most difficult and costly pieces of civil engineering ever undertaken.

The political engineering required may be even more daunting. The major reason the United States and its Coalition partners went to war was not to guarantee the West a supply of cheap oil, much as America would welcome that resource. Neither did they act out of any great love of Kuwait, a land whose wealth and arrogance many less fortunate Arab neighbors view with bitterness. They went to war in part because they hoped to establish the United Nations and the rule of law, not force of arms, as the final arbiters in international disputes. They also fought to restore the fragile balance of power that has kept the Middle East, if not peaceful, then at least somewhat predictable in its instability. An Iraq devastated by eight years of needless war with Iran was still a powerful force to help keep Iran and Syria in check. An Iraq with access to Kuwait's vast riches would have controlled one-fourth of the world's oil reserves and easily dominated the region. Neither the West nor the Middle East could allow a man with Saddam Hussein's record of aggression to gather that much power.

The Coalition succeeded in half its goals; the judgments of the United Nations Security Council carry much more weight today than they did before the Gulf War. But like the infrastructure of Iraq and Kuwait, the political and military balance that existed before August 1990 is now a shambles. Each of the countries involved faces special problems in adapting to the postwar situation.

Iraq lost more than its army, weapons, and personnel in the war. The moment it invaded Kuwait, it lost whatever trust its neighbors formerly granted it. And no matter how much love Saddam Hussein may have won among Palestinians, Jordanians, and Arab extremists, the loss of his armies has destroyed his nation's influence in the region. Iraq must now find some way to restore its position within the fractious brotherhood of Middle Eastern nations.

Kuwait's royal family, the al-Sabah, has already found that ascending their thrones was the easy part of returning to their country. Simply being attacked, undermined—at least to some degree—their legitimacy as the absolute rulers of the wealthiest nation in the Gulf region. Saddam's blistering attacks on them, as corrupt wastrels who live in luxury while neighboring Arabs starve, won a large and sympathetic audience. The Kuwaiti resistance fighters know they worked to save their country while the royals lived in comfortable exile in London, New York, and Aspen; they want a say in its future. The al-Sabah must reestablish themselves as effective leaders, grant a minimum of democracy, and work harder to help develop the region's poorer nations before their position will again be secure. One necessary step will be to restore the Kuwaiti parliament, which was suspended in 1986, when it developed ambitions of having an effective voice in government.

Saudi Arabia's monarchy also faces rising democratic sentiment in their land. "The decision to go to war was correct; I support it," one of their subjects observed. "But like everything else, it was a decision made by the king and the princes. I suddenly realized that we have no say in our own fates." The king's challenge is to accommodate the Saudi people's need to share at least a little of the power without losing his hold on the country. During the Gulf War, he revived plans for a Majlis al-Shura, a royally appointed assembly in which commoners can offer their opinions and advice. In a land as rigidly governed as Saudi Arabia, that idea is almost revolutionary. It is the least he can do.

Jordan must make amends for aligning itself with the aggressor in the Gulf War. That task will prove simple, but not at all easy, as we will see in Chapter 14.

Throughout the region, nations must find some way to defuse other time bombs. They must make and maintain peace between Israel and the Palestinians, a topic we will also hold for the next chapter. And they must find some way to bring stability to Lebanon, where war was a way of life years before Saddam came to power. To date, peace there, such as it is, depends for its existence on Syrian ruthlesness with its local dependents, and on the lightly armed troops of the United Nations Interim Force near the border with Israel.

Finally, the United States must formulate a reasonable long-term policy for its relations with the Middle East. In its relentless focus on the short term, Washington has often backed losers and created Frankenstein monsters. For decades, it supported the Shah of Iran, only to see his government displaced by the rabidly anti-American Khomeini regime. To counterbalance Iranian power, it helped Saddam Hussein build the armies that made him a threat to the entire Middle East. Most recently, in its eagerness to build a coalition against Iraq, it has allied itself with Syria, even though Hafez al-Assad's regime is still on the U.S. State Department's list of nations supporting terrorism. Stability will not come to the Middle East until the United States breaks this unfortunate habit. There seems at least a chance that the Gulf War has finally taught Washington the lesson it has so long resisted.

One crucial part of the Middle East's future will be an international program to support reconstruction and development throughout the region. It will operate much like the Marshall Plan, which helped Europe rebuild after the Second World War. This will be a more complex undertaking than the original Marshall Plan, in part because Europe itself was a simpler place in the 1940s and '50s than the Arab regions are today. After World War II, there was little need to consider balancing the interests of nations crippled by war with those made more powerful by it, nor those of poor lands with the priorities of the wealthy. In Europe, everyone was impoverished and crippled by the war, victors and vanquished alike. In the Middle East, only Iraq and Kuwait have been crippled. Their adversaries in Iran have had at least some chance to rebuild after the eight-year war. Syria, too, remains unimpaired. Saudi Arabia plans to double the size of its air force, expand its army, and install a $3 billion electronic security system along its seven-hundred-mile border with Yemen. And all the oil states are still rich, while their neighbors remain poor. Add America's reluctance to give any of the Arab states enough power to threaten Israel, and the situation becomes even more complex. Tact, negotiating skill, and a keen sense of long-term strategy—three areas in which the United States has occasionally proved deficient—will be at least as important as money during this period.

(Even money is now a problem for the United States, whose streets less fortunate countries once said were paved with gold. The spectacle of American diplomats going hat-in-hand around the developed worled, asking for contributions to help pay for their commitment in the Middle East, will be repeated frequently during the years to come.)

One of the countries that needs this generosity most is Iraq. During the Gulf War, President Bush often denied any intention to destroy his opponent, either as a nation or as a military force. The Coalition proved that, in its ground campaign, when its troops could have driven the 150 or so miles to Baghdad unopposed, but resisted the temptation. Yet Iraq's infrastructure and industrial base were largely destroyed by the bombing that preceded the invasion. Simply supplying Baghdad with electricity will take at least a year—all ten of the city's major substations were obliterated—and neither water nor sanitation in the city will be reliable until that is accomplished. The same story is told repeatedly on a smaller scale throughout the country. Iraq must be prosperous enough to support its people; abject poverty breeds totalitarian extremism, as the world learned in Weimar Germany and has seen many times since then.

Even during the Gulf War, we would have sworn that the United States would lead the effort to rebuild Iraq. It is not to be. Though America has provided a little humanitarian aid for the victims of its bombs, its traditional generosity has been overwhelmed by Iraqi brutality to the Kuwaiti people and to a few of the prisoners of war, and by the suspicion that Iraq holds the raw materials for nuclear weapons. It will not recover until Saddam Hussein passes from the scene.

The United States will be more willing to help the blameless needy of the Middle East, whether or not they aided it in the Gulf War. Whether the Arab nations will be willing to accept its aid is another matter. After years of reviling America, they have either allied themselves with the hated enemy or have stood aside and watched it destroy a fellow Arab land. Every nation in the region has its quota of extremists whose sense of Islamic purity has already been offended by the presence of Westerners in the land of Mecca and Medina. Saudi Arabia often has been criticized bitterly for being too heavily influenced by the West, though it considers the Koran to be its constitution, adheres strictly to Islamic law, and has proved its loyalty to the Arab cause by bankrolling the Palestine Liberation Organization for more than twenty years. Syria claims that 85 percent of its people disapproved of its involvement in the Coalition against Iraq. The spectacle of American bombs raining down on Arab civilians, even if only by accident, further inflamed that passion. Accepting further involvement by Western powers, no matter how much it is needed, almost inevitably will inspire further outrage.

If the United States and its allies are to promote stability in the Middle East, they must find some way to deal with an Arab population that embraces religious fanaticism of a kind virtually unknown in the West since the Middle Ages, one whose mission is still to spread Islam and its puritanical life-style throughout the world and that views Americans as infidels. It is a task at which American governments have consistently failed.

Yet it may be that Iraq and the other poor nations of the Middle East have no choice but to accept Western aid, at least for the time being. Saudi Arabia and the oil states might help to pay the costs of reconstruction and development, but the wealthiest—Saudi Arabia and Kuwait—already have mammoth expenses of their own. Simply restoring Kuwait's water, electricity, and sanitation and getting oil production started again, will cost some $2 billion. Kuwaiti planners estimated that the price of restoring their nation's infrastructure completely would total as much as $45 billion, and that was before retreating Iraqi soldiers destroyed as much of the nation's infrastructure as they could; when the final bill is tallied, it could near $100 billion. The remaining oil states—Oman, Quatar, Bahrain, and the United Arab Emirates—have seldom been generous to their poorer brethren, who are more than ten times as numerous. The six-nation Gulf Cooperation Council has offered to set up a regional development fund with a total of $15 billion to lend impoverished Arab states. There is little reason to hope that they will ever add to that fund. If Egypt, Iraq, Syria, and Jordan hope to improve the lives of their people, they will do it largely with

Western money. Any future Palestinian state will find itself equally dependent on Western good will.

For the moment, the Gulf War has left the region more volatile, not at all the peaceful community that Coalition leaders liked to picture while justifying their war against Saddam Hussein. The near-destruction of Iraq has left a power vacuum that other states could be tempted to fill. Iran, Syria, and Turkey all claim title to parts of Iraq's territory; they could decide to occupy it while Baghdad's ability to defend itself is at a nadir. Western diplomacy, and the memory of Western power, will restrain that impulse.

Yet, in the long run, the new Middle East should be a more stable place, less buffeted by mutual antagonisms and would-be empire-builders. Secretary of State James Baker and his colleagues have pinned their hopes for continued peace on the establishment of a Gulf-states equivalent of NATO. Italian diplomats have suggested uniting the countries of the Mediterranean and the Middle East in a peacemaking organization modeled on the Conference on Security and Cooperation in Europe. And Egypt's semioffical newspaper, *Al Ahram,* has suggested that the Arab nations should set up a standing army of perhaps twelve armored divisions to quash any future war in the area as soon as it begins. The idea that the fratricidal nations of the Middle East could cooperate to enforce their own peace seems more wishful thinking than serious diplomacy. Yet Saddam Hussein's nearly successful attempt to dominate the region has left others more eager to defend against any repetition of the experience. Less than one month after the end of the Gulf War, Kuwait, Saudi Arabia, and other oil states offered to pay the costs of a regional defense force if Egypt and Syria would provide the manpower. Egypt has agreed. If the general hostility in the Middle East can be reduced, they may yet join hands for the common good. That is by far this troubled region's best hope for peace and prosperity.

C H A P T E R   1 4

....

Israel and Its Neighbors: A Bomb Defused

"By 2000, and probably several years earlier, the long, bloody war between Israel and its neighbors will be over."

....

In a Third World that seems made up almost exclusively of tinderboxes, the most unstable region is the Middle East, as Iraq has just reminded the world. And the nation most likely to face its violence is Israel, which claims to want peace but refuses all efforts to broker negotiations with its neighbors. In the next ten years, Israel will get its elusive peace, whether or not it wants to make the concessions required of it. Ironically, it will have Saddam Hussein to thank. The crisis in Kuwait has paved the way for a Palestinian settlement guaranteed by the world community.

For years—essentially since the Six-Day War in 1967—the Arab-Israeli conflict has been frozen in place. The Palestinians have demanded a homeland in Gaza and the West Bank; Israel has slowly deepened its control over those regions as it has established Jewish settlements in the disputed territory; the PLO and allied groups have maintained their smoldering war of terrorism, despite Yasir Arafat's statement recognizing Israel's right to exist and renouncing violence against nonmilitary targets; hard-liners throughout the Arab world call for a holy war against Israel and its allies in the West. And so it goes. The 1973 Yom Kippur War did nothing to change the situation. Massacres by Palestinian guerillas in 1974 and 1975 left Israel in control of the contested lands. The Camp David Accords signed by Israel and Egypt in 1979 died with Anwar Sadat two years later. Israel's attempt to drive the PLO from Lebanon in 1982 had no lasting effect. Even the years of the *intifada,* the Palestinian uprising in the territories occupied by Israel, have achieved little more than the deaths of one thousand Palestinians, mostly at the hands of their Palestinian brothers. Israel, it seems, is no closer to withdrawing from the regions they call Judea and Samaria; the Palestinians are no closer to self-rule in the land they consider their home.

In fact, the Arab efforts have hardened Israel's resolve never to return the West Bank and Gaza to Arab control. From the time Israel was founded, in 1949, until after the Yom Kippur War, the Labor party ran the nation almost without opposition. Its leaders have at least been willing to consider making peace with their neighbors. Since 1977, the hard-line Likud party has not lost a major election outright, in large part because it refuses every attempt at conciliation with the Palestinians. Israel has moved its official capital to Jerusalem. It has settled many of its new Russian immigrants on the West Bank, using American aid money to build homes for them in Arab East Jerusalem, despite Washington's loud objections. These are not the actions of a nation interested in reconciling its differences with the Palestinians.

Yet the recent Gulf War fundamentally changed the equations of power and trust throughout the Middle East. The new conditions permit, and almost surely will produce, a permanent settlement of the Palestinian problem in the forseeable future.

For its part, Israel showed remarkable and uncharacteristic restraint during the Gulf War. In 1981, faced with the threat that Iraq might someday be able to build atomic weapons, Israelis blasted a reactor near Baghdad out of existence. Ten years later, faced with the reality of an attack with Scud missiles, Israel did nothing. This strongly suggests that the Shamir government, for all its bluster, is capable of behaving reasonably when given good reason to do so. This is a development that would-be negotiators can only welcome.

There is another factor here as well, and it may be even more significant. Had Israel responded to Saddam Hussein's provocations, Egypt, Saudi Arabia, Syria, Kuwait, and the other Arab members of the U.N. coalition would have found themselves allied with their erstwhile enemy against an Arab brother, a position that would have undermined their support at home and their standing within the region. Because Israel did not act when it had every right to do so, the moderate Arab nations—and some, such as Syria, that have never been particularly moderate—are in its debt, and they know it. Whenever they can do so without losing their Arab credentials, they will pay off that obligation by supporting a peace settlement.

Other crucial relationships have also changed. Iran, once the most militant of the Middle Eastern states, managed to control the enthusiasm of its fundamentalist extremists for an anti-Western *jihad,* something that American diplomats were not sure President Hashemi Rafsanjani could do. By remaining aside from the battle, Iran has bought itself new credibility. Suddenly, it appears to be a nation that would-be deal-makers in the West can deal with. This offers the hope that the European Community, and perhaps even the United States, will provide the aid and trade that Iran desperately needs to rebuild its economy. Teheran will not risk that opportunity by supporting Palestinian extremists or otherwise interfering with a settlement in Israel. At the least, this is one increment of tension that has now relaxed.

Syria has achieved much the same transformation. In 1983, it supported the bombings that killed nearly three hundred American diplomats and servicemen in Beirut. In 1986, the European Community imposed limited economic sanctions against Syria, a response to its support for terrorism. Until shortly before the start of the Gulf War, Damascus was the PLO's home. Suddenly, because Syrian president Hafez al-Assad hated Saddam Hussein more than he disliked the West, Syria joined the coalition against Iraq. Immediately, the West conveniently forgot the past. Syria, too, has built the foundations of a new relationship with its former enemies. Even before the end of the Gulf War, Syrian diplomats quietly spoke of joining in a settlement with Israel. When the time comes, they will swallow hard and endorse a peace that provides secure borders for both the Palestinians and the Israelis.

Egypt was long an outcast among Arab states, thanks to acceptance of the camp David Accords, declaring peace with Israel. In recent years, as President Hosni Mubarak has toughened his attitude toward the Shamir government, it has regained some of its lost standing. The Gulf War has completed that process without requiring a return to the hard-line anti-Israel camp. After fighting side-by-side with Syria, Egypt can no longer be considered an outcast from the Arab community. Its views will now be heard and respected. That includes its willingness to deal with Israel.

Jordan and the Palestinians lost heavily in the Gulf War. Faced with rabid anti-American sentiment, King Hussein was forced, despite his American wife, into a Faustian alliance with Iraq. By aligning themselves with Saddam Hussein, they cut themselves off from vital support in Saudi Arabia and Kuwait. The Gulf states used to give Jordan some $550 million in aid each year. About 315,000 Jordanians lived and worked in the Gulf region, sending another $600 million per year in wages back to Amman. Saudi Arabia and the Gulf states bankrolled the PLO. All that changed when the Palestinians and Jordan threw their support to Iraq. According to one estimate, lost jobs, taxes, and subsidies will cost the Palestinians $1.5 billion per year. King Hussein must find some way to make up with his former supporters. Yasir Arafat has even more pressing problems. He retains control over the Palestine Liberation Organization, but his blunder has cost him much of his prestige. It will not be easy to find a replacement, but mistakes in the Arab world carry severe penalties. If Arafat wishes to retain his position, and perhaps even his life, he will have to find some way to regain the outside support he has lost. He will do it by making peace. Neither man is in a position to resist a settlement backed by their former allies.

That leaves only two key players in the region: the United States and—perhaps—the Soviet Union. Their roles have yet to be settled.

Exactly how the Soviet Union will influence progress in the Middle East is difficult to predict. Not long ago, when *glasnost* was in flower, Moscow had virtually abandoned the Middle East, to deal with its internal problems. Its actions during the Gulf War made it clear that the "cold warriors" of the Red Army and the KGB had temporarily regained their hold on the government. Soviet peace-making efforts then seemed less an attempt to end the war than a bid to assert the Soviet Union's identity as a "great power" and to offset the growing American influence in the region. They will continue this new activity in the Middle East and may be tempted to act as a "spoiler" if not allowed to help shape the new alignment of power in the region. However, it seems unlikely that they have the interest or the resources to prevent an eventual peace. The Soviet economy desperately needs all the aid the West can provide, and Moscow hopes that the West will continue to give only token support to Baltic separatists and to Boris Yeltsin's reform movement. There seems little chance that either the United States or the European Community will withdraw their support from Soviet reformers, but Moscow will not jeopardize either of its major goals, simply to flex Soviet muscles in the Middle East.

The role of the United States is easier to foresee. America was once anathema to the entire Arab world, with the exception of Egypt, Saudi Arabia, and Kuwait. That, too, has changed. It has now fought a war at the side of at least some Arabs who until 1990 were its sworn enemies. It has also backed two resolutions in the United Nations Security Council condemning Israel's actions against the Palestinians. Remaining in the region permanently could cost it the capital it has unexpectedly earned, but it will not make that mistake. By withdrawing its forces from the Middle East as quickly as it can, the United States will demonstrate that it truly has no colonial ambitions there. All these actions confirm that America is, after all, a nation that Arabs can deal with.

In addition, the United States is the only country in the world that can wield any leverage against Israel. In the past, Arab onlookers have believed that America's powerful Jewish bloc, combined with the efforts of Israeli-funded political action committees, made it impossible for Washington to coerce Israel to the bargaining table. That has never been entirely true, and it is less so now than in the past. Only 22 percent of America's 5.9 million Jews support Israeli annexation of the West Bank and Gaza, according to recent polls. And a survey of 780 leaders of American Jewish organizations found that three out of four supported both talks with the PLO and the return of at least some territory as part of a peace plan. According to a *New York Times/CBS* poll in 1990, nearly half of American Jews favor the establishment of a Palestinian homeland in the West Bank and Gaza. When the time comes for peace talks, Washington will have a free hand to promote them in any way it can.

That time will come sooner than many people expect, for one

more influence now growing in the Middle East could derail the peace process if talks are put off too long. The Muslim fundamentalism that sprang up in Shiite Iran in the late 1970s is now making itself felt throughout the much larger Sunni Muslim world. In Jordan, Algeria, and Egypt, and to lesser extents throughout the Middle East, Sunni fundamentalist movements are agitating for the establishment of Islamic states. As they continue to gain support among grass-roots Arabs, the regimes they hope to displace will find it increasingly difficult to make controversial decisions. Acceptance of Israel's right to exist within secure borders will be one of the more difficult challenges they face in the 1990s. Because it is also one of the most necessary, all the parties concerned will, in some cases reluctantly, seize the opportunity while it still exists.

Before 1992 is very old, and conceivably by the end of 1991, the United Nations will sponsor a conference on peace in the Middle East. It will deal with many issues, as we saw in the last chapter, but resolving the Palestinian conflict will be one of the most important. Israel will refuse to participate at first, claiming that the U.N. has no place meddling in the affairs of Samaria and Judea, which it considers to be its own land. The Shamir government will also refuse to sit at the same table with the PLO representative to the U.N. Persuasion—and, if need be, overwhelming pressure—by the United States will quickly overcome that reluctance.

One by one, the barriers to peace will come down. First among them will be Israel's refusal to accept the Palestine Liberation Organization as spokesmen for the Palestinians of the West Bank and Gaza. The PLO won its Palestinian following in the disputed territories, not so much because it has fought Israel at every turn, though that was important, but because it funded schools, hospitals, and other communal services. That funding came to a halt when Yasir Arafat led the organization into Saddam Hussein's camp. Even before the invasion, Kuwait had cut off its payments to the PLO and formed ties with Hamas, a militant Islamic group in the territories. Israel may be little more interested in talking with Hamas than it was with the PLO, but its history of conflict with the newer organization is much shorter, the mutual hatreds less entrenched. With encouragement from Saudi Arabia, Kuwait, and Syria, Hamas—or some proxy yet to be identified—will find Palestinian representatives that Israel can accept. With encouragement from the United States, Israel will allow the Palestinians of the occupied territories to elect those candidates to speak on their behalf; the U.N. will monitor the voting. And then, with whatever quiet encouragement the United States has to exert, Israel will sit down and talk with them.

Even then, of course, peace will not be easy to achieve. Israelis and Palestinians are separated by more than years of bitterness and simple bullheadedness. If Israel gives up Gaza, the West Bank, and the Golan Heights, it will need some other guarantee for its security. Arab extremists must be restrained from using the formerly occupied lands to stage terrorist attacks on the Jewish state. Everyone of significance in the area will have to accept formally, Israel's right to exist within whatever boundaries are set by the peace talks. The Palestinians need assurance that they too can live at peace within their new homeland. They will need economic help to rebuild what little is left of their economy. And the Arabs within Israel must find some voice in the government; at present, though they make up 16 percent of the Israeli population, they are unrepresented. And Muslims everywhere will need some resolution of Jerusalem's status. They will not accept the city's absorption into Israel. None of these issues will be resolved easily.

The agreement that emerges from this drawn-out process will look something like this: Israel will give up Gaza, much of the West Bank, and a token from the Golan Heights. This will satisfy the terms of U.N. Resolution 242, which requires only that Israel give up "occupied land," not necessarily all of the land it occupies. As a reward for siding with Saddam Hussein, Jordan will be required to contribute much of the East Bank to the Palestinians; it has already given up its claim to the West Bank. This territory will constitute the new Palestinian homeland. Israelis now living in the West Bank and Gaza will remain citizens of Israel and will receive a grace period—perhaps five years—in which to resettle within their own homeland's borders. Jerusalem will remain Israel's capital, but the crucial Temple Mount/Dome of the Rock area will come under international control, with a status much like that of the Vatican. A United Nations peacekeeping force will occupy the border between Israel and the new Palestine to guarantee the security of both until Palestinians and Jews agree that it is no longer needed. And the West will supply the funds required to develop a stable Palestinian economy. Once these or equivalent terms are signed, peace will at last be at hand.

We suspect that it will take two years to begin formal talks, two to three years longer to achieve a settlement. But by 2000, and probably several years earlier, the long, bloody war between Israel and its neighbors will be over.

CHAPTER 15

Terrorism into the 21st Century

"Terrorism is a relatively inexpensive political tool for poor nations to use against the rich."

Since the hostage-taking in Teheran more than a decade ago, Americans have tended to regard terrorism as largely a Middle Eastern phenomenon. That is far from correct. Most terrorist acts against U.S. citizens have occurred in Latin America and Europe. In 1985, for instance, eighty-six incidents of terrorism were directed against Americans in Latin America, sixty-one in Western Europe, and only sixteen in the Middle East. Terrorism against the inhabitants of these countries operates on a much grander scale. Shining Path guerillas have killed thousands of Peruvian officials and civilians, as well as Americans and others. Colombian drug lords have waged war on the central government to discourage it from extraditing them to the United States. Brazilian right-wingers "liquidate" the unwanted children of the *favelas*. Throughout much of Latin America, terror is nearly as common as poverty.

Yet in the West, it is the Middle Eastern terrorists who have won the greatest media attention, for their spectacular attacks at targets from airports to cruise ships. That makes them the most successful terrorists in the world, because terrorism is less a variety of war than an extreme form of public relations. Its purpose is not to destroy military targets, but to unnerve governments and their citizens, in the hope that they will eventually give in to the terrorists' demands. Carl G. Persson, a past president of Interpol, the International Criminal Police Organization, favors the definition of terrorism as "the deliberate and systemic murder, maiming, and menacing of the innocent to inspire fear for political ends."

Terrorism is frightening and effective, specifically because it is aimed at the innocent. In a nation suffering the terrorist plague, bombings, assassination, and kidnapping can strike anyone without warning. Yet this is not random violence. Strikes are usually carefully planned and orchestrated.

They can also be highly effective, particularly when they bring their cause wide publicity. The most extensively covered terrorist incident occurred after the massacre at the 1972 Munich Olympics; it had an estimated television audience of 500 million people. No one has ever quantified what immediate effect that incident had on the viewers, but one recent *threat* of terrorism clearly changed the plans of its target audience. Although the odds of being attacked by terrorists are extremely low, many would-be American tourists opted to stay at home during the Persian Gulf crisis. Even Las Vegas, about as far from the front as it is possible to get, suffered a decline of tourism during the war.

Many people have suggested that if the news media were to ignore terrorist acts, they might fade away. We suspect that terrorists would simply escalate their ferocity to a point at which they could no longer be ignored.

Yet terrorism can also be too effective. It is difficult to gain both attention and sympathy when purposely engaging in acts of violence. For this reason, these groups employ "selective terrorism"; that is, they usually strike at "combative" targets—military, police, or government officials—rather than at civilians. If terrorists kill too many civilians in too brutal a manner, public opinion screams for retaliation rather than sympathy. Many onlookers called the U.S. government a "hostage" of the Iranian crisis in 1979, and it certainly behaved as one. As a bid for publicity, taking the staff of the American embassy in Teheran could hardly have been more successful. But in the long run, it may have hurt the kidnappers' cause. Many Americans still hate Iran and everything connected with it. Iran desperately needs Western aid and trade assistance; even after their restrained role in the

Gulf crisis, there is little chance that they will get it.

Some of the most sophisticated terrorist incidents carried out by "private" organizations in recent years have been the work of the Irish Republican Army. Several of its most dramatic attacks came even while Britain prepared for the wave of terrorism that Saddam Hussein promised would follow the outbreak of the Gulf War. As Prime Minister John Major conferred with his War Cabinet, the IRA launched three mortar bombs from the back of a van. One of the bombs struck the garden of 10 Downing Street. Major, displaying both typical British nonchalance and his resigned awareness that the IRA will not cease its struggle, continued his meeting in another room. Eleven days later, IRA bombings at Victoria and Paddington Stations curtailed rail transportation. A bomb threat shut down Heathrow Airport for ninety minutes. Police noted that they were handling approximately six threats per day in central London. In a particularly ugly development, the IRA has also begun to use unwilling civilians to carry out its plots. In Northern Ireland, the IRA has coerced several men with threats to their families, to drive vans loaded with explosives to military check-points. There is little doubt that incidents of this type will be repeated often throughout the 1990s.

Madrid could be another hotbed of terrorist violence, particularly in 1992. Not only is the European Community dropping its trade barriers that year, the Olympics will be held in Barcelona, the World's Fair in Seville, and all of Spain will celebrate the 500th anniversary of Columbus's voyage to America. All this should boost *Hispanidad*. But the Basque Homeland and Liberty (ETA) separatist group has announced that it also has plans for the year. Spanish police have already unraveled a complicated plot involving a shoot-out in Seville, three hundred kilos of explosives, and nine accomplices, including a Benedictine monk. The ETA kills, on average, one person every twenty-one days.

The future of the badly splintered Palestine Liberation Organization (PLO) is not quite so clear. It may well be looking for a new leader. Yasir Arafat damaged both his own prestige and the PLO's reputation by allying himself with Saddam Hussein during the Persian Gulf crisis. When Israel forced the PLO to retreat from Beirut in 1982, Arafat was able to claim victory because he took his troops out carrying their weapons; this time he has no such opportunity. Both as a negotiator and as a threat, the PLO has lost its credibility. Arafat's Al-Fatah faction may return to terrorism in an effort to reclaim its Palestinian following.

Abu Nidal's Fatah Revolutionary Council broke with Al-Fatah in 1973 over Arafat's willingness to negotiate peace. Its operations have aimed to sabotage PLO policies. Abu Nidal worked closely with Syria and Libya, until he broke relations with both and allied himself with Iraq during the Gulf War. His followers have carried out at least sixty terrorist acts in over twenty countries. They (as well as the Iranian-backed Lebanese Hezbollah) are among the main suspects in the bombing of Pan Am Flight 103 over Lockerbie, Scotland in 1988. A November 1989 purge killed 150 guerillas in a power struggle. This organization will remain one of the world's most dangerous terrorist groups.

Muhammad Abbas (leader of the Palestine Liberation Front), was quoted in the *National Review* on September 1, 1989, as declaring, "We believe that the main losses are not in the number of those killed. The main objective is to keep the conflict alive, escalate it, destroy traditional enemy measures against us, and inflict losses on the enemy's political, material, economic, and military structure." Abul Abbas was responsible for the *Archille Lauro* hijacking and a frustrated attempt to launch a speedboat attack on a beach filled with Israeli vacationers. Other active PLO factions include Ahmad Jibril's Popular Front for the Liberation of Palestine-General Command (PFLP-GC) and Abu Musa's Fatah-Uprising, headquartered in Syria. There is little chance that any of them will lay down their weapons in the near future.

The Rand Corporation and Aberdeen University have estimated that one-quarter of all terrorist acts have been supported by governments. This is, at best, an imprecise way to promote national policies. *Aviation Week and Space Technology* recently quoted an Israeli official who noted that "One of the characteristics of these [terrorist groups] is that they are never under control, not even by the nations that provide all their support. They have their own goals, agendas and scores to settle."

There is one form of terrorism that seems to be on the decline, at least for the moment. In years past, the Soviet Union has lent ideological or policy support to many terrorist organizations, while its satellites and client states directly supported revolutionary insurgencies and sometimes lesser terrorist acts. Bulgaria sheltered the would-be assassin of Pope John Paul II. The East German Stasi aided the Red Brigade in undermining the Federal Republic. Cuba prided itself on its ability to export revolution. And the Sandinistas supported their leftist brethren in El Salvador's insurgency. This support may be a thing of the past. The Soviet Union no longer has the money to export revolution or conflict abroad, and it seems to have abandoned the adventurism on which that policy was based. Its dire need for Western financial aid places close restrictions on its ability to give aid and comfort to terrorist groups.

Other countries, most of them in the Middle East, have become much more involved in the operational details of terrorism than the Soviet Union ever was. Iran, Libya, Syria, and Iraq have all funded terrorist groups and have given them the space and freedom to train for their activities. Terrorism is, after all, a relatively inexpensive political tool for poor nations to use against the rich.

The regime in postrevolutionary Teheran consolidated its domestic following for years, by promoting religious fervor and a hatred of the West. (This last seems odd for a theocracy that claims to worship Allah, whose most important characteristics are benevolence and mercy.) Terrorism has been a favorite tool. Iranians have perpetrated some of the most unforgettable acts of terrorism, including the most effective—the seizure of the U.S. Embassy and personnel in Tehran, in November 1979. Iran has also been blamed for the suicide bombing of the barracks in Beirut that left 241 marines dead, though Syria may also have borne responsibility for that incident. The Ayatollah Khomeini's death threat against Salman Rushdie, author of the *Satanic Verses,* reflected both his sect's hard-line Shi'ism and its hatred of the West. Khomeini sought to inspire devout Moslems to kill Rushdie and is also thought to have alerted the worldwide terrorist network that Iran built. One of the main cogs of this system is the Guardians of the Islamic Revolution, which has hijacked aircraft, killed a German businessman who sold weapons to Iraq during the eight-year war, and claimed credit for the bombing of Pan Am Flight 103 (although many experts believe a PLO faction to be the guilty party).

More recently, Iran appears to have restrained its violent impulses. The reason is much the same as that behind the Soviet change of heart: Without Western patronage, Teheran has no chance of repairing what is left of its economy after years of retreating into the thirteenth century, followed by its war with Iraq. It will have to go one major step farther before it can hope for better relations with the United States and Europe, however. Until the hostages taken by pro-Iranian terrorist groups in Lebanon are released, it will remain an outcast nation. The pressure to meet that demand will grow as Iran watches Western aid helping to upgrade life in neighboring Arab states.

Libya, too, has lowered the volume of its strident pronouncements by decibels in recent years, and with much more immediate motivation. After Libya was implicated in the bombing of La Bella Berlin, the disco that was frequented by American servicemen, U.S. fighter jets bombed Tripoli and some of its chemical weapons facilities. The "hit squads" of terrorists meant to assassinate U.S. officials in response, never materialized. When strongman Muammar Qaddafi asked a terrorist leader to leave Libya, in late 1990, Colonel Qaddafi renounced terrorism. He remains anti-American, but has made his support of terrorists less obvious.

Syria manipulates Palestinian terrorist groups for its own gain in the Middle Eastern power struggle. This tool, combined with outright military force, has been so successful that Damascus now dominates Lebanon, which has practically become its satellite. Syrian President Hafez al-Assad has also supported splinter factions of the PLO, as a personal affront to Yasir Arafat and to thwart any move toward a peace settlement or the recognition of Israel. Now that Assad's formerly unbending hatred of the Jewish state seems to be easing slightly, Syria, too, may depend less on terrorism and more on diplomacy to advance its ends.

Yet the real surprise in the terrorist world has been Saddam Hussein's Iraq. If any nation was equipped to set off a wave of terror throughout the world, it was Iraq before the Gulf War. Many terrorists found safe harbor in Baghdad: Abu Nidal's Fatah Revolutionary Council; Abul Abbas's Palestine National Front; George Habash's Popular Front for the Liberation of Palestine (PFLP); Ahmed Jibril of the PFLP-General Command (also a suspect in the Pan Am bombing over Lockerbie, Scotland); Abu Ibrahim has "retired" to Iraq; and Abu Iyad moved to Iraq in

June 1990. In 1990, many analysts forecast that terrorist attacks would trigger the coming war, just as the Abu Nidal group's assassination of the Israeli ambassador to England prompted the Israeli invasion of Lebanon in 1982.

When the war finally came, Saddam declared his cause to be a jihad, thereby giving any Moslem license to strike at the United States and its allies. In the first three weeks of the war, some eighty terrorist attacks struck Coalition targets—four times the "normal" rate, according to the *Economist*. Bombs struck diplomatic centers owned by the United States, Britain, France, Italy, and Saudi Arabia. There were more attacks in the Middle Eastern theater: sixteen in Lebanon, eleven in Turkey, six in Greece, and four in Yemen. Yet in the United States itself, nothing happened. The closest America came to terrorism was a time bomb planted in a giant alcohol-storage facility near the Norfolk Naval Base. It was first presumed to have been placed by Iraqi agents; then the local police department arrested the tank farm's owner for attempted insurance fraud. As worldwide waves of terror go, it was something of a bust.

Only three incidents could be directly attributed to Baghdad—even though radio messages on February 5 and 6 ominously announced: "From the headquarters to Urwah: this is your day. From Mahyub to Ayman: we are waiting to hear your voice. Mahyub to Mudar Salim: do not hesitate." No doubt these were instructions to the far-flung Iraqi terror network, which includes its diplomats. Iraqis bungled their job in Manila—both by accidentally blowing up one of their own men and by revealing that Iraq's embassies were integral to the terrorist effort. Most of the allied countries immediately sent all but a minimum of Iraqi diplomats packing.

So long as Saddam Hussein rules Baghdad, there is a chance that terrorists will strike Western targets in his name; if he should die violently, a burst of terrorist reprisals against Israel is almost inevitable, whether that country had anything to do with it or not. But these excuses, too, will fade away as the United States and Europe make it clear that they wish to help the Middle East, not to dominate it. As a weapon of state, terrorism is going out of fashion.

Unfortunately, that does not mean that terrorism will pass from the world scene as the twentieth century does. It will continue as long as frustrated political movements see no other effective way to advance their policies. Terrorist attacks will prove even more effective as psychological weapons, as mass communications continue to increase the size of the target audiences.

Technology will also give terrorists a variety of new targets with which to make their political points. One reason is that technology encourages concentration: Manufacturing depends on fewer people in the more developed countries, where a larger percentage of the labor force works in service industries. The concentration of industry provides select targets, offering terrorists the opportunity to do maximum damage with minimum effort. In 1988, a suburban Chicago telephone switching office suffered an accidental fire that blocked telephone service for weeks in the areas it served; a well-planned attack could leave an area without vital services for long periods.

Computer facilities have already become popular targets. The Red Brigades of Italy, a troupe of "neo-Luddites," often blow up computers, which they regard as symbols of America's imperialist and technological hegemony. France's Action Direct has targeted them as well. And in Germany, twenty-four computer centers were bombed in a single year.

A less obvious danger, but an even greater one in the 1990s, will be the risk of potential for more insidious attacks on the data stored in computers. In one recent incident, computerized spies in Germany worked their way through the international telecommunications networks, through a university bookkeeping computer in California, and into a number of American defense systems. In this case, the information stolen was relatively insignificant. But many corporate computer systems are no better protected than the military computers were. Changing or erasing the data in a crucial computer system could shut down a city transportation network, cut off electricity to millions of people, or disrupt a nation's financial system. Computer "viruses"—programs hidden within other software that erase part or all of the system's information—are discovered almost every month. In one recent incident, a virus slowed or halted computer operations at more than one hundred American laboratories and universities. Defending against these attacks will be costly. It will be expensive to develop and install adequate security systems, and adopting more restrictive access controls will reduce the efficiency of the facilities using them. But this is one hazard that, though unlikely to strike any particular computer system, can be so destructive that there is little choice but to prepare for it. Many private corporations, as well as government agencies, will feel themselves forced to accept this extra expense in the 1990s.

Nuclear power plants are stressed to withstand the impact of a crashing airplane. But few are able to withstand a determined terrorist who understands how the system works. Antinuclear activists in Spain and France have already managed to shut down reactors temporarily. More ruthless enemies might have done enough damage to release radiation over a wide area.

The United States is particularly vulnerable to this kind of high-tech attack on critical facilities where critical assets are concentrated. Virtually all the telephone communications in all the large cities of the United States flow through just ten regional switching stations. All the north-south rail traffic east of the Mississippi River passes over two bridges, one over the Ohio River, the other over the Potomac. And two pipelines in Louisiana supply nearly all of the natural gas used in the northeastern U.S. Any of these bottleneck installations could be put out of action with a minimum of effort. The pipelines use imported pumps that would take months to replace. The bridges could be out of service for a year or more.

Finally, technology has brought new weapons to defend against:

Intelligence estimates say that perhaps a dozen of the shoulder-fired Stinger antiaircraft missiles donated to Afghan rebels found their way into Iran, where they have almost surely been passed on to terrorist organizations. They are extraordinarily effective. Afghan *mujahedin* fired 340 of them at Soviet aircraft; 269 of the targets went down. A civilian airliner could well be next.

A new variation on computer terrorism is the electromagnetic pulse generator. Hooked into the power line feeding a major computer center, the power surge it creates could erase all the data in the system's memory. Such devices are not difficult to build.

As far as we know, no one has yet implanted explosives into the body of a suicidally fanatical terrorist, but many volunteers for such a mission can be found in the Moslem countries. It could be done easily, and no security technique now in use could screen him out of the passengers boarding an airliner.

Somehow, terrorists have largely overlooked biological and chemical weapons, despite their practical advantages for small and ruthless organizations. Biological and chemical weapons are the ultimate weapons of psychological warfare. A bomb blows up only once; toxins can thrive for minutes, or years. While not very dangerous, they inspire great fear. Some are not very difficult to manufacture, as the German Red Army Faction, French Action Direct, Libya, and Iraq have discovered. Yet William E. Gutman reports in *Omni* magazine that the CIA recorded only twenty-two incidents between 1968 and 1980 in which terrorists used "exotic pollutants" such as chemical, biological, and radiological materials. Injections of mercury into Israeli and Spanish fruit in 1978 accounted for the bulk of these occurrences. Other terrorists—or perhaps just domestic "crazies"—have filled Contac, Teldrin, and Dietac capsules with rat poison. In Britain, someone purposely contaminated milk with gasoline. Cyanide, injected into a few Chilean grapes, so frightened Western consumers that some nations banned the entire crop. The potential for this kind of terrorism remains great. We will look at chemical and biological warfare more closely in Chapter 26, and will discover just how easily they could be turned to the terrorists' purposes.

Fortunately, the overwhelming dread inspired by chemical and biological weapons may be the greatest argument against their use. Even the Iraqis did not deploy them during the Persian Gulf War. Weapons of mass destruction seldom translate easily into political gain. Terrorists want to shock their target audiences into giving them recognition and sympathy. It does them little good to have the general populace turn in horror against their cause. Thus the deadliest of terrorist acts may remain simply a nightmare, and not become reality.

The key to living with the threat of terrorism is to make sure it never becomes more than a threat. It can be done. The U.S. Federal Bureau of Investigation reduced the number of terrorist incidents in America by more than ten times, between the 1970s and the 1980s. Threats must be taken seriously; the public must understand the dangers of terrorism. The deaths over Lockerbie might never have occurred if the authorities had acted on warnings that terrorists soon intended to destroy an airliner on that route.

The first priority is to gather intelligence about would-be terrorists and to analyze it accurately. Agencies involved in counterterrorism must coordinate their activities, not only on a domestic level, such as between the CIA and the FBI, but also on an international scale. Interpol will take the lead in coordinating the efforts of national police forces, as it does in many other fields of crime. One of its units maintains a database on terrorists and their activities. Ultimately, it will be able to track their movements.

The European Community has formed the Trevi Group of interior/justice ministers that handles problems of terrorism. The twelve countries share information and jointly bar suspects from entering Europe. The U.S. formed a joint affiliation with the Trevi Group in 1986.

In order to curry favor in negotiations with the United States about Israeli-Palestinian issues, the PLO has provided information on possible planned terrorist actions in Europe. The reports did not prove helpful on that occasion; they included nothing that American counterterrorism experts did not already know. But there is at least the possibility that the organization will someday provide more timely warning of a planned attack. Another goal of law enforcement officials is to understand the inner workings of terrorist organizations, and in this the PLO can clearly be of help. Its current willingness to cooperate should be exploited at every opportunity.

Coordinated counterterrorism efforts like these will bring terrorists to justice. Simultaneously, governments will forgo short-term deals with terrorists in favor of a long-term strategy of not dealing, or negotiating, with terrorists.

To date, few terrorists have ever ended up in jail. The United States has been particularly determined to correct that. A 1984 law made overseas hijacking a U.S. crime if American citizens became victims. The 1986 Diplomatic Security and Allied Terrorism Act made it a federal crime to assault or kill Americans overseas as an act of terrorism. Another 1986 act gave U.S. intelligence agents the right to seize suspects in foreign countries. Yet, by 1989, only one terrorist, Fawaz Younis, had been brought to trial, for hijacking a Royal Jordanian jet in 1985.

In the 1990s, more effective measures will be developed. Instead of trying to extend national law to cover international crimes, the problem of terrorism will be regarded as an international problem. The U.N. General Assembly passed an antiterrorism resolution in 1972, which it reemphasized in 1985. The International Court of Justice (ICJ) may also join in the effort. Thus far, it tries only cases championed by opposing states. That could change in the 1990s. Unlike the states, terrorists would not necessarily be represented by their client state(s) and would not have to consent to the ICJ's jurisdiction. This could be one of the most effective weapons against terrorism in the early twenty-first century.

THE HAVE-NOTS:

Africa

Rich in Resources, Poor in Prospects

"Slow economic growth, coupled with rapid population growth, will push sub-Saharan Africa's portion of the world's poor from 16 percent in 1985 to over 30 percent by 2000."

This giant, troublesome continent has had a difficult past, and there is regrettably little that is good to be said about its future. Slight economic improvement combined with a rapidly growing population spells ruin for Africa. At the continent's current rate of growth, the population will double in twenty-two years. Living standards already have fallen to 1960 levels. Desertification, drought, and famine remain constant threats. The next ten years will be bleak ones for the dark continent.

To say the least, Africa has been badly served by its colonial history. The borders drawn by European powers, like those in the Middle East, did not create true nation-states, where people linked by similar ethnic or cultural backgrounds can manage their affairs as a relatively homogeneous group. Instead, they forced native peoples together without regard for tribal identities and animosities. This has permanently scarred African politics.

South of the Sahara, nations fall conveniently into two groups: those once colonized by Great Britain, and those formerly governed by other European nations. Where Britain ruled, mainly in eastern Africa along the route to India, it trained a native infrastructure capable of governing an independent country. Other imperial powers, in contrast, insisted on running the infrastructure of the countries themselves. Portugal, for example, was a relatively poor and populous land; it could afford to send its citizens abroad to run Angola. When the Portuguese left West Africa, they took with them the know-how required to run the country. Loath to leave, the Portuguese also did as much as they could to ruin the countries they had exploited; the last settlers poured cement down elevator shafts, damaged industrial structures, and wreaked general havoc. As a result of this difference, most of Britain's former colonies are now relatively prosperous and stable, at least by African standards; other ex-colonies are not.

Sub-Saharan Africa accounts for a much greater share of global poverty than of population. The entire continent's gross domestic product in 1988 was only $135 billion, nearly $20 billion less than the GNP of Belgium, a country with fewer than ten million people. Of the 180 million poor in this region, the World Bank classifies 120 million as being extremely poor. The proportion is about the same in North Africa and the Middle East.

And unlike some regions, Africa is growing more impoverished, not less so. Recession in the 1980s cut real wages by 20 percent throughout sub-Saharan Africa and by nearly 60 percent in some cities. The real incomes of self-employed peasants have declined by nearly one-third. Living standards fell by an estimated 15 percent in just the seven years ending in 1985. The economic downturn also reduced adjusted per capita spending on education and health, with predictable results. In sub-Saharan Africa, mortality under the age of five measures 196 per thousand, life expectancy only fifty years, and only 56 percent of children are enrolled in primary school. Northern Africa and the Middle East fare somewhat better: Under-five mortality registers 148 per thousand; life expectancy, sixty-one years; net primary school enrollment, 75 percent.

Africa's basic problem is not its lack of resources, its inept governments, or its lack of infrastructure. It simply has too many mouths to feed, a problem that worsens daily. The United Nations estimates that if the rate of population growth in Africa had been limited even to that of Latin America during the 1980s, all else being equal, Africa could have avoided its deepening poverty. But the population is now growing at more than 3 percent per year, the fastest in the continent's recorded history and at least 1 percent faster than on any other continent. By the end of the 1980s, the African economy had actually grown for several years. Yet because the population grew even faster, per capita income continued to decline.

This pattern will hold true throughout the 1990s. Sub-Saharan Africa's gross domestic product will grow by more than 3 percent annually, but population growth will continue to outpace it. Thus, even more people will suffer from poverty. If current trends continue, sub-Saharan Africa's population of 450 million will rise to 615 million in this decade, while per capita incomes will decline by another 20 percent. Even today, per capita income on this continent barely reaches the subsistence level. By 2000, an additional seventy million people will live in poverty.

Birth control seems an obvious solution, but traditional African societies frown upon many such measures. Fewer than 5 percent of African women use modern birth control methods, and men often regard condoms as an affront. The American antiabortion lobby has blocked U.S.-funded attempts to promote several other methods of family planning. And throughout most of Africa, having many sons is a matter of both pride and necessity. Many poor rural families depend on having many children to help out on the land. Where the state does not (or cannot) provide retirement benefits, children are expected to look after their parents; they are needed as a cultural, rather than political, form of old-age insurance. Given the high child mortality rate, many women are inclined to have many children to be sure that some will survive into adulthood. In the United States, the average woman has a total of fourteen children, grandchildren, and great-grandchildren. In Africa, the number is 258.

Three-fourths of the people in southern Africa are small-scale farmers and herders. They account for most of the poor in Botswana, the Ivory Coast, Ghana, Kenya, Nigeria, and Tanzania. Farm work tends to be highly seasonal or part-time, and incomes peak with the harvest and fall into the "hungry season," when illness and starvation are most common. In most countries, the few large farmers have been able to manipulate product pricing and government support programs in their favor, to the detriment of the poor; this has been most flagrant in Nigeria, Senegal, and Tanzania. Few of the small farmers have been able to develop or adopt improved technologies. Favorable weather conditions over most of the continent, in the late 1980s, yielded bountiful harvests, but population pressures nearly matched the increase. And this brief improvement was an exception to the long-term trend.

Africa grew more food than it could eat in the 1960s. Changing climatic conditions, growing population, civil wars, and other problems have hurt the continent's ability to feed itself. Desertification has ruined farmland; the Sahara spreads at rates of up to ninety miles a year. Only 3 percent of the farms in Africa are irrigated; most farmers depend on rain to water their crops. In the Sahelian countries, just south of the Sahara, there is half as much rainfall today as there was in the 1950s. In a normal year, without drought or other emergencies, Africa grows some ten million tons less food than it needs. By 2000, the United Nations estimates that Africa will need forty to fifty million tons more food than it currently grows each year.

And that is in an average year. Drought makes the situation far worse. In the mid-1980s, drought-related famine in Sudan killed hundreds of thousands of people. In 1990, inadequate rainfall again virtually destroyed crops in the region. At year's end, observers feared that hunger would be even more widespread this time than in the last famine. It was expected to affect one-third of the nation's twenty-six million people.

It already takes $1 billion worth of food aid each year just to keep the majority of Africans alive, and even that is far from enough. Malnutrition rose in the region throughout the 1980s. Conditions improved briefly in Benin, Burkina Faso (the former Upper Volta), Ghana, and Togo, but have again entered a decline. Ethiopia, Lesotho, Madagascar, Niger, and Rwanda have suffered more persistent hunger. Angola, Chad, Ethiopia, Malawi, Mali, Mozambique, Niger, and the Sudan are perennially near famine.

Starvation is not always caused by a scarcity of food, however; sometimes food is available, but only at prices the poor cannot afford to pay. Some countries have realized that widespread distribution of government food stocks or imports can stabilize prices and alleviate the diminished purchasing power of the poor.

In 1984, the Kenyan government organized commercial food imports that arrived just as domestic food stocks ran out—three months before foreign food aid arrived. The government of Cape Verde sold food on the open market to finance public employment programs.

Too often, political conflicts exacerbate poverty. The end of the cold war should have brought peace to the continent. It did not. Governments still squander their money on weaponry to keep themselves in power, when they should be spending it on food, education, and health care. Many of these countries suffer from civil wars, and both governments and rebels often block the delivery of food to the starving:

• Angola's Marxist government will not allow the U.N. to send food to the UNITA rebels through its "peace corridors."

• In Ethiopia, the province of Tigre continues to revolt against the government, while the Eritrean People's Liberation Front (EPLF) recently triumphed in a second, unrelated rebellion. For the moment, all are permitting food to pass through their territories to the other groups, but they all have long histories of blocking aid shipments in order to starve their opponents.

• Samuel Doe's bloody fall has weakened Liberia and plunged the country even more deeply into civil war, fought among three main factions. According to the U.N.'s World Food Program, less than half of the required six thousand tons of rice needed each month arrived in Monrovia in January 1991.

• The soldiers who overthrew Sudan's democracy in 1990 asked that Western relief organizations *not* send the 1.2 million tons of grain needed to relieve an impending famine. (The ministry of finance sent written requests to embassies asking them to send food, however.) The government of Omar el Bashir claims that the nation's grain shortfall is not so severe as others believe. Meanwhile, a civil war continues with the non-Muslim south. The government's slogan has been "We eat what we grow, we wear what we make." It is, they appear to feel, much better to starve than relent.

These nations are far from unique in a continent where tribal hatreds often dominate national life, and the niceties that usually receive at least lip service in European wars are seldom observed.

In this context, aid is both desperately needed and difficult to use. Other countries either lent or donated more than $100 billion in the 1980s, with little to show for it. In 1988, the United States sent about $750 million to Africa, 11 percent of U.S. foreign aid; that was about one-third less than in the early 1980s. Other nations have donated more, however. Sub-Saharan Africa, which is home to less than one-eighth of the Third World's population, now receives more than one-third of worldwide aid, up from less than one-fifth in 1975.

Unfortunately, economic aid is much like food: Little of what is sent to Africa reaches the people who need it. As debt accumulates, the debtor state has less incentive and opportunity to invest in its resources rather then to consume them for short-term profit. With less investment, the economy stagnates, further reducing the chance that the debt will be repaid. Sub-Saharan Africa (not including Nigeria) paid $2.9 billion in interest on its debts in 1988. That money, equal to more than one-fourth of all aid and development assistance received that year, consumed funds that had been meant to increase investment and consumption and to decrease poverty. Nineteen-ninety marked the fifth consecutive year in which sub-Saharan Africa repaid more to the International Monetary Fund than it received in new loans.

According to the World Bank, twenty-four of the world's twenty-six severely indebted, low-income countries are found in sub-Saharan Africa. The total debt of all the low-income countries amounted to $103 billion in 1988—relatively low compared to the combined debt of $156 billion in the middle-income countries. But the debt burden is harder for the sub-Saharan countries to support. Compared with their GNPs, they owed slightly over twice as much as the middle-income debtors.

Sixteen of the sub-Saharan countries have rescheduled their debt under the protocol of the 1988 Toronto Summit's Special Program for Africa. This program included plans for partial write-offs, longer repayment periods, and lower interest rates. Without such measures, these countries simply cannot pay back the money that they owe. Even with debt reduction, sub-Saharan Africa's per capita incomes will rise only after the mid-1990s, and then will grow by only one percent a year, until 2000.

Some of the world's poor nations can hope for partial debt relief under the plan suggested in 1989 by U.S. Treasury Secretary James Brady. Directed at nineteen middle-income countries that hold primarily commercial debts, the Brady initiative asks banks to forgive part of their debts in return for international guarantees that the rest will be repaid. The goal is to strengthen the nations' adjustment programs and mobilize private investment. But of all the African countries, only Morocco qualifies for relief. The African countries owe more than 65 percent of their foreign debt to official, noncommercial institutions. Commercial lenders prefer to deal with middle-income, resource-rich countries, such as most of the countries in Latin America. They have left it to the International Monetary Fund (IMF) to lend to the lower-income countries of Africa.

Five of the IMF's worst debtors are African countries. Somalia and Sudan each have overdue bills worth nearly three times their total annual exports. In the 1980s, some of the IMF's leading members wrote off $1.6 billion of loans to Africa and agreed to many reschedulings. A decade later, the IMF has concluded that writing the loans off would do more harm than good. Instead, the Fund has devised a "rights-accumulation program" (RAP) in which a debtor who makes IMF-approved economic reforms earns "rights" to borrow, although the country cannot yet obtain fresh money. When the debtor country has earned enough "rights" to equal the value of the remaining debt, other governments will join to provide a bridging loan to pay off the money owed. The IMF heavily influences governments and commercial creditors in their deliberations over whether or not to lend to a specific country. Nigeria, for one, negotiates the right to borrow from the IMF even though it has no intention of doing so; Nigeria needs the Fund's endorsement to enable it to borrow from other sources. Guyana has followed the RAP procedure, and Zambia hopes to take the RAP as well.

Some other countries have become "hooked" on aid. Sudan and Zaire received $9.6 billion and $5.8 billion, respectively, between 1970 and 1988. Other large recipients include Mozambique, Niger, and Togo. None of these countries has acted effectively to reduce the poverty of its citizens.

In these and many other African nations, borrowing has been used to mask great imbalances in local economies that sustained overvalued exchange rates and discouraged export trade. These debts have done little to help build a modern infrastructure, reduce dependence on exports of primary commodities, or improve managerial capacity. Together, these weaknesses have severely impaired Africa's ability to license foreign technology. The few multinational corporations interested in Africa have preferred to invest directly in such labor-intensive industries. Thus, little technology has been transferred, and many African countries are forced to depend on foreign corporations to provide jobs—a sort of forced "Irelandization."

Outside companies have little cause to spend their money in Africa, however. It costs half again as much to build and operate a factory in Africa as it would elsewhere. Companies have to provide their own electricity and use radios to communicate with the outside world; telephones are unknown outside major cities, and seldom work even when available. Return on investment in the continent during the 1980s averaged a miserable 2.5 percent per year. In southern Asia, the return is 22.4 percent annually. Understandably, private outside investment in Africa has plummeted, from a total of $2.3 billion in 1982 to less than $500 million. French companies alone have cut their investment from $1 billion per year in the early 1980s to less than $50 million in 1990. This, too, has hurt the sub-Saharan region. Its share of the world's export trade has declined by half in the last thirty years, largely because of competition from more productive Third World lands.

This has made it difficult to diversify Africa's ability productive base and to add value to its primary commodities, which are subject to price fluctuations on the world market. Sub-Saharan Africa's exports of primary commodities fell in the mid-1980s and stagnated throughout the remainder of the decade. The drop in prices for commodities cost the continent 15 percent of its importing power. Meanwhile, the volume of Africa's exports fell by 8 percent, and the value of imports rose by 10 percent, to $76 billion.

A few of Africa's countries have a chance to do better than their neighbors. Ghana is one. In the 1980s, the government in Accra tried hard to reform the nation's economy, with considerable success. As a result, Ghana has prospered. Its economy grew by more than 5 percent in 1989. Between 1974 and 1983 GDP fell 20 percent and export volume plunged by 40 percent. By 1989, though, output climbed an annual average of 6 percent and exports by 12 percent. Inflation fell from 70 percent to 30 percent in the same period.

Tiny Mauritius may be the model that other African countries wish to follow. Wages and profits continue to rise, unemployment has nearly been eliminated, and the European Community has granted it privileged status for trade in its sugar, textiles, and clothing. Interracial conflict remains low even though half the island is of Hindu descent.

There is also some hope for Africa's oil-producing nations, which were hard hit when the price of crude fell in the late 1980s. During the 1990s, the rising demand for petroleum and the declining share of non-OPEC production will again raise the price of oil if only temporarily. The World Bank plans to use some of its $8 billion reserve fund to buy oil for Africa's poorest non-producing countries, as the price rises. This will do nothing to improve the infrastructure and earning capacity of the recipients, however.

Rising oil production and high prices will clearly benefit Nigeria, and there is at least some evidence that the income will be used more wisely than in the past. Traditionally, when Lagos has received income, it has quickly squandered it on ill-conceived development programs and other forms of waste. But when oil prices spiked during the Gulf War, Nigeria established a stabilization fund with which to begin paying off its $32 billion in debt. The quick collapse of the oil market gave the country little to work with, but there is room to hope that they will be equally sensible when prices begin to rise again.

On the other hand, Nigeria's current political situation is so bizarre that it is difficult to be sure what will happen there. Soldiers have ruled the country for twenty-one of its thirty years of independence. Two attempts at democracy have only inflamed racial hatred and collapsed. President Ibrahim Babangida has promised another try in 1992. It will be an odd form of democracy. Babangida himself has created the only two parties that will be allowed to compete in the coming election—the Social Democrats and the National Republican Convention; no tribes need apply. Babangida has organized everything for the two groups, ranging from their constitutions to their official colors. All past and present politicians will be banned from running. The two parties are intended to compete on the basis of policy, and nothing else. Babangida seeks to avoid divisive debate over tribal loyalties, economics, or religion. Tribalism is particularly volatile in Nigeria, where over five thousand people died in the 1980 Muslim-Christian riots. It will be interesting to see where this effort leads.

Democracy is further along in Mozambique, where President Joaquim Chissano's ruling Frelimo party relaxed its monopoly on power, at the end of November 1990. A day after the new constitution went into effect, the Renamo rebel movement consented to a cease-fire on two railway lines. As of early 1991, the first free election was slated for the dry season, later in the year. If the voting goes smoothly, the success will encourage donors from whom Mozambique receives $900 million in foreign aid each year. Market-oriented reforms after Mozambique's conversion from communism will encourage investment and help keep the economy growing at 4 to 5 percent per year.

Zimbabwe also benefits from the easing of tensions in neighboring Mozambique. The civil war—especially the incursions of Renamo forces into Zimbabwe—cost the government in Harare $500,000 per day. Like Mozambique's Chissano, President Robert Mugabe has learned the value of both national reconciliation and market reforms. December 1987's Unity Agreement between his own Zimbabwe African National Union (ZANU) and Joshua Nkomo's People's Union has smoothed over tensions between the parties and lessened tribal rivalries. Mugabe refused ZANU's requests to expropriate the property of five thousand white farmers. In 1989, though, Mugabe promised to purchase half of the remaining white farmland. The Commercial Farmers Union opposes such a move, because it would take the land away from its supporters and might impair Zimbabwe's ability to feed itself. According to some estimates, forcing the whites to sell fifteen million acres could cut national farm production by three-quarters, and exports by a third. Mugabe disagrees, citing a World Bank report that shows that Zimbabwe could exist on a commercial farming industry half of its current size. The government ultimately will back private ownership rather than collectivization. Previous attempts at collective farming after independence in 1980, proved cooperatives to be a costly folly. The most successful farmers—not the poorest—will be allowed to pay for title deeds over a period of twenty years.

It is clear, however, that these potential success stories are the exception in Africa, not the rule. Slow economic growth, coupled with rapid population growth, will push sub-Saharan Africa's portion of the world's poor from 16 percent in 1985 to over 30 percent by 2000. Child mortality under age five will remain the world's highest, at 135 deaths per thousand; and universal enrollment in primary school will cost more than the impoverished governments can hope to afford. According to the World Bank, just to hold the number of poor steady, would take Herculean efforts: a GDP growth of 5.5 percent per year; the restructuring of industry; more technology and incentives for agriculture; higher spending on primary education, health care, nutrition, and most important, family planning. To accomplish all this, African governments must spend more on social needs, and donors must step up their aid.

Neither will be easy. A 10 percent reduction of NATO expenditures could be used to double American aid to all poverty-stricken countries, but the United States has many commitments outside Africa and is finding it increasingly difficult to meet them. Relying on a trickle-down effect from the economic success of the industrialized world, to raise per capita incomes in Africa, will not work. The 3 percent growth in GDP expected from the developed world will raise per capita incomes in sub-Saharan Africa by only one-half percent—most of which will be derived from the benefits of aid.

Neither can the African nations hope to spend much more on their own development. Short-term increases in the prices of oil and minerals will raise the region's export earnings to $67 billion. Yet North Africa will see its per capita GDP grow by only 2.1 percent a year during the 1990s—much less than the rate of population growth.

Nor is there any possibility that Africa will be able to build its own economic bloc, like those now growing in the developed nations, and thereby raise its standard of living through internal trade. Intra-African trade composed less than 5 percent of the total trade in the 1980s. It will not increase significantly. Economic unity in Africa will remain extremely unlikely through 2000; the countries are simply too poor.

It would help if Africa could build some mechanism for settling its many political disputes peaceably. The six-nation Economic Community of West African States, led primarily by Nigeria, could set an example for the entire continent.

Yet, not even a miraculous level of political stability could save Africa. With the continuing population explosion, the number of poor will grow. This will mitigate any economic gains.

For the rest of the world, throughout the foreseeable future, Africa will remain a source of oil; scarce, nonrenewable resources; and worry. To its own inhabitants, Africa offers little more than survival, and in many cases not even that. It will benefit little, and late, from the burst of prosperity that seem ready to overtake the developed world.

••

CHAPTER 17

Africa's 20th-Century Plague

"In Joseph Conrad's Heart of Darkness, *the future has be-come much darker than any writer could have imagined."*

••

The most significant factor in sub-Saharan Africa is not one of politics or resources, but one of medicine and science: the human immunodeficiency virus (HIV) and its result, the acquired im-mune deficiency syndrome, or AIDS. For many millions of Afri-cans, and perhaps as many other people around the world, the future is meaningless, because they will not be alive to see it.

For a time, HIV appeared to spread fastest in the developed countries, where testing was available even for people without symptoms. According to Dr. Michael Merson, director of the World Health Organization's Global Program on AIDS, about half the world's known HIV infections in 1985 occurred in the industrialized nations, and most of them appeared in the United States. On that basis, the World Health Organization (WHO) originally believed that fifteen million to twenty million cases would appear by the turn of the century.

But even as the virus has begun to slow its spread in the devel-oped countries, the epidemic is still growing geometrically in poorer lands. By 1990, two-thirds of the eight million or so known infections were in the less developed countries. Ten years later, about three-fourths of the cases expected throughout the world will occur in those areas. WHO now expects that twenty-five million to thirty million people will contract HIV by the end of this decade. That may well be a conservative estimate.

HIV has been at its most destructive in Africa, where medical researchers believe it first evolved and entered the human population. South of the Sahara, AIDS cases doubled from an estimated 2.5 million in 1987 to five million in 1990. About one adult in forty was infected, throughout the region.

In some cities the rate is much higher. In Nairobi, 5 percent of adults were infected by mid-1990. In Lusaka, Zambia, and Kampala, Uganda, more than one adult in five carried HIV. In the Ivory Coast city of Abidjan, AIDS is the leading cause of death, according to a report by researchers from the American Centers for Disease Control and the University of Abidjan. In 1988 and 1989, the team examined roughly 40 percent of the adult cadavers in the city's two largest morgues. More than 40 percent of the male cadavers and nearly one-third of the female cadavers were infected by HIV. The researchers estimated that one-sixth of the deaths among men and one-eighth of those among women had been caused by AIDS. In the West, only homosexual men and the most concentrated populations of intravenous drug users face similar devastation.

Nor is AIDS still confined to African cities and to a few high-risk groups—prostitutes and their most active customers: soldiers, long-distance truck drivers, and migrant workers—as it was for the first few years of the epidemic. In the 1990s, AIDS has begun to spread among the rural villages, where between 50 and 80 percent of the African population lives. In southwestern Uganda and nearby Tanzania, one villager in eight is infected by HIV; in market towns, the figure is one in three.

Though people in the West tend to think of AIDS as a disease of men, in sub-Saharan Africa it is now the leading cause of death among women between the ages of twenty and forty. In some central African cities, up to 40 percent of women in the 30 to 34 age group are infected. Among pregnant women of all ages, the rate is between 10 and 20 percent in some areas. Health officials in Balantyre, Malawi, say that the infection rate among pregnant women jumped from 2 percent in 1987 to 22 percent only three years later. In Kigali, Rwanda, 30 percent of pregnant women carry HIV. In southern Zambia, the number is 8 percent, and rising.

Many of the people who will die of AIDS during the 1990s

have yet to be born. Children of women with AIDS have about one chance in three of being born infected with the virus. By the end of 1992, according to a report from the World Health Organization, African AIDS victims will have given birth to about four million babies, at least one million of whom will die of AIDS within their first year of life. Dr. Merson estimates that some ten million children will have developed the disease by the end of the 1990s. Most will already have died by the year 2000.

A few bright spots remain in this extraordinarily bleak picture. Some parts of Africa are oddly unaffected by AIDS. Nigeria is home to 120 million, more than one fifth of the people south of the great desert. Infection rates at some clinics there top out at only 5 percent. Overall, HIV carriers make up less than 1 percent of the population. And in Zaire, even before AIDS-prevention programs got under way, the infection rate among pregnant women had stabilized at about 8 percent. Why these regions seem to resist the spread of AIDS is a mystery that epidemiologists would dearly love to understand.

But experience in Africa may have explained another mystery. In the developed countries, AIDS appeared almost exclusively among homosexual men, intravenous drug users, and those who received contaminated blood during a transfusion. In the United States and most of Europe, there are signs that heterosexual transmission of HIV is becoming more significant. Yet it remains limited almost exclusively to prostitutes, their clients, and people whose sexual partners contracted the disease by one of the traditional routes.

In other regions, the pattern has been very different. By 1990, some 60 percent of reported cases worldwide were believed to have begun with heterosexual acts. At least 5 million Africans have already been infected with HIV, 80 percent of them by heterosexual transmission. By 2000, four out of five cases throughout the world will be spread by heterosexual contact.

At first, medical researchers were startled by the ease with which HIV spreads among African heterosexuals, but they now believe they have found at least part of the explanation. Genital ulcers, such as those caused by syphilis, herpes, or chancroid, provide an easy pathway into the body and dramatically raise the risk of infection. Chancroid ulcers tend to fester more than those of other venereal infections, and so may allow the passage of

HIV virus more easily. Women with chancroid have about triple the normal risk of contracting HIV from a male sexual partner, and they are at least five times as likely to transmit HIV as those without the extra risk factor. Men face more than one chance in twenty of receiving AIDS from a woman who carries both HIV and chancroid, and at least one chance in ten if the man is uncircumcised, as many African men are. Though chancroid is relatively rare in the West, it is common in Africa and parts of Asia where AIDS has spread rapidly.

In some areas, these factors have been aggravated by a strong tradition of promiscuity and the maintenance of multiple or serial sexual relationships. A recent survey in Zambia found that 40 percent of married men admitted to having had at least one extramarital sexual partner within the previous year. In Nigeria, one-third of married women and more than half of married men said they had a sexual partner other than their spouse. Similar results have been found in Uganda, Zaire, and other countries where AIDS is at its most common. The wide networks of sexual contact built up by this promiscuity virtually guarantee the rapid spread of any venereal infection.

Other circumstances have also tended to complicate the situation. For one thing, AIDS is not caused by one virus in Africa, but by two. In the West, virtually all AIDS patients carry a virus known as HIV-1; most cases in Africa also involved this virus. But in 1986, researchers in West Africa discovered a second virus in AIDS patients and named it HIV-2. Relatively little is known about HIV-2. The evidence suggests that it existed in some parts of Africa for twenty years or more, before it was recognized. It appears slightly less contagious than HIV-1 and is slower to cause clinical AIDS. But there is no doubt that it, too, can kill. In Guinea-Bissau, a small, swampy ex-colony of Portugal located south of Senegal on the Atlantic coast, HIV-2 infects up to 10 percent of the population, about one hundred thousand people. In Angola, 14 percent of the patients at one sexually transmitted disease clinic had HIV-2, 14 percent had HIV-1, and some patients had both forms of the virus. And in Dakar, Senegal, about 10 percent of prostitutes were infected with HIV-2 in 1990, compared with only 3 percent who carried HIV-1. Many cases of HIV-2 infection may have been overlooked in the early stages of the epidemic, simply because the virus had not yet been identified, and the standard tests for HIV-1 do not react for HIV-2 positive patients. Also, only a small proportion of the AIDS patients in Africa are tested for HIV-1, because a positive test is of little value for a patient whose immune system has already been damaged. Such tests continue to be prohibitively expensive for mass screening of asymptomatic individuals—cases where early intervention might be of more benefit.

Because sanitation and public health care are less well developed in Africa than in the industrialized nations, AIDS also tends to be complicated by a different group of opportunistic diseases. Severe diarrhea is common. So are several forms of cancer, in addition to the Kaposi's sarcoma, familiar in Western AIDS clinics. And the spread of HIV seems to be promoting a sharp rise in tuberculosis cases. Tuberculosis is usually transmitted by the wracking coughs of its victims. Up to 70 percent of people in some parts of Africa carry the infection, but in nine carriers out of ten their immune systems repress it well enough to limit symptoms and transmission of the disease. But in AIDS patients, the damage to the immune system allows the disease to become active. More than half of the new TB patients identified in the Central African Republic since 1988 also suffered from AIDS. In Zaire, up to 40 percent of new TB patients are infected by HIV. Doctors in Africa now consider multiple infections with TB to be a major indicator of clinical AIDS, which WHO defines in Africa by groups of symptoms, rather than by a positive HIV antibody test. Tuberculosis cases in sub-Saharan Africa had been declining at a rate of 2 to 3 percent per year for more than two decades. Now public health workers fear that TB could again spread rapidly.

The nations of Africa are ill-equipped to cope with such an epidemic on their own. In Uganda, where one million people (in a population of sixteen million) were infected by 1990, the national health budget amounts to less than one dollar per person, per year. Few of Uganda's neighbors can do much better. The World Health Organization spent some $90 million on AIDS prevention and treatment in 1990, half of it in Africa. Other public agencies and private foundations donated another $60 million or so to African AIDS programs. But even with that, funds are woefully inadequate to provide the treatment needed by existing patients, much less to prepare for those yet undiscovered. AZT, the only drug, so far, widely used in the West to slow the progress of HIV and AIDS, is too expensive for African health-care systems to provide. The standard of care in Africa is far below that of the U.S., and will probably never come close, given the desperate economic situation. Hospitals throughout much of sub-Saharan Africa already are forced to send home AIDS patients with TB, diarrhea, pneumonia, cancers, and the other ills that chronically afflict AIDS patients there. Nor is there room for patients with diseases such as typhus and hepatitis, which though serious are less certainly fatal than AIDS.

These problems can only grow worse. The number of adult AIDS patients south of the Sahara will double or triple by 1995, and may double again by the end of the century. And that does not count HIV-infected babies. At least half a million will be born in the region between 1990 and 1992. In Zimbabwe, AIDS is already the leading killer of infants; according to the Red Cross, more than one-fourth of children under the age of four carry the AIDS virus.

Many of Africa's plague-ridden lands were reluctant at first to acknowledge the problem, but most are now developing extensive AIDS education and prevention programs. Most now routinely test donated blood for HIV. In Kampala, Uganda, the continent's first anonymous testing and counseling service opened its doors in 1990. In Zambia, a new system of medical clinics has cut the incidence of sexually transmitted diseases by 15 percent. Zaire has begun an aggressive campaign to distribute condoms donated by the United States Agency for International Development. Until 1988, only half a million condoms per year were sold in this country of more than thirty-six million; in 1990, the program distributed nearly nine million condoms. And in Kenya, doctors estimate that a project distributing condoms to the prostitutes of a single red light district is preventing between six thousand and ten thousand new cases of AIDS each year. The prostitutes themselves have reported an increased demand for condoms among clients.

One country that has yet to face the reality of AIDS is South Africa. In 1989, South Africa spent just $2 million for AIDS education and research. Until recently, more had not seemed necessary. A nation of thirty-seven million people, South Africa had reported only five hundred cases of AIDS by mid-1990. Most of them afflicted white homosexuals. Ironically, the otherwise pernicious isolation of apartheid may have slowed the spread of the infection into the black population. Still, an estimated one percent of black adults also carried HIV virus at mid-year. By the end of 1991, according to one research study, nearly half a million South Africans could be infected. Another found that one-fifth of the schoolgirls in Natal province suffer from AIDS. And even that is likely to be just the beginning. Health officials doubt that the spread of AIDS could be stopped before at least 5 percent of black South Africans contract the disease, even with a vigorous program of education and prevention. The reality is likely to be far worse, because the puritanical white majority have found it impossible to face the need for sex education or a campaign to promote the use of condoms, while many blacks still view condoms as part of a white plot to inhibit the growth of the black population.

No one yet knows the full impact of HIV on life in Africa, but a few developments are already obvious. Family life has been mutating rapidly under the pressure of the disease. AIDS has cut the middle from many families; grandparents and grandchildren now struggle together to cope with the loss of the intermediate generation. When parents die, other children move in with aunts and uncles. Some families struggle on with older brothers or sisters caring for younger siblings. One study, sponsored by UNICEF, estimates that in ten countries of central and east Africa, up to six million children will lose at least one parent during the 1990s. Most will lose both.

Socially, AIDS is causing the most profound changes since European colonialism. In Zambia, the tradition in some tribes required a man's widows to be purged of his spirit by a cleansing ritual that included having sex with a member of his family. In the age of AIDS, alternative procedures have been adopted. A growing number of people in the traditionally polygamous African societies have opted for monogamy. People are marrying earlier to avoid the risk of contracting AIDS in premarital sex. A few even say they will not marry at all unless their potential spouse joins them in an AIDS test.

The economic impact of this twentieth-century plague also remains poorly understood. There is more to it than the cost of caring for patients, and eventually burying them. More than thirty thousand young men from Malawi used to work the mines in South Africa; in 1986, they sent home $21 million. But South Africa now requires that potential guest workers be examined for AIDS, and the Malawian government refuses to permit the tests. Few Malawian men are left in South Africa, and their contributions to Malawi's economy have dropped by more than $15 million per year. Even that will be only a small part of the ultimate cost. Some parts of Africa are being deprived of up to one-fifth of their working-age men and women. The value they would have contributed to their nations has simply vanished. South Africa could be particularly vulnerable. Its economy depends on the exploitation of cheap labor from a large pool of black workers. If 10 percent of the nation's black men were to die of AIDS—a reasonable guess based on experience elsewhere in Africa—the resulting economic damage could end any hope that growing freedom will raise the living standards of the black community there.

This potential catastrophe could be repeated in other countries that have tried to hide from the threat of AIDS. One is mainland China. Until 1990, medical authorities there had discovered only forty-eight cases of AIDS, and all but seven of them had occurred in visiting foreigners. Then 146 peasants from Yunan province appeared with the disease. Yunan, near the famed "Golden Triangle" opium growing area of Burma, Thailand, and Laos, has a growing drug problem, and the farmers had shared contaminated needles. Despite China's draconian anti-drug laws, this incident will not be the last of its kind.

The Soviet Union, too, once denied the existence of an AIDS problem within its borders. But recently, the Soviet weekly magazine *Ogonyk* forecast that between 1989 and 2000, the number of AIDS victims in the USSR alone could total twenty million. After the turn of the century, it said, the cost of combatting the epidemic could exceed $3 trillion per year—more than the nation's GNP in 1989. By 2010, it suggested, up to 40 percent of Soviet young people could be infected. The cause was not sexual promiscuity or drug use, but an acute shortage of medical supplies. In 1990, the report estimated, Soviet hospitals would receive only about 650 million syringes, fewer than one-tenth as many as were needed. As a result, syringes are reused, though only one hospital in three is equipped to sterilize them. Any undetected HIV infection in one hospital patient will very likely be passed on to others.

And yet even this pales by comparison with the long-term threat facing sub-Saharan Africa. A recent study by the United States Census Bureau and the U.S. Agency for International Development paints a more horrifying picture still. By 2015, the researchers believe, AIDS will kill more than three-fourths of the women who die during their childbearing years, 2.4 million women in that year alone. In some ethnic groups, the disease will kill up to one-third of working-age men. It will cut life expectancy in some cities by nearly twenty years. And it will orphan some sixteen million children. By 2015, the report forecasts, fully 17 percent of the African population will be infected by HIV, seventy million people in all.

Africa was the laboratory in which nature first created man. That same center of evolutionary research has now produced a disease with the power to destroy much of the civilization that humanity has built in the last few centuries. Enlightened public-health and education programs will eventually slow or halt the spread of AIDS; science will produce vaccines that can prevent infection and drugs to control or cure it. But for Africa, these developments will come too late. In Joseph Conrad's "heart of darkness," the future has become much darker than any writer could have imagined.

CHAPTER 18

The Bitter End of Apartheid

"Conventional wisdom has it that divisive forces will prevent de Klerk and Mandela from reaching the kind of compromise needed to bring peace and democracy to South Africa. We believe they will force an accommodation."

As recently as February 1990, when President Frederik Willem de Klerk legalized the African National Congress and released Nelson Mandela from prison, it seemed that this potentially wealthy land might at last be ready to heal its divisions. President de Klerk has tried to continue easing the restrictions on non-whites. In 1990 and the first months of 1991, he directed that his own National party open itself to blacks and proposed to remove from the books all laws discriminating between the races. In June, the legislature removed the last of the laws that underlay apartheid, save the Constitution itself. Yet the nearer South Africa approaches to the end of apartheid, the more difficult further progress seems to become. The pattern of two steps forward, something more than one step back will dominate South African politics and society until the mid-1990s. Yet by the end of the decade, this racist land will have achieved something approaching full democracy.

Credit for this change belongs, of course, to just two remarkable men: Nelson Mandela and F.W. de Klerk.

Nearly three decades ago, Mandela was a lawyer widely respected in the black community. His prominence in the banned

African National Congress (ANC) earned him twenty-seven years in Cape Town's Victor Verser prison. Now seventy-three and in failing health, he seems amazingly free of bitterness and able to work with the white oligarchy. His dedication to the well-being of all South Africans, not just to fulfilling the demands of his own constituents, is one of the reasons we are optimistic about the nation's future.

In some ways, de Klerk is an even more remarkable figure, for he has changed more and in far less time. Like the Soviet Union's Mikhail Gorbachev, he has not always been a reformer. He spent more than sixteen years in his nation's parliament, and throughout that time hewed to the National party line. He supported the idea that races should live in separate areas, work under discriminatory conditions, and use segregated public facilities. He denied blacks the right to strike, or even to form trade unions. He refused them the privilege of settling permanently in white areas. When de Klerk ran for the presidency in 1989, he campaigned on a strong pro-apartheid platform.

But even then, it was clear that apartheid could not last. South Africa was growing progressively harder to govern. Rent strikes and boycotts were common in black neighborhoods throughout the country. In local elections, few blacks went to the polls. In Natal province alone, nearly four thousand people were killed for political reasons, between 1985 and 1990. The system of so-called "homelands" for blacks was also breaking down. Between 1987 and 1989, the homeland governments of Transkei, Ciskei, and Venda were all overthrown black soldiers who favored the ANC. The pretence that apartheid gave each race the right to run its own affairs was collapsing. The Dutch Reformed Church even declared that apartheid was a sin.

In 1989, the ANC gave de Klerk its terms for negotiation. In the Harare Declaration, it demanded an end to the state of emergency, legalization of the ANC and other banned organizations, the release of political prisoners including Nelson Mandela, an end to executions, removal of troops from the black townships, and the elimination of security restrictions. de Klerk granted almost all of them, early in 1990. Only Natal, where the violence was at its worst, remained under a state of emergency; only those ANC members who had been convicted of arson or murder remained in prison. Shortly after the government released Nelson Mandela, preliminary negotiations began.

To date, they have not led very far. This is not the fault of Mandela and de Klerk, who clearly want to smooth the transition from apartheid to whatever more equitable system of government follows it. But as they try to unite South Africa, life and politics there have become increasingly fragmented.

On Mandela's side, two separate power struggles have broken out for control of the black community, both during negotiations and after the end of apartheid. One is between the ANC and Chief Mangosuthu Buthelezi's Inkatha movement. The other is within the African National Congress itself.

The conflict between the ANC and Inkatha mirrors similar antagonisms that have occurred whenever central governments have tried to take power in the nations of Africa: The existing tribal authorities have no interest in losing their positions, and they have done everything possible to obstruct the national government from exercising control. In this case, the central power is the ANC, which aspires to govern a united black South Africa. Like other tribal leaders before him, Chief Buthelezi wants to maintain his regional power in largely Zulu, Natal. He does not mind shedding blood to accomplish his goal. Throughout the country, four thousand were killed in overtly political violence in 1990. Another twelve thousand South Africans died that year in violent crimes. In the Johannesburg area, nearly 800 people died in less than two months.

This battle had cost the ANC some of its prestige. Buthelezi has tried to depict the group as a Xhosa tribal organization comparable to his own Inkatha. Nelson Mandela's position as a Xhosa prince gives the idea some credibility. And on that basis, Inkatha may have a clearer right to represent South African blacks than the ANC does. Buthelezi claims his organization has 1.6 million members. That is probably exaggerated, and most onlookers believe the Congress has considerably more members. Two polls in 1990 found that some 64 percent of urban blacks, and 38 percent of all blacks outside Natal, said they felt closest to the ANC. Only one percent in the cities and two percent in the country at large favored Inkatha. Yet, as a banned organization, the ANC kept no membership records, and when it tried to recruit official members in 1990, only 150,000 people signed up.

Inkatha violence undermined the ANC in another way. In September 1990, the Pretoria regime cracked down on township bloodshed in "Operation Iron Fist." The move gave authorities the power to ban gatherings in the "unrest areas" and to detain suspects without charge. Residents were forbidden to carry the weapons used in the fighting—axes, knives, spears, pitchforks, and machetes. Later it imposed a 9:00 P.M. curfew in townships around Johannesburg and drafted provincial and reservist police into the area to combat out-of-control mobs. The killings declined rapidly. Unfortunately, so did faith in the idea that the ANC could successfully negotiate with Pretoria to end the repression.

Several less violent organizations have also been competing for the ANC's constituency. The Pan African Congress and the Azanian People's Organization (AZAPO) both oppose any talks with Pretoria. Both have strong followings among South Africa's black intelligentsia.

This has helped to fuel a schism within the ANC itself. The organization's leadership consists of three groups: former exiles, former prisoners, and activists who worked underground while the Congress was banned. Like Nelson Mandela, they tend to be over forty and dedicated to negotiating for a peaceful end to apartheid. But more than 40 percent of black South Africans are under age fifteen, and young people make up a large proportion of the ANC's rank and file. They are a radical, impatient constituency, hard to control and suspicious of their organization's leaders. Though Mandela remains widely respected for his years in prison, many young ANC members feel he has lost touch with the harsh realities of life in the streets. Other senior ANC officials are unpopular with younger members, who suspect them of corruption.

This mirrors the long-standing division within the American civil rights movement. As early as 1895, the radical black leader W. E. B. Du Bois fell out with the acclaimed educator and activist Booker T. Washington over Washington's belief that demands for social equality were useless until blacks achieved economic independence. More than half a century later, the rift appeared again, when respected leaders such as Martin Luther

King and Roy McInnes were challenged by the younger militants of the radical Black Panthers and similar organizations. If the situation in South Africa develops as that in the United States did, violent radicalism will accomplish little but to trigger a white backlash against any progress toward black equality.

ANC's radicals are gaining power within the organization. The Congress's first conference held in South Africa in thirty years was marred by clashes between older leaders and the younger hard-liners. ANC President Oliver Tambo, recently returned from exile, suggested easing economic sanctions, but the proposal was voted down. Mandela was loudly criticized for talking with the Pretoria government without first putting the matter to a vote by the membership. A recent ANC document, reflecting the radical position, declared "the strength of the ANC on the ground must be felt and feared."

The Congress had scheduled a national conference for November 1990. The meeting has since been postponed to June 1991, a decision supported by both sides of the schism. ANC leaders worry that young hard-liners will take over in the election to be held at the general meeting, while more radical members fear that the election will be rigged in favor of current officials if it is held before all the organization's young exiles return to South Africa. Unless the meeting is postponed again, the election's results will be known by the time this book appears. It seems safe to predict that neither side will be fully happy with them.

Nelson Mandela's own family is playing out this division within the ANC. Shortly after his return from prison, Mandela insisted that his wife, Winnie, be appointed head of the ANC social welfare program. Organization moderates protested, because Winnie Mandela is far more radical than her husband. Hard-liners have given her their enthusiastic support. Winnie Mandela does have the credentials for the job; she was the first black in South Africa to qualify as a social worker. Yet how long she will hold her first official role with the Congress remains unclear.

More detrimental has been the conviction of Winnie Mandela for kidnapping and assault in the death of fourteen-year-old Stompie Seipei, in December 1988. Jerry Richardson, leader of the "Mandela Football Team" that acted as her unofficial bodyguards, has been sentenced to both death and eighteen years imprisonment for crimes including the murder of Seipei. Witnesses say Winnie Mandela took a very active part in beating suspected collaborators. Her trial temporarily came to a halt after the disappearance of a key witness against her, an incident that critics said smacks of mob rule.

For Nelson Mandela, his wife's legal problems are more than a personal tragedy. Those who know him well say that he is following Xhosa tradition, which says that a husband must take responsibility for his wife's actions. If so, his tribal loyalty may have subverted his devotion to South Africa. His unwavering support for his wife, however commendable under other circumstances, could well undermine his credibility with moderates on both sides of the color barrier.

F.W. de Klerk faces growing problems as well. Since he repealed the Separate Amenities Law, which separated races in public facilities, some towns dominated by the Conservative Party have imposed user fees at pools and libraries in the hope that blacks will be unable to afford to use them. Conservative leaders have talked of withholding taxes from Pretoria as a way to force de Klerk into calling early elections.

Even farther to the right, more pressures are growing. The Boerstaat party, formed in 1988 by Robert Van Tonder, hopes to restore the old Boer republics of the Orange Free State, the Transvaal, and Vryheid. In twenty years, Van Tonder believes, South Africa will be a confederation of largely autonomous nation-states, some white and others black, cooperating for the common good.

Wim Booyse, a risk analyst, compiled a list of seventy right-wing organizations that have sprung up to oppose any relaxation of apartheid. Among them are eight paramilitary units and twenty-eight smaller terrorist groups.

And a commission appointed by President de Klerk found that thirty police officers had acted illegally by firing into a black crowd in March 1990, killing five and wounding two hundred. The commission said the incident had been caused by a lack of discipline and control over the ranks and recommended that the officers be prosecuted. de Klerk, apparently fearing to challenge the police, dropped the matter without action. Even more disastrous was the revelation that De Klerk's government has funded several Inkatha rallies. The resulting scandal has undermined De Klerk's authority and destroyed whatever trust he had earned from ANC leaders. There is a chance, though no more than a chance, that it could eventually bring down his administration.

Conventional wisdom has it that these divisive forces will prevent de Klerk and Mandela from reaching the kind of compromise needed to bring peace and democracy to South Africa. We believe they will force an accommodation. Under the current constitution, de Klerk's National Party faces an election no later than 1994. According to opinion polls, the Conservative party, which has reluctantly supported de Klerk's reforms, and the smaller white extremist parties, would win any all-white election if they joined forces to defeat the National Party. For its part, the ANC fears that failure to come to an agreement that gives blacks substantial power would destroy its following. Opening the voting to blacks is the best hope either organization has of retaining any of its power.

Whether the African National Congress decides to reshape itself into a political party and take direct control of the country or simply to maintain its coalition with the National Party, it is certain to gain a much greater say in the country's affairs. A rumored deal between Mandela and de Klerk would put ANC members into de Klerk's cabinet. Whether or not that agreement has yet been reached, a National Party that maintains its power beyond 1994 will owe so much to Nelson Mandela and his supporters that it cannot avoid giving them a place in government.

No matter who is running South Africa, they will face problems that would be difficult even for a unified nation to solve. One problem is its changing population. As of 1990, there were about thirty-five million people in South Africa, twenty-eight million of them black. At the turn of the century, the population will have grown to more than forty-five million. Whites will contribute little if any to the increase; at the moment, their numbers are declining by nearly one percent per year. By 2010, there will be almost nine times as many black South Africans, as white. As whites find themselves ever more outnumbered, it will take a government skilled in diplomacy to keep their fear of black domination under control. Neither Nelson Mandela nor F. W. de Klerk will be there to ease the process.

Another problem is urbanization. South Africa's cities are

growing faster than any on the continent. In 1985, only sixteen million people lived in the nation's cities; by 2000, nearly thirty-six million will do so. In the last ten years of the century, populations will double in Pretoria, Johannesburg, Cape Town, and other major cities. Durban and Cape Town will have populations of seven million. "PWV," the region from Pretoria in the north, the Witwatersrand in the center, and Vereeniging in the south, will coalesce into a single megalopolis. By 2010, its population will reach 16.5 million.

According to one estimate, the flight of rural blacks to the cities will require the construction of two million new homes by end of century. In fact, at least that many are needed now. Some seven million people are already living in shanty towns built of tarpaper, cardboard, and plastic sheeting. Rather than trying to provide them with electricity, water, and sanitation, city governments have been trying to reverse overcrowding by demolishing squatter camps. It is a wrong-headed policy at best. The number of people living in the camps will double by 1996.

Apartheid has done even more than population growth, to cause this massive shift in population. For years, South African law prohibited landless blacks from moving to the city. Apartheid even tried to reverse the flow, shipping blacks en masse to barren homelands that could not support them. Overcrowding and ecological devastation followed quickly. Pretoria lifted the ban on black migration to the cities in 1986, and the flood began. Only five years later, South Africa's rural areas are populated mainly by women, children, and old men. (The world has seen this pattern before, in the United States of the 1920s, when jobless black men from the South moved to northern cities in search of work. Their descendents still crowd the ghettos of New York, Boston, and Chicago.)

Yet, South Africa's most pressing problems are economic. The country qualifies as a developed nation, but it remains at the low end of the economic spectrum. Its per capita GNP is roughly equal to those of Yugoslavia, Portugal, and most South American countries. Its medical and financial infrastructures are among the most sophisticated in the world, but most industries are distinctly medium-tech. South Africa has abundant minerals, including gold, diamonds, platinum, and many of the strategic metals, but export demand has grown slowly in the face of

American and United Nations sanctions. Gold prices dropped throughout most of the last decade. The 1980s brought severe drought that damaged farm crops.

These and other problems have hit the South African economy hard. Though unemployment is all but unknown among whites, up to 30 percent of blacks are jobless. Inflation averaged nearly 14 percent between 1980 and 1988, and is still rising. And foreign exchange is in short supply. The country has had to reschedule its debts, and the payments still cost about $1.5 billion per year. More than $1 billion more is lost through private investment outside the country.

There is reason to wonder whether the African National Congress has what it takes to repair South Africa's damaged economy. After decades of exploitation by white landowners and businessmen, many blacks equate capitalism with apartheid. ANC members are no exception. According to ANC's military commander, Chris Hani, 27 of the organization's 35 National Executive Committee members also belong to the South African Communist party, which remained banned until July 1990. The Communists are particularly influential in the black trade-union movement, whose support the ANC urgently needs. The ANC's 1955 Freedom Charter declared that "the mineral wealth beneath the soil, the banks and monopoly industry shall be transferred to the ownership of the people as a whole." As of spring 1990, the ANC still planned to nationalize the mining industry.

The ANC may yet back away from this policy, for virtually all of South Africa's neighbors have shown how self-destructive central economic planning can be. Most of the national economies in sub-Saharan Africa (not counting South Africa itself) have been government controlled. Over the last three decades, their per capita incomes have grown by no more than one-third of one percent per year, on average. More than half have actually declined. Thirty countries in the region are now scrapping government ownership and controls, with promising results. In 1989, the 18 countries that have made the most progress toward free-market economies grew by 3.7 percent. Ghana devalued its currency and freed commodities prices in 1984, and its economy has grown by 5.5 percent per year.

In South Africa itself, a new department has begun to privatize and deregulate economy. Though many cities have resisted the program, Welkom, in the Orange Free State, privatized bus services, saving $1 million per year; expanded the fleet of black taxis from 400 to 1,500; and privatized the local airport and other municipal facilities. Welkom now claims to have highest per capita income in the country and to be South Africa's fastest-growing city.

An entrepreneurial movement is even growing among South Africa's black community. One development is the growth of "spaza shops" catering to blacks. Like the corner markets in American cities, they sell convenience foods at high prices, but they are so close to home that the extra cost is worth paying. There are an estimated fifteen thousand spaza shops in the Johannesburg area alone. Street hawkers offer fast foods, fruit, and other products in the cities. A "black taxi" industry has sprung up as well. Drivers use 12- to 15-seat minibuses to carry black city-dwellers to work quickly and conveniently. The industry already employs an estimated 300,000 people, two-thirds as many as mining. Some economists believe this "informal economy" already accounts for 35 percent of South Africa's gross domestic product.

Once South Africa rids itself of apartheid, its economic health could improve quickly. Many of the economic sanctions against South Africa could soon be lifted. The 1989 United Nations resolution under which most sanctions were imposed allows member states to end their boycott, not when apartheid is at last gone, but when South Africa shows signs of "irreversible progress" toward that goal. President Bush declared South Africa's changes "irreversible" as early as President de Klerk's visit to the United States in 1990.

The European Community has already proposed to lift its embargo on imports of South African iron, steel, and gold coins once racial classification and segregation laws are lifted, a condition now met. The British Commonwealth's Committee of Foreign Ministers on South Africa has voted to retain its sanctions until Pretoria removes the last of its apartheid laws; the Commonwealth summit will make the final decision in October 1991. But as a member of the European Community, Britain could be forced to end its sanctions even before other Commonwealth members get the chance to vote again.

Most South African forecasters project a dismal future for

their nation. The population will grow, of course, so housing and public facilities will be ever less adequate. The tentative move toward a free-market economy will come to a halt as the government tries to cope with international economic sanctions, so employment will decline and inflation will continue to rise. And growing political conflict will make it impossible to solve the nation's other problems. At worst, growing black frustration could erupt into civil war.

We expect a very different scenario. The de Klerk government, we believe, repeal the Group Areas Act and the Two Lands Act, which provide for the separation of the races. The government is also likely to release the last of its 1,300 political prisoners. That done, the way will be open for formal negotiation between the government and the ANC. Before the 1994 elections, the two will agree to some form of political compromise. The resulting government will be something less than a strict one-man, one-vote democracy—the white minority fears that unlimited majority rule would be used to strip them completely of their wealth and power—but it will give South African blacks the right to vote for and to hold public office. The coalition government will continue to deregulate and privatize the economy, and if sanctions are still in place, the ANC will ask that they be ended. These changes will give South Africa an economic boost that will reduce the inflation rate, ease unemployment, and raise the standard of living for all. And that, in turn, will relieve much of the social tension that now plagues the nation.

South Africa will not eliminate all its problems by the turn of the century. As we saw in the last chapter, it faces an AIDS epidemic that will strain even its well-developed medical system. But ten years from now, it will be clear that apartheid is just an evil memory. South Africa will be healing its self-inflicted wounds.

THE HAVE-NOTS:

LATIN AMERICA

•••

The Struggle for Democracy and Survival

"The Latin American governments that hope to survive must also give their people a decent living by stemming hyperinflation and eradicating the terrible poverty."

•••

Throughout history, Central and South America have suffered from several almost universal problems. Most nations of this region are divided into two mutually hostile camps: the tiny minority of wealthy families who control the economy and government, and the vast majority of the population, who lack both capital and influence. The poverty and overpopulation endemic to Latin America grow directly from this social division. Because the poor have no effective voice in government, there are few social programs to help them, and those few are uniformly ineffective. As in Africa, instead of Social Security, the poor have children, in hope that the next generation will be able to support them in their old age. The population grows constantly, and scarce resources must be spread ever more thinly.

The result can be seen in Argentina, where there have been six military coups in the twentieth century. Argentina has all the economic advantages that most Latin American countries can only wish for: fertile farmlands that provide enough food to support the population, vast reserves of hydroelectric power, natural resources including oil, and a well-educated labor force capable of competing in the modern world. It even has a slight, positive balance of trade.

Almost by tradition, Argentina has long had some of the most inept government policies ever to subvert a promising economy. Vast social programs have driven the government budget to well over $30 billion per year, or just under one-third of the GNP. Nationalization has crippled many of Argentina's basic industries. Inflation peaked in 1989 at 6,000 percent, but has declined since then to merely horrendous levels. And foreign debt payments cripple development, despite frequent refinancing and restructuring.

Argentina's crippling problems are replayed in neighboring Brazil on an even larger scale. Brazil has a well diversified economy and reserves of oil, precious metals, copper, and iron that should support a thriving nation. They do not.

In November 1989, Brazilians voted in their first direct presidential election in 29 years. The new president inherited an economy so unstable that it is difficult to understand why anyone wanted the office. Fully half the wealth in Brazil is owned by only one percent of the population, a guarantee of civil unrest anywhere in the world. Inflation ran more than 900 percent in 1988 and neared 1,200 percent the following year. The good news that year was that, after eight years of little or no growth, the gross domestic product advanced—by 0.3 percent. Under such poor conditions, there seems little hope that President Fernando Collor de Mello can either repair his nation's ailing economy, or even retain power.

Latin America's smaller nations face many of the problems of Argentina and Brazil, and often unique challenges of their own. Bolivia is hobbled by civil unrest and an economy heavily dependent on coca production. El Salvador remains divided between left-wing insurgents and a right-wing government whose "death squads" maintain a low profile out of deference to American sensibilities, but could easily slip out of control at any moment. Nicaragua at last lives under what passes for an elective government, but there is little sign that the wounds of its long civil war have even begun to heal. In all this region, only Costa Rica, Venezuela, and perhaps Chile show any sign of building stable and prosperous societies.

In time, democratic government might cure the inequities that prevail throughout this region, but Latin America lacks a strong tradition of democracy. For many years now, politics throughout much of Latin America has followed a dismal cycle: when majority rule does take hold, however briefly, its leaders are often so committed to an unrealistic populism that their social programs threaten to bankrupt the country. Public unrest returns, and military rule soon follows. Eventually, the military turns its power over to civilian leaders, and the cycle begins again.

Yet in the past ten years, democracy has made remarkable strides throughout most of the Latin American countries. Only the governments of Cuba and Suriname continue to lack the claim of having been democratically chosen by their people. Not everyone is convinced that those elections were fair; many votes have been contested, including those in El Salvador and Mexico. Yet on the whole, the continent has made great strides by replacing the military dictatorships of a decade ago with more legitimate leaders. Pressing questions remain to be answered during the 1990s. Will the new democratic governments survive? And will their more market-oriented economic policies at last relieve the crushing poverty and extreme income disparities?

The answers to these and other mysteries depend on the actions of the three forces that have long competed for control of most Latin countries: the military, the ideologically-controlled labor unions, and the Catholic church.

On the face of it, the military has suffered most from recent developments. The decline of communism in the East has eroded the generals' claim that national security required military control of their nations. Rebellions remain active in several Latin countries, but they fight on, with much less foreign assistance. Now that the Soviet Union has withdrawn its support, Cuba lacks the funds to foment revolutionary movements in neighboring lands. With that threat vanished, large military budgets place unreasonable strains on weak national economies.

Yet the military machines that supported past authoritarian regimes have not disappeared. They continue to play an important role in the political process—for better or, more often, worse. While none of the major Latin American countries faces an immediate coup, military restlessness undermines the authority of the elected government and destabilizes the political situation. Chile's former strongman leader, General Augusto Pinochet, continues to head the nation's army. Against the advice and warnings of her vice-president, Victor Godoy, and the UNO coalition, Nicaraguan president Violeta de Chamorro allowed the Sandinista Humberto Ortega to remain as the head of the armed forces in hopes that her decision would preserve a sense of unity and continuity. Bolivia's military is apt to resume power in an attempt to bring order and stability to the troubled country. The government in San Salvador cannot exert full control over its military in its fight against the leftist rebels.

"Caste militaries"—armed forces headed by an educated, social elite—retain their unofficial power in Brazil and Argentina. In Brazil, right-wing death squads routinely attempt to clear the country of "undesirables." Recently, paramilitary groups have earned international condemnation by killing the unwanted and often, homeless children of the slums.

The military also makes its presence strongly felt in Argentina, which it ruled by junta from 1976 to 1983. During that time, military death squads murdered more than nine thousand Argentine civilians during their so-called dirty war against the left. Over the years, the military has collected a large stock of resentments that make it highly volatile. It lost power when it forfeited its prestige in the short and disastrous war over the Falkland Islands (or Malvinas, as Argentina prefers) in the early 1980s, an embarrassment that still rankles. The army also objects to being called upon to help stem regional drug trafficking—a demeaning task for an institution that regards itself as the defender of the national honor.

President Carlos Menem walks a dangerously fine line in trying to placate this powerful military establishment. As the only Latin American leader to send troops in support of "Operation Desert Shield" in the Persian Gulf, he risked restoring the military's lost prestige. And although the army supported the elected government during an attempted coup in December 1990, it exacted a stiff price: Menem was forced to accept the demands of the arch-nationalistic army faction of *carapintadas* (painted faces) by releasing five senior officers jailed for the their part in the "disappearances" of civilians during the junta's rule. The officers still refuse to admit their involvement in those murders, but the widespread belief in their guilt inflamed popular bitterness at their perceived escape from justice.

Menem's concessions will be only the first of many needed to soothe the uneasy, brass-heavy military. He and his successors will have a difficult time persuading the army to stay in its barracks.

Costa Rica shows what South American countries can accomplish when they manage to get rid of the disruptive military influence. It owes its remarkable stability mainly to the fact that it abolished its army in 1951. According to policy, the police eschew guns in favor of more practical screwdrivers: violators of traffic laws have their license plates removed and must venture downtown to reclaim them. Even during the tumultuous 1980s, when regional pressures might have encouraged San Jose's leaders to form a stronger defensive force, then-president, and Nobel Peace Prize winner, Oscar Arias spearheaded a peace plan abroad and continued to stress education over the military at home. The tiny country devotes just over 3 percent of the government budget to self-defense and spends nearly one-quarter on health. The theme of "more teachers than soldiers" has produced Central America's most literate population and a government that will continue to transfer power smoothly through democratic elections.

In most of Latin America, the only force that opposes the military right wing is organized labor, on the left. The collapse of socialism has undercut the labor unions even more directly than has the military. Just as Cuba cannot afford to prop up insurrections, it cannot donate funds to the unions, and some of the Communist-supported unions have found their coffers shrinking. The push toward privatization of state-owned companies and free-market economics has also weakened union bargaining positions. In Argentina, President Menem gratefully accepted the traditional union support for his Peronist party. Yet after being elected, he determined to sell some of the state-owned enterprises that had served as union strongholds. Among them are such giants as the telephone industry, the electric company, the oil company, the shipping line, the railroads, the port authority, and the government's share of the hydroelectric plant on the border with Uruguay. That Menem could afford to "betray" organized labor in this fashion is clear proof of the unions' waning power.

The unions are not likely to recoup their former power. In the more developed nations, automation and robotics are already beginning to raise the demand for highly skilled workers in less labor-intensive industries while they are replacing the unskilled and semiskilled laborers who make up the unions' rank and file.

Yet they will remain a potent force in Latin life well into the next century. If they do not share their government's vision of development, they can still provoke time-consuming and expensive conflicts. Some countries, such as Mexico and Venezuela, have taken precautions against severe labor disruptions by bringing the unions' leaders into the governmental structure. Where economic reform is successful, it will be because governments wisely found some way to work with the unions, not against them.

The power bloc least affected by the changes of the 1980s is the Catholic church. Its influence over the social structure in Latin America will remain powerful well beyond the next ten years, particularly in Mexico, Colombia, and Nicaragua. Although Argentina's Peronist government claims to have freed itself from the church, vestiges of its former ties remain; for instance, the constitution requires that the elected president must be Catholic. The Catholic church may even grow stronger in Panama now that it has received access to former strongman Manuel Noriega's radio network. One welcome change will be the taming of "liberation theology." This socially activist branch of the church will remain popular with the poor, but it will discard its most strident Marxist overtones.

During the 1980s, for the first time, Protestant evangelists have been giving the established church serious competition in the once solidly Catholic continent. Their message of hard work and prayer appeals to the poor, who seek to improve their lives. And for probably the first time, non-Catholic presidents have climbed to power in Peru in 1990 and in Guatemala the following year. This trend seems likely to continue for the remainder of the century.

Will Latin America's democracies last? Some will; some will not. Governments in Nicaragua, El Salvador, Brazil, Peru, and perhaps Argentina are at risk. The democracies of Costa Rica and Venezuela are the most entrenched and stable. The ones that endure will be those that can rein in or coopt their rivals for power—the military, labor unions, and the Catholic church. Just as important, the Latin American governments that hope to survive must also give their people a decent living.

It will not be easy. In 1989, Latin America's regional GDP grew at a mere 1.1 percent (the level for 1978), following a scant showing of 0.6 percent in 1988. Meanwhile, the annual rate of inflation soared at an average of 1,000 percent. The larger economies of Argentina, Venezuela, and Peru brought down the average, registering declines of 5.5 percent, 8.5 percent, and 10 percent, respectively; other countries did far worse.

Though average per capita incomes in Latin America are six times higher than those of sub-Saharan Africa, the extremes of poverty and wealth in this region are the most pronounced in the developing world. One-fifth of the continent's population lives in poverty; in some countries, the proportion is much higher. The need to improve their lot has long been Latin America's most daunting problem. Raising the poor to, or slightly above, the poverty line would take only a 2 percent personal income tax on the wealthiest one-fifth of the population—an amount equal to 0.7 percent of the regional GDP. Even that modest change has been difficult or impossible to enact.

One of the better ways to measure poverty is to look at its effects on the lives of people who suffer it. Typical factors examined include the average number of calories consumed per person per day, daily grams of protein consumed per capita, life expectancy at birth, and rate of literacy. By these measures, the poverty in Latin America and the Caribbean ranks as the third most extreme by region after sub-Saharan Africa and the Middle East/North Africa. Probably due in part to the Spanish tradition of reading, Latin America's literacy rate is relatively high for an underdeveloped area. Since there are great differences in types and degrees of poverty, Latin America's urban and rural poor should be considered separately.

Poverty is at its worst in the rural areas, even when we account for the higher cost of living in the cities. Most of the rural poor are small-scale farmers who cannot exist on their meager plots. Twenty-seven percent of Brazil's population lives in its rural northeast region, for example, but these people account for over half of the country's poor. Similarly stricken regions include the Andean highlands of Bolivia, Ecuador, Guatemala, and Peru. The land here is isolated and undesirable; the altitude is so high that most foreigners have difficulty breathing unless they take proper medication in advance. Arable land is scarce, and agricultural production low.

Certain groups endure more than their share of deprivation. The continent's indigenous Indians tend to suffer more than the general population, especially in Bolivia, Ecuador, Guatemala, Mexico, and Peru. Women and children in particular tend to be the hardest hit; both their life expectancies and their levels of education are lower than those of men.

In the *barrios* of Caracas and *favelas* of Rio de Janeiro, the urban poor also live in squalor. Overcrowding is at its most obvious in São Paolo, where the population may reach twenty million early in the next century; almost 30 years ago, there were already more than two million people living in the São Paolo city dump. The squatter settlements are unsanitary and badly overcrowded. Fires are a hazard. Water is contaminated.

Yet the urban poor have some advantages that their rural cousins lack. The contrast between their shantytowns and the modern high-rises makes their plight harder to ignore. They also form a more politicized, vociferous bloc than the rural poor, who tend to be overlooked in comparison. And there is generally more infrastructure in the cities than in countryside. Most of the ghetto's inhabitants migrated there from the countryside in order to try to find work. Very few return to their former homes.

Because the urban poor in many Latin American countries have more political influence than their rural cousins, agricultural policies made in the capitals tend to favor the cities and industry. Taxation and subsidized credit in Brazil, for instance, favor large farmers and the bulk of labor. Agricultural policies have actually reduced labor demand and have also made it practically impossible for the poor to buy their own land to farm. In Bolivia, the government gave large agricultural companies most of the land for raising livestock and forestry. It is easy to understand why land reform and redistribution present such prickly political questions in Latin America.

One measure of the "skewedness" of income distribution is the Gini coefficient. In a society where income is evenly distributed, where one percent of the population earns one percent of the available income, the Gini coefficient is zero; conversely, when one percent of the population earns all the available income, the Gini coefficient is one.

In 1970, Brazil had a Gini coefficient of 0.50. Since then it has worsened considerably. Brazil has one of the most lopsided income distributions in the world. Less than one percent of the population owns more than 50 percent of the wealth, enough to compromise the nation's stability.

Similar disparities are seen throughout Latin America. In 1986, the wealthiest tenth of Costa Rica's population owned nearly 40 percent of the wealth; in 1987 Venezuela's top tenth claimed 34 percent; and in 1988 in Colombia, the richest 10 percent of the population owned 37 percent.

Colombia is one of the very few Latin American countries that has partially reduced the inequality of its income distribution. Its Gini coefficient dropped from 0.54 in 1971 to 0.48 in 1978. During that time, wages for the unskilled rose 6.6 percent a year, while GNP grew at only 3.9 percent and worker productivity improved slightly. Hence, the distribution of income shifted in favor of the underclass.

Few countries in the region can boast of similar improvements. Incomes in Latin America fell in the 1980s, and living standards for millions there are now lower than in the early 1970s. The World Bank has called the 1980s a "lost decade" for the undeveloped regions of the world.

Reducing poverty and increasing social stability in Latin America requires internal reform more than external aid. Controlling inflation is one key; without this, consumer and investor confidence will remain shaky, and economic crises will continue in an ever-widening spiral. Price and financial policies that emphasize productive labor-intensive employment in both rural and urban areas can promote greater equality, as long as governments stress the development of infrastructure as well. And Latin American countries must find some way to cope with the massive foreign debts they incurred in the 1970s, when banks were eager to recycle their petrodollars. The following chapter will focus on that debt, which amounts to almost one-fifth of Latin America's export revenues.

To some extent, how well Latin America fares in the decade to come rests on the progress and prosperity of the developed world. If terms of its international trade are unfavorable and the demand for exports falls, an additional 5 percent of the region's population will be condemned to poverty by the year 2000. To help with Latin America's development, the industrialized countries must bring to the table a growth rate of about 3 percent, lower interest rates, and an improvement in the terms of trade. None of these is guaranteed.

In all, Latin America faces an uncertain future. The region will remain populated by a very few "haves" and many "have-nots" for many years to come. Yet the 1990s offer the best opportunities for improvement that Latin America has ever had. The political commitment to democracy and market reforms combined with a strong global economy offer glimmers of hope. If governments rely on economic growth to improve the plight of the poor, and neglect social services, the poor will be unable to take advantage of any new opportunities. Yet prospects for increased trade—both with the U.S. and among the Latin American countries themselves—will benefit the region the most in the long term. If these opportunities are managed well, the 1990s need not be another lost decade.

C H A P T E R   2 0

···

Overdue Bills

"Growing trade will someday enable the Latin American economies to survive without the help of their richer neighbors. But debt slows growth, especially when meeting the payments costs nearly one-fifth of export revenues."

···

Since the early 1980s, American economists have spent a significant part of their time wondering when the "debt bomb," the mass of unrepaid and unrepayable Latin American borrowing, would finally go off, destroying many of the largest U.S. banks, and perhaps even the American banking system. In the 1990s, the debt bomb still will not go off; instead, it will begin to go away.

When President George Bush returned from his tour of five Latin American countries in late 1990, he left a region that was $429 billion dollars in debt—$24 billion of that in overdue interest payments to commercial banks. Brazil and Argentina owe nearly 40 percent of the entire Third World's debt between them. These countries, as well as Chile, Uruguay, and Venezuela, have undertaken major efforts to restructure their economies. More than their ability to repay their tremendous debts, will hinge on the success of the reforms. The stability of these new democracies also hangs in the balance.

North American banks that were eager to recycle their large holdings of petrodollars fueled large government deficits in the late 1970s and early 1980s. Regional governments took advantage of the easy cash to begin ambitious development plans. When the easy money supply slowed in the 1980s, many Latin American governments borrowed at home and printed more money. Inflation in the severely indebted, middle-income Latin American countries spiraled out of control by the late eighties. Inflation measured at over 100 percent between 1980 and 1987. In 1989 the Brazilian government called a 30 percent *monthly* inflation rate "stable." Because the debtor countries had been living beyond their means, they were forced to reduce demand. The resulting recessions squeezed the incomes of the poor, who were the most vulnerable to the drop in the demand for labor.

The economies of the Latin American countries were further shocked by a combination of higher interest rates and less favorable terms of trade that cut real incomes. Lower commodity prices hurt the value of Mexico and Venezuela's oil exports. They also indirectly damaged the non-oil producing countries of Cuba and Brazil. The Soviet Union had allowed its island client to reexport any leftover oil from the heavily subsidized oil-for-sugar swaps. Until oil prices fell, Cuba had been able to rake in a handsome profit—in fact, up to 40 percent of its hard currency. Brazil, recognizing that its oil dependency compromised its national security, invested heavily in a "gasahol" program. While oil prices soared, the Brazilian program bolstered national morale and remained relatively cost-efficient. The lower oil prices, however, made gasahol seem extravagant. (The conversion to gasahol was never completed, however. Brazil still imports a significant amount of oil; the Persian Gulf War has cost it several billion dollars in higher petroleum prices.)

The Latin American countries have pursued different approaches for managing their problems of debt. Mexico ($97.4 billion in debt at the end of 1989) and Chile ($18.9 billion) have regularly serviced their debts without overdue interest payments. Chile has determined to stop borrowing from the IMF until 1992.

Colombia ($17 billion) and Venezuela ($33 billion) have faithfully serviced their debts and have negotiated to refinance them when necessary.

Peru ($20.3 billion) and Ecuador ($11.4 billion) stopped paying their debts in 1985 and 1987, respectively. Peru owes at least $5 billion to its creditors; President Alberto Fujimori's new government has tried to make amends for the repudiation in order to become eligible again for IMF funding. Ecuador's outstanding commercial interest payments constitute $1.6 billion of its total obligations.

Argentina and Brazil are the worst violators of international financial agreements. Argentina ($59.9 billion) fell increasingly behind in interest payments in the 1980s and stopped servicing most of its commerical debt in 1988; it now lags $7.8 billion behind on those obligations and $4 billion behind on payments to non-bank creditors. Brazil ($114.7 billion) has fallen $8 billion behind in interest outlays, which it has not paid since the summer of 1989. Both the Sarney and Collor governments have claimed that they intend to pay back the money and will not repudiate the loans.

In June 1990, President Bush set his goals for the "Enterprise for the Americas" program:

• First, the United States hopes to develop free trade among open markets throughout the hemisphere. In addition to structural reforms in most of the Latin American countries, this will require the gradual elimination of subsidies and trade barriers. A hemispheric trade agreement would encompass 411 million people and 7.7 million square miles—clearly the largest market ever created.

• Second, the Latin debtor nations must find some way to reduce their enormous debts. The Brady Plan, discussed in Chapter 16, has been moderately successful in reducing commercial debts to date; the Bush administration has higher hopes for the future. The U.S. has also announced that it will supply an additional $100 million to guarantee loans if the European Community and Japan will do the same.

• Third, the U.S. advocates a new economic partnership, maintaining that prosperity depends on "trade not aid."

Even though the Enterprise for the Americas plan offers some help in reducing the enormous Latin American debts, it does not go far enough. The free trade initiative would forgive no more than $12 billion in debt. Far more is needed, for these economies are not yet stable or mature enough to stand on their own. Growing trade will someday enable the Latin American economies to survive without the help of their richer neighbors. But debt slows growth, especially when meeting the payments cost nearly one-fifth of export revenues. With reduced debt, countries can spend that money to strengthen their economies, which will then draw otherwise timid investors. But debt relief is their only way to get there.

Many skeptics regard Bush's Enterprise for the Americas as merely a symbolic reminder that Latin America has not been forgotten in American foreign policy, even though the U.S. been preoccupied by events in Europe, the Soviet Union, and the Persian Gulf. In this view, it may be no more than rhetoric, much like the Bush administration's publicized but unfunded drive to put a manned space colony on Mars. In fact, the plan presents an ideal—something the Latin American countries can aim for while they undergo painful economic restructuring at home. Yet many countries need a trade framework sooner than Bush's loftly proposal offers. Latin America will watch closely for any progress on U.S. plans for a free trade and investment agreement (FTA) with Mexico to determine just how serious Bush's offer really was.

Latin American schemes for economic integration have long consisted of wishes rather than reality. Nonetheless, with the demise of the military governments and the ensuing relaxation of tensions, some programs are in the planning stages.

The Caribbean Basin Initiative (CBI), passed by the U.S. Congress in October 1990, was intended to encourage and support market reforms, debt reduction, and sustenance of the environment. It aims to promote economic growth, stability, and diversification by giving certain products duty-free access to the large American market. The measure has assisted twenty-three beneficiary countries in Central America and the Caribbean by drawing the attention of potential investors to them. Although the CBI has brought some jobs to the islands, little technology has been transferred; most of the businesses that have set up shop in the region are in the apparel industries. Further, it is estimated that for every hundred dollars of revenue, 80 dollars "repatriates" to the mainland.

By the end of 1994, the nations of the Southern Cone—Argentina, Brazil, Paraguay, and Uruguay, but not Chile—hope to erect a tariff-free common market, opening their markets to competition. Such a move could serve as a major impetus for

Bush's hemispheric trade zone ranging from Tierra del Fuego to the western-most tip of Alaska. Tariffs will be lowered by 20 percent each year until none remain. The number of exceptions to free trade will be cut at the same rate.

Similarly, the Andean countries of Bolivia, Colombia, Ecuador, and Peru are moving to expand their trade with one another. To encourage this effort, the United States Congress will consider legislation to lift duties from some of the region's products. Congress will target this extra support largely toward impoverished populations of these countries, in hope of reducing their dependence on the lucrative cocaine trade.

Mexico, El Salvador, Costa Rica, and Panama established a Caribbean Free Trade Zone in early 1991. This could affect Mexico's proposed FTA with the United States, even though the other members are all signatories of the CBI.

Many people have made quick comparisons between economic integration in Latin America and European integration in 1992. Few such comparisons are valid because Latin America lags far behind the EC's tremendous progress. The current situation in Latin America more resembles the European Economic Community of the 1950s, when tariff barriers were cut, but political and further economic integration were still far off. Latin America will not open its borders to allow the free movement of persons, goods, services, and capital for some time to come. Common agricultural policies and the creation of formal institutions are no closer. And so far, no strong, visionary leaders, such as Jean Monnet or Robert Schuman, have stepped forward to lead these efforts.

Latin America simply lacks the philosophical and political motivation that war-torn Europe held. Latin America's drive is not that of the idealist decades following World War II but that of the bottom-line mind-set of the 1990s. Latin leaders recognize that the increasing globalization of trade could make the region insignificant.

A variety of difficult problems will slow the course of Latin American integration. Tremendous poverty is one; inflation, so extreme that it makes official exchange rates meaningless, is another. And the countries often compete in the same markets with very similar products; they have not carved out market niches for themselves. Protectionism and subsidies are also more severe than those in Europe, and the economic systems are not as mature, stable, or uniform. Coordinating auto-industry policies alone will present a difficult challenge, especially as Brazil's gasohol program is unique to the region. Business environments in Great Britain and Portugal are dissimilar, of course, but the gulf between Chile and Peru is much more vast. When a recession occurs in Chile, residents of Santiago have to forgo wine with their dinners (which is not so terrible, considering the quality of some of the formerly state-produced vintages); citizens of Peru are lucky to have a dinner to eat.

Chile has largely disowned its less successful neighbors in the region. Rather than joining a regional free trade agreement, Chile would prefer one directly with the U.S., much like the proposed FTA with Mexico. Chilean industry lacks the subsidies and nontariff barriers that cripple trade between countries. In short, Chile has embraced free-market reforms more lovingly than even Mexico. President Patricio Alwyn has courted foreign investors and would like to privatize the remaining state-owned companies. Although the economy is not as large, and the distance from the U.S. is greater, the signal given by any pact between Chile and the U.S. will be clear to the other Latin American countries. Chile's example should inspire a stronger push for reforms and privatization throughout the region.

In addition to these efforts at regional integration, the Latin American nations have signed a number of bilateral agreements. This is typical of the early days of economic unification. Even the EEC jump-started itself with a series of bilateral and trilateral treaties. The Benelux countries proved in the late 1940s that a customs union could be successful. And the European Coal and Steel Cooperation helped to knit together the economies of France and Germany. The two former adversaries had fought over the resource-rich region of Alsace-Lorraine in several wars, trading it back and forth. The ECSC proved to be a peaceful solution to an historically vexing problem.

Energy and security concern most of Latin America's treaties. Argentina, Brazil, and Uruguay have cooperated on the construction of a major hydroelectric dam on their borders. Although Argentina is almost bankrupt, it has agreed to start paying its natural gas bills to Bolivia. Venezuela has declared its willingness to cooperate within the region by selling oil to its neighbors at less than market prices. In November 1990, Argentina and Brazil signed a nuclear pact to provide for inspections of each other's plants. Argentina, Brazil, and Chile have also signed a security pact to help with drug interdiction and environmental protection.

Bilateral agreements have also promoted economic growth in some parts of Latin America. Trade between Argentina and Brazil, the region's two largest powers, increased from $1 billion in 1985 to $2.3 billion in 1990. Companies on both sides of the border have opened offices on the other side to examine trade possibilities. Argentina and Brazil have also agreed to reduce tariffs by 40 percent within a year and to implement further reductions of 7 percent by the end of 1994.

The debt crisis triggered the current trend toward privatization. Throughout the region, governments have begun to sell state-owned enterprises to private owners or to shift the operation to private-sector managers. Most have finally acted because they could not afford to support state-owned enterprises that lost money; some have grudging accepted that privatization will ease the burdens of bureaucracy. State-owned enterprises have seldom proved to be efficient producers of high-quality products. Instead, they often have drained government coffers in the name of the national interest. For example, losses from the Dominican Republic's state-owned enterprises reached 3.6 percent of the island's GDP in 1987.

Privatization has not always gone smoothly. In one of Argentina's periodic cabinet reshufflings, early in 1991, the minister who planned to sell off Argentina's 150 state-owned companies lost his portfolio, and his ministry was dismantled. Later that January, with no warning, inflation soared out of control, and the markets panicked after several months of welcome stability. Privatization will probably continue out of economic necessity, though many Peronists find the planned sales of the railroads and the national mint especially galling. Potential investors must be careful to keep a low profile, so as not to antagonize other Latin Americans who resent the fire sale—especially to foreigners—of their cherished communications systems, power companies, shipping lines, port authorities, and oil companies, no matter how ineptly they have been handled in the past.

Brazil, the region's other heavy debtor, plans to sell its steel company and four other state companies valued at $5 billion, by March 1991. By 1992, President Collor hopes to sell twenty other companies worth $19 billion.

Plans for privatization are similar to the start of a game of Monopoly, when everything is up for sale by the bank. In this Latin American version of the game, however, not everyone begins with the same amount of money. Those who already have money are bound to prosper. Those who lack capital are in danger of being worse off than they were before the game started. (At least in Latin America, unlike Eastern Europe, the players can agree in advance who owns the land, and the players understand the rules.) If privatization is to improve life in Latin America, governments there must use the money they receive to ensure that the poor do not suffer during the economic transition.

For its part, as the United States encourages the structural reforms now taking place in the indebted countries, it will arrange to write off more of the debt, using credits for American products, much as it forgave the loans made to Europe during the World Wars. (Only Finland ever repaid its debt.) Parts of Latin America need a new Marshall Plan almost as much as Europe did then. In the long run, generosity in the 1990s will bring the United States future rewards: A stronger hemisphere will provide better markets for its goods and make it easier to stem the migration northward. Full Latin American integration will not take place by 2000, or for several years after that. Partial integration on a smaller scale, such as a free trade area among the countries of the Southern Cone, will be well under way by the turn of the century.

··

Saving the Amazon and the Economy

··

"Brazil will work to conserve parts of the rain forest if the U.S. will forgive portions of its enormous foreign debt. It is little to ask: Brazil refuses to service its debt until it can renegotiate its loans, while lenders refuse to renegotiate until Brazil ends its undeclared moratorium."

··

Latin America's financial efforts alone will not solve the continent's problems. Anticipating future recovery, most commercial banks are reluctant to write off the enormous debts completely. Debt-for-nature swaps, modeled on earlier debt-for-equity swaps, may provide some long-term relief for both troubled economies and beleaguered environments.

Rain forests exist as narrow bands around the equator and account for 6 percent of the earth's land surface. Brazil holds 30 percent of the world's rain forests. The Amazon River basin covers 3.6 million square miles, twice the size of India. On average, 96 inches of rain falls there each year. Most of this precipitation falls daily during the afternoon showers in the wet season. The Amazon river disgorges 170 billion gallons of water each hour into the Atlantic.

Over half of all the earth's life forms are found in the rain forests; this includes 90 percent of all insect species. More species of plants live in Brazil's tropical forest than in any other country. This includes one fabled rubber tree with fruit that explodes in order to scatter its seeds over 20 yards away. One-fifth of all bird species inhabit this region, as do some mammals ranging from three-toed tree sloths to pink porpoises.

But while the rain forest hosts a plethora of species, many species are represented by very few members. Forest areas 50 miles from each other have been shown to share only one percent of their species. Thus the destruction of small segments of rain forest dooms certain species to extinction and reduces biodiversity. This is cause for practical as well as ethical concern, for the rain forest has been dubbed a "living pharmacy." One-fourth of all prescription drugs contain ingredients derived from tropical plants. Less than one percent of the plants have been studied. Some may not survive long enough to be collected and examined; some could offer cures for cancer or AIDS or clues that would lead to them. Decreases in the ecosystem's biodiversity also means that fewer pools of genetic materials will be available to add to cultivated plants. A lesson from the 1845 Irish potato famine: diversity helps limit the damage of widespread disease.

Since preindustrial times, one-fifth of all forests have disappeared. Much of the loss occurred in temperate North America and Europe. Until recently, the largely inaccessible rain forests have been spared. According to the World Resources Institute, tropical deforestation now clears 16.4 to 20.4 million hectares a year, an area the size of Washington state. Brazil endures the greatest losses of any one country. The National Space Research Institute of Brazil used infrared satellite images showing smoke from fires to calculate that eight million hectares were lost in 1987. In the past decade, fires and chain saws have consumed over 10 percent of the rain forest. During the "burning season," the two-month period between the dry and wet seasons, many Amazonians (mostly rich ranchers and small farmers) set fires to clear out fields or recently deforested land. Living trees consume carbon and emit oxygen; burning trees release carbon, double jeopardy for the massing carbon in the earth's atmosphere. Climatologists in Brazil estimate that the burning of the Amazon contributes one-fourth of all global carbon dioxide emissions.

Every day, between 70,000 and 140,000 acres of rain forest are cleared for timber, cattle husbandry, and agriculture. The International Timber Organization found that only 0.13 percent of the rain forest logging can be classified as sustainable. Nearly 80 percent of the would-be farmers cannot subsist on the land that they have altered. Many, instead of giving up, try and try again by moving farther into the rain forest. Brasilia estimates that land-grabbing farmers have already destroyed 5 percent of the jungle; some scientists claim that between 7 and 12 percent is more realistic.

Widespread deforestation brings far-reaching changes in the tropical forest ecosystems which can no longer help to retain water, control the climate, and conserve the soil. The forests may even promote rainfall, rather than merely soak up the downpours; that is, if the forest were to disappear, so might the rain. The region would then be afflicted by higher temperatures, drought, and perhaps eventual desertification.

Brasilia has fallen under growing scrutiny as it seeks to take advantage of the country's resources. Two studies conducted by the World Bank, by Hans Binswanger and Dennis Mahar, showed that subsidies and tax allowances have spurred deforestation. (The Brazilian government has characterized the clearing of the rain forest as "improvement." However, in 1988 the government repealed old tax laws that promoted the clearing of the forest.) Clearly, the destruction of the rain forest is a loss for both the world and the Brazilian government. But these programs continue because they benefit the powerful, who are close to the government while the poor forest-dwellers lack influence.

Pressured by the U.S. Congress to adopt a new policy of refusing to support development that destroys the rain forest, the World Bank and the Inter-American Development Bank suspended loans of the $300 million needed for paving the road to Rio Branco, Acre's state capital. Financial officials were not impressed when Brazil failed to create the forest reserves that it had promised. Earlier, the BR364 highway between Cuiaba and Porto Velho opened Rondônia state to the hundreds of thousands of settlers who destroyed 23 percent of the state's forest before determining that the land there is unsuitable for farming.

Japanese banks, on the other hand, are eager to fund a new road through the jungle that will link Brazil to Peru's network of the trans-Andean highway, giving Brazil access to the Pacific Ocean. Brazil asserts that Acre needs to be freed of its isolation. The distance to the Pacific Coast via Peru will be half as short as the length to Brazilian ports. Japan currently buys 40 percent of the world market's supply of tropical logs. But since Indonesia and Malaysia have banned the export of their logs, Japan has sought a new supply. Until now, logging has caused less than 5 percent of the rain forest's damage. This fraction will grow when the road is completed.

U.S. Senators Timothy Worth and Albert Gore protested to Japanese member of Parliament Yoshiro Mori. The senators asked that Japanese banks demand environmental standards like those applied by the World Bank when issuing loans. President Bush also discussed the matter with former Japanese prime minister Noboru Takeshita at Emperor Hirohito's funeral. Former president Jose Sarney became so enraged at this "meddling" that he named the highway a national priority, with or without Japanese credits.

Yet Brasilia has met opposition to its development ambitions at home as well. Government planners intend the Amazon region to provide one-third of the country's energy by 2010. The $5.8 billion Kararao hydroelectric dam on the Xingu River will flood Indian lands and virgin forest. Brazil rejects protests by Indians and ecologists, noting that it must import expensive oil and has been discouraged from working on its nuclear program. The outcry will grow louder in the next few years when Brazil attempts to exploit its rich deposits of iron ore and other minerals.

Francisco Alves "Chico" Mendes Filho, the leader of the rubber tappers and a conservationist who had organized the native Indians, has become a martyr for those who oppose the burning of the jungle. In December 1990 two ranchers were convicted for his murder two years earlier. Had Chico Mendes not been so popular abroad, they probably would not have been brought to justice. The Americas Watch noted, in a February 1991 report, that in Brazilian land disputes between 1964 and 1989, only 17 trials and eight convictions resulted from the murders of 1,566 farm and church workers and other activists. The paper noted that "violence is the quick and dirty way for rural elites to dispose of community and union 'troublemakers' who dispute their right to maintain thousands of acres of land uncultivated."

While Brazil possesses the largest rain forest of any country, the Amazon jungle crosses over national borders. The different countries have adopted their own approaches to managing this vital resource. The Colombian government granted its native Indians rights to land twice the size of Scotland. While Bogota gave away one-third of the country's territory, it retained the mineral rights. The European Community donated $386,000 to assist the Indians who will administer this inaccessible region, which has also been plagued by sporadic guerilla activity and drug-running. Peru and Venezuela have yielded tracts of forest to their Indians, but these small areas are inadequate for the Indians' migratory mix of hunting and cultivation. Technically, Brazil has given Indians forest reserves but has often abused the land anyway.

Brazil's desperate economic straits make it difficult to focus on the environment when there are so many people who clamor to be fed and housed first. The United Nations noted in its *Environmental Perspective to the Year 2000 and Beyond* that mass poverty is at the root of environmental degradation; sustained development will require equitable access to environmental resources. And because environmental changes in one sector affect others, international cooperation and conflict resolution is needed. The safeguarding of species "is a moral obligation humankind, and should improve and sustain human well-being," the U.N. has declared.

Brazil has taken quick offense to efforts by the United States to "dictate" to it about the need for conservation. Brazil regards this as a breach of its sovereignty. It also considers the U.S. as hypocritical in its concern. After all, Brazilians point out, American colonialists and pioneers cleared out temperate forests to make room for civilization with scant regard for native Americans. The U.S. responds that it wronged the native Americans, and that there is no need to repeat its mistakes. Further, America's westward expansion occurred over many decades. Brazilian development has produced a sudden and dramatic threat to the worldwide environment.

Another parallel may be more valid: The U.S. continues to cut down its forest in the Tomgass in northern Alaska. American taxpayers shell out $100 million each year to cover the costs of harvesting the cheap timber. Subsidies thus encourage logging in America's last great temperate rain forest where it is too arid and too cold for the forest to grow back.

Brazil also objects to American "intervention" because the industrialized countries have contributed far more to pollution by emitting gasses that deplete the ozone layer. The average American uses up 15 times more energy than the average Brazilian. And Americans have happily furnished their houses with Amazonian wood. Brazilians want the U.S. to put its money where its mouth is.

Brasilia first saw the concept of "debt-for-nature swaps" as "environmental colonialism"; President Sarney feared that debt-for-nature swaps could transform the jungle into an international zone, a "green Persian Gulf." (Considering that the world has acted to safeguard its vital interests in the Persian Gulf, Sarney may have had something of a point.) Since then, though, Brazil has realized that these financial transactions can serve its interests well, and the government now seems willing to pursue the debt-for-nature swaps. That is, Brazil will work to conserve parts of the rain forest if the U.S. will forgive portions of its enormous foreign debt. It is relatively little to ask: Brazil refuses to service its debt until it can renegotiate the terms of its loans, while the lending agencies refuse to renegotiate until Brazil ends its undeclared moratorium.

A debt-for-nature swap involves the release of local currency for conservation at home together with the cancellation of debt abroad. It is more or less a "win-win" situation for the concerned country. The bank holding a country's debt writes off the face value from taxes after selling the loan to conservationists at a deep discount. The country's central bank then redeems the debt and issues local currency bonds equal to the amount of the entire debt. Local conservation groups then may use the interest on the bonds for their own projects. World Wildlife Fund (WWF) Director Thomas Lovejoy proposed the transactions in 1984 to help the economically poor but environmentally rich countries. Development aid, such as the roads and dam featured above, often hurts ecology.

Such arrangements have met with success in smaller Costa Rica, Ecuador, and Bolivia since 1987. In Costa Rica, the Nature Conservancy, the WWF, and others purchased $11 million worth of debt in 1987 and again in 1989 to preserve and increase parklands. If Costa Rica had continued clearing 7.4 percent of its forest a year (the 1983 rate figured by the World Resources Institute), almost all of the country's forest would have been destroyed by 2000. In Ecuador the WWF contributed to reducing

$10 million of debt in order to protect and manage national parks both on the mainland and the symbolically important Galapagos Islands where Charles Darwin observed finches and formulated his theory of natural selection. Conservation International bought $650,000 of external debt to allow the Bolivian government to reserve 3.7 million acres of tropical forest.

To save the forests of Mata Atlantica, the region between Rio de Janeiro and São Paulo, conservation groups were able to purchase up to $100 million of Brazil's debt at a discount. Brazil's central bank then issued local currency bonds with a face value worth the amount of the original debt, and local environmental groups now use the interest for their projects. Luis Inacio "Lula" da Silva, a former union leader and contender for the presidency in 1989, applauded the linkage of Brazil's foreign debt to protection of the Amazon. "If the Amazon is the lungs of the planet, then Brazil's foreign debt is the pneumonia," he declared.

Debt-for-nature swaps are not a solution by themselves, but they will play a significant part in the recovery of the Latin American economies and the preservation of the rain forest for the next ten years and beyond. They still have a few drawbacks that must be monitored closely—especially their contribution to future inflation when they increase domestic spending.

Conservation has been proven to be much more profitable, economically as well as ecologically, than the slashing-and-burning of the rain forest. Environmentalists have regarded the free market with skepticism, imagining robber barons interested in quick profit turnarounds and little else. But market mechanisms may be one of the most sensible and persuasive ways to convince politicians that saving the environment is in their own best interest. For instance, governments that control the forests located on public lands have allowed heavy logging but do not auction off logging rights (as the U.S. auctions off oil-drilling rights). If they would sell the rights, conservationists could bid in order to have the trees left alone. The value of selling the logs would not be as great, especially when compared to the costs of extra carbon in the atmosphere, less rainfall, decreased water supplies, soil erosion, and silting rivers. (A complication to this plan would be bidding by the Japanese, once the road to Peru has been built.)

Charles Peters, Alwyn Gentry, and Robert Mendelsohn have shown that harvesting rubber, acai (the fruit of the palm tree), and nine other fruits and saps yielded twice the average Peruvian wage for the people of Combu. The *WorldPaper* reports that fifteen natural products growing on one hectare can be worth as much as $8,500, compared to $1,000 for the wood or $2,900 in cattle that destroy the forest. Other studies have revealed that one acre of sustained rain forest is worth approximately three times as much as an acre of cattle pasture and twice as much as the timber on it. The exact figures do not matter as much as the illustration that the living rain forest is worth much more than the "improvements" the Brazilian government has been determined to make. To compensate for the cost-ineffectiveness of the cattle ranchers, for instance, Brasilia has subsidized beef so heavily that local meat costs four times as much as imported beef.

The marketing of the rain forest will not be easy, however. The lack of infrastructure makes it difficult to transport products, especially from deep inside where there are no roads. The development of roads would be a Catch-22: they would make it easier to enter the depths of the rain forest to retrieve renewable resources; and because ranchers and farmers would quickly take advantage of the opening of new land, roads could destroy the rain forest they were meant to save. The complexity of the rain forest will make developing homogeneous products difficult unless products are derived from the same area consistently.

Markets still must be created for many of the products. This process has already begun. U.S. companies have come up with novel ways to "save the rain forest." Cultural Survival, Inc., formed the Rain Forest Marketing Project in 1989 to develop international markets for non-timber and nonharmful rain forest products. Cultural Survival brings more than two hundred products out of Brazil, including nuts, dried fruits, frozen fruit pulp, oils, and pigments. But the nonprofit trading group, while funneling ever-increasing profits back into Brazil, has not yet attracted any mainstream companies.

Cultural Survival's largest customer is Ben Cohen's new company Community Products, Inc., which had projected 1990 sales of its Rain Forest Crunch candy to be over $1.5 million. Half of its Brazil nut and cashew brittle goes to the Vermont headquarters of Ben & Jerry's Homemade, Inc., makers of Ben & Jerry's ice cream, of course, and their newest flavor is Rain Forest Crunch. Ben & Jerry's donates 7.5 percent of pretax profits to nonprofit groups; Community Products has pledged 60 percent of its profits to a variety of groups.

Cultural Survival also buys Brazilian products for The Body Shop, a natural cosmetic shop chain that markets organic products. The British firm, which has a reputation for its staunch opposition to animal testing, hopes to create a line of products derived from the rain forest. A Brazil nut hair conditioner will soon join the some three hundred items in the product line.

The Tagua Initiative, spearheaded by Conservation International, persuaded Patagonia, Inc., and Smith & Hawken to buy buttons made from the tagua nut in order to provide economic incentive to thousands of Ecuadorians. Loblaw International hopes to add rain forest products to its already established $21 million "ecologically friendly" Green Line in its supermarket chains.

The United Nations has suggested that every country should consider the environment when formulating plans. It will play a larger role in environmental policy in the next ten years. To prevent singling out "environmental thugs" such as Brazil, the U.N. will agree to tie talks on the conservation of the rain forest to other environmental conventions. For instance, a conference should cover not only the "greenhouse" effect, to which the burning of the rain forest contributes, but also such related issues as air pollution, ozone depletion, water use, and sea pollution.

Such a conference has been scheduled for 1992. The U.N. Conference on Development and Environment will mark the largest environmental event in the last 30 years. Government representatives will take stock of events in the last few decades and will develop a road map for the years ahead. Many of their concerns over biodiversity, the greenhouse effect, land degradation, and deforestation will involve the future of the Amazon rain forest. In this unavoidably politicized setting, the industrialized countries will have to pledge to cut back on their own emissions if they hope to persuade Brazil to stop squandering its treasure. Brazil can be convinced by the continuation of debt-for-nature swaps and the complete end of aid for development that harms the environment. Further encouragement will include tax breaks for companies that market the Amazon's renewable resources.

The message will get through. Already, more than 75 percent

of those surveyed for a Harris poll in Latin America, Asia, and Africa voiced concern over the loss of trees in their homeland and elsewhere. Even in relatively undemocratic lands, that degree of support for the environment will eventually change government policies.

In the next few years, conservationists hope to change significantly the way ecological decisions are made. If they have their way, governments will allocate at least 10 percent of the rain forest as pristine parkland. State-of-the-country addresses will discuss changes in the environment. Filing environmental impact statements will become de rigueur. By the turn of the century, many such measures will be enacted.

THE HAVE-NOTS:

The Other Asia

•••

Lands Without Hope

"For countries with few internal resources, the only way to raise the standard of living is to buy needed supplies and technology from outside. Those purchases must be paid for with export profits. In Asia, these are difficult to come by, even in the best of times."

•••

We have saved for last, in this "Have-not" section, the region with the most uniformly dismal prospects, not merely for the remainder of this century, but as far into the next as can be glimpsed, however dimly. Outside the Pacific Rim trading nations, the countries of Asia share a variety of problems, any one of which would make it difficult to improve their economic and social conditions. All are burdened by poverty and overpopulation. They have few natural resources on which to build a more modern economy. All suffer from governments that are corrupt, inefficient, or repressive, and frequently all three.

And there is war. Since the Japanese invaded the region in the early days of World War II, bullets and bombs have been almost constant companions throughout much of Asia.

Vietnam, Laos, and Cambodia were virtually destroyed by the French Indochina and Vietnam Wars, a period of uninterrupted combat that lasted for 26 years. An estimated 1.5 million people died in Vietnam between 1961 and 1972. Another 6.5 million became refugees. Massive American bombings obliterated industry in the northern part of the country, and lesser assaults damaged much of the productive capacity in the south. Neither part of Vietnam has ever recovered from the destruction.

India and Pakistan have fought each other three times in four decades, not counting frequent border clashes. The two first went to war in 1948, only a year after they were granted independence from Britain, over the question of which owned the wealthy provinces of Kashmir and Jammu. The same argument led to war again in 1965, and in 1971 a Bengali uprising in Pakistan flared into a two-week battle.

The battle was longer and far more destructive in Bangladesh, which gained its existence when India and Pakistan declared their most recent truce. During nine months of fighting, an estimated one million Bengalis were killed in what was then East Pakistan, and ten million more fled to India.

India seems perpetually on the edge of several revolutions at once. Hindus battle Muslims, Sikh separatists wage a terrorist campaign to establish their own state, and several lesser ethnic groups are seeking independence. We will examine these movements more closely in the next chapter.

In Myanmar, still better known as Burma, at least 20 small insurgent groups struggle for independence against the bloody martial-law regime. The Karen minority have been fighting continuously for independence since Burma received its sovereignty in 1949.

Cambodia has been at war with itself and its neighbors since 1969, when American bombers began to attack Vietcong and North Vietnamese troops based there. In just four years in the late 1970s, under the communist Khmer Rouge occupation, more than one million of its people fell victim to deliberate starvation, overwork, and the firing squad. Since then, the Khmer Rouge and two non-communist resistance groups have been fighting the Vietnamese-backed government.

This chapter will be brief, for there is very little to be said about the future of these lands. For most, the years to come will differ little from the recent past. Stability will elude them. Their populations will continue to grow. And despite tentative investments by a few Pacific Rim corporations, no end to their poverty is yet in sight. Only India and Vietnam seem to hold any possibility of change, and we will save them for later chapters.

A few basic numbers show how far these countries must go

to provide their people with a decent living, and how difficult it will be for them to get there:

• Bangladesh packs 118 million people into an area less than half the size of Italy, or roughly as large as the American state of North Carolina—more than two thousand per square mile and the number is growing by nearly 3 percent per year. Each square mile of potential farmland must feed nearly 3,200 people, using technologies most of which were available a millennium ago. Per capita GNP is about $150, per capita income $120. There is only one doctor to every 6,200 people. Life expectancy for men is 54; for women it is 53. Fourteen children out of every hundred die in infancy. And in 1988, 1989, and 1990 flooding and other natural disasters rendered some thirty-million people homeless and killed several hundred-thousand.

• Cambodia has a population just under seven million. Only 16 percent of its land is arable, so each square mile under cultivation must support 625 individuals. Its people produce $960 worth of goods and services each year. Since the bloody reign of the Khmer Rouge, there have been too few doctors in Cambodia to be statistically or medically significant. The average man lives only 47 years, the average woman, only 50. The infant mortality rate is more than 13 percent.

• Laos has a population of four million. Only 3,700 square miles of its territory is suitable for farming; the rest is jungle. There are so few doctors that each must serve 6,500 potential patients. Life expectancy is 48 years for men, 51 for women. Nearly thirteen of every hundred children die in their first years of life. With a gross national product equal to less than $125 per person, Laos may be the poorest nation in the world. Uganda, Malawi, and Guinea-Bissau are wealthier than Laos.

• Myanmar is home to some 41 million people and over 1,040 per square miles of crop land. As of 1989, its per capita income was $210. There is one doctor for every 3,500 people. Newborn males can look forward to 53 years of life, newborn females to 56 years. One child in ten dies before maturity.

• Pakistan meagerly supports 1,460 people per square mile of arable land, over 113 million in all. With a per capita income of $360 and only one physician for every 2,200 people, the Pakistani people have a life expectancy of about 55 Roughly one in eight dies an infant.

For a sense of scale, contrast these statistics with those of Portugal, the poorest nation in the European Community. Some 10.5 million Portuguese inhabit an area of little more than 36,000 square miles. Just under one-third of that land mass is arable, so Portugal must support more than 900 people per square mile of potential farmland. Per capita income in 1986 was already nearly $3,000. There is one doctor for every 388 people. Men live an average of 71 years, women 78. Fewer than one infant in sixty-five dies.

Look also at the United States, still the world's richest land, though Japan will soon overtake it. The U.S. population is just over 250 million people. American farmers support 330 people per square mile of potential farmland, and still managed to export more than $41 billion worth of agricultural commodities in 1989. America's GNP of $4.8 trillion in 1988 was $19,200 per capita, the highest in the world. Per capita income was $16,444, also the current record. The United States has one doctor for every 410 people, one hospital bed for every 188. Its life expectancy is 71 for men, 79 for women. Its infant mortality rate is ten per thousand.

People traditionally divided the world into East and West and spoke of the philosophical and material gulf between them. More recently, it has become fashionable to speak of a gap between the North and the South, between the wealthy, industrialized hemisphere and the poor, agrarian one. Yet there are more fundamental differences than location between the wealthy lands of the West and the poor ones of Asia. Singapore, after all, comfortably supports more than 2.7 million people with less than twenty-five square miles of arable land. Its per capita GNP in 1988 was nearly $8,800. It has less in common with its poorer neighbors than with Paris or New York.

One factor that dooms Asia to continuing poverty is its birth rate. Portugal's population is growing at a rate of only half a percent per year, that of the United States by 0.6 percent—one-fourth of the Asian average. Despite its high rate of infant mortality, Bangladesh ended 1990 with over 3.5 million more people than it had when the year began. Pakistan's population grows by nearly 3 percent each year, the populations of Cambodia, Laos, and Myanmar by more than 2 percent. Simply to avoid sinking deeper into poverty, their economies must grow as much as their populations do every year. It will not happen.

Almost uniformly, these are agricultural economies. In Laos, 85 percent of the labor force works in farming, only 6 percent in industry. Pakistan's economy is the most industrialized in the region. Yet more than half of the nation's people still toil on its farms; only 13 percent work in industry. In any of these lands, crop failure means starvation.

For countries with few internal resources, the only way to raise the standard of living is to buy needed supplies and technology from outside. Those purchases must be paid for with export profits. In Asia, these are difficult to come by even in the best of times. Bangladesh produces most of the world's jute, weaving some of it into burlap before shipment; this one industry accounts for a large part of the country's external sales. Cambodia's only significant industries are rice milling, wood, and natural rubber. Laos depends almost solely on forest products. Myanmar and Pakistan have modest reserves of oil and natural gas, but they rely on agriculture for much of their foreign trade. Natural rubber, and to some extent jute, are quickly being replaced by synthetic materials, and many of the food products grown in the region face competition from the European Community's subsidized exports. These are not commodities on which to build a stable, profitable economy.

Even within the limits set by their resources, the poor nations of Asia have not prospered. With export sales of $4.5 billion in 1988, Pakistan has by far the region's largest income from foreign trade. But that amounts to less than 40 dollars per capita. In the same year, Myanmar earned only $3.36 per person in foreign trade, Cambodia $1.32. For comparison, Portugal exports $1,187 per person per year, the United States $1,452, and Japan more than $2,205. In all these lands, imports take out of the country far more currency than exports bring in. In Pakistan and Myanmar, the net value of imports is more than half again the value of exports. In the neighboring lands, it is three to five times more.

One reason for this is a nearly complete lack of the basic infrastructure needed to conduct business. Roads, transportation, and communications networks are primitive throughout the region. Pakistan has the best supply of cars, trucks, and telephones among these lands. There is one car for every 210 people, one commercial vehicle for every 715. Telephones are somewhat more common, but at one for every 159 people, they are still too scarce to support a modern economy. Bangladesh is far worse off: It has only one passenger car for every 2,900 residents, only one commercial vehicle per 4,720, and 568 people have to share each telephone. Laos has one radio for every ten people, but virtually no televisions or telephones outside the capital of Vientiane. Throughout much of Asia, it is nearly impossible to ship products from field to factory to port, or to report their arrival and arrange their sale once they get there.

The other obstacle in each of these nations is the government that purports to administer them. Bangladesh officially is an Islamic republic; Pakistan, a parliamentary democracy. Laos is a communist state; Myanmar, a military dictatorship. Amid Cambodia's decades-long civil war, there is no effective government at all. None of these regimes has the popular support necessary to guarantee its own existence or the effective control over its territory required to promote the welfare of its citizens, assuming it were inclined to do so.

Ironically, the most durable of these regimes is probably the communist government of Laos, where any possible administration would have the least to offer its people. Its reign has been essentially unchallenged since 1975, when Pathet Lao forces vanquished the army of the coalition government led by Prince Souvanna Phouma. But approximate stability is all the communists have brought to Laos, which remains mired in poverty. To support their ineffectual rule, the communists spend more than 10 percent of the nation's GNP on defense.

To some extent, Bangladesh and Pakistan resemble the countries of Latin America. They are nations where the forms of democracy may be observed, but the substance has never developed (though in Latin America at least, this may finally be changing).

Until recently, Bangladesh was ruled by General Hussain Mohammad Ershad, who took power in a bloodless coup in 1982. Late in 1990, Ershad resigned after a series of increasingly violent protests against corruption and voter fraud. Early in 1991, new elections had yet to be held. There seems little prospect that any new leader will succeed in stabilizing this trouble-prone country.

And without an effective mandate, he will be no more able to ease the chronic destitution of his people than Ershad has been. Bangladesh will not become significantly more stable or prosperous in the remainder of the 1990s.

In Pakistan, the first elected government since the 1970s was dissolved by a semi-constitutional coup after only two years in power. During that time, Benazir Bhutto's administration built little more than a reputation for corruption and incompetence. Her brief tenure has been replaced by a coalition of nine mostly right-wing parties with relatively little in common but their opposition to Bhutto. The coalition, known collectively as the Islamic Democratic Alliance, seems unlikely to achieve much in the way of stability. In that case, the coming decade will see a resurgence of the deep-seated ethnic rivalries between the Punjab majority and the Sindhi, Pushtun, Urdu, and Baluchi minorities. Pakistan's $17.2 billion foreign debt rose quickly during the recent Persian Gulf War, and the need to repay that borrowing will prevent any rapid expansion of development programs. In short, Pakistan's future seems likely to be indistinguishable from its past.

Myanmar's military rulers have turned the former Burma into a "terror state," according to Amnesty International. The description seems apt. They promised to yield power to the National League for Democracy (NLD), which won a landslide victory in the May 1990 elections, but soon reneged. In November, they imprisoned 14 NLD officials and raided 133 Buddhist monasteries whose monks had refused to minister to military families. Since mid-year, the army has expanded to put a quarter of a million men under arms and bought a variety of sophisticated new weapons. It now seems poised to mount an attack on the two dozen or so rebel groups and drug-smuggling gangs that maintain their own armies in Myanmar. As the army has grown stronger, the rebels have weakened. The Burmese communist party, whose army was once the most powerful of the revolutionary groups, has abandoned politics for the more lucrative heroin trade. Karen forces, who had been the strongest of the ethnic rebel groups, have lost many of their men in battle. In the next four or five years, Myanmar will become a more peaceful place, if only because the antigovernment forces will be largely wiped out. This will do nothing to bring democracy or prosperity to this beleaguered land.

That leaves Cambodia, where in 1990 the United Nations worked hard to end the nation's twelve-year civil war, even after developments in the Middle East distracted most of the world's attention. Under the U.N. plan, the government—Pol Pot's Khmer Rouge, and two other warring factions—would have been disarmed and the administration run by United Nations officials until free elections could be held. The scheme collapsed under fears that (1) it would be impossible to verify disarmament of the Khmer Rouge and the other insurgent groups and that (2) turning government ministries over to officials who did not speak the native Khmer language would lead to chaos. The one person who might be capable of reconciling the opposing factions, Prince Norodom Sihanouk, seems unwilling either to throw his support behind any of the competitors or to act as an impartial mediator. In June 1991, the beligerents managed to declare another truce and to renounce foreign military aid. Yet neither the government nor the Khmer Rouge holds a commanding advantage over the other factions, so the situation appears destined to remain as it is, each group running part of the country and no one really in charge.

Economically, it almost does not matter who governs. Cambodia has depended for years on Soviet aid and trade for much of its income and has been hard hit by the USSR's new demand for hard currency and pay-as-you-go approach. Cambodia is doomed to growing poverty, without a new sponsor. None is likely to appear.

If the impoverished nations of Asia hope to improve their living standards, they must find new sources of income. For a time, the flowering of the ASEAN Four inspired a fragile hope that new prosperity would spread throughout Asia. And, in fact, some of the region's wealthier lands are trying to help their less fortunate neighbors. At their government's urging, companies in Thailand have invested in banks in Laos and hotels in Cambodia. But in business there is an old saying: "You can always tell the pioneers; they are the ones lying in the sand with arrows in their backs." There seems little chance that business development in this region will prove profitable. And without that, few new investors are likely to follow these leaders, and the ground-breaking ventures will soon be abandoned.

In all these nations, the economic and political situations appear to be growing worse, not better. None can soon be expected to win even a tiny fraction of the stability and prosperity that we believe the major trading nations will enjoy in the 1990s. More than anywhere else on earth, this is a region without hope.

....

India: Caste, Creed, and Civil War

"One of the most troublesome influences working to undermine India's domestic tranquility is the government itself, and the political elite that dominates it."

....

Throughout the decades of the 1920s, '30s, and '40s, the residents of India strove to gain their freedom from British rule. In the 1990s, they may regret their decision. The order that the Raj impressed on the subcontinent may have been imposed violently and at the behest of a foreign monarch, but it was order nonetheless, and native Indians in the nineteenth century enjoyed all the rights accorded to any subject of the Empire. As the twentieth century nears its end, both order and personal rights are an increasingly distant memory.

Late in 1990, the government proposed to reserve 27 percent of all civil service jobs for "backward classes," a category that includes more than 3,000 ethnic and social groups and half the Indian population. (Another 22.5 percent of government jobs are already reserved for untouchables and members of other "scheduled castes" at the bottom of the rigid Hindu social structure.) At stake were an estimated 50,000 government jobs formerly open to upper-caste Indians. At least 40 young, upper-caste Hindu men and women protested by committing suicide through self-immolation; three times that many more attempted suicide by fire. The government rescinded its order.

A month later, mobs tried to tear down the 462-year-old

mosque in Ayodhya and erect in its place a shrine to the Hindu god Rama. Some 250 people died there, and roughly 300 more were killed in "sympathy" riots in cities in six other states. Another 100,000 were arrested.

In Punjab, where in 1984 government troops stormed the Golden Temple at Amritsar to put down a Sikh rebellion, the separatist movement has grown ever bloodier. At the end of 1990, Sikhs and Hindus in the state were killing each other at a rate of 600 per month. Another separatist rebellion was beginning to simmer in Assam, far to the northeast.

And in Kashmir, which is also claimed by Pakistan, the Indian Border Security Force has tried to repress Muslim insurgents by burning some 4,000 homes and shops and beating, raping, torturing, and often killing those suspected of separatist leanings. The Indian government admits that more than one thousand Kashmiris died in the first year, after a minor insurrection began in the state in the winter of 1989.

This chaos will grow worse for at least the next five years.

One of the most troublesome influences working to undermine India's domestic tranquility is the government itself, and the political elite that dominates it. The last two prime ministers have taken office at the head of fragile coalitions of parties ranging from the religious Right to the Marxist Left. None but the prime minister's own party intended them to last. They were meant only to keep stronger candidates out of office until one of the major opposing factions could gather enough support to seize the position more permanently.

Four major parties are striving to dominate this mess. Each supports one side or the other in the nation's ethnic rivalries, and each has diligently promoted its own cause by fanning extremist passions.

One is the Janata Dal party (JDP) of V.P. Singh, the first of the lame-duck prime ministers. Singh was elected late in 1989 as a reform alternative to the late Rajiv Gandhi. A series of minor scandals during Singh's administration cost him support, and many viewed his attempt to set aside government jobs for the "backward classes" as flagrant vote-buying. Singh won strong Muslim support for his defense of the Ayodyha mosque, but the Muslim vote in parliament was too small to save him when other backers pulled out of the coalition.

The Janata Dal (S) party of Singh's successor, Chandra Shekhar, is a splinter group from the JDP. The "S" stands for Socialist, Shekhar's guiding policy and a popular one in Indian politics.

Rajiv Gandhi's Congress party, the party of his mother, Indira Gandhi, and of Jawaharlal Nehru before her, has led India throughout most of its history as a sovereign nation. It retains a large following among the Hindu majority, but fell into disarray following Rajiv Gandhi's traumatic assassination during the elections of mid-1991.

The fourth major party in Indian politics is the Bharatiya Janata Dal (BJD), a militant Hindu organization. Its long-term goal is to turn India into a "Hindu republic," much as many nations with Muslim majorities have rebuilt their political and legal systems around their dominant religion. The BJD was a major force in the movement to destroy the Ayodhya mosque. An unofficial but popular BJD slogan holds that "The only place for Muslims is in Pakistan or the grave."

The relationship between these contenders has been changing rapidly in the last two years. BJD support went a long way toward keeping former prime minister V.P. Singh in office. His abortive job program for the disadvantaged eroded that cooperation, because it earned Janata Dal a following among lower-caste Hindus, a group the BJD considers their own voting bloc. BJD forced Singh into an unsuccessful vote of confidence when the government arrested party leader Lal Krishnan Advani for fomenting trouble between India's Hindu and Muslim populations. The BJD is now standing aside, trying to build its power base.

Under Singh, the Congress party was out of power. For the moment, it supported Chandra Shekhar's coalition government, an administration it could count on to be easily dislodged when the Congress party had regrouped. It backed out of the arrangement in March 1991, forcing Shekhar out of office. If he hadn't been assassinated, Gandhi could have become prime minister.

In the long run, the BJD may decide India's future. In the last elections, the party won 11 percent of the votes and 86 parliamentary seats. It hopes to double that in the next election, and it may well succeed. Before the decade is over, it could well have enough support among the Hindu community to form its own government. A bloody civil war almost surely would follow.

Muslims form only 11 percent of the population, Sikhs just two percent. But in a population as vast as India's, that amounts to more than 110 million people, all of whom would consider a BJD victory tantamount to a declaration of war against the nation's minorities.

This growing instability could soon begin to inhibit what has been a dramatic improvement in India's standard of living.

Historically, India's trade barriers have been among the highest in the world. Import duties protected native industries from outside competition; even high-tech equipment and capital goods that could not be produced within the country were subjected to stiff tariffs. Businesses were taxed so heavily that it made little sense to accept the risks of starting one. And they were subject to the dictates of a vast bureaucracy, slow-moving, meddlesome, and corrupt. India's economy managed to grow at a rate of about three percent per year, despite this interference. But with the population growing at two percent per year, economic development had little effect on the nation's standard of living.

That changed abruptly in the late 1980s. Many imports are still heavily taxed, but barriers against high-tech goods and production equipment have come down. Business taxes have also been reduced. As a result, real GNP growth jumped to an average of 5.5 percent per year between 1986 and 1989; at times, it touched seven percent. The population is still growing by two percent per year, but that leaves between three and four percent per year of real growth in the standard of living. According to one estimate, this burst of prosperity has lifted more than fifty million people out of poverty in the last five years. Somewhere between 10 and 20 percent of the Indian population now qualifies as middle class.

How long this unaccustomed progress might continue remains unclear. The World Bank has forecast that the Indian GNP will grow by six percent per year in the first half of the 1990s, but that assumes that the country will remain stable. In the late 1980s, India's unique ethnic and social conflicts simmered quietly. Only the tiny Sikh minority developed a coherent separatist movement, and the police siege at the Golden Temple at Amritsar in 1984 appeared to have repressed its most fervent members. As we have seen, that peace is fragile at best.

The subcontinent's traditional flash point is Kashmir, the

northernmost state in India, which was partitioned by the border with Pakistan. Allocation of the predominantly Muslim section of Kashmir to Pakistan and of the mostly Hindu region to India is still disputed by both countries. In 1948, in 1965, and again in 1971, India and Pakistan went to war for possession of Kashmir. The stronger Indian army has always won quickly.

There are signs that war is again not far off, and this time it could be much more destructive. Since 1989, the native Kashmiri separatist movement has grown steadily more active, despite the efforts of 150,000 soldiers and paramilitary men sent in by the New Delhi government to quell it. Benazir Bhutto restrained the Pakistani army, whose sympathies lie with the Muslim insurgents, and held talks with Indian officials in hopes of preventing yet a fourth war between the two countries. Since Bhutto and her civilian government were purged, there have been several border clashes, including at least one involving mortars and heavier artillery. Pakistan appears to have offered sanctuary to the Kashmiri insurgents, and India has accused its neighbor of providing them with training and supplies. So far, the Muslim minority in India proper has tried to distance itself from the problems in Kashmir, fearing that the bloody crackdown against the separatists could grow into a pogrom against all Muslims. The growing threat of the BJD could put an end to that restraint. Any outbreak of war between Muslim Pakistan and Hindu India could rapidly turn into a general revolution in India.

Even if the two sides manage to avert open war, the trend is clearly toward more incidents of rioting, more and more active separatist movements, and more clashes between the Hindu castes. And the issue of the Ayodhya mosque is far from settled. Perhaps adroit politicking by Rajiv Gandhi could have kept these conflicts under approximate control in the next few years, but his assassination leaves little hope that India will escape the 1990s without at least one major breakdown of civil order.

We said in the last chapter that, unlike most of the impoverished countries of Asia, India offers the possibility of change. We did not say that the change would be for the better.

Vietnam: The Last True Communist State?

"For an international pariah, Vietnam has a lot to offer potential investors—cheap labor, tungsten, rare earths, high-grade coking coal, and iron ore. And, of course, there is oil, much of it uncovered by American oil companies working under licenses from the South Vietnamese government in the early 1970s."

In Europe, even the hardest of hard-line Communist governments have fallen or been forced to change their ways. In Romania, the Ceausescus are dead. In Bulgaria, where intelligence sources once estimated that one adult in four worked at least part-time for the secret police, Todor Zhivkov is in prison, and the first non-Communist president has taken office. Even Albania has grudgingly opened itself to multiparty elections.

It's different in Asia. Vietnam shows no sign of opening its doors to political dissent. To prepare for celebrations in spring of 1990, police in Ho Chi Minh City arrested dozens of suspected dissidents who might otherwise have led embarrassing demonstrations. And one Politburo member lost his job for suggesting that Vietnam must liberalize or risk the fate of Eastern Europe. In this country, at least, the ban on multiparty democracy and open dissent remains absolute.

This unfashionably doctrinaire communism is one legacy of the long, bitter Vietnam War. Now more than 15 years into the past, the war remains with Vietnam each day. There is more to it than the napalm scars and healed wounds still to be seen here and there throughout the country. The real loser in the war was not the United States or South Vietnam but the economy of the entire nation. In addition to the estimated 900,000 North Vietnamese and 400,000 in the South who died in the war, virtually all of the industry in the North was destroyed, while in the South battles damaged or destroyed many factories. Wholesale exile of city dwellers to the country and "reeducation camps" also disrupted the lives of professionals and skilled workers who might otherwise have kept at least part of the economy running during the postwar years. Little or none of the vanished infrastructure has been rebuilt.

One reason is simple poverty. Neither half of Vietnam was ever rich, and the war consumed the nation's capital as efficiently as it did the Vietnamese people themselves. Only outside investors could have paid for the reconstruction, and few capitalists would have been inclined to put their money into a country ruled by Communist hard-liners, even if their Western influence had been welcome.

The other major obstacle is the United States, which placed an embargo on trade with Vietnam immediately after the war and has maintained it ever since. Cut off from what was then the world's most generous source of both aid and trade, Vietnam had to depend on whatever assistance the Soviet Union and mainland China chose to provide. Both proved unreliable.

Yet the economy is showing signs of recovery. Despite their theoretical orthodxy, Vietnam has made some of the most radical economic changes in the communist and formerly communist world. Its version of *perestroika* is called *doi moi*. Private businesses and family farms were legalized in 1987. Two years later, Hanoi abandoned nearly all of its state price controls and dropped its remaining restrictions on private investment and hiring. In fact, all these decisions simply made official what had already become the status quo. Consumer goods were already flooding into the country—some through trade with China, some sent home by Vietnamese "guest workers" in other countries, and many with the aid of an active smuggling industry—and their prices were already being set by the market.

Since then, privately owned restaurants, bars, gas stations, and video shops have been springing up all over Hanoi. Press officers in Ho Chi Minh City have developed a lucrative business renting out government cars for weddings, while foreign ministry photographers use their cameras to take wedding pictures, which they develop in the ministry darkroom.

Hanoi has also ended its subsidies for state-run industries and ordered its companies to find some way to operate at a profit. In some cases, the results have been dramatic. Vietnam has one of the world's worst rail systems. Until recently, it took the nation's antiquated trains three days to go the 1,200 miles from Hanoi to Ho Chi Minh City. The new profit motive has shortened the journey to 52 hours and cut the work force by nearly one-third. In an effort to drum up new business, railroad managers have been delivering tickets to their passengers' homes, offering free breakfasts and newspapers on the trains, and providing taxis and trucks to get passengers and cargo to the station. Prices went up by one-fifth in 1989, but passenger traffic rose by nearly one-third.

A dose of capitalism has clearly helped the failing Vietnamese economy. Vietnam has been on the edge of famine for years. In 1989, it suddenly became the world's third-largest exporter of rice, putting 1.4 million tons on the market. Inflation is down to an estimated 30 percent per year. And Hanoi says that personal incomes are rising at last. Prime Minister Do Muoi forecasts that per capita income in Vietnam will grow from its current level of about $200 per year to $500 by the turn of the century.

It will not be easy, for Vietnam has lost several of the sources of income it depended on to stay afloat. The Soviet Union has put trade with Vietnam on the same pay-as-you-go, cash-only basis it now uses with all its former dependents. Hanoi worries that Moscow could even demand repayment of its long-term debt, estimated at up to $18 billion. And somewhere between $15 billion and $2 billion in aid and subsidized trade vanished when its former allies in Eastern Europe threw off their communist governments.

Until recently, "guest workers" in Eastern Europe and the Middle East contributed vital foreign exchange to Vietnam's meager earnings. Sixteen thousand were stranded in Iraq, where their labor on roads and irrigation projects was helping to pay off the $400 million Vietnam owes for oil purchases. Up to 200,000 have been working at factories in East Germany, Bulgaria, and Czechoslovakia. Some 60,000 have returned home from the former East Germany. Twenty thousand more will return from Bulgaria when their contracts run out in 1992. About 37,000 will come back from Czechoslovakia by 1995. Only the Soviet Union has retained all its Vietnamese guest workers, about 80,000 of them, and there is no telling how long they will be allowed to remain.

Returning workers have also aggravated a worsening unemployment problem. The Hanoi government admits to 1.7 million jobless, but outside observers say there are closer to six million unemployed. The problem has been growing for many years, because Vietnam's population expands faster than its economy. The country needs over one million new jobs annually just to keep from falling further behind. The problem grew more acute in 1989, when the International Monetary Fund stepped in to help Hanoi control its hyperinflation. The body engineered a credit crunch that depressed prices, but also cut consumer spending. At the same time, 500,000 soldiers were released from duty in Cambodia. Unemployment shot up to at least 20 percent. And there are still some 54,000 Vietnamese facing involuntary repatriation from internment camps in Hong Kong. This is the major reason Vietnam is looking for foreign investment, even though outsiders carry the risk of ideological contamination.

Many potential investors have been easy to sell on Vietnam. For an international pariah, Vietnam has a lot to offer potential investors—cheap labor, tungsten, rare earths, high-grade coking coal, and iron ore. And, of course, there is oil, much of it uncovered by American oil companies working under licenses from the South Vietnamese government in the early 1970s. Petroleum geologists estimate that Vietnam could produce 2.5 billion barrels of oil over the next 15 years. Some 325 million barrels have already been confirmed in the Bach Ho region, and there is that much or more in the Haiphong area. When all this is developed, Vietnam could be as big a producer as Malaysia. A Vietnamese-Soviet joint venture already has been pumping oil from offshore deposits found by Mobil early in the 1970s, and firms including

British Petroleum, Petrofina, Royal Dutch/Shell, and Compagnie Française des Petroles have contracted to develop other fields. About one-third of Vietnam's foreign trade to date is with Japan, but others are hastening to enter the market. Siemens, the German electronics giant, landed a contract in 1990 to set up a telecommunications link between Hanoi and Ho Chi Minh City. Companies in Thailand have been angling for a joint venture in steel. French banks and textile makers are setting up shop. By the end of 1990, the government had managed to sign nearly two hundred foreign investment deals with a net worth approaching $2 billion.

These potential profits tempt American companies just as strongly as their competitors in Europe and Asia. Several have found ways to do business directly with Vietnam, using a variety of methods to skirt the ban on sending money there. Ted Turner's Cable News Network has added a satellite downlink to carry its programs into Vietnam. To avoid the embargo, it is not charging for its programming. American Telephone & Telegraph has agreed to begin long-distance phone service to Vietnam. The company will pay satellite and earth-station fees run up by Vietnam and will put any remaining payments due in escrow until the embargo ends. And Mobil has been trying to find some formula that would let it return to Vietnam's oil fields. The Vietnamese would welcome it back, because American technology is superior for recovering oil from offshore wells.

Even American consumer goods are reaching the Vietnamese market. Marlboro cigarettes are for sale there. So are Band-Aids, M&Ms, and even Post-It pads. To date, though, such deals can be made only through middlemen in Thailand and Singapore, who siphon off profits that might otherwise return to the United States.

Recently, the United States business community has begun a quiet but powerful effort to end Washington's postwar trade embargo against Vietnam. The U.S. Chamber of Commerce recently helped about 30 companies and trade organizations set up a "Vietnam normalization coalition" to promote the resumption of trade between the two nations. The effort may take some time, for two major obstacles still stand in the way of a reconciliation.

One is the American soldiers still missing in action after the Vietnam War. There is nothing terribly new about having men unaccounted for after a war. More than 45 years after the end of the Second World War, 78,750 Americans remain to be found. Another 8,200 are still listed as missing in action in Korea. Yet the missing remain a powerfully emotional issue among the American electorate. The National League of Families, a support group for families of men lost in the Vietnam War, says that 2,302 Americans have yet to be returned. Of these, 1,112 are known to be dead, but their bodies were never returned for burial at home. The remaining 1,190 are considered possible prisoners of war. According to a 1990 poll, two-thirds of all Americans and 84 percent of ex-servicemen believe that living American prisoners are still being held in Vietnam.

The other problem is Cambodia. When the Khmer Rouge, under Pol Pot, dismantled the nation, executing professionals and sending virtually the entire urban population to clear the jungles, Vietnam invaded and deposed them. Since 1979, the Hanoi-backed government of Prime Minister Hun Sen has been fighting to keep the Khmer Rouge and two allied guerrilla factions from regaining power. For a decade, Vietnamese troops were there with them. Bringing them home was a major precondition for any resumption of trade with the United States.

Hanoi is as eager for American investment as American companies are for Vietnamese profits, and it has worked hard to meet Washington's demands. Vietnam pulled its troops out of Cambodia in 1989. A year later, Foreign Minister Nguyen Co Thach journeyed to Washington to promise greater cooperation in locating the remains of Americans missing in action since the Vietnam War. It was the first time a high-ranking Vietnamese official had visited the city since 1975. Washington now demands a comprehensive settlement of the Cambodian civil war before it will end its embargo. As we saw in Chapter 22, that condition could be difficult to meet. Yet even without peace in Cambodia, there is a chance that the United States could soon end its embargo. Vietnam's latest concession is an offer to let American ships use the naval facilities built by U.S. soldiers at Cam Ranh Bay. The port could go a long way toward making up for the loss of bases in the Philippines. If the Aquino government and its successors continue to demand a hasty withdrawal of American troops, the embargo could end well before Cambodia's civil war does.

Cambodia has also poisoned Vietnam's once-close relationship with the People's Republic of China, which sponsors the Khmer

Rouge. When Vietnam invaded Cambodia in 1979, China cut off its aid and heavy fighting broke out on the border between them. In the last year, Vietnam has sent several representatives to Beijing, asking that trade and rail routes between the countries be restored. So far, it has little to show for its efforts. If Beijing has made any concrete offers, news of them has not reached the West, but it seems a good guess that relations between the two countries will remain chilly until a Cambodian settlement is reached.

Once that issue is resolved and the American embargo is lifted, Vietnam will still have adjustments to make before many foreign companies will be comfortable trading there. It has yet to set up the formal structure of banking and commercial law required to let investors know exactly where they stand. In 1990, hundreds of Vietnam's small credit cooperatives went broke. They were neither regulated nor insured, and their depositors wound up losing all they had saved. In April 1991, Hanoi made it officially legal for private citizens over age 18 to set up their own businesses. State officials and military personnel were banned from doing so, apparently in an effort to avoid corruption. Under the new law, private entrepreneurs are guaranteed the right to own the means of production and to pass along both capital and property to their heirs. This is at least a step in the right direction. Vietnam is clearly so eager for investment that more progress can be expected in the near future.

In the next ten years, Vietnam could reverse itself periodically, as we expect China and the Soviet Union to do. The Communist government will find it difficult to accept that capitalist prosperity requires democracy, and is worth the trouble democracy causes. Until it does, foreign contacts will seem threatening, no matter how clearly they are necessary. Western prosperity will almost surely bring Western-style dissent as well, and the government will crack down occasionally to maintain its own position. Yet Vietnam will soon come to depend heavily on outside investment and technology. In a few years, even political change will seem less threatening than the loss of business that would follow repression on the scale of Tiananmen. Slowly, liberalism will creep in, whether it is welcome or not.

We do not expect multiparty elections to flower in Vietnam as quickly as they did in most Eastern Europe. But by the turn of the century, or soon thereafter, this last true Communist state could become the newest democracy in Asia.

P A R T   F I V E

THE NEW WORLD ORDER

INTRODUCTION

In previous sections of this book, we have examined several major trends now reshaping the economic and political structures that have ruled the world since the end of World War II:

The regional economies are becoming integrated into three major trading blocs.

Politically, some parts of the world are also drawing together. The Germanys have already healed their long-standing division. The Chinas will reunite, and the Koreas may follow suit. There is even a chance that the two North American nations, the United States and Canada, may become one (with the exception of Quebec, of course) for the first time since they were fellow colonies of the British Empire.

And, almost universally, democracy and capitalism have triumphed over their totalitarian adversaries. In Eastern Europe, the former satellites of the Soviet Union are either building multiparty electoral governments or threaten to collapse into chaos because the existing regimes have yet to accept the democratic will of their people. In Latin America, only two of the region's nations have yet to elect their first governments that at least claim democratic support. Even in the Soviet Union itself, the demand for a working democracy now seems too strong to be silenced, save by means that Moscow can no longer afford to use. This transformation has occurred, not because the authoritarians saw the error of their ways, though Soviet Premier Mikhail Gorbachev deserves credit for at least attempting to bow gracefully before the inevitable, but because centrally planned economies have proved themselves incapable of providing for the needs of their people.

These are fundamental changes in the rules by which the modern world operates. They have clearly invalidated the bipolar alliances, based on superpower politics, that have governed international relations for nearly five decades. In the remainder of the 1990s, this obsolete structure will be replaced by a form of consensus rule centered in the United Nations, much like the coalition formed by the United States during the Persian Gulf crisis. Because technology has given new power to some nationalistic Third World nations that previously counted for little in world affairs, this new global system will face serious challenges throughout the foreseeable future. In Part 5, we turn to the structure and function of this new world order.

C H A P T E R 2 5

••

Ceding Sovereignty for the Global Good

"The Iraqi invasion of Kuwait went a long way toward so-lidifying the U.N.'s role in preserving the world's collective security. Where the superpowers had long competed for in-fluence, they now chose to work together."

••

Nearly five decades ago, most of the globe's individual countries banded together to form the United Nations, an organization built on the idea that international law can and must reign in national rivalries. The idea had been attempted once before, in the ill-fated League of Nations, three decades and one world war earlier. The League survived, if in name only, for twenty-five years and during that time accomplished very little. For most of its history, it has seemed that the U.N. would meet the same fate as its predecessor. It might endure, but would remain forever paralyzed by the conflicts between its largest members. But since 1988, the role of the United Nations in world affairs has grown rapidly. Its sanction of the Gulf War, and the decision of the great powers to abide by its decisions, constitutes the first major expression of a new era in which collective action will be used to settle regional conflicts and to attack common global problems.

As we have seen throughout this book, the United Nations is only the largest of the international bodies to which individual nations are surrendering some of their powers in hopes of promoting the collective good. On the Continent, the twelve member states of the European Community are quickly handing over many of their sovereign rights to the Brussels bureaucracy. In North America, Canada and the United States have already given up some of their independence to regulate trade between their nations; by 2000, one of them may even give up its own existence to join the other.

Internally, also, many countries are finding it necessary to forfeit some of their accustomed powers to local minorities. This trend has been strongest in the Soviet Union and its former satellites of Eastern Europe. In the vacuum left by the relaxation of Moscow's control, a host of nearly forgotten ethnic groups are seeking the right to rule themselves. In Yugoslavia, Croats and Slovenes are struggling to end Serbian domination of their home territories. In the Russian republic, there are 16 autonomous ethnic regions, nine of which have declared their sovereignty—and won approval from the republic's president, Boris Yeltsin. Similar movements are in progress throughout the Soviet empire, while others either have occurred or soon will in various parts of the Middle East, Asia, and even the Americas. The long-running Irish rebellion is one such movement. So is *Quebecois* separatism in Canada.

These trends will be among the most important features of international politics in the remainder of the century, and well into the next. Both are guided by a single principle: Problems should be handled at the level on which they occur. International issues—war, environmental pollution, economics, terrorism, human rights—require international responses. Local issues require action within the nation faced by them, and that does not necessarily mean within the state borders that exist today.

Revolutionary as that principle seems to anyone schooled in the politics of the twentieth century, these trends are simply returning world affairs to something more closely resembling their natural, logical condition. Few of the so-called nation-states we have known during this century have any natural reason to exist at all. They were cobbled together from the remains of nineteenth-century empires: the British and French, the Hapsburg and Ottoman. Yugoslavia and Czechoslovakia are classic examples, and the resurgence of supposedly forgotten ethnic hatreds within them clearly demonstrates how artificial their existence has been. More than 90 of the 159 member states of the United Nations have come into being since the end of World War II, most often by secession from these post-colonial artifacts. Included among them are some of the world's perpetual trouble spots. Most of the boundaries among Africa's 50 or so states were set by the great European empires at the Berlin Conference of 1884. Their purpose was not build states to fit the needs of African ethnic, linguistic, and cultural groups, but to balance the powers of Europe. The resulting distortions caused civil wars in Angola, Ethiopia, Mozambique, Nigeria, and Sudan, among many others. The Middle East, too, was carved up after World War I by the European powers that dominated the region, with similar results. Iraq's attempt to annex Kuwait would simply have restored the status quo that existed before the British apportioned regional power to suit their own convenience. Syria covets Lebanon for similar reasons. Even the Vietnam War can be traced to the artificial boundaries drawn by French empire-builders. When these deformations are corrected, the world will be a more peaceful place.

The need for some such change was obvious before the United Nations was born. After World War II, many people began to question the utility of the state. Power politics had spilled much blood. Politicians had exploited nationalism to promote themselves and their ambitions at great cost. In an article in *International Affairs,* David Mitrany introduced the concept of functionalism: governments, on behalf of the commonwealth, should band together to provide services for health, the environment, education, telecommunications, the infrastructure, and other mutual concerns. Mitrany asserted that this functional approach "should help shift the emphasis from power to problem and purpose." Such tasks could be delegated to bureaus, staffed by apolitical technocrats, that would provide a unified service for all the member states. Mitrany hoped that nationalism would fade and people would shift their allegiance to a world federalist system. This process would eventually make war less feasible. "The task that is facing us is how to build up the reality of a common interest in peace. . . . Not a peace that would keep the nations quietly apart, but a peace that would bring them actively together; not the old static and strategic view of peace, but a social view of it," Mitrany held. The United Nations incorporated much of his blueprint in such agencies as the World Health Organization, the International Labor Organization, and the United Nations Educational, Scientific, and Cultural Organization.

During the Cold War years, superpower politics reduced the U.N. to near uselessness, but a wave of successes eventually recalled the institution's noble purpose of collective security. A U.N. mediator in Afghanistan led the talks in which the Soviets agreed to pull their troops out. A Security Council plan outlined a cease-fire between Iraq and Iran. The U.N. Transition Assistance Group helped out with the elections in the new state of Namibia. The U.N. also helped to end fighting in the western Sahara and Cyprus. The five permanent members of the Security Council agreed to a truce and administration for war-shredded Cambodia until new elections could be held, an effort that paved the way for the home-grown truce of mid-1991. U.N.-brokered discussions, agreed to by leftist guerillas (FMLN) and San Salvador, sought to end civil war in El Salvador. In February 1990 the U.N. observed Nicaragua's first free elections; banners proclaimed, "your vote is secret." Soon after, the contra camps in Honduras were disarmed under U.N. supervision.

Yet, in all these triumphs, there was less substance than met the eye. In most, the conflict had already started to subside. The U.N. did not end the wars or work out political solutions. It only served to facilitate the ends of the crises. The United Nations can only be effective when the "Big Five" will it to be. Their vetoes can preclude any action; their support is needed to enforce directives. In a more reasonable world, the U.N. would be able to project more power. If current trends continue and necessary reforms are enacted, it will.

The Iraqi invasion of Kuwait went a long way toward solidifying the U.N.'s role in preserving the world's collective security. Where the superpowers had long competed for influence, they now chose to work together; the Soviet Union even sided with the United States, its former enemy, against Iraq, its former ally. When diplomatic boycotts and economic embargoes failed to halt the unrepentant Saddam Hussein, war became inevitable. But this time, for the first time since the Korean "police action" of the early 1950s, the war was an internationally sanctioned use of collective force to punish an aggressor. It was an affirmation that international law, not national interest and power, would rule.

President George Bush made the crucial decision when he claimed that the Security Council's authorization to use force after January 15 meant that he did not have to go to Congress for a declaration of war; Congress had, he pointed out, already ratified the U.N. charter. Though done for reasons of internal politics, Bush's pronouncement marks the first time that the U.S. government has granted that its own laws are not the highest that it must obey. It was a remarkable departure from the policies of the Reagan administration, which mined Nicaraguan harbors and announced that the World Court held no jurisdiction over the United States.

The U.N. will continue to grow in stature if it can develop credible methods to fulfill its four basic tasks: peacemaking (diplomacy), peacekeeping (police actions), peace-enforcing (U.N.-sponsored war), and peace-building (attacking potential causes of conflict, such as poverty). International law will never quite have the enforcement power of national law, but during the 1990s U.N. members will give it more "bite," so that all but the most foolhardy of potential aggressors will abide by its decisions. Until that occurs, international law will exist only to be manipulated by the powerful, as it was during the grim days of the cold war.

The fundamental change will be to strengthen the U.N.'s peacekeeping powers. One likely development is a permanent fund to support U.N. intervention in crisis areas, so the Security Council can act without having to scramble for funds at the last minute. Former Soviet Foreign Minister Eduard Shevardnadze suggested that the U.N. revive its moribund Military Staff Committee, which in theory consists of the Chiefs of Staff of the "Big Five" and advises the Security Council on military matters. The Committee is also supposed to organize and command any armed forces the council uses to enforce its decisions. There have been several proposals as well, to give the U.N. a permanent military force of its own. As a first step, the Scandinavian countries have suggested placing units of national armies under the control of the United Nations. Later, the organization may be able to recruit its own permanent peacekeeping brigade, and perhaps a strike force to handle hostage situations and other such emergencies.

The U.N. desperately needs at least one more power: the right to step in to resolve conflicts on its own decision. Its "blue helmets" have been successful in policing danger zones, but they can act only where both parties consent. Ethiopia, Sudan, Somalia, Mozambique, and Sri Lanka have all rejected U.N. mediation in their internal conflicts. In the post–Gulf War era, there is at least a chance that member nations will at last grant the U.N. the right to intercede even when it is not wanted. This would be the ultimate cession of sovereignty and would do more to promote peace in the world than any other single action the national governments could take.

Some change is also needed to restructure the veto power of the Security Council. As things stand, any of the council's permanent members can veto resolutions not compatible with their own foreign policy. And some major nations do not enjoy such representation, including the strongest powers in Europe and Asia: Germany and Japan. Brazil has proposed that the U.N. add Third World members to the Security Council; its candidates include Brazil itself, Egypt, India, and Nigeria, in addition to Japan and Germany. Another idea is to eliminate the single-nation veto. Under this proposal, three of the permanent Security Council members would have to vote against a resolution to overrule the decisions of the other permanent and rotating members. There is no guarantee that any of these specific ideas will be enacted during the 1990s. However, some change seems inevitable. It should give the United Nations a stronger voice in world affairs.

Yet the U.N. may never approach being the "world government" that some of its early supporters once hoped to see. Even the United States, the largest and strongest proponent of the "new world order," remains unwilling to surrender much of its sovereignty for the common good. Witness its refusal to accept the recent international treaty intended to combat global warming. One political theorist, Stanley Hoffmann, likens nation-states to artichokes. Although you can peel off the leaves of functional tasks (such as health, energy, and the environment), sovereignty remains at the heart of the nation-state. You can remove leaves, but the heart will remain, even when all else is stripped away.

In its most extended form, functionalism ultimately fails; it can never completely erase sovereignty or its most basic elements, such as foreign policy and defense. The U.N. can counter aggression against politically weak states and may even intervene in their affairs. No such action will ever be taken against any of the five permanent Security Council members or the other nuclear powers. Yet the United Nations can effectively promote the global good. It will be particularly helpful in mediating issues that affect many countries, such as the environment or drug-running or refugees. Its power and prestige can only grow in the decade to come.

•••

Coping with Third World Superweapons

"As a terror weapon, bacteria are inviting. In theory, a few grains of botulin toxin in, say, New York City's water supply would slaughter the innocent by the thousands."

•••

Little that was televised of the Persian Gulf War struck home as hard as the scenes of Israeli families wearing gas masks in the privacy of their own living rooms. Nothing hammered home as forcefully as Saddam Hussein's message to the world about how ruthlessly he was willing to wage this war. And nothing conveyed how far modern warfare had come, better than those simple pictures of ordinary people trying to lead normal lives, while wearing gas masks inside rooms sealed off from the outside world by plastic sheets and masking tape.

The "poor man's atom bomb" is what some weapons experts call the poison gases that everybody hoped had been scrapped, after they were used to such horrifying effect in World War I. Iraq used mustard gas to kill almost 6,000 Kurdish rebels in its eight-year war with Iran and then used the same gas with even deadlier results against as many as 10,000 Iranian foot soldiers. Some Western nations imposed sanctions against Iraq, but all that meant was placing export controls on the raw chemicals Iraq needed to make more poison gas. The Geneva Protocol of 1925 banned the use of chemical weapons; Iraq signed it in 1931 but never ratified it. The world fell silent on Iraq's use of gas in its war with Iran largely because few nations wanted to be seen siding with Iran.

Iraq has also been hard at work on the other low-budget weapon of mass destruction: deadly bacteria and natural toxins. Anthrax, botulism, plague, and tularemia are all favorites of the biological weapons designer's trade. Iraq is believed to have experimented with all these diseases. According to rumor, they used Rift Valley fever against their own Kurdish population. Unlike poison gasses—the most powerful of which seldom kill more than five percent of the people attacked, even when the victims are unprotected—tularemia kills up to 60 percent of patients who go untreated; anthrax kills up to 95 percent. Often, these days, bacteria are genetically engineered to increase their killing power and to make the infections more difficult to cure. This is a technique that any bright high school biology student can learn.

Just when the world thought it was safe from the threat of nuclear war, a new and horrible kind of war is being brewed in the chemical plants and biological laboratories of Third World nations who cannot afford to own and test atomic weapons. *Omni* magazine called it the "new shape of death," a new kind of war that makes savage brews to "spread disease for military goals, make an enemy's air unbreathable, and seed clouds with substances that turn rain into liquid death." Iraq was merely the first of the modern poisoners to use its weapons.

It may all sound new and threatening, but chemical and biological warfare are almost as old as battle itself. At the height of the second Peloponnesian War in 450 B.C., the Spartans burned pitch and sulfur to flood poison fumes under the enemy's city walls. Greek fire was used at sea as early as 1200 B.C., then on land for more than one thousand years thereafter. Biological weapons appeared in 1347 when, during the siege of Kaffa, the Mongols threw the bodies of plague victims over the walls of the city. The first wholesale use of toxic agents took place in 1915 at Ypres when the Germans fired chlorine gas bombs on French and British troops. The French retaliated with "blood gases," and the Germans came back with mustard gas and the Americans with choking phosgene gas. By the time the miasma cleared in 1918, more than 100,000 of World War I's nine million dead had been felled by poison gas.

Saddam Hussein's gas of choice has been nitrogen mustard, which attacks the body's bone marrow and destroys the ability to produce the white blood cells that fight off infection. It is a little like being attacked by the AIDS virus. Those who do not suffocate from a mustard gas attack suffer huge, ulcerated blisters that cover the armpits and the groin, and succumb to death in a matter of days at least and weeks at most. Saddam Hussein's gas arsenal also included at least three kinds of nerve gas, whose victims' first warning is a blurring of their vision. Then, as if an invisible vise were being tightened around their chests, they are forced to battle for every breath. Death is invariably caused by asphyxiation but only after continuous attacks of muscle spasm, vomiting, and diarrhea. United Nations teams sent to examine the bodies of thousands of victims of at least three Iraqi gas attacks in 1988, found evidence that mustard gas had been used. The perception that Iran may have sued for peace because its troops were demoralized by Iraqi gas attacks did nothing to dim their luster as an effective weapon in parts of the Third World.

Though the use of poison gas weapons was banned in 1925, nothing was done to prevent their manufacture and stockpile. In 1969, talks were begun to ban the possession of chemical weapons. If anything, the situation has gotten worse in the more than 20 years since then. Great Britain abandoned chemical weapons in 1956, but France, the Soviet Union, and the United States have set about modernizing their stockpiles. Iraq ignored the talks completely and has gone about systematically building up one of the largest stocks of poison gas anywhere in the world. China, Egypt, Ethiopia, Iran, Israel, Libya, Myanmar, Somalia, Syria, Taiwan, and Vietnam all possess both poison gas and the means to deliver it. One reason Iraq did not use poison gas in the early weeks of the war in the Gulf may have been that its Scud missiles did not have the "throw weight" to carry gas projectiles into Israel and Saudi Arabia. Fortunately, the aircraft that could have carried gas bombs over both countries were demolished by Allied bombs, hidden in bunkers to protect them from attack, or flown to sanctuary in Iran to keep them from being destroyed.

Biological weapons, too, have been banned by the international community since 1975. Even then, there was little chance that any relatively civilized nation would use them, for most armed forces had concluded long before that disease-causing bacteria were too hard to control for use in war. In the 1940s, Great Britain experimented with biological attack on the island of Guernsey, in the English Channel. They used anthrax, a disease that causes fever, shock, and acute respiratory distress. More than four decades later, the bacteria remain just as virulent as they were when released.

Saddam Hussein's use of chemical, and perhaps biological, weapons against defenseless Kurds and Iranians once again raises the horrifying possibility that a ruthless or unstable dictator will be tempted to use them against anybody who threatens him. Poison gas, especially, is diabolically easy to make and use. The technology for making mustard gas is a century old, and it takes only a few turns of a valve to switch a factory from making pesticides and herbicides to turning out lethal nerve agents. Making and delivering chemical warheads is almost as simple. The world arms market is overrun by outdated short-range ballistic missiles, like the Soviet Scud and Chinese Silkworm, that can quickly be changed over to carry gas. Iraq began manufacturing nerve gas at a so-called pesticide plant in Samarra that was hidden from Western intelligence eyes for almost ten years.

Saddam Hussein learned the chemical warfare trade from another Arab bully, Libyan dictator Muammar Qaddafi. Like Hussein, a friend of terrorists and a sworn enemy of Israel, Qaddafi became frustrated by his inability to buy or steal black market nuclear weapons and turned to poison gas as the easiest and cheapest alternative. Almost like a precursor of Hussein, Qaddafi bought the technology for his poison gas factory from West Germany, where there were enough capitalist renegades to sell the Libyan leader everything required to put together the Middle East's first chemical plant for producing gas weapons of death.

The story of Qaddafi and his German chemical suppliers is now a classic; *New York Times* columnist William Safire refers to it as "Auschwitz in the sand." The Bonn government had long known more about German involvement in the Libyan affair than it cared to admit. Finally, in January 1989, a Bonn spokesman conceded that since October 1988, West German intelligence had possessed "serious information" about what it called the "Libyan project." Bonn quickly announced tighter export controls. But the feeble attempts to appease outside anger could not erase the appalling fact that German companies helped to create a poison gas factory in the Libyan town of Rabta, 40 miles south of Tripoli. The Libyan cover story was that the factory produced drugs, pesticides, and plastics. The truth was that a few pipes and valves and one or two different starting materials was all that stood between those products and mustard gas, the disabling and disfiguring agent that Libya is still suspected of making in Rabta. Both are made by mixing certain carbon-containing chemicals with chlorine and sulfur.

The German company central to the whole affair was called Imhausen, located in Lahr in southern Germany, where it was frequently called a "poison kitchen" by the town's inhabitants. From 1977 to 1989, the firm notified the Munich patent office of three innovations, two for new ways of producing carbonic acid ethylester and carbonic acid alkylester. The patent applications were accompanied by rather unusual requests that the inventor go unnamed. Still a third application involved a new way to remove hydrogen sulfide from exhaust gases in an unidentified chemical process. All were applicable to the manufacture of poison gas. Imhausen was not new to scandal. In 1985, Bonn gave a list of chemicals to the Organization of the Chemical Industry (VCI) and asked it to determine which were produced in Germany. Among them was pinakolyl alcohol, which can be used to make a deadly poison gas called Soman. Pinakolyl alcohol has almost no industrial significance. The VCI asked Imhausen if it was making the chemical. Imhausen declined to answer.

The Libyan project was run under the name "Pharma 150." In Hong Kong, a company called Pen-Tsao-Materia-Medica-Center, Ltd., was allegedly using Imhausen blueprints to build a chemical plant with the project name Pharma-150. Pen-Tsao shared its Hong Kong headquarters with the Dee Trading Co., Imhausen's largest stockholder. What was Pen-Tsao's role? It ordered chemicals and parts from Pharma 150 in Hong Kong, all of them shipped out through Antwerp, Belgium. Before the ships carrying the parts and chemicals had reached the North Sea, both the documents and the ship's destination had changed to Pharma 150 in Libya. German workers have since testified that the construction site for the Libyan Pharma 150 was located far from what Libya described as chemical plants. There were other differences as well. Pharma 150 was surrounded by guards; the chemical plants were not. Building 2 at Pharma 150, they said, had a door that measured 80 feet by 20 feet, serviced by a moving crane that could handle 500 tons at a time. Its floor was made of steel plates almost an inch thick, and it was surrounded by an earthen wall kept under constant observation by video cameras. Its loading dock was covered by camouflage nets and protected by radar and surface-to-air missiles. The precautions did not stop there. At every pipe connection in the plant, there were sensors and alarms to warn of leaks and escaping gas. The conclusion of Western intelligence experts was that the Libyan plant had a capacity to make roughly 40 tons of mustard and nerve gas a month. It was the largest chemical-weapons complex ever built in the Third World.

If the past is any kind of prologue, and it almost always is, the prospects for putting a strong leash on chemical warfare do not look good. The story of the Libyan plant is one of missed chances and repeated frustrations for the world community. It hardly bodes well for those who, like Britain's John Major and America's George Bush, claim to have made it a priority to stop the spread of chemical and biological weapons. At least 16 nations are said to possess some stockpile of chemical and biological weapons; another ten are "thought" to possess at least one chemical or biological weapon in some kind of standby stockpile, and 12 more are thought to be seeking the same kind of curious security blanket for themselves. The Libyan story was repeated, almost word for word, in Iraq. Even the same German companies were involved, and one of George Bush's stated objectives for launching Operation Desert Storm was the destruction of Iraq's chemical and biological weapons factories. Still, the potential for global disaster as a result of chemical weapons is nowhere greater than it is in the cauldron of the Middle East. If Libya and Iraq set out to acquire a chemical arsenal, it seems likely that Syria, Iran, Egypt, the Sudan, and even Jordan have at least made the effort at some time in the recent past.

This is why the success of the Libyans and Iraqis, and the failure of the U.S., Britain, and anybody else to stop them, is especially troubling. For more than a year and a half starting in 1987, U.S. intelligence had strong evidence suggesting that Libya was building a chemical weapons plant at Rabta. The most galling thing of all is that the assistance the Libyans were getting came from West Germany and Japan, two of America's closest allies and the two countries that have pledged themselves more to peace than any other nations on Earth. While accumulating evidence that the Libyan plant under construction was designed to produce war gases, the U.S. got almost no cooperation in its attempts to have the plant's building permit revoked. American officials who approached Tokyo in 1988 to inquire about the role of Japanese companies in Libya say now that they were purposefully misled. When a firm named Japan Steel Works was identified as having assisted the Libyan venture, company officials told visiting American senators that they were only building a desalinization plant. Given the plant's desolate, inland location, intelligence officials regard that assertion as an outright lie. Later that year, a Japanese diplomat in Washington told an American official watching the whole affair that the company's employees had left their uniforms behind and that "certain oriental gentlemen" were now wearing them. "Who are these oriental gentlemen?" the American asked. "They might be Thai," the Japanese diplomat replied. In fact, U.S. government officials said, Japan Steel Works had built a metal-working plant within walking distance of the chemical factory; its purpose was the manufacture of bomb casings. Intelligence authorities later documented the movement of chemicals from the chemical plant to the metal-working facility.

One more category of weapon sure to wind up in Third World hands need not be obtained through such elaborate schemes. The industrialized countries are sure to sell them. These are the next generation of "smart" weapons, due to enter the U.S. inventory by 1995. The world got a good look at the efficiency of laser-guided bombs in Iraq and Kuwait: where the old "iron bombs" would have had trouble hitting a narrow target like a bridge, the new munitions can almost find the white line down the middle. The bombs now under development will do it without human guidance. The "Sensor-Fuzed Weapon" is a bomb containing 40 separate warheads, each of which can guide itself to individual targets, such as tanks. "Silent Soldier" is a self-contained weapon that can be dropped into the battlefield and left to fire itself at an oncoming tank. "Thirsty Saber" is a cruise missile that can find its way to enemy territory, search out its own targets, blast them with self-guided warheads, and return for another load. And the jet-propelled "Tacit Rainbow" can "loiter" for up to an hour, watching for enemy radar, then home in and destroy it. Based on past marketing practices, all these weapons will be available to the Third World in the first year or two of the next century.

In sharp contrast, the developed world will at least try to police chemical and biological weapons. It is a far more difficult task than it is to regulate the manufacture of nuclear weapons. Not long ago, North and South Korea, Brazil, Argentina, and Egypt all were believed to be within a few years of building atomic devices; the threat of international sanctions appears to have dissuaded them. Like many Third World countries, they seem to have given up their quest to join the nuclear club. Pakistan has never given up, in large part because its unfriendly neighbor, India, already possesses nuclear weapons. But the world has had a treaty to stop the spread of atomic weapons for years, a treaty that most nations have signed and ratified and that is supported by regular inspection of nuclear facilities throughout the world. There is no way to examine every factory and laboratory suited to the production of chemical and biological weapons.

We are not terribly concerned about biological weapons, simply because they are so horrifying. Saddam Hussein's suspected use of Rift Valley fever, if it occurred, is an example that few despots would care to follow. In a normal war, they are as likely to kill the troops who used them as they are the enemy, and they make it impossible to occupy the conquered territory safely. As a terror weapon, bacteria are more inviting. In theory, a few grams of botulin toxin in, say, New York City's water supply, would slaughter the innocent by the thousands. But the leader who used biological weapons on the battlefield would be known, while the perpetrator of a terrorist crime would risk being found out. Both would find themselves reviled by their enemies and ostracized by their former friends. Neither could hope to die peacefully in his sleep.

But gas has been used at least six times in the last ten years, in part because there is no treaty to stop the spread of chemical weapons and in part because they are more controllable than biological weapons and are somewhat less likely to trigger a deadly reprisal. The ease with which they can be made, and the ease with which they can be concealed, makes it all the more imperative that something be done to stop the spread of chemical weapons. With the proliferation of more accurate intermediate-range ballistic missiles today, the stakes are especially high. This is one of the most important strategic issues facing the world in the 1990s and the early years of the twenty-first century.

CHAPTER 27

NATO Finds a New Purpose

"Reluctant as they have been to admit it, NATO has lost its reason for being. The once-credible military threat to Western Europe has disappeared; a single, strong and united Germany now forms a bulwark against whatever hazards remain to its East. If NATO is to survive beyond the year 2000, it must find a new purpose based on the same unanimity that so quickly emerged in 1949."

The last time Europe staggered into such a crossroads was in 1945, when nations changed themselves and their relations with their neighbors, their allies, and their enemies. The victorious Allies divided Germany into two, seemingly for forever, and faced off in a cold war that might last as long as the division itself. Now, once again, Europe is at a crossroads. There are no longer two Germanys, there is no longer a satellite bloc of the Soviet Union. The iron curtain that once stretched, as Churchill said, "from Stettin in the Baltic to Trieste in the Adriatic" lies in ruins, alongside the toppled bricks of the Berlin Wall. As Europe looks ahead from its new crossroads, the result could be a continent defying its history and at peace with itself for years to come. Just as simply, it could be a Europe doomed to repeat its history and stumble once again into conflict. The end of the process now beginning could be the collapse of the New European order, with the New World once more a bystander to the quarrels of the Old.

After more than 40 largely successful years, the West—and especially Western Europe—lacks a common sense of mission or a strategy for coping with the rapid changes taking both ends of the European continent by storm. While stormy themselves, the last four decades never lacked a sense of purpose. From the day the North Atlantic Treaty Organization was born on May 29, 1949, the Western powers quickly established NATO as the political and military response to the threat they perceived building in the East, which began with the Communist coup d'état in Prague. NATO and the Marshall Plan behind it brought millions in economic aid to Europe and established the America-centered "free world" in which the capitalist, democratic countries decided to organize themselves. If nothing else, there was a remarkable consensus from the very beginning on the best way to proceed.

But having won the Cold War that so dominated Western political life after World War II, the North Atlantic Treaty Organization faces the far tougher challenge of how to even survive the peaceful years ahead. Reluctant as it has been to admit it, NATO has lost its reason for being. The once-credible military threat to Western Europe has disappeared; a single, strong, and united Germany now forms a bulwark against whatever hazards remain to its East. If NATO is to survive beyond the year 2000, it must find a new purpose, based on the same unanimity that so quickly emerged in 1949. But today, even a modest consensus is harder to sell. Led by a revitalized Germany, enough NATO states now want real change in the alliance's defense posture. That may make it impossible to reach any new consensus, much less to preserve the one from which NATO grew.

NATO thrived for years on fears of Soviet expansionism, supported by American prosperity and West European dependence on that wealth. Together, they provided a solid foundation that kept the alliance intact through an endless sea of change. These three conditions persisted for so long that they seemed a perpetual way of life. The Soviets could almost always be counted on to make menacing noises, rattle their sabers and missiles, crack down on their satellite states, and make a constant stew of mischief throughout the Third World. While they moved in only 20 years from the economic and political backwash to being king of the hill, the Americans naively believed they could both afford and accomplish anything in the world they wanted to do. For their part, the West Europeans were quite content to let Washington make all the big decisions on war and peace. They were just as happy to concentrate their efforts to make Western Europe richer than it had ever been. Almost needless to say, all three of these conditions have dramatically changed or completely disappeared.

The coming of Gorbachev, the dissolution of the Soviet Union's satellite bloc, and the collapse of the Warsaw pact have weakened the sense of threat that held NATO together. The risks to the Atlantic alliance have been reduced, transformed, or eliminated in a few swiftly passing years. In fact, NATO's cold war victory began in 1983, when the alliance withstood the anxious oversimplifications of the European peace movement and deployed the short-range Pershing II nuclear missile warheads. Whatever hope of triumph the Soviet Union may have had in a battle with Western Europe was gone. From then on, the emerging Kremlin leadership began to recognize the futility of maintaining the same old foreign policy.

That policy had no objective more cherished than the division of Germany. "How long do you believe there will be two Germanys?" Soviet foreign ministers were always asked. With a smile, they always responded, "Who knows?" Then came the collapse of the bloc and the loss of East Germany.

Suddenly, the greatest Soviet nightmares of the last 40 years came to pass right before the Kremlin's eyes. But incredibly, the Soviet Union under Gorbachev steeled itself to the changes and became almost models of restraint and cooperation. Freedom of expression that was unthinkable five years ago is possible in the USSR today. The Kremlin has made sweeping arms control proposals, undertaken unilateral cuts in its armed forces, and pressed diplomatic talk and summit meetings as a way of negotiating their numerous differences with the West. Much of this transformation has come out of economic desperation, but that does not make it any less real. And while many of Gorbachev's movements toward democracy have met with stiff opposition from the Old Guard, the USSR is less and less likely to fall back on its old repressive ways, even in the wake of the August 1991 coup attempt. The Soviet Union would have to pay too high a price at home and abroad, its thirst for capital is too great, and it can no longer restrain the forces that it has unleashed in its own empire. The result, as Ronald Steel has put it, is that the "Soviet element in the global power equation has diminished sharply."

The American element in the global equation has diminished as well. The old cartoon of a beefy Uncle Sam with his pockets bulging with money has become little more than a joke. Much of Western Europe is more productive, enjoys a higher standard of living, and offers its citizens more comfort and security than does its traditional protector on the far side of the Atlantic. Europeans also buy a large portion of the Treasury bonds that finance the U.S. trade and budget deficits. Western Europe remains militarily dependent on America, but the economic conditions that created that dependency have long ceased to exist. Having overcome its bloodied past, Western Europe has become a haven of wealth, security, and justice in a world where those qualities are in scarce supply. Inspired by their own prosperity and the belief that the Soviet threat has passed, the West Europeans have focused on their own economic and political agendas. Those agendas include the full integration of their economies by the end of 1992.

Meanwhile, the United States has been slowly suffering an overdue retrenchment. The alliance was built on the premise that America had inexhaustible wealth, which turned it into the West's perpetually reliable creditor. Having now become the world's most ravenous debtor, the U.S. finds it ever more difficult to sustain its standard of living, behave like the world's last superpower, and maintain its traditional commitments. Once an obligation, later a manageable burden, NATO has become a drain on diminishing American resources. The allies have become "freeloaders," told they must take on "their fair share of the burden," and are threatened with U.S. troop withdrawals if they do not fall into line. Our allies have a different view of the world than Washington does. They have long ceased to consider the Soviets a significant threat, have little interest in spending money to counter radical Third World movements, and think their own military budgets adequate to preserve their freedom. The idea of an unprovoked Soviet attack strikes most of them these days as ridiculous. Together with other European attitudes, this has eroded NATO's American constituency.

If one stops there, NATO is left with an uncertain future. But there are still many reasons to be concerned with Europe's military security.

A Warsaw Pact assault on the Fulda Gap is no longer a danger, but peace and security have not yet come to the East. Gorbachev's experiment with *perestroika* may still fail, and while outright Stalinism may no longer be likely in the Soviet Union, even less virulent forms of totalitarianism are not to be taken lightly. The August coup in the Kremlin may have undermined Congressional ratification of the Strategic Arms Reduction Treaty (START) between the U.S. and Soviet Union. And even if a START agreement is ratified quickly, it would still leave the Soviets with 9,000 strategic nuclear warheads and a total arsenal of more than 20,000 nuclear weapons. A START II accord, which could take us out to the turn of the century, seems unlikely to be negotiated, or even attempted, and in any case would not reduce Soviet forces to less than 5,000 strategic nuclear warheads. These weapon systems are paid for, cheap to maintain, contribute to less than 20 percent of the Soviet defense budget, and are still ten times more numerous than the combined British and French nuclear arsenals. While this remains true, NATO will have a role to play.

There is another. In a moment of frustration, Chancellor Helmut Kohl once pointed out to then–Prime Minister Margaret Thatcher that Germany had proved itself a good European neighbor for 45 years. What more was needed, he asked, before England would give his country the trust it had earned? Thatcher's answer: "Another 45 years!"

Europeans are seldom that open about it, but in their hidden hearts many still share the Soviet Union's almost instinctive fear of a unified Germany. The agony of defeat in World War II and the 45 years of division that followed have clearly damped Germany's enthusiasm for war. Yet that may not last forever, or so the suspicion runs. Left to itself, with its growing excitement about being the Old Germany and its almost brute economic force, Germany might recover its pre-1945 sense of destiny.

There are more concrete reasons as well for Europe to wish for a counterbalance to German power. While pledging their allegiance to NATO, most German politicians and diplomats would like to see it replaced eventually by the 34-nation (CSCE). This may be for the best for the rest of Europe; weighted representation will ensure that Germany does not dominate the forum. And there is no question that Germany has its own priorities. Though Chancellor Kohl vows to instill fresh momentum into the European Community's drive toward political and economic union, Bonn's recent treaty of friendship with Moscow and the proximity of new East European economic markets are likely to turn much of Germany's attention eastward. The rest of Europe has other priorities.

Europe itself must provide the balance to keep Germany in the fold. Yet neither CSCE nor the collective neutrality that some emerging Eastern European nations seem to support will do the trick. Only American power, which remains unequaled on Earth, can be relied on to keep Germany in line, and only NATO offers that support. In this context, NATO has once again become relevant, not so much for its military hardware, but as an instrument for forging Europe's political future.

Two events that took place late in 1990 will shape NATO's future. The "Declaration of London" made the organization's continued existence palatable to both the new Germany and the Soviet Union. The Soviet Union found comfort in NATO's pledges that it will "never . . . be the first to use force" and will make its nuclear arsenal "truly weapons of last resort." For Germany, the declaration offered to abolish the short-range nuclear weapons that would kill Germans in the event of a European war.

Of course, keeping the peace need not be NATO's job alone. This brings up the second critical event of late 1990, the Conference on Security and Cooperation in Europe, held in Paris that November. In front of 12 neutral countries at the Salle des Fêtes, at the Elysée Palace, the 16 NATO countries and the six Warsaw Pact nations signed an agreement to cut arms in Europe dramatically and to bless German unification. Among the godparents of the pact, the Soviet Union and Germany were the most enthusiastic, the Americans and British the least enthusiastic, and the French somewhere in between. At the end, the 34 nations involved (the United States, Canada, and all of Europe, Albania has since joined) agreed to set up a secretariat in Prague, a Conflict Prevention Center in Vienna, and an office in Warsaw to gather data on elections and possibly even to monitor them. The secretariat will prepare yearly meetings of a council of ministers. There will also be a parliamentary wing, called the Assembly of Europe.

The plan remains vague, but it is a first step in the right direction. Modest as it is, the CSCE at least gave East Europeans a way to join fully with the rest of Europe, and it did this without isolating the Russians. The need not to shut them out was well expressed in French by Polish Prime Minister Tadeusz Mazowiecki and in "solid school German" by Hungarian Prime Minister Jozsef Antall. Their message was that Europe, though at last rescued from the threat of war, now risks being divided into haves and have-nots. Antall spoke darkly of a "welfare wall" rising to replace the iron curtain. The East Europeans also warned of rising national frictions. Their concerns were borne out in the first few months of 1991 by the harsh Soviet crackdowns in Lithuania, Latvia, and several other republics and by the Kremlin coup that followed.

If that were not evidence enough that NATO has lost little of its relevance, the war in the Persian Gulf also demonstrated the organization's continuing importance. More than a few of the world's experts felt that Iraq's invasion of Kuwait would encourage other global bullies to attack their neighbors. At the very least, analysts said, the invasion of Kuwait has forced many countries to reappraise what they spend on defense. Wolfgang Demisch, of UBS Securities in New York, a leading defense securities analyst, believes there is more recklessness loose in the world. "Argentina and Chile almost went to war over some useless islands," Demisch says. "This is the kind of thing we can expect more of." He likens the global situation today to the historical hostility that exists between Greece and Turkey, which have long spent 5 to 6 percent of their gross national products to arm themselves against each other. "As far as global unrest goes," Demisch says, "we'll have a lot more Greece and Turkey situations."

If anything holds them in check, it will be the memory of the strong response by the United Nations Security Council to Saddam Hussein's aggression. It was no accident that the air and ground assaults against Iraq and occupied Kuwait were led by American and British forces, with strong supporting roles played by French, Italian, and Dutch aircraft, in addition to Middle

Eastern troops. The shared outlook between the NATO countries remains key to the relationship. NATO's charter forbids it from acting as NATO per se outside of Europe. NATO could have acted in the Persian Gulf only to protect Turkey from an Iraqi assault. Otherwise, NATO had no legal role to play. Instead, however, several NATO countries decided individually to send forces. This remarkable consensus allowed these countries to serve under the U.S. command even though they could not claim the NATO banner. Just as NATO will be refashioned to feature rapid deployment forces, it may also consider changing its charter to allow for such "out-of-area" involvement.

Epilogue

....

Life in the New Global Society

"We will soon enjoy a burst of prosperity much like the one that buoyed the United States during the 1950s. This time, the entire developed and developing world will share in it."

....

"**T**he world, it was the old world yet," as A. E. Housman observed under somewhat different circumstances. A few of the rules have changed in the field of international affairs, and some of the most difficult problems of the post–World War II years at last show signs of easing. But even if all the contentious political issues of the past were to disappear magically in the next decade, much more would still remain to be accomplished. All the fundamental obstacles to a decent life have been largely neglected in the decades of jockeying for political and military advantage. Poverty, disease, overcrowding, pollution, and ignorance remain to be conquered.

For the industrialized nations, and for the developing countries on their borders, the next ten years will be a time of consolidation and economic growth. Mikhail Gorbachev canceled the cold war because the traditional Soviet expansionism wasted resources desperately needed for the more useful purpose of raising his nation's standard of living. In doing so, he gave the same opportunity to his former enemies in the West. The nations of Eastern Europe, now freed from Soviet domination, form a reserve of unused productive capacity that, when modernized, will add to the goods and services that make life more comfortable. So do the hundreds of millions of dollars worth of weapons and military research formerly devoted to making sure the cold war would never turn hot. Factor in as well, the market efficiencies offered by the removal of trade barriers within and between the three great blocs now being formed, and we will soon enjoy a burst of prosperity much like the one that buoyed the United States during the 1950s. This time, the entire developed and developing world will share in it.

Yet, for much of the Third World, the political and economic changes of the 1990s will go largely unnoticed. In the preindustrial countries of Asia, Africa, and Latin America, life will remain stark and brief; Africa faces the appalling devastation of AIDS, in addition to its more familiar problems. Nothing the developed lands can do in the 1990s can significantly change those constants.

Even in Europe, where the "new world order" will bring its earliest and greatest rewards, the millennium is at hand only in the literal sense. The tasks of modernizing Eastern Europe's productive capacity and cleaning up the pollution left by decades of unregulated industrial waste will absorb much of the Continent's attention in the coming years. And as we have seen, the withdrawal of Soviet force from Eastern Europe, and its relaxation within the USSR itself, has released the petty nationalistic quarrels of past centuries; the pitched battles already seen in Armenia and Georgia will all too likely be replayed in Kosovo and neighboring areas of the Balkans. The proto-democracies of Poland, Hungary, and the other former Soviet vassal states all must develop the habits of tolerance and compromise, without which popular rule brings only the tyranny of the largest voting bloc.

The vast economic power of the unified European Community will ease many of these problems; EC patronage will be needed to pay the cost of bringing Eastern Europe into the modern world, and it will go primarily to the nations that show the most promise of using it wisely. This is a huge incentive for healing the Continent's regional and ethnic animosities. As summer of 1991 warms the northern hemisphere, it even seems possible that Serbia may ease its hold on the rest of Yugoslavia in response to large but peaceful protests; if so, it will be clear proof that Belgrade understands how much it would lose by alienating Brussels.

Many other conflicts will be difficult to resolve because there is no structure equivalent to the European Community that can peacefully enforce order outside the great trading blocs, between them, and sometimes within their individual member states. The devastation that Saddam Hussein brought on his nation in the Gulf War is just one symptom of the need for more effective ways to keep the peace. The IRA bombings in the United Kingdom, Basque separatist murders in Spain, and generalized religious and ethnic rage in India are others. There is no significant possibility of violence between the developed nations—we believe the leaders of the major blocs have at last grown too sensible to indulge even in trade wars, much less the more savage kind—but minor-power conflicts, revolutions, and terrorism will continue almost at their accustomed pace. They will grow more threatening as nuclear weapons and ballistic missiles continue their spread to the less developed and less stable nations.

At this point, only one country has the power to return the world to a new cold war—the same country whose internal reform movement finally brought an end to the last one. The Soviet Union finds itself in a position all too reminiscent of Weimar Germany. Once more, a great military power, often gripped by unthinking nationalism has been humiliated on the world stage. Its economy is in ruins. Its ethnic minorities are at each other's throats. It changes things little that Germany's downfall was brought about by war and that the Soviet Union's has been caused by the inherent inefficiency of its governmental system. In fact, this may make the situation even less stable. In Weimar Germany, the leaders responsible for their nation's destruction were stripped of their authority at the war's end. In the Soviet Union, the Party and its hard-liners retain much of their power. They will inevitably lose their position, probably before the turn of the twenty-first century, but there could be more than one cycle of reform and retrenchment between now and then. Whenever Moscow cracks down on its dissidents, the West will begin to wonder whether it can yet afford to beat its missiles into plowshares.

For most citizens of the developed nations, these will be matters for the morning paper and the evening television news programs. The hardship facing the undeveloped countries will affect us only when the United Nations calls up troops from its member states to quell regional disorders or when the wealthy nations enlist volunteers for programs, like the American Peace Corps, to ease the suffering of less fortunate lands. As always, the vast majority will be more concerned with challenges much closer to home. The steady loss of manufacturing jobs from the developed nations to the developing ones will continue as it did in the 1980s; so will the growing demand for professionals and information workers. The small farms of Europe will succumb to competition from their more efficient counterparts in the United States and the Third World. These trends will continue to mean hard times for those who, owing to age or education, cannot make the transition to the new economy. Yet most of us will experience the nineties as a time of growing well-being. It will be the first of several such decades.

There is a chance that the future will be even brighter than it now seems. We have had to narrow our view of the world in this book, partially in order to remain within the space of a single volume and partially because of the realities of modern publishing; with only rare exceptions, writers must complete their work in a year or two at most, not the decades Gibbon devoted to *The Rise and Fall of the Roman Empire*. For these reasons, we have concentrated on international politics and economics, excluding other factors that will do much to shape the world of the next century. Those factors remain beyond the scope of this book, but the most important of them deserves at least a mention. This is the rapid growth of science and technology. The sum total of all human knowledge amassed throughout history is only one percent of the information that will be available to us by 2050. No fewer than 80 percent of the scientists, engineers, anthropologists, sociologists, and operations researchers who ever lived are alive today. In the years to come, their work will take us in directions we cannot envision, before we arrive at our destination. Yet, at least a few of the most fertile grounds are obvious. The tools and insights they offer will illuminate the world around us in ways never before available.

New developments in electronics and telecommunications will be among the first to make their impact. Before 1995, the industrialized nations will adopt the first cellular telephone system that uses satellite technology to relay calls anywhere in the world. High-definition television will surely arrive well before the turn of the century. And the 1990s may at last be the decade when so-called "home computers" truly find a role in the home. There seems little chance that any of these developments will change our lives as fundamentally as television did in the 1950s and 1960s, or as personal computers did in the 1980s, but some are likely to surprise us.

In the more distant future, space technology may finally come into its own. There is no longer any doubt that such Buck Rogers fantasies as solar power satellites and asteroid mining could be turned into practical realities if only we had the will to pursue them; in fact, there has been no doubt of it since the basic research and engineering studies were completed nearly 20 years ago. It would take two decades to build enough solar power satellites to replace the polluting coal and oil on which the world's economy now depends, and somewhat longer to retrieve the vast supply of iron, nickel, and other resources available in a single asteroid. But the rewards would more than repay the investment of time, effort, and money required to secure them. Now that the Soviet Union has offered to merge its space program with those of the West, there is at least a chance the work could begin by the turn of the century.

In basic science, there is the Human Genome Project, one of the most important, complex, and fascinating scientific endeavors yet undertaken. Its goal is nothing less than to map the entire human genetic structure, the 50,000 to 100,000 bits of DNA in which nature has coded the instructions needed to build a complete person. (For details of this epochal work, see Robert Shapiro's *The Human Blueprint; The Race To Unlock the Secrets of Our Genetic Script,* St. Martin's Press, 1991.) This breathtaking effort will illuminate the processes by which the human organism grows and operates. Its discoveries will change medicine and biotechnology even more profoundly than the end of the cold war has changed international affairs.

And in medicine, researchers have discovered that drugs such as melatonin (which nature uses to regulate the body's internal clocks) and deprenyl (used for the treatment of Parkinson's disease) can dramatically extend the lives of laboratory animals. Other lines of research promise to ease or eliminate the suffering caused by Alzheimer's syndrome and the other ills of aging. By the end of the century, we should know whether the same techniques work with human beings. Very probably, they will. Those of us who are alive in the year 2000 could well have personal access to the vast knowledge available in 2050. There has never been, and will never be, a more fundamental transformation in the ground rules according to which we human beings live our lives.

These and many other developments in science and technology will bring new challenges. Some of them may be even more difficult to solve than the political issues now facing the world. They will arrive before we are fully prepared to face them. But in the 1990s, humanity and its governing institutions at last show signs of maturing. We enter the decade groping for peaceable, cooperative ways to resolve our differences; we will enter the next century with the new world order firmly established. "The world will be a more peaceful and prosperous place in the 1990s than it has been in the decades since World War II, because the premises by which it is governed have changed. In the coming years, it will no longer be ruled to suit the needs of ideological and military competition, but instead, to promote international trade and the well-being of the trading nations." We believed that when we began the prologue to this book nearly a year ago. Events since then have done nothing to undermine our faith in the decade now opening. The changes we are witnessing today will leave us far better equipped to face the challenges yet to come.

Appendix A

90 MAJOR TRENDS NOW CHANGING OUR WORLD

Population

1. In the industrialized countries, the "birth dearth" has cut growth almost to nothing; in the developing world, the population bomb is still exploding.
   - The rich get richer, the poor have children: Throughout the industrialized world, workers can look forward to national retirement programs or social security. In the developing lands, those too old for labor rely on their children to support them—so they have as many as they can.
   - Thanks to better health care, children have a greater chance to survive into adulthood and produce children of their own. This will accelerate population growth.
2. The AIDS epidemic will slaughter the defenseless by the millions.
   - According to the World Health Organization, AIDS-causing HIV will infect up to 40 million people by 2000.
   - By 1990, some five million people in sub-Saharan Africa already carried the disease, twice as many as just three years earlier. In some cities, up to 40 percent of the population may be infected. By the year 2000, 90 percent of the sub-Saharan population will test HIV-positive.
   - Seventy percent of the prostitutes in southern India tested HIV-positive in a recent study.

1.a

1.b

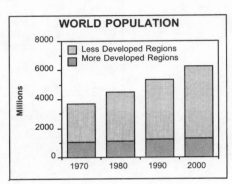

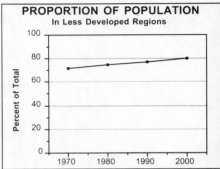

1.c

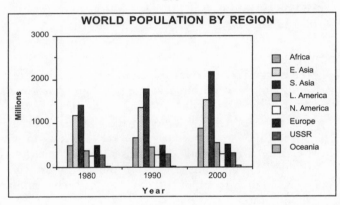

1.d

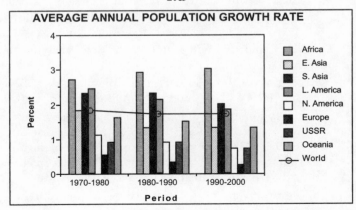

1.e

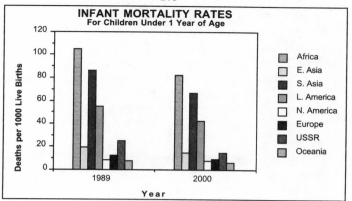

- In an attempt to halt the spread of AIDS, China has forbidden prostitutes to solicit Westerners.
3. A host of new medical technologies will make life longer and more comfortable in the industrialized world; it will be many years before these technologies spread to the developing countries.

The Technologies

- Colleges, government agencies, and private companies will pour $100 billion into genetic engineering by 2000. They will soon churn out artificial blood and natural medicines such as human growth hormone and insulin (already in production). Soon after, doctors will be able to tamper with fetal genes, making babies immune to some diseases.
- A new generation of CAT-like scanners will give such detailed views of the body that doctors can eliminate most exploratory surgery.
- Laser surgery will reduce patient trauma, shortening hospital stays and lowering medical costs.
- Biomedical engineering will create new and better bionic limbs, practical artificial hearts, and body monitors to detect oncoming heart attacks, strokes, and epileptic attacks before they occur.
- Experimental brain–cell transplants will aid victims of retardation and head trauma by 2001. Surgeons will repair sick hearts by grafting in healthy muscle from other parts of the body. In many operations, laborato-

ry-grown bone, skin, muscle, and blood cells will replace donor tissues.

• The first anti-aging treatments will extend the human
lifespan to more than a century of vigorous health.
Best bet: melatonin, the natural hormone that regulates
the body's "clocks," which prevents many of the effects of aging in animals and extends their lifespans by
20 percent, without adverse side effects.

The Profession

• Medical knowledge is doubling every eight years.

• Organ transplants, artificial organs, genetic engineering, and a host of other developments have made
it possible to prolong life almost indefinitely, but they
raise a host of disturbing ethical and moral issues, such
as surrogate motherhood, how to distribute medical
resources fairly, and when to withdraw life support.
Well into the next century, the developed nations will
still be trying to resolve these and similar dilemmas.

• By 2001, the United States will have 100,000 more
physicians than it needs. The result: doctors will pay
closer attention to their patients, open their offices on
evenings and weekends, and even begin to make house
calls again. Some may leave the U.S. to practice in less
crowded nations.

4. As the West grows ever more concerned with physical
culture and personal health, the developing countries are
adopting the unhealthy practices that wealthier nations
are trying to cast off: smoking, high-fat diets, and seden-
tary lifestyles. To the people in developing countries,
these deadly luxuries are symbols of success.

• By 2001, nine out of ten American insurance companies will expand coverage or cut premiums for policy-
holders with healthy lifestyles. Their contemporaries
in Europe will soon follow.

• Growing health-consciousness will create mini-boom
industries in participant sports, exercise equipment,
home gyms, and employee fitness programs.

• Two-thirds of the people surveyed in a recent Harris
poll claimed to have changed their eating habits in the
last two years. Americans today consume fifteen
pounds more chicken, one pound more fish, and twen-

ty-two gallons more low-fat milk per capita each year than in 1976. This trend will spread through the developed world.

• U.S. alcohol consumption has dropped from two gallons per capita per year in 1979 to 1.6 gallons in 1987. Instead of hard liquor, Americans are drinking beer, wine, and sparkling water. Europeans are beginning to follow their lead.

• In the U.S., smokers are kicking the habit. Only 35 percent of American men smoke, down from 52 percent twenty years ago; 29 percent of women smoke, down from a peak of 34 percent.

• However, the developing world continues to smoke more each year; even Europe shows little sign of solving this problem.

• Drug abuse appears to be leveling off in the United States; in the 1990s, drug traffickers will begin to focus on potential markets in the Soviet Union, eastern Europe, and Africa.

• The next major trend in personal fitness will be stress control. Ninety percent of all diseases are stress-related.

4.a

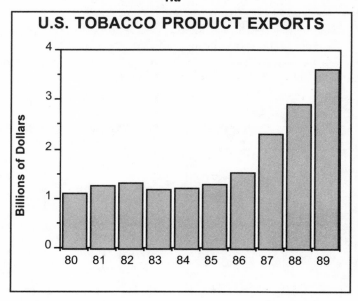

5. Better nutrition and the "wellness" movement will raise life expectancy.
  • In the developed countries, children born in the 1980s will live to an average age of seventy (male) or seventy-seven (female); in the developing world, life expectancy will remain stalled at fifty-nine (male) and sixty-one (female).

5.a

LIFE EXPECTANCY AT BIRTH

(Bar chart showing "Years of Life" on the vertical axis from 0 to 80, with groups for 1989 and 2000. Bars labeled "More Developed Regions", "World", and "Less Developed Regions".)

6. In the developed world, the vast Baby Boom generation is approaching middle age, and threatening to overwhelm both medical and social security programs. These costs will consume an increasing portion of national budgets until about 2020.

6.a   **6.b**

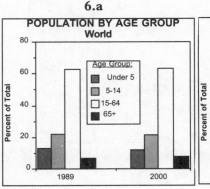

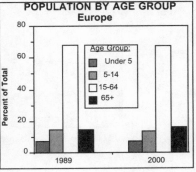

7. Look for the United Nations to take on even more of the work of relieving hunger and poverty in the developing world.

- Growing population problems will force the industrialized nations to spend more on the World Health Organization.

- UNESCO, the relatively obscure United Nations Educational, Scientific, and Cultural Organization, will also grow sharply in the 1990s.

- The developed world will continue to pour more money into famine-, plague-, and disaster-relief. The U.N. and the Red Cross/Red Crescent will coordinate many of these programs.

Food

8. Farmers will continue to harvest more food than the world really needs, but inefficient delivery systems will prevent it from reaching the hungry.

- According to the World Bank, some 800 million people are chronically malnourished by U.N. standards. As the world population grows, that number can only rise.

- Hunger is slowly losing its role as a political weapon. By the turn of the century, fewer governments will feel free to starve their opponents into submission.

- Food quality and health standards pioneered in the United States are now spreading to the European Community. The trend will quickly spread to less developed lands.

- The trend in some developing countries to adopt Western diets will do more than raise the risk of heart attack and stroke. Because a cow eats more calories than its meat provides, overall food production may plateau, or even decline.

- Though trade negotiations have deadlocked over the issue of national agricultural subsidies—the United States and other food exporters would like to do away with them; Japan, South Korea, and the European Community refuse to give them up—tariffs are on their way out. Most will be gone by 2000.

9. Packers will be freezing more of their merchandise,

wrapping it better, adopting the *sous vide* (cook/chill) process, and even zapping your peas with radiation, all in an effort to make food last longer. Soon consumers will enjoy products much like army "MREs" (Meals Ready to Eat), which can now survive unrefrigerated for up to eighteen months.

10. Farms themselves are changing rapidly.

   • In the United States, the family farm is quickly disappearing. Giant agro-businesses will reap vast profits, while small, part-time "hobby" farms also survive. This trend will begin to affect other developed nations during the 1990s, and will eventually spread to the rest of the world.

   • Former Iron Curtain countries will find it difficult to turn their huge, inefficient collective farms back to private owners; progress in this effort will be uneven.

   • Land reform in the Philippines and Latin America will move at a glacial pace, showing progress only when revolution threatens. Most of the vast holdings now owned by the rich and worked by the poor will survive well into the twenty-first century.

11. Science is increasing the world's supply of food.

   • According to the U.S. Office of Technology Assessment, biotechnology and other yield-increasing developments will account for five-sixths of the growth in world harvests by 2000; the rest will come from newly cultivated croplands.

   • Biotechnology is bringing new protein to developing countries. Bovine growth hormone can produce 20 percent more milk per pound of cattle feed, while genetic engineering is creating fish that grow faster in aqua-farms. Use of biopharmaceuticals and new farm chemicals should grow by nine percent in the next decade.

   • Gene-splicers are creating plants that require less water, grow faster, and resist disease better than their natural ancestors. They can be planted where growing seasons are too short for traditional strains or produce extra crops each year.

12. Water will be plentiful in most regions. Total use of water worldwide by 2000 will be less than half of the stable

renewable supply. Yet some parched, populous areas will run short.

- The Middle East and the American West, in particular, are in for dry times by the turn of the century. Two decades later, as many as twenty-five African nations may face serious water shortages.
- The amount of water needed in Western Asia will double between 1980 and 2000.
- Southern and Eastern Europe must keep a close eye on their supples; so must Central and Southern Asia.
- Coordinating the use of ground and surface water will make irrigation more efficient. Brackish water and treated waste water will soon be used to irrigate salt-tolerant crops and for some industrial applications.
- We already know how to cut water use and waste water flows by up to 90 percent. In the next decade, the industrialized countries will finally adopt many of these water-saving techniques.
- Farm regions will improve and expand their irrigation systems, and build a host of new ones. Where ecologically acceptable, they will also build more dams to gather the life-giving water that in many areas, such as the American West, is already in short supply.
- Cheaper, more effective desalination methods are on the horizon. In the next twenty years, they will make it easier to live in many desert areas.
- New, less expensive technology will soon make it practical to drill more and deeper wells.
- Developing countries reuse little of their waste water, because they lack the sewage systems required to collect it. By 2000, building this needed infrastructure will become a high priority in many parched lands.
- Progressively more of our water will be reused, as the scarcity of fresh water makes the cost of recycling competitive.

13. Food supplies will become healthier and more wholesome.
    - Most nations will adopt higher and more uniform standards of hygiene and quality, the better to market their food products internationally. Consumers the world over will benefit.

- To meet the needs of a growing health-conscious segment of the population, especially in the developed world, food processors will continue to introduce products that are less carcinogenic and contain less cholesterol and fat.

14. The U.N. Food and Agriculture Organization will take on a much larger role in the world's food production and distribution.

Energy

15. Despite all the calls to develop alternative sources of energy, oil will provide more of the world's power in 2000 than it did in 1990.

- OPEC will supply most of it. Demand for OPEC oil grew from 15 million barrels a day in 1986 to over 20 million barrels just three years later. By 2000, it will easily top 25 million barrels daily.

- If oil production outside the OPEC nations has not yet peaked, that day will come soon. Existing wells and refineries are operating near capacity, and few non-OPEC lands have enough reserves to justify building more. By 2000, or very soon after, both America's Prudhoe Bay and Britain's North Sea oil fields will run dry.

- OPEC will easily make up the deficit.

16. Contrary to popular belief, the world is not about to run out of oil.

15.a   **15.b**

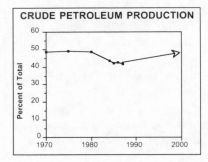

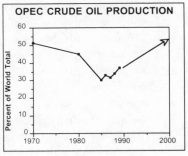

15.c

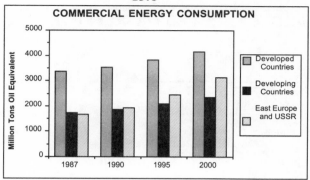

- The world's proven oil reserves have nearly doubled in the last ten years as a result of intensive exploration.
- If the price of oil starts to rise, new methods for recovering oil from old wells will become cost effective. Techniques already developed could add nearly fifty percent to the world's recoverable oil supply.

16.a

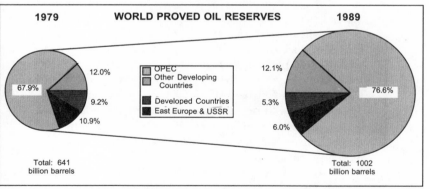

- The "huff and puff" technique, whereby carbon dioxide is pumped into old wells to force previously unrecoverable oil to the surface, is currently showing promise.
17. Oil prices are not likely to rise; instead, by 2000 they will plummet to between seven and nine dollars per barrel.
   - The United Nations, in its *Global Outlook 2000* report, predicts costs will lie in the $15 to $25 per barrel range (in 1987 dollars) for the rest of this century: The mar-

16.c

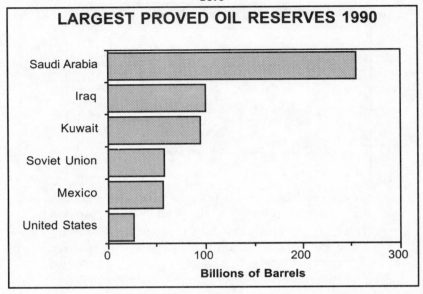

LARGEST PROVED OIL RESERVES 1990

Saudi Arabia
Iraq
Kuwait
Soviet Union
Mexico
United States

0   100   200   300

Billions of Barrels

ket will not bear the cost of oil over $25 for an extended period of time. The report also argues that oil prices will not drop below $15 per barrel for extended periods, since this would stifle production in high cost regions. OPEC members also will not jeopardize their countries' economic development by letting the price fall lower. In fact, OPEC describes a price below $18 per barrel as a "price collapse." The U.N. report overlooks a number of factors that will undermine oil prices within the next ten years. One is that oil is inherently cheap. It costs only $1.38 per barrel to lift Saudi oil out of the ground. Even Prudhoe Bay and North Sea oil cost only $5 per barrel.

• The twenty most industrialized countries all have three-month supplies of oil in tankers and storage tanks. Most have another three months-worth in "strategic reserves." If OPEC raises its prices too high, their customers can afford to stop buying until the costs come down. This was not the case during the 1970s oil shocks.

• OPEC is not very good at throttling back production to keep prices up when their market is glutted. They will not get any better at it in the 1990s.

• The Persian Gulf war showed how vulnerable oil prices really are. The attack on Kuwait more than doubled oil prices for a few weeks; they fell back to nearly pre-war levels long before the war ended. Not even the destruction of Kuwait's oil fields could keep oil prices high.

18. Growing competition from other energy sources will also help to limit the price of oil.

• Natural gas burns cleanly—and there is enough of it available to supply the world's entire energy need for the next two hundred years.

• Nuclear plants will supply 12 percent of the energy in Eastern Europe and the Soviet Union by the end of the century.

• Solar, geothermal, wind, and wave energy will ease power problems where these energy sources are most readily available, but they will contribute only a small fraction of the world's energy in the foreseeable future.

• Nuclear fusion, the energy produced when small atoms are combined to form larger ones, probably will not supply practical power before 2020.

• Even later, a costly but pollution-free hydrogen economy may at last become practical.

The Environment

19. People the world over will become increasingly sensitive to environmental issues as the consequences of neglect, indifference, and ignorance become ever more apparent. Policies and programs on global, regional, and national levels will emerge to repair damage already done and to prevent future damage. International organizations, particularly the U.N., will help to coordinate and carry out these efforts.

20. In the 1990s, air is not just for breathing any more; it's for debating, regulating, and cleaning. Air pollution and other atmospheric issues will dominate eco-policy discussions for years to come.

• Soot and other particulates will come in for growing scrutiny in the near future. Recent evidence shows that they are far more dangerous than sulfur dioxide and other gaseous pollutants formerly believed to present major health risks. In the United States alone, medical researchers estimate that as many as 60,000 people may die each year as a direct result of breathing particulates. Most are elderly and already suffering from respiratory illness.

- By 1985 the concentration of carbon dioxide in the atmosphere had increased 25 times since pre-industrial days; by 2050 the concentration is likely to increase another 40 percent if energy use continues to grow at its current pace. Burning fossil fuel will spew about 7 billion tons of carbon into the air each year by 2000, 10 to 14 billion tons in 2030, and 13 to 23 billion in 2050.

- Blame global warming for at least some of the spread of Africa's deserts. Before the process runs its course, two-fifths of Africa's remaining fertile land could become arid wasteland. Up to one-third of Asia's non-desert land and one-fifth of Latin America's may follow. Global warming will not only hurt agriculture but will also raise sea levels, inundating low-lying coastal areas such as river deltas, flood plains, and seashores that are now home to millions of people. The entire nation of Bangladesh could eventually be under water. In an effort to stem the tide, 137 countries will likely sign the far-reaching World Climate Treaty in Brazil in February 1992.

- The global average level of stratospheric ozone, which filters out cancer-causing ultraviolet radiation, fell by about five percent from 1979 to 1986.

- The 1987 Montreal Protocol on Substances That Deplete the Ozone Layer, which went into effect at the beginning of 1989, asks nations to cut production and use of harmful chlorofluorocarbons (CFCs) by half from 1986 to 1999, with a ten-year delay allowed for developing countries that consume less than 0.3 kg per capita.

- In the May 1989 Helsinki Declaration on the Protection of the Ozone Layer, 81 countries and the European Community agreed to phase out CFCs completely by 2000, if not sooner.

- Less damaging (but not benign) hydrochlorofluorocarbons (HCFCs) will gradually supplant CFCs until environmentally acceptable replacement products are developed.

- Having announced in 1988 its intention to phase out CFC production, Du Pont recently unveiled a new generation of refrigerants that will replace CFCs in new air conditioning and refrigeration equipment, and produce only ten percent of the global warming effect attributed to CFCs.

- Brazil and other nations will soon halt the irrevocable destruction of the earth's rain forests for economic gain. Those countries will need economic help to make the transition. The World Bank and the International Monetary Fund will help underwrite alternatives to rain forest destruction.

- "Acid rain" like that afflicting the United States and Canada will appear whenever designers of new power plants and factories neglect emission control equipment. Watch for it in most of the developing countries.

21. Efforts to save whales, dolphins, spotted owls, snail darters, and old-growth forests are just the first of many such campaigns. Proposed dams, factories, landfills, housing developments built on wetlands, and the like will have to survive more environmental impact studies, and more comprehensive ones, before breaking ground. Court orders and demonstrations by ecologically concerned citizens groups will block a steady stream of construction projects, both in the West and in a growing number of developing countries.

22. If you live in a developed nation and are not yet recycling your garbage, you have something to look forward to. Within the next decade, most of the industrialized world will all but run out of space in its landfills.

- The Environmental Protection Agency estimates that existing technologies could reduce the total amount of hazardous waste generated in the U.S. by 15 to 30 percent by 2000.

- Governments will respond with a flood of new regulations and waste management programs designed to turn back the tide of trash.

- For now, recycling is a necessary nuisance. By 2000,

it will become a valuable resource, as research finds profitable new uses for materials still being discarded. Recycling will save energy as well; remanufacturing takes less power than the full iron-ore-to-Cadillac production process.

• One other development will help: new packaging materials and techniques that produce less waste. Many of them will appear on store shelves in the next ten years. Already, McDonald's is handing out its Big Macs in cardboard containers instead of ozone-destroying plastic; some businesses have replaced Styrofoam "packing peanuts" with unsalted popcorn.

23. Protecting the environment will become the hot new growth industry of the 1990s and early twenty-first century. Entrepreneurs will strike gold in marketing environmentally safe products, developing ways to monitor pollutants, and cleaning up after disasters such as oil spills.

• Ruptured oil tankers are a major threat. Double-hulled ships would reduce the risk; by 2000, many Western nations will require double hulls on all new tankers.

24. Insurance-like programs to pay or repair environmental damage will proliferate. The U.S. has had its "Superfund" to pay for cleaning up toxic waste sites for several years. The European Community will soon establish a similar fund.

Warfare

25. Mikhail Gorbachev's "new thinking" has cut the risk of widespread nuclear war almost to zero, but it has also made the world safer for local and regional conflicts. During the Cold War, the superpowers could restrain their aggressive junior allies from attacking their neighbors. With the nuclear threat effectively gone, would-be antagonists feel less inhibited. Saddam Hussein was only the first of many small despots who will try to win by conquest what cannot be achieved by negotiation.

• The United States and the Soviet Union will sign a long procession of arms treaties in the next decade. The two countries will make a virtue of necessity, but both will act primarily to cut expensive military programs from their budgets.

• With the demise of the Warsaw Pact, NATO must seek a new purpose—it will eventually become an emergency strike force for the United Nations—the number of guns, tanks, and military planes in Europe will fall to little more than half their peak levels.

• By 2000 or so, the most influential man in the Soviet Union will be neither Mikhail Gorbachev nor Boris Yeltsin—nor one of the Communist hard-liners now hoping to restore the pre-Gorbachev status quo. Instead, it will be former Foreign Minister Eduard Shevardnadze, who retains many friends in the Moscow government, but will return to teaching and mold the thinking of the next generation of Soviet leaders. In the long run, it is Shevardnadze who will make permanent the political and economic revolution now taking place in his nation, and the new era of superpower peace.

26. These changes will allow the superpowers to cut military spending in half. The money saved will be used for social programs in the West, economic development in the East; some will help to balance national budgets. It may be less than originally hoped because troops and conventional weapons cost more, on a "bang-for-the-buck" basis, than nuclear arms.

27. International bodies will take over much of the peace-keeping role now being abandoned by the superpowers.

• U.N. peace-keeping forces will suppress conflicts in the Middle East and in Southwest Asia.

• The Warsaw Pact has already disappeared; NATO will be radically transformed now that it is no longer needed to defend against a Soviet invasion of Europe. Both may be replaced by the Conference on Security and Cooperation in Europe, a group of 34 nations, including the U.S. and the Soviet Union.

28. Soviet-American cooperation in the Persian Gulf crisis was just the first step in an emerging new relationship between the former antagonists. In the years to come, they will often act together to meet international crises. Their competing intelligence organizations will even begin to share their findings—but only with regard to other countries.

• By 1995, and perhaps much sooner, the U.S. and the

U.S.S.R. will act jointly to promote international talks on a comprehensive Middle East settlement.

29. Tactical alliances formed by common interests to meet immediate needs will replace long-term commitments among nations.

  • Iran and Iraq will tolerate each other in their stronger hatred for the West.

  • The U.S. and Syria will never be friends but both dislike Iraq; in the Middle East, "the enemy of your enemy is your friend."

  • Turkey and Greece will be hard-pressed to overlook their differences about Cyprus but may do so in an effort to counter terrorism.

30. Brushfire wars will grow more frequent and bloody. Four of the most likely:

  • Israel vs. the Arab countries—We foresee one last conflict in this region before the peace that now seems near actually becomes reality. Israel will win this one, too.

  • India vs. Pakistan—The two have feuded with each other since the British left in 1947; religious differences, separatism in Kashmir, and small stocks of nuclear weapons make this a hot spot to watch carefully.

  • Greece vs. Turkey—Over 15 years ago, Turkey invaded the northern part of Cyprus, disrupting life on the island and producing a conflict within NATO. There is not much chance for resolution while Greece's New Democratic Party remains unable to take bold initiatives (since it holds only a slight majority in the Parliament) and as the "Davos Spirit" of reconciliation breaks down.

  • Northern Ireland vs. itself—This perpetually troubled land will remain its own worst enemy. In trying to keep Ireland under control, the British face an increasingly unpleasant task.

31. Look for a new wave of terrorism:

  • The IRA has stepped up its violence in recent months, sometimes forcing civilians to cooperate in missions such as car bombings of British checkpoints. This is a clear sign of things to come.

  • Abul Abbas leads one of the extremist PLO factions inflamed by Saddam Hussein's aggression. Muammar

Qadhafi, a long-time ally, recently kicked him out of
Libya. Some observers believe that Qadhafi may have
been trying to curry favor with the West; we suspect
that it was just a falling out among thieves.

- Abu Nidal, who heads another of the PLO's innumer-
able splinter groups, also has ties to Saddam. After
Iraq's bloody defeat, he is almost surely plotting
against the West.
- And in Northern Spain, Basque separatists of the ETA
are still fighting for autonomy. They will neither receive it nor give up the fight in the 1990s.

32. The development of nuclear, biological, and chemical
weapons will continue to grow. Some Third World
powers will be tempted to use them. Cheap, easy to
make, easy to conceal chemical and biological weapons
could become the terrorist threat of the future.

World Economy

33. The world economy will grow rapidly in the foreseeable
future, becoming ever more tightly integrated.

- World trade will grow at a brisk 4.5 percent annually
in the next decade. As one result, foreign competition
will continue to cost jobs and income in the developed
market economies.
- The GDPs of the developed market economies will
grow at 3.1 percent on average in the 1990s as investment demand increases and the economic integration
in Europe improves capital efficiency.
- The economies of Eastern Europe and the U.S.S.R.
may recover with a GDP growth rate of 3.6 percent.
- The developing countries will fall further and further
behind the industrialized nations, largely because their
populations continue to rise faster than their incomes.
GDPs in the developing economies will grow by 4.3
percent per year (well below the 5.1 percent rate they
enjoyed in the 1970s). In the 1970s, their per-capita
GDP was one-tenth that of the developed countries.
By 1985, it had fallen to one-twelfth. By 2000, it will
be one-thirteenth.

- By reducing military budgets, the fabled "new world
order" will make more money available for business.
- By 2000 or so, all national currencies will be convert-

33.a

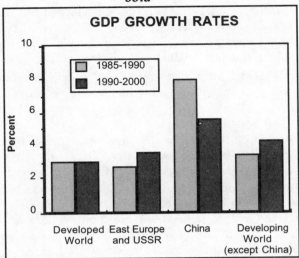

GDP GROWTH RATES

| 1985-1990 |
| 1990-2000 |

Developed World · East Europe and USSR · China · Developing World (except China)

ible, following a model similar to the European Community's Exchange Rate Mechanism.

- It is becoming almost impossible to label a product by nation—for example, "Japanese cars"—since parts often come from several countries, to be assembled elsewhere and sold in yet other lands. Already, 39 percent of the parts for goods "manufactured" in the United States are imported from other countries. Protective tariffs will therefore become obsolete—for the good of the worldwide economy.

- Stock and commodities markets, too, are becoming ever more tightly bound together. Witness the stock crash of October 19, 1987, when falling prices in New York touched off even greater collapses as far away as Singapore. Currency traders routinely stay awake nights to keep watch on markets in New York, London, and Tokyo.

34. The world is quickly dividing itself into three major blocs: the European Community, the North American free-trade zone, and Japan's informal but very real Pacific development area. Other regions will ally themselves with these giants—Eastern Europe with the EC, Mexico with the U.S.-Canada free-trade agreement. The nations of the Latin American Economic System will slowly build ties with their neighbors to the North. The Australia-New Zealand bloc is still trying to make

up its mind which of these units to join—the Pacific Rim, where its nearest markets are, or Europe and North America, where its emotional bonds are strongest.

- The economic structure of all these regions is changing rapidly. All but the least developed nations are moving out of agriculture. Service sectors are growing rapidly in the mature economies, while manufacturing is being transferred to the world's developing economies.

- Within the new economic blocs, multi-national corporations will not replace the nation-state, but they will become far more powerful, especially as governments relinquish aspects of social responsibility to employers.

34.a

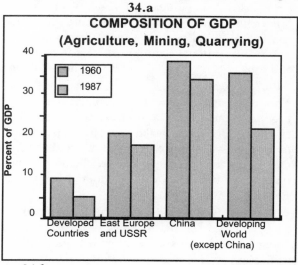

34.b

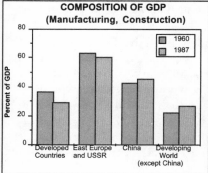

34.c

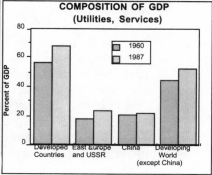

35. The European Community is destined to become an even stronger economic power than the United States or Japan.

   • By 1992, the EC will represent an integrated economy of 325 million people, with a Gross Domestic Product of $4 trillion.

   • By 1996, the European Free Trade Association (EFTA) countries will join with the EC to create a market of 400 million people with a $5 trillion GDP. Sweden, Norway, Finland, Austria, and Switzerland will join the founding twelve.

   • By 2000, most of the former East Bloc countries will become associate members of the EC. Bulgaria, Czechoslovakia, Hungary, Poland, Romania, and the Soviet Union will wish to be associate members. Austria will also seek associate membership after stipulating a constitutional requirement that it remain neutral and thus outside the EC's foreign policy–making apparatus.

   • The most rigid barrier to international trade will be product standards; as some have suggested, it will be easier for Britain to make standards agreements with Japan than with France. Most U.S. standards for high-tech in the aerospace, electronics, chemicals, and pharmaceuticals industries will be adopted or modified for EC use.

36. Even before the fall of socialism, most governments had come to understand that security seldom requires maintaining unprofitable state enterprises, and without that justification it is not in the national interest. Government enterprises the world over are therefore being returned to private hands, a trend that will grow steadily in the coming decade.

   • Western Europe ranges widely from the Thatcher revolution in Britain, which by all accounts was most likely to privatize, to the Socialists in Spain and Portugal, who discovered that government coffers would benefit as privatization made the economy grow.

   • Eastern Europe and the U.S.S.R. clearly recognize that future prosperity requires the loosening of the central government's monopoly on capital. Poland is taking the lead.

- In Latin America, after decades of tight government control, even the Peronists in Argentina and Mexico's so-called Party of the Institutionalized Revolution are relenting. The continent's economies are struggling to climb out of debt and end hyperinflation. Privatization may provide the needed miracle. It is the only course left that has not already failed repeatedly.
- And in the Pacific the outgoing Labor governments of Australia and New Zealand began the privatization process; the new Conservative governments are not likely to stop it. Even China is attempting, albeit feebly, to put its state-run businesses on a profit-making basis.

37. The 25 most industrialized nations will devote two to three percent of their Gross Domestic Products to help their poor neighbors.
    - Much of this will be money that formerly would have gone to pay military budgets.
    - The World Bank and IMF will help distribute funds.
    - Loans and grants may require developing nations to set up population control programs.

38. Western bankers will at last accept the obvious truth: many Third-World debtors have no hope of ever paying back overdue loans. Creditors will thus forgive one-third of these debts. This will save some of the developing nations from bankruptcy and probably dictatorship.

38.a

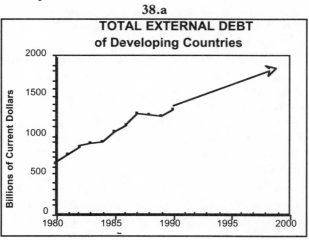

TOTAL EXTERNAL DEBT of Developing Countries

- Recall that arguments for the forgiveness of Egypt's $7 billion military debt held that Egypt had proved a valuable ally in the Persian Gulf crisis and that Cairo could not afford to pay back the money anyway.

39. Developing nations once nationalized plants and industries when they became desperate to pay their debts. In future, the World Bank and International Monetary Fund will refuse to lend to nations that take this easy way out. (Debtors, such as Peru, are eager to make amends to these organizations.) Instead, indebted lands will promote private industry in hope of raising needed income.

40. Washington, D.C., will supplant New York as the world financial capital. The stock exchanges and other financial institutions, especially those involved with international transactions, will move south to be near Congress, the World Bank, and key regulatory bodies.

- Among the key economic players already in the Capitol: the Federal Reserve Board; the embassies and commercial/cultural attachés of nearly every country in the world; and the headquarters of many multinational and foreign corporations.

- In addition, several agencies of the United Nations, including the International Monetary Fund and the General Agreement on Tariffs and Trade are headquartered or routinely conduct much of their business in Washington.

- The Developers Network has established the Wall Street DC 2000 Committee to promote Washington as the world's new financial center.

- The Center for European Community Studies, a unique research and teaching resource focused on the international business aspects of the EC, recently opened at George Mason University's International Institute in Arlington, Virginia, a Washington suburb.

- Improved communications technology no longer makes it essential to be close to the New York Stock Exchange.

- New York City suffers from high real estate costs and taxes totalling $9 to $12 per square foot downtown. These have had a greater impact in times of weakening financial market and dropping business volume.

- New York's economy will continue its current slump. For the past two decades, the headquarters of many non-financial corporations have fled.
- City and state governments had, in effect, to bribe (with $145 million in tax relief and other incentives) four major commodities exchanges to build a new headquarters in Manhattan instead of moving elsewhere.
- Drexel Burnham Lambert moved a section of its bond division to California; Morgan Stanley & Co., Smith Barney Harris Upham & Co., and Prudential-Bache Securities Inc., are currently considering moving out of the city by the end of the decade.
- Computer centers of some of the larger financial firms have also left.

Science & Technology

41. Technology has come to dominate the economy and society in the developed world. Its central role can only grow.

- Such technological advances as the computer, robotics, and CAD/CAM directly affect the way many people live and work.
- For some economists, the numbers of cars, computers, telephones, facsimile machines, and copiers in a nation define how "developed" the country is.
- Personal robots will enter the home by 2000. Robots will take on mundane commercial and service jobs, and environmentally dangerous tasks such as repairing space-station components in orbit.
- Computers will become part of our environment rather than just tools we use for specific tasks. Portable computers will give us wireless access to data wherever we go.
- "Wireless hook-up" will simplify relocation of personnel, minimize delays in setting up new installations, and permit computer terminals to travel with the user, rather than forcing the user to travel to the terminal.
- By 2001, most companies and government agencies will be using artificial intelligence (AI) to help assimilate data and solve problems beyond the range of to-

day's computers. Various forms of AI—expert systems, robotics, machine vision, voice recognition, speech synthesis—will find uses in data processing, health and human services, business and government administration, and airline pilot assistance.

• Expert systems will be the most productive form of AI in the near future. By 2001, they will be in universal use in manufacturing, energy prospecting, automotive diagnostics, medicine, insurance underwriting, and law enforcement. Industries that will benefit from expert systems include insurance, investments and banking, manufacturing and process control, equipment problem diagnosis, and quality control.

• Revenues from off-the-shelf expert system application software is rising exponentially, and is expected to continue.

41.a

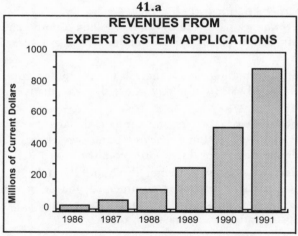

REVENUES FROM
EXPERT SYSTEM APPLICATIONS

• Superconductors operating at room temperature will be in commercial use by 2001. Products based on them will include supercomputers the size of three-pound coffee cans, electric motors 75 percent smaller and lighter than today's, practical hydrogen-fusion power plants, analyzers that can chart the interaction of brain cells, and 300 mph "maglev" trains that float on electromagnetic cushions.

42. The technology gap between developed and developing countries will continue to widen.

- The developed countries have ten times as many scientists and engineers per capita as the developing. The gap between their spending on research and development grew three-fold from 1970 to 1980.
- The technologically underdeveloped lands are marked by antiquated or nonexistent production facilities, a dearth of useful knowledge, ineffective organization and management, and a lack of technical abilities and skills. Under these conditions, underdevelopment is often self-perpetuating, which weakens the country's ability to compete in international markets.
- The widening technology gap will aggravate the disparity in North-South trade, with the developed nations of the northern hemisphere supplying more and more high-tech goods, while the less developed countries of the South become even more restricted to exporting natural resources and relatively unprofitable low-tech manufactured products.

43. Nations will exchange scientific information more freely, but will continue to hold back technological data.
   - Fifty-three percent of Ph.D. candidates in science and engineering programs in the United States are from other countries. Anything they learn will return to their homelands when they do.
   - Basic research is done principally in universities, which have a tradition of communicating their findings.
   - Technological discoveries, in contrast, often spring from corporate laboratories, whose sponsors have a keen interest in keeping them proprietary. More than half of the technology transferred between countries will move between giant corporations and their overseas branches or as part of joint ventures by multinationals and foreign partners.
   - The space-faring nations—soon to include Japan—will share their findings more freely.
   - Despite teleconferencing, computer networks, and other advanced communications methods, face-to-face meetings will remain the most effective method for transferring scientific information.

44. Turnover rates in high technology are accelerating.
   - All the technological knowledge we work with today

will represent only one percent of the information that will be available in 2050.

- The development cycle—idea, invention (a patentable product), innovation (production of a working proto-type), imitation (the rise of competing products in the marketplace)—is growing steadily shorter.
- Products must reach the market quickly to be successful.
- The U.S. will continue to generate more ideas than any other country, but the Japanese will lengthen their lead in getting products to market.
- Computer-aided design, used widely in the automobile and aerospace industries and now spreading into many others, shortens the amount of time between idea and finished design.
- Manufacturers will continue to adopt new production technologies as fast as they can, shortening the development cycle even further.

45. Research and development will play an ever greater role in the economy.

45.a

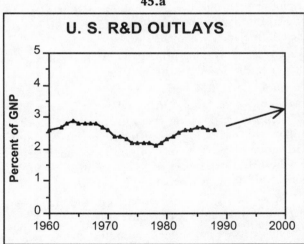

- R&D outlays in the United States have varied narrowly (between 2.1 and 2.8 percent of the GNP) since 1960 and have been rising generally since 1978.
- R&D spending is growing most rapidly in the elec-

45.b

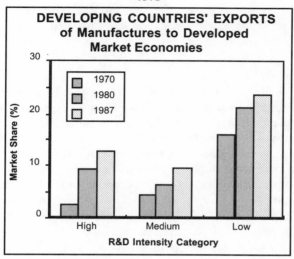

DEVELOPING COUNTRIES' EXPORTS
of Manufactures to Developed
Market Economies

tronics, aerospace, pharmaceuticals, and chemical industries.

46. Technological advances in transportation will soon avert the growing threat of national gridlock in the air and on land. These developments will also enable less advanced countries to expand their transportation systems while bypassing some of the growth problems that beset the industrialized countries.

- Rails, but not trains, are on the way out. By the turn of the century, magnetically levitated trains will begin to replace the spokes (short hops of 100 to 500 miles) of the airline industry's existing "hub-and-spoke" networks.

- The next generation of airliners will carry up to 1,000 passengers. Washington, New York, Tokyo, and Frankfurt will become major transfer points for passengers of supersonic aircraft.

- New automobile technologies will give us the "smart car," equipped with antilock brakes, computer-orchestrated fuel-injection systems, continuously variable transmissions, active suspension, and similar innovations. By 2000, the first practical battery-powered cars will be on California highways.

- Highway technology, however, will lag vehicle improvements. High cost and the need for standards will delay for many years new technologies that allow signal lights and the roadbed itself to keep track of cars issue traffic advisories.

Separatism

47. The information revolution has enabled many people formerly insulated from outside influences to compare their lives with those of people in other countries. This knowledge has often raised their expectations, and citizens in many backward and repressed lands have begun to demand change. This trend can only spread as world communications networks become ever more tightly linked.

    • East Germans learned of reforms elsewhere in Eastern Europe via West German television; Romanians found out through Hungarian media.

    • The Voice of America has informed and inspired dissidents throughout eastern Europe.

48. Politically, the world's most important trend is for nations to form loose confederations, either by breaking up the most centralized nations along ethnic and religious lines or by uniting independent countries in international alliances.

    • *Eastern Europe:* Yugoslavia will soon split into a loose confederation, based on the region's three dominant religions: Greek Orthodoxy, Roman Catholicism, and Islam. Czechoslovakia is already loosening the ties between its Czech and Slovak regions. And, following a brief, unsuccessful attempt at new repression by the right wing of the Communist Party, the Soviet Union will reorganize itself into a confederation of fifteen largely-independent states.

    • *European Community:* The Continent will form an effective confederation of twelve states in 1992, seventeen by 1996. Eastern European states will become associate members by 2000.

    • *North America:* After Quebec secedes from Canada, probably in 1996, the four Eastern provinces will join the United States by 2004, the Western provinces by 2010.

    • *Asia:* The leases are about to run out on Hong Kong and Macao; the British and Portuguese colonies will rejoin mainland China no later than 1997. If Beijing lives up to its promise to preserve their capitalist lifestyles, Taiwan will seek to join the People's Republic shortly after that. Even the two Koreas will reunite before 2000.

- *Middle East:* Saddam Hussein inadvertently gave Israel and its Arab neighbors their best chance for peace in forty years—and they seem to be throwing it away. Fortunately, leaders on both sides recognize the blunder, even if they cannot prevent it. Hostilities will escalate there again, but this time Israel will trade its captured lands for peace. By 2000, economic and political ties will start to bind the region into a prosperous and tranquil community.

International Organizations

49. The major international organizations will take on a far greater role in the "new world order."

- The United Nations will finally be able to carry out its missions of keeping the peace and promoting social welfare. For domestic political reasons, U.S. President Bush acknowledged that his nation is subject to the dictates of the World Court; with this precedent, that body will enjoy growing prestige throughout the 1990s. UNESCO's food, literacy, and children's health funds will all receive added money from the industrialized nations, enabling that agency to accomplish more. Growing donations will also enable WHO to expand its disease eradication, inoculation, and training programs, while the FOA will bolster its starvation relief efforts and programs to help teach farming methods.
- More countries will reform their economies and politics to meet requirements for IMF loans and World Bank programs that provide development funds, grants, and education funds.
- The Red Cross and Red Crescent will step up their blood and disaster relief programs.
- Interpol, the CIA, the KGB, and other intelligence organizations will cooperate to monitor terrorism, control anti-terrorist programs and coordinate crime-fighting worldwide.

50. The Conference on Security and Cooperation in Europe (CSCE) will pick up where NATO and the Warsaw Pact left off by creating a pan-European security structure.

   • This change will transform what has been an intermittent diplomatic process into a permanent institution.

   • CSCE will have to revise its voting rules; as things stand, each of the thirty-five member nations can veto any Conference proposal.

51. The field of public diplomacy will grow, spurred by advances in communication and the importance of international organizations.

Communications

52. Communications and information are the lifeblood of a world economy. Thus, the world's communications networks will grow ever more rapidly in the next decade.

   • A constellation of satellites providing position-fixing and two-way communication on Earth, 24 hours/day will be established in the 1990s. A person equipped with a mini-transceiver will be able to send or receive a message anywhere in the world.

   • The number of cellular telephones is growing exponentially in the United States and will increase by 50 percent per year through 1995.

   • AT&T expects to have a worldwide 800 toll-free telephone number system in place by 1992. It will soon be possible to call an 800 number in any country to order a product or service from a different country. For example: Call Russia for caviar, France for a special wine or champagne, Norway for salmon, Germany for special wursts.

   • The revolution in communications technologies offers hope that developing countries can catch up with the developed world. However, few have yet been able to profit from the new age of information. In 1985, developing countries owned only 5.7 percent of the computers in the world. Most of their computers are used mainly for accounting, payroll processing, and similar low-payoff operations.

53. The growing power and versatility of computers will continue to change the way companies, individuals, and nations do their business.

   • Processing power and operating speeds are still increasing. By 2000, the average personal computer will have at least fifty times the power of the first IBM PCs and one-hundred or more times the power of the original Apple II.

   • Computers are becoming both smaller and cheaper. Portable computers have liberated many salespeople and consultants from the office; many more will follow. By 2000, more than one-fifth of the U.S. workforce will work primarily at home or on the road.

   • Computers and communications are quickly finding their way into information synthesis and decision-making. "Automatic typewriters" will soon be able to transcribe dictation through voice recognition. Computers will also translate documents into various languages; today's best can already handle a 30,000-word vocabulary in nine languages.

54. Continuing development of mass media in telecommunications and printing.

   • Telecommunications is quickly removing geographic barriers: The national newspaper USA Today, relying on satellite communications, is printed simultaneously at multiple sites every day. Satellite-transmitted data can be entered into a computer in, say, a Caribbean country by two people (for greater accuracy) earning 50 cents per hour and transmitted back to the United States for less than $1.50; in the United States, having one person enter the data costs $5.00 per hour.

   • An "integrated information appliance" will combine a telephone, facsimile machine, copier, scanner, computer, and laser printer in one economical unit. The first multifunction communications machines are already on the market.

   • Many popular magazines and special-interest journals in the year 2001 will be on floppy disks which allow the "reader" to manipulate and interact with the information on his computer. (Today, such publications are limited to computer hobbyists.)

   • Mass media will become more personalized as consumers turn to pay-for-view television to select movies and entertainment. Viewers will down-load their choices from a teledelivery service, paying for the program when they view it.

• As of 1991, 52 percent of U.S. homes have cable TV; cable will reach 87 percent of American homes by 2000.

54.a

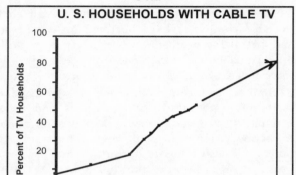

• Fiber optics, improved lasers, and a wide variety of other new data-transmission technologies will make it possible to send data many thousands of times faster than today's equipment allows.

• ISDN (Integrated Services Digital Network) will make it possible to transmit data in digital form without expensive modems, and will allow data to share telephone and radio links with voice messages. This will make for cheaper and more efficient use of switching and transmission equipment and cut the cost of telecommunications.

• ISDN will bring large-scale data processing to the relatively small user by 2001. ISDN will provide access to real estate listings, inventory, financial information, and many other databases at much less cost and over much greater distances.

• Advanced data-transmission methods will make telecommunication far easier to use. New equipment will coordinate multiple expert systems, providing (for example) medical advice in advance of likely illnesses, executing financial transactions, offering travel and entertainment options while it is still possible to get reservations, and delivering all forms of education.

• Readers will be able to prepare their own personalized newspapers by logging onto news-service data bases at night, selecting stories, laying them out, setting the headlines in sizes that reflect their importance to the reader, and adding pictures. After the reader enters his preferences into the computer the first time, the process will be automatic.

Labor & Lifestyle

55. The world's labor force will grow by only 1.5 percent per year during the 1990s, much less quickly than in recent decades, but fast enough to provide most countries with the workers they need. In contrast, the United States faces shortages of labor in general, especially of low wage-rate workers.

55.a

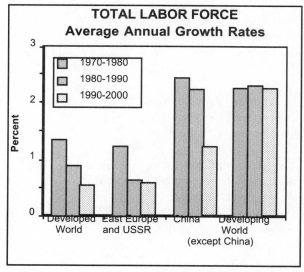

• The decline in the American birthrate in the 1960s and early 1970s means that relatively few young people are entering the job market today. The number of jobs is increasing, creating entry-level labor shortages that are expected to tighten in the 1990s, especially in the service sector.

• This may open more entry-level job opportunities for

55.b

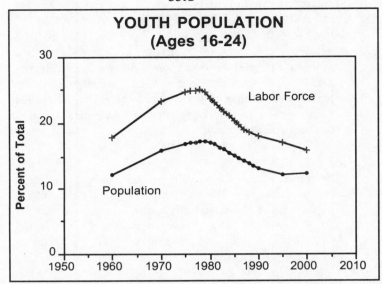

**YOUTH POPULATION
(Ages 16-24)**

Labor Force

Population

Percent of Total

high school graduates, as companies accept the need to train them on the job.

- In the 1990s, the American economy will create about one million new jobs in the less-skilled and laborer categories.
- Institutions of higher education, business, and the military will all vie for youths 16 to 24 years old as this group shrinks from 20 percent of the U.S. labor force in 1985 to 16 percent in 2000.
- The U.S. military has already seen a drop in the education levels of recruits as competition from the private sector intensifies.
- Hotels, restaurants, fast-food places, convenience stores, retailers, and businesses needing beginning computer and clerical skills will be especially hard hit by this labor shortage.
- Untapped labor force resources include the retarded and handicapped, and stay-at-home mothers. Businesses will recruit workers from these groups and also will seek to attract more foreign workers. Whatever shortage remains will be made up by increased automation.
- Multinational companies may find their operations

handicapped by loss of employees and potential workers to the worldwide epidemic of AIDS, especially in Africa, since many firms rely on indigenous workers.

• Shorter work weeks are coming in most of the Western industrialized nations: Sweden is now at 36 hours and Germany is at 37, headed for 35 hours.

56. The shrinking supply of young workers means that the overall labor force is aging rapidly.

• Persons from age 25 to 59 accounted for 65 percent of the world labor force in 1985; almost all growth of the labor force over the next decade will occur in this age group.

56.a

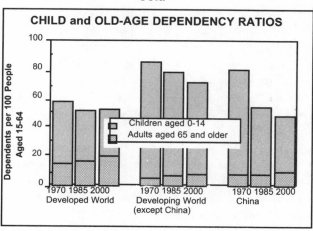

57. Unions will continue to lose their hold on labor.

• Union membership is declining steadily in the United States. It reached 17.5 percent in 1986. According to the United Auto Workers, it will fall to 14 percent by 1990, 12 percent by 1995, and less than 10 percent by 2000.

• Increased use of robots, CAD/CAM, flexible manufacturing complexes can cut a company's workforce by up to one-third.

• Growing use of artificial intelligence, which improves productivity and product quality, will make the companies adopting it more competitive, but will reduce the need for workers in the highly unionized manufacturing industries.

57.a

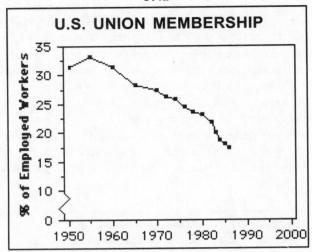

U.S. UNION MEMBERSHIP

• Unionization in Latin America will remain about the same as in the 1980s.

• In the Pacific Rim, unionization will remain low.

• Union membership in the developing world will remain extremely low.

58. People will change residences, jobs, and even occupations ever more frequently, especially in the developed world.

• High speed, magnetically-levitated trains will allow daily commutes of up to 500 miles.

• The number of people who retrain for new careers, one measure of occupational mobility, has been increasing steadily.

• The new information-based organizational management methods—non-hierarchical, organic systems that can respond quickly to environmental changes—foster greater occupational flexibility and autonomy.

• Job mobility—changing location or firm, but doing the same work—also will increase. Even in traditionally stable industries, people will become used to the idea of changing jobs several times in their lifetimes.

59. Changing careers will become increasingly common. By the early 21st century, the average worker will change his career every ten years.

• A recent Louis Harris poll revealed how little commitment American workers have for their jobs: only 39 percent of workers said they intended to hold the same job five years from now; 31 percent said they planned to leave their current work; 29 percent did not know.

60. Two-income couples are also on the rise. In 1960, only 28.5 percent of American couples both held jobs. By 1970, the number was 37.7 percent. A decade later, it was 46.2 percent, and by 1985 it had climbed to 49.0 percent. Forecasting International believes the figure will reach 75 percent by 2000. Similar trends will be seen throughout the industrialized world.

60.a

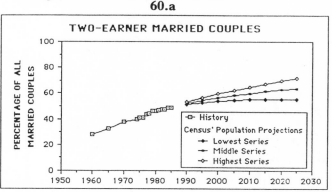

61. The long-standing trend toward specialization will continue.

- In medicine, law, engineering, and the other professions, the body of knowledge that must be mastered in order to excel in any particular area precludes excellence across all areas.

- The same principle applies to artisans such as auto and aviation mechanics, house builders, and repairmen of all kinds.

- The emerging information-based organization is built on its teams of task-focused specialists.

- For hundreds of special tasks, corporations will turn to consultants and independent contractors, who will specialize more and more finely as markets globalize and technologies differentiate.

- In the next decade, close to six million jobs will open up in the United States alone in the highly skilled executive, professional, and technical occupations.

- Two of the fastest growing fields will be among the most specialized: engineering technology and the health industries; many new biotechnology jobs also will open up.
62. The growth of information industries will move the developed countries toward an "information society."
   - By the year 2000, Forecasting International believes that 85 percent of the labor force will be working in the service sector, many of them in information industries, and many others working with computerized equipment.

62.a

U.S. INFORMATION INDUSTRY EMPLOYMENT IN 2000

☐ Growth/Extraction Sector
▦ Fabrication Sector
Service Sector:
  Information Industry:
  ▨ Working at home
  ☐ Not working at home
▨ Other industries

- Computer competence will approach 100 percent in U.S. urban areas by 2000. The developing world will be far less well equipped for the next century. Some former Eastern Bloc scientists worry that, after several generations, a computer competency gap might be harder to bridge than technological gaps have been in the past.
- Seventy percent of U.S. homes will have computers in 2001, compared with 24 percent now; more than three-fourths will be equipped to permit communication with the public data network.
- Computers in the home will give us vast new power over information and services dealing with education,

work, health care, shopping, banking and finance, reservations, and other such data-based fields.

- The amount of information accessible through home computers (from telephone links and from disks with thousands of times the capacity of present-day floppies) will be so vast that we will require the services of artificially intelligent electronic assistants to sort through it.

- Interactive cable television makes possible transactions from home, such as electronic newspapers, electronic shopping, and electronic banking.

- Personal computers will be used to vote, fill out income tax returns, apply for auto license plates, and take tests such as college entrance exams and professional accreditations.

- High technology industries are being encouraged in many states' economic development plans, yet these industries account for only 4 to 5 percent of the new jobs created each year in the United States. Far more new jobs are opening up in businesses that use computers and other high-tech equipment.

63. The rise of knowledge industries will make Western society far more dependent on information.

- About half of all service workers (43 percent of U.S. labor force by 2000) will be involved in collecting, analyzing, synthesizing, structuring, storing, or retrieving information.

- Half of these people will opt for "flex-time, flex-place" arrangements that allow them to work at home, communicating with the office via computer terminals.

- Developers of hardware and software will still enjoy vast opportunities. Five of the ten fastest growing careers between now and 2001 will be computer-related, with the demand for programmers and systems analysts growing by 70 percent.

- Many encyclopedic works, large reference volumes, and heavily illustrated manuals will be more economical to produce and sell on videodiscs, particularly when they must be updated frequently.

64. The wave of new entrepreneurs that appeared in the United States during the 1970s and '80s is just the leading edge of a much broader trend.

- Between 1950 and 1970, the number of new business incorporations in the U.S. jumped from under 100,000 to nearly 300,000 annually; in 1986 the number of new business start-ups hit a record 700,000. A similar trend has appeared in Western Europe, where would-be entrepreneurs were until recently viewed with suspicion. And a new generation of entrepreneurs is growing throughout Eastern Europe. Even in Japan, the entrepreneurial spirit is beginning to make itself felt.

64.a

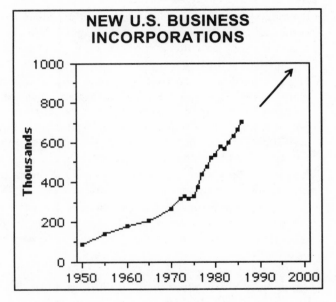

NEW U.S. BUSINESS INCORPORATIONS

- Mid-career professionals increasingly will found their own businesses as new management techniques squeeze many of the executives out of large companies. For many, it will be the only career advancement possible: by 2001 only one American in fifty will be promoted; in 1987, it was one in twenty.
- More and more women are starting up small businesses. Like generations before them, many women are still leaving traditional jobs to have children—but they are building home-based careers as well.
- During the decade from 1970 to 1980, small businesses started by entrepreneurs accounted for most of the 20

million new American jobs created. In 1987, small businesses produced one million new jobs, compared with 97,000 from larger companies.

- By 2000, 85 percent of the U.S. labor force will be working for firms employing fewer than two-hundred people.

65. Throughout the developed world, employment in the service sector will continue to grow rapidly.

- The U.S. Bureau of Labor Statistics projects that service industries will employ 74.4 percent American workers by 1995, 77.4 percent by 2000. Forecasting International's estimate for 2000 is about 85 percent.

- Service jobs have replaced the many well-paying jobs lost in manufacturing, transportation, and agriculture. These new positions often are part-time and offer about half the wages of manufacturing jobs.

65.a

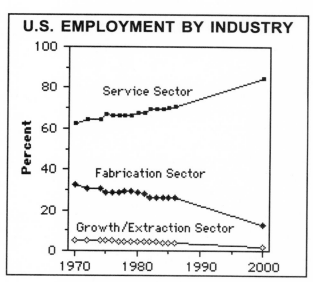

66. In contrast, employment in the agricultural and manufacturing sectors will continue to plummet in the industrialized lands.

- U.S. agriculture and mining are declining slowly, largely because they employ so little of the workforce already. In 1990, only 3.3 percent of American workers held jobs in these sectors. By 1995, the number will stabilize at 3.0 percent.

• There will be 1.25 million farmers in the U.S. in 2000; this is 900,000 fewer than today.

• Manufacturing jobs are disappearing far more quickly as computer-aided design and manufacturing and other new production technologies replace unskilled and semiskilled workers. A full 1.7 million were lost between 1979 and 1985.

• Construction and manufacturing will continue their steady decline. In 1990, they employed 23.2 percent of American workers. By 1995, the number will be 22.6 percent. Five years later, it will have fallen to 19.6 percent. Similar trends can be found in Europe, and even Japan. In contrast, farm laborers are streaming off the land and into factories throughout the developing economies of the Pacific Rim, just as American and European workers did earlier in this century.

• The projections above come from the U.S. Bureau of Labor Statistics. Forecasting International believes they are far too optimistic. By 2000, agriculture and mining will employ only 2.7 percent of American workers, fabrication only 13 percent.

• By 2001, only 9.7 percent of the American labor force will hold jobs in manufacturing, down from 18 percent in 1987. However, productivity will have increased by 500 percent in those industries which have automated, added robotics, and implemented flexible manufacturing technology.

67. More women will continue to enter the labor force.

• Three factors are driving this trend: the growing volume of work that can be done at home, thanks in part to computers and telecommunications; the growth of child-care facilities and services; and the economic need for income from both spouses. In addition, businesses will seek to fill labor shortages with stay-at-home mothers by offering child-care programs and job sharing.

• In both developed and developing regions, the percentage of economically active women has risen since 1950. Women represented 36.5 percent of the world's labor force in 1985. This growth is expected to continue at a moderate rate, with developed nations showing the fastest increases. Some 63 percent of new entrants into the American labor force between 1985 and 2000 will be women.

67.a

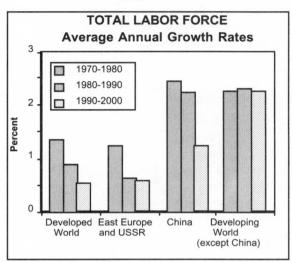

67.b

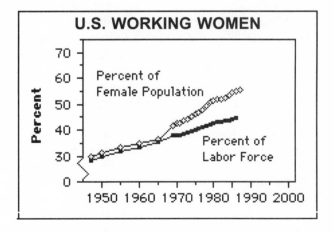

• Working U.S. women, as a percentage of the female population, took a sharp turn upward in the mid-1960s; as a percentage of the total labor force, growth has been slower but steady since World War II. These trends will accelerate for several years, as employers try to cope with the dearth of younger workers, but will slow in the late 1990s, as virtually all women who need or want jobs will have them.

• For similar reasons, the number of women holding formal jobs will grow quickly in Japan, which traditionally has neglected this segment of the potential labor market. The change will appear larger than it really is, however, as many light manufacturing jobs in Japan are carried out on a piecework basis; the man officially holds the job, but the entire family pitches in.

68. These new job opportunities will bring new life to the women's movement.

• "Old girl" networks will become increasingly effective as women fill more positions in middle and upper management.

• A comparable infrastructure is evolving in politics that allows women to make more decisions and to exercise greater control over government policy. Women will use that new power to secure more child-care services, greater employment opportunities, and pay rates more nearly equal to those of men in similar jobs.

• One indication of America's growing dependence on the wife's income: life insurance companies in the U.S. today are selling more policies to women than to men.

69. Diversity is a growing, explicit value throughout much of the developed world.

• The old idea was to conform, blend in with the group; this is giving way in the United States, especially among minorities, to pride in cultural heritage and a general acceptance of differences in all aspects of society. The interest and acclaim which Alex Haley's book *Roots* generated is one example. Greater tolerance for unconventional sexual preferences is another.

• Ethnic pride is also re-emerging in former Communist Bloc countries. As an unfortunate result, historical animosities long suppressed are undergoing a dramatic revival. In the 1990s, they will create civil unrest, and perhaps even civil war. The strife of the Hungarian minority in Romania, and clashes between Armenians and Azerbajianis in the Soviet Union are cases in point.

70. Throughout the world, aspirations are rising, even among people who would have had little reason for hope a generation ago, and growing numbers of people look forward to a modern lifestyle and economic success.

70.a

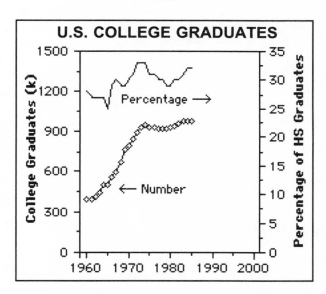

- Aspirations are not enough without the means to fulfill them. Even in the United States, only one in three high school graduates goes on to graduate from college—and one-fourth of high-school students drop out before graduation. The percentage of college graduates is far lower in most other countries.
- Without higher education, young people probably will never live up to their expectations. In 1986, U.S. male high school graduates not enrolling in college were earning an average of 28 percent less in constant dollars than in 1973.
- There are, in addition, more young Americans who report no earnings, up from 7 percent of all 20- to 24-year-old men in 1973 to 12 percent in 1984.

71. The work ethic is in decline.

- Job security and high pay are not the motivators they once were because there is a high degree of social mo-

bility and people value job fulfillment more than traditional rewards; 48 percent of Americans responding in
a recent Louis Harris poll said they work because it
"gives feeling of real accomplishment."

- Fifty-five percent of the top U.S. executives inter-
viewed in the poll said that erosion of the work ethic
will have a major negative effect on corporate performance in the future.

- Even in Japan, the last bastion of the work ethic,
young people say they have no interest in the life of
hard labor their parents endured, even if the reward is
a lifetime of security and affluence. Many now take
only part-time jobs.

72. Automation and other computer applications will
shorten the average workweek. Among the most important are computer aided design and manufacturing
and computer integrated manufacturing which will dramatically reduce the amount of human labor that goes
into many products. In the United States, the workweek
will shrink to 32 hours by 2000, creating more leisure
time. Similar trends can be seen throughout the industrialized world.

73. Tourism, vacationing, and travel (especially international travel) will be among the fastest-growing activities.

- When both spouses work, the couple has more disposable income to spend on leisure activities.

- The number of U.S. travelers to foreign countries (excluding Canada and Mexico) increased at an average
annual rate of 8.8 percent between 1981 and 1988, and
4.4 percent per year even during the less affluent half
of the period, from 1985 onward.

- The number of overseas travelers to the United States
increased at an average rate of 4.7 percent per year
from 1981 through 1988, and fully 18.3 percent between 1985 and 1988.

- International currency exchange rates directly affect
travel. When the dollar falls, the United States can expect more foreign visitors; when it rises, it is the
Americans who travel abroad.

- By 2001, the volume of air travel for both business and
pleasure will double from the level in 1985.

73.a

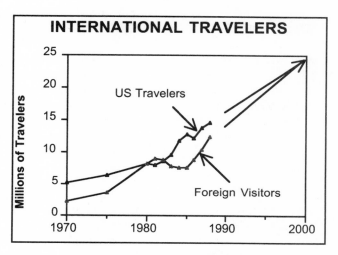

INTERNATIONAL TRAVELERS

- More persuasive electronic marketing will spur tourism as well. Attention-getting videos with up-to-date information about vacation destinations are supplanting printed brochures. Video programs include current, detailed information on accommodations, climate, culture, currency, language, immunization, and passport requirements. (Real estate agents and salespeople in many other fields are adopting similar techniques.)
- By 2000, one of every nine people in the United States will work for the hospitality industry—hotels and motels, restaurants, travel and tour agencies, airlines, cruise ships, and theme parks.
- People are coming to prefer many short vacations spread throughout the year to the traditional two-week vacation.

74. Consumerism, already a potent force in Western society, will gain even greater power.
   - One reason is that consumers are becoming more organized. New consumer agencies and organizations appear almost daily.
   - Consumer information, such as unit pricing and content labels, will spread through more informative packaging, television programs, government regulation, and special studies and reports.

• This wealth of information will enable consumers to become smarter buyers. They will demand quality, service, dependability, and fair prices.

• Former Communist Bloc countries represent a vast new market for consumer goods now that they are adopting market economies and making their currencies convertible. This market will build gradually, paced by the consumers' affluence, which will grow slowly at first and then will accelerate.

Industry

75. Large businesses are quickly changing their organizational structure to take advantage of new information technologies. In future, most will be composed of specialists, usually operating in project-oriented teams, who rely on information from colleagues, customers, and headquarters to guide their actions.

• Decision processes, management structure, and work methods are being transformed as businesses take the first steps from struggling to cope with unprocessed data to using information—data that has been analyzed and organized in a useful way.

• The advent of vast, high-speed data-processing capability has made this transition possible.

• Information-based organizations require more specialists in field operations, not at corporate headquarters. As a result, many American companies have shrunk their headquarters staffs dramatically. In the 1990s, both Europe and Japan will be forced to follow the U.S. lead.

76. The traditional command-and-control, "company-as-army," model of management will all but disappear as information-based organizations proliferate.

• Manual and clerical workers are fast being replaced by knowledge workers. By 1995, 80 percent of all managers will fall into this new and growing category.

• This requires a marked change from the old, rigid hierarchical management styles toward more participation by workers, who will act largely as consultants for management.

77. The actual work will be done by task-focused teams of specialists.
    - The traditional department will assign the specialists, set standards, and serve as the center for training.
    - Instead of keeping each stage of product development separate, specialists from research, development, marketing, and manufacturing will work together as a team in all stages.

78. A typical large business in 2010 will have fewer than half the management levels of its counterpart today, and about one-third the number of managers.
    - More than ever before, upper management will be responsible for clearly stating performance expectations for the organization, its parts, and its specialists, and supplying the feedback necessary to determine whether results have met expectations.
    - With traditional methods, executives could effectively manage only six subordinates; with computers, they can oversee 21. So fewer mid-level managers are needed.
    - Middle management will all but disappear as information flows directly to upper management for analysis.
    - As major firms "trim the fat," the organizational pyramid will flatten, with the specialists on the bottom.
    - Opportunities for advancement to upper level management will shrink, because candidates will come from within narrow specialties, and few will have the broad view of business required of corporate leaders.
    - Because each specific industry requires unique qualifications of its leaders, and they will become increasingly necessary under the new management methods, finding top executives will be extremely difficult.
    - This will require companies to develop ways of preparing specialists for broader roles as business executives and business leaders in their organizations.
    - These specialists often work more for job satisfaction than for pay or security. Thus, the values and compensation structure of business will have to change radically.

79. International and multinational corporations will continue to grow, and many new ones will appear.

- Companies will expand their operations beyond national borders. Joint ventures and mergers with foreign firms are common ways. Recent examples include:

—Matra Marconi Space, called "the first international space company," a joint venture of Marconi Space Systems, a British General Electric company, and Matra Espace, in France;

—BMW Rolls-Royce, a German-based venture of BMW and Rolls-Royce;

—Aerospatiale in France and Deutsche Aerospace (MBB) are planning to merge their helicopter divisions under a new Eurocopter company late in 1991.

- Many other companies will go international by locating new facilities in countries that provide a labor force and benefits such as preferential tax treatment, but do not otherwise participate in the operation. Ireland pioneered this practice with U.S. companies in the insurance, electronics, and automobile industries. It found that when companies leave, for whatever reason, the country loses revenue and gains an unemployed labor force.

80. Both companies and governments need to anticipate the consequences of expensive or irreversible acts before they act on new ideas. As a result, they are sponsoring more futures studies and political and economic forecasts every year.

- In crisis-oriented democracies, where the political will to solve problems develops only when it becomes too inconvenient to ignore them, it is particularly important to anticipate problems that could someday require attention.

- Political and economic forecasters and other future-oriented organizations will increasingly influence decision-making in government, business, and industry in the years ahead. Leading companies are now stretching their long-range planning horizon to seven to fifteen years; not long ago a three-year horizon was considered "long-range."

- In the late 1970s, the World Future Society estimated that there were 300 futures-oriented organizations in the world; the number has more than doubled since then.

- The Congressional Clearinghouse for Futures Research has become one of the most active research organizations in the United States.
- The World Future Society's membership has reached nearly 35,000 people in over 80 countries, and continues to grow rapidly.

81. Public officials in the Western democracies face growing demand for accountability in government spending and policy.

- In the United States, for example, both voters and legislators will focus on the results of public education, rather than being content to look at budgets, employment roles, and other secondary issues. NASA's beleaguered space program has already had to face this new scrutiny.
- Computers make it easier to maintain audit trails and place the blame for waste and mismanagement on those who deserve it.

82. Corporations face similar demands for greater social responsibility.

- A wide variety of environmental disasters and public health issues have drawn public attention to the effects of corporate negligence, and to situations in which business can help solve public problems not necessarily of their own making:

—Union Carbide's accidental release of toxic chemicals in Bhopal, India, is a classic case in point;

—So is the *Exxon Valdez* oil spill in Prince William Sound, Alaska;

—The release of radiation from the government-operated Chernobyl power plant in the Soviet Union has also focused concern on privately owned reactors in the West;

—The law requiring new cars to carry seat belts compels auto makers to help ease the problem of traffic deaths, which are caused largely by the negligence of drivers.

- In future, companies increasingly will be judged on how they treat the environment—and forced to clean up any damage resulting from their activities.
- Government intervention will supplant deregulation in key industries. The airlines will be compelled to provide greater safety and services; the financial service in-

dustry will be regulated to reduce economic instability and costs; electric utilities will be held responsible for nuclear problems; and chemicals manufacturers will have to cope with their own toxic wastes.

• With five percent of the world's population and two-thirds percent of the lawyers on the planet, U.S. citizens will resort even more to litigation if their demands are not met.

83. In business, the big get bigger, the small survive, and the middle-sized are squeezed out. (At Forecasting International, we somewhat ponderously call this the "bimodal distribution of institutions.") This trend appeared in the United States in the 1980s. It has now spread to Europe and will continue until virtually all of today's mid-sized corporations either have been absorbed by larger competitors or have been driven out of business.

• Nine domestic U.S. airlines today control 80 percent of the market, leaving the smaller carriers with only 20 percent. By 2001 there will be only four major domestic carriers.

• As of 1991, there are 20 major auto makers around the world with market shares ranging from 18.1 percent (GM) to 1.0 percent (BMW). By 2001, only five giant automobile firms will be left; production and assembly will be centered in the U.S., Korea, Italy, and Latin America.

• By 2000, there will be just three major corporations dominating the U.S. computer hardware industry: IBM, Digital, and Apple.

• The 1990s will be the decade of "micro-segmentation" as more and more highly-specialized businesses and entrepreneurs search for even tinier markets.

• The bimodal trend has hit almost all industries:

—Stores: The best-run chain department stores discounters profit from the mass market, while specialty boutiques prosper in niche markets. Mid-sized family-oriented stores that lack special appeal are going broke *en masse*.

—Hotels: Large hotel chains and the economy hotels thrive; so do elegant inns and quaint bed-and-breakfasts. Those in the middle become large, are absorbed, or fail.

—Restaurants: Elegant dining and cheap fast-food restaurants are making it at the expense of sit-down family restaurants in the middle.

—Health Care: Both huge hospital corporations and walk-in medical centers are growing rapidly, while free-standing community hospitals are going out of business.

—Agriculture: Agribusinesses making over $500,000 are flourishing; individual farmers make under $100,000 are surviving, often because they hold outside jobs; it is the middle-income farmer who is going bankrupt.

—Banks: Interstate and international banks are growing rapidly, and local banks that specialize in personal service are succeeding; the rest are being gobbled up by larger banking chains or are going under.

—Financial Institutions: Large brokerage houses are growing larger still, as witness the recent merger of E.F. Hutton and Shearson-Lehman Brothers, while local brokers are making it through personal attention to their customers.

—Aerospace: Four major German aerospace companies have combined into a single group, Deutsche Aerospace. In Italy, Aeritalia and Selenia are merging to form a new company called Alenia. The low end of this industry, would-be private launch services and small engineering firms, are still trying to carve out markets.

—Electronics: Tiny makers of high-performance loud-speakers and other equipment for discerning audiophiles prosper, but in such consumer markets as televisions and VCRs, only the giants survive. The Plessey electronics group, which in smaller industries might qualify as a giant, has been absorbed by Britain's General Electric Company and Siemens of Germany.

• Speculation: U.S. government regulators are beginning to wonder whether breaking up AT&T was a good idea. The telecommunications giant may be reconsolidated in the mid-1990s.

Education & Training

84. A vast new wave of education and job training and re-training will sweep the Western world in the 1990s, and particularly the United States.

• No population burdened by illiteracy can conceivably

cope with modern technology. The United States is the worst-afflicted of the great industrial nations.

• Throughout the world, education—especially the basic literacy learned in primary school—remains a major goal for development as well as a means of improving health, labor productivity, GDP growth, and social integration.

—Most developed countries have literacy rates over 95 percent. The increasing levels of technological "savvy" demanded by modern life, however, often are more than people are prepared to meet, even in the most modern societies.

—The proportion of illiterates among the world's adult population has steadily decreased, although the absolute number has grown. The literacy rate in developing countries will have risen from 61 percent, on average, in 1985 to 72 percent by 2000. Yet the number of illiterate adults will have climbed from 910 million to 920 million in the same period.

84.a

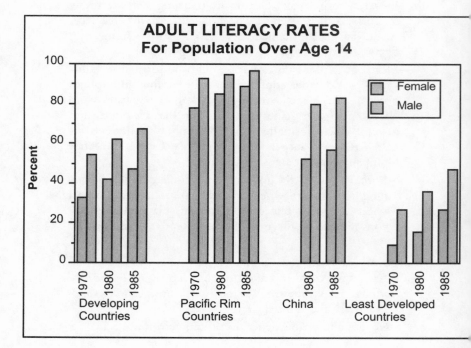

ADULT LITERACY RATES
For Population Over Age 14

84.b

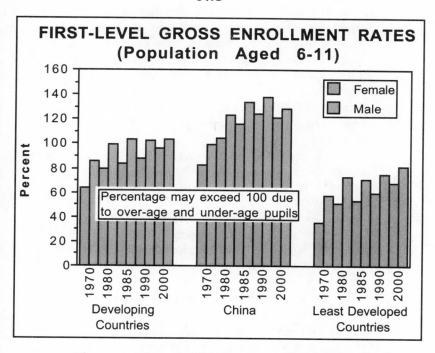

FIRST-LEVEL GROSS ENROLLMENT RATES
(Population Aged 6-11)

• The proportion of children not enrolled in school will fall from 26 percent in 1985 to 18 percent by 2000.

—Children in developing countries often fail to enroll in school, for various reasons. Sometimes classrooms are too crowded to admit new students. Students who need transportation, often cannot find it. And some cultures still discourage girls from attending. Most of these practices are changing, though slowly.

—Enrollment in primary school has risen dramatically in most of the developing world, but Africa is an unfortunate exception. In 31 sub-Saharan countries reporting their enrollment rates, the rates for boys had fallen in 13, and the rates for girls in 15.

• Useful, job-oriented knowledge is becoming increasingly perishable. The half-life of an engineer's professional information today is five years; in ten years, ninety percent of what he knows will be available on computer, while he will be expected to learn new techniques and skills throughout his working life. Eighty-five percent of the information in U.S. National Institutes of Health computers is upgraded in five years.

- Both job markets and technologies are changing so quickly that all but the least skilled among us will require increased training for at least the next generation. This probably is a permanent change in the working world.

- Because of fundamental changes in the economy, fewer and fewer well-paying jobs can be had without advanced training.

- Up to 4 percent of the U.S. labor force will be in job retraining programs by the 1990s, upgrading their skills to keep pace with changing technologies and working conditions.

- American schools soon will train both children and adults around the clock. The academic day will stretch to seven hours for children. Adults will work a 32-hour workweek and prepare for their next jobs in the remaining hours.

- State, local, and private agencies will help in this training by offering internships, apprenticeships, pre-employment classes, and adult education.

- To prepare students better for advanced education, high school and college faculties will build new cooperative learning programs in all but the most isolated regions.

85. Educational "perestroika" is changing American schools. In the long run, this will repair the nation's competitive position in the world economy.

- The information economy's need for skilled workers requires educational reform.

- The lackluster performance of U.S. students on standardized tests has helped to build a constituency for reform.

- Science and engineering schools will be actively recruiting more students.

- Foreign exchange programs will grow markedly in an attempt to bolster the competence of American students in international affairs.

- In the midst of this reform, there will be a severe shortage of qualified teachers in the United States. An estimated one million new teachers will be needed between 1989 and 1993. The need to cut average class size from 17.8 students to ten will aggravate this deficit.

• Also needed in the U.S.: an annual increase of $5 billion in federal spending for programs such as the Head Start preschool program, federal aid for disadvantaged children, the Job Corps, and the Job Training Partnership Act.

86. Business is taking on a far greater role in training and education. This trend will accelerate dramatically in the United States in the 1990s and will appear in other nations.

• Automation and computers will replace unskilled jobs with positions requiring a high degree of literacy. Businesses will have to provide continual training so that their workers can keep up with the greater demands.

• More companies will contribute resources and personnel to schools, job-training programs, and community service programs, both in the United States and in Europe. In the Pacific Rim nations, Japanese companies will take on the same role in an effort to ensure the supply of qualified labor in their client nations.

• The corporate investment in employee education and retraining, is now some $80 billion a year in the United States. It will approach $200 billion by 2001.

• Most new jobs are generated by businesses too small to pay for training; one-half of all funding for formal training comes from 200 to 300 large companies in business and industry.

• The U.S. Job Training Partnership Act, now funded at a rate of $4.5 billion per year, calls on private business to help direct the training of the unemployed. This helps ensure that training will prepare students for jobs that are actually available, rather than for trades now on the decline.

87. Technologies will revolutionize both basic education and job training.

• Cockpit simulators for pilots were only the first of many artificial work environments. Job simulators that combine computers, videodiscs, and instrumentation now train ship's captains and nuclear power-plant operators. In the 1990s, they will find roles in most complex industries.

• Many rural schools are broadening their curricula with televised courses from other school districts, states, or even countries. Others are linking themselves to larger and more prosperous schools through computer networks.

• By 2001, nearly all college textbooks and many high school and junior high books will come with computer disks to aid in learning.

• Computers will provide access to all the card catalogs of all major libraries in the world by the late 1990s. Not long after, it will be possible to call up on a PC screen millions of volumes from distant libraries. Videodiscs will enhance books by providing visual and audio information.

• Most universities today can receive satellite communications. By 2000, virtually all will be able to send by satellite as well, so that worldwide interactive video teleconferencing will be possible. This will supplement symposia and other meeting formats.

• Interactive computers, videodisc, and other new media are making it possible to individualize courses so that students can learn according to their needs and abilities.

• Personal computers with ultra-high resolution screens, 3-D graphics, high-level interactivity, and artificial intelligence will enhance game-playing and simulations used in education and training.

88. New discoveries in pedagogy—the science of learning—will bring a host of more effective teaching methods in the next decade.

• Schools will find ways to use the growing knowledge about individual learning styles to coursework. For example, the Key School, in Cincinnati, Ohio, has built an entire new grammar school curriculum based on theoretical psychology and has proved uniquely successful in teaching even severely disadvantaged children.

• Schools will be less important in future. Individuals will learn more often on their own, the "places" of learning will be more dispersed, and the age at which subjects are learned will depend on the individual, not tradition.

- Students at all levels will learn as few but doctoral candidates do today, by consulting books, journals, and primary resources.

- Unconventional techniques such as sleep learning and role playing will help boost memory skills.

- Computerized learning will improve teaching methods, helping students to learn more in less time. The result may be a one-sixth reduction in overall learning time for the basic curriculum.

89. Universities will stress development of the whole student, not just academic learning.

- School administrators are growing more willing to support class-related activities beyond traditional coursework.

- Schools are also giving students more advice about academic programs and career paths.

90. Higher education is changing as quickly as primary and secondary schools.

- The soaring cost of higher education may force program cuts. (If so, the developing countries face an ultimate loss of foreign exchange, as their industries fall further behind those of cheaper, more efficient competitors.)

- Post-high school education costs far more than secondary or primary education. Public spending throughout the world averaged $2,642 in 1980, $2,636 in 1985 (in constant 1980 dollars).

- There are too few jobs for liberal arts college graduates in many developing countries. Egypt cannot keep its promise to give a job to every graduate; the civil service is grossly overstaffed already. Zimbabwe cannot place its graduates, a cause of civil unrest. And in India, riots broke out when then Prime Minister V.P. Singh announced that many relatively scarce civil service positions would be reserved for those of middle and lower caste.

- By 2001, America will have too few adolescents to fill its colleges and universities. Schools will close their doors, merge with other institutions, and reduce fac-

90.a

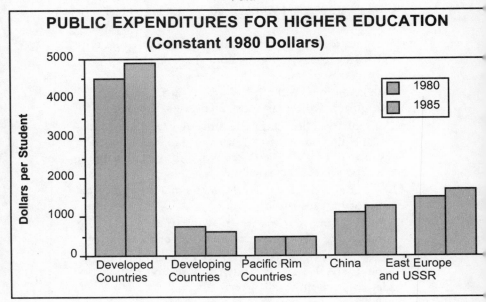

PUBLIC EXPENDITURES FOR HIGHER EDUCATION
(Constant 1980 Dollars)

ulty size and class offerings. Colleges and universities will also recruit older students, including retirees. By 1995, half of all college and university students will be age 25 or older.

90.b

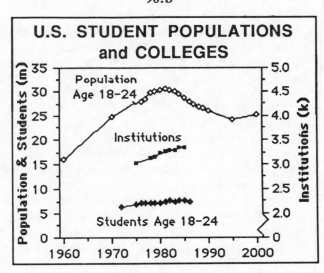

U.S. STUDENT POPULATIONS and COLLEGES

- Displaced college and university instructors will find employment at secondary schools, in business-based education programs, and in producing educational computer software.
- More and more businesses will conduct their own research, augmenting or supplanting that traditionally performed by colleges and universities.
- The concept of "university" is changing. Increasingly, major corporations are collaborating with universities to establish degree-granting corporate schools and programs. Examples include: The General Motors Institute, Pennsylvania State's affiliation with a major electronics company, General Electric; and Rutgers University's arrangement with Johnson & Johnson, a major pharmaceutical house.
- More private companies will market large electronic databases, eventually replacing university libraries.

Appendix B

PROFILES: 30 COUNTRIES THAT POINT TO THE FUTURE

Of necessity, the main text of this book has concentrated on a number of key issues and a few influential nations whose circumstance and policies will dominate the course of world events in the coming decade. In following this course, we have largely neglected less powerful countries, and often the details of politics, demographics, and economics in even the major trading nations. This capsule will fill in some of the lacunae.

The capsule portraits below have been pieced together from a wide variety of materials. Much of the economic information comes from the World Bank. Demographic data most often originated with the United Nations. Reports of current events were culled from a wide variety of public and privileged authorities. Extensive additional information in the public domain has been drawn from the Central Intelligence Agency and other high-confidence sources.

Argentina

The second largest country in South America suffers some of the continent's worst economic and political headaches. This former Spanish colony recovered from a protracted ten-year war of independence in 1820 as it discovered that foreign markets and open borders created vast wealth and spurred immigration for the *Tierra del Fuego* (Land of Fire), a previously poor and sparsely inhabited country. In 1910, Argentina's economy ranked tenth in the world. Buenos Aires rivaled Washington, D.C. as a hemispheric power. But six coups within the twentieth century have wrecked havoc on this sometimes democratic republic. The frequent switches back and forth between military and civilian governments have all but ruined the once prosperous economy. In 1943, the second military coup gave Juan Domingo Peron the seat of power and an influence that impacts on the Argentine system today. Overly politicized labor unions and a strident military (although suffering from loss of prestige over its debacle in the Falkland Islands, or Malvinas), once the base of Peronist power, plague the system today—an attempted military coup embarrassed President Carlos Saul Menem during U.S. President George Bush's visit to Argentina during his tour to launch the "Enterprise for the Americas."

Although the Peronist candidate, President Carlos Saul Menem has reversed his party's policies to cut social programs and has started a privatization program, beginning with the indebted telephone company ENTel. Foreign investment in other state firms such as the national airline Aerolineas, the railroad, YPF oil, ports, and the Somisa industrial export firm, should help Argentina pay its $66 billion foreign debt. Not only will the hard currency bolster coffers in Buenos Aires but it will also stave off the $4 billion annual drain on the central budget Yet there remains some resistance from those who fear that these acts amount to "selling your house to buy food."

Argentina today boasts tremendous natural resources, wheat, and beef. If Argentina can steady itself economically by succeeding at privatization and repaying its debt, its literate people and the diversified economy could help the country regain a sense of its former glory—when it was frequently remarked that "God must be an Argentine."

Australia

Australia has become one of the most popular places for people to immigrate to; one of every five Australians is foreign-born. The total population on the world's smallest continent has more than doubled since World War II. Four-fifths of the more than 4.5 million migrants have settled there to stay. In addition to the normal immigration program, Australia safely harbors roughly 12,000 refugee immigrants per year. Since 1975, the Land Down Under has accepted over 114,000 Indochinese refugees as permanent residents.

The country boasts diversified and mature manufacturing and service sectors. These greatly benefit from Australia's bountiful natural resources, which include aluminum, bauxite, cobalt, copper, industrial diamonds, gold, iron ore, lead, nickel, silver, and uranium. Further, deposits of coal, natural gas, and liquid petroleum gas have made Australia a net exporter of energy products. Yet the country has been led to the brink of recession.

During Labour's fourth consecutive term, high interest rates (three times those of either Germany or Japan), overvalued currency, damaging trade barriers, labor costs, and a current-account deficit that has grown to become proportionately the second-largest in the industrialized world have brought the economy to a standstill. Prime minister Robert J. L. Hawke has focused on liberalizing the economy and encouraging industrial competitiveness. Treasurer Paul Keating plans to partially privatize the Commonwealth Bank—the Labour Party's sacred cow—in order to bail out the ailing State Bank of Victoria. Keating also wants to privatize the overseas telephone service (OTC) and the satellite service, Aussat; the domestic telephone service, Telecom, will remain publicly owned but will be exposed to unlimited competition for the first time.

Protectionism has damaged the economy. Symptomatic of these tendencies, the Australian Manufacturing Council recommended in July 1990 that the government intervene to protect industry and exports. Internal barriers have prevented Australia from exploiting the Asian markets. Nearly one-third of its high-tech exports go to New Zealand or Papua New Guinea. The "Closer Economic Relationship" trade agreement with New Zealand now being implemented will be a boon only if Australia explores its other trade possibilities as well. The Labour Party needs to adopt a broader trade policy and to reduce Australia's self-imposed restraints if it wishes to compete, to avoid recession, and to ward off a routing in the next polls by opposition leader John Hewson.

Austria

Austria has enjoyed remarkable political and economic stability since the end of World War II. Although the economy began to taper off in the early 1980s, the inflation rate has been kept as one of the lowest in Europe. Like their counterparts in the Federal Republic of Germany (FRG), Austria's independent, conservative banks follow strict anti-inflationary policies. The Central Bank has maintained a hard schilling policy to ward off "imported" inflation.

Austria's homogeneous, 98 percent ethnic German population has helped build the strong bilateral Austrian-German economic relationship—what some refer to as a virtual "economic Anschluss." In 1989 over one-third of Austria's exports went to the FRG, and Austria imported 43.4 percent of its goods from the FRG. German companies regularly buy out Austrian ones. Austria makes spare parts for German automobiles. Tellingly, the schilling has been pegged to the German mark.

Austria has forged strong relations with the European Community and will seek membership after 1993, once it smooths out the neutrality question. As a member of the European Free Trade Association (EFTA), Austria has concluded bilateral free trade agreements with the EC. Since July 1977 the exchange of nearly all industrial goods between Austria and the EC has been free from tariff barriers.

Vienna has been active in "bridge building to the East" which involved increasing contacts at all levels with Eastern Europe and the Soviet Union. Considered the gateway to the Danube River basin, Austria will prove an excellent launching pad for businesses interested in Eastern Europe—especially to those who can take advantage of Austria's historical, close ties to Hungary. Austria already serves as non-Soviet Eastern Europe's second largest Western trading partner (after Germany), with 10 percent of the region's total trade with the West, and it accounts for close to 14 percent of Hungary's Western trade. In all, Austria has been well positioned geographically and demographically to take advantage of the growing, lucrative markets in both the EC and Eastern Europe.

Bolivia

Bolivia's unfortunate geography has made it rich in mineral deposits but little else. Without access to ocean, Bolivia has been cut off from much of the world. Its harsh climate, which averages 10 degrees centigrade, and its high altitude, in the Andes, tend to make foreigners ill—thus further limiting foreign exchange. Bolivia's borders with five Latin American states have caused it countless headaches, disputes, and wars. Decades of political turmoil and confusion have taken their toll as numerous military dictatorships have stymied development. The army remains strong, claiming 16.6 percent of central government expenditures, and will be apt to intervene, even though Bolivia plans to move toward a more open political process.

Rather than the military, the unorganized society presents the greatest threat to the fledgling democracy. Bolivia stands as the least-developed country in South America. Two-thirds of the population lives in poverty and suffers from a high mortality rate, with an average age of mortality of only 53 years. Health care and transportation are extremely mediocre. Investors will have a difficult time since the unskilled and poorly educated labor force will not easily be geared toward sophisticated production. The lack of telephones renders communication difficult.

President Jaime Paz Zamora's economic plan for his term of office, through 1993, stresses the continuation of free-market policies, a single realistic exchange rate, the elimination of unjustifiable subsidies, and wages kept in line with a maximum inflation rate of 9 percent—a difficult goal considering that Bolivia has suffered the effects of a rampant

482 percent annualized inflation rate. Yet, due to tighter fiscal policies, inflation may be only 12 percent in 1990—one of the lowest rates in the region. Despite his bold plans, the outlook remains grim. The loss in export competitiveness will step up devaluation. A better trade performance could certainly boost the current account. A new law protecting foreign investments may prove to be enticing, especially as the Bolivian Congress encourages investment in mining, oil, and gas. The scheduled 19.8 percent increase in oil production will be a needed boon, as will a new deal that gets Argentina to pay its bills for the natural gas that makes up approximately 40 percent of Bolivia's exports. Even with these reforms, Bolivia remains the most impoverished country in South America.

Brazil

Brazilians voted in their first direct presidential election in twenty-nine years in November 1989. The ballots reflected the public's frustration with President José Costa Sarney's ruling Brazilian Democratic Movement party (PMDB) after his government failed to deliver the country from its economic and social woes. Fernando Collor de Mello, a former governor of the northeastern state, Alagoas, finished first among the 22 candidates seeking the presidency. Later, he narrowly defeated the leftist contender in the run-offs. Collor's campaign platform consisted of planks promoting wide-reaching agrarian, administrative, patrimonial, fiscal, and debt reforms.

Still, Brazil's economy remains precarious. Currently, one percent of the population owns half of the wealth. In September 1989, prices soared to a record high, 36 percent over those of the previous month. Prices in 1988 climbed 933.6 percent; by November 1989 inflation neared a 1200 percent annual rate. Brazilian politicians define "stability" as holding inflation down to a 30 percent monthly rate. The gigantic internal debt fuels the widespread fear of hyperinflation. The 1989 deficit exceeded 6 percent of GDP. After eight years of low or zero growth, GDP grew by 0.3 percent in the first eight months of 1989, compared to a negligible 0.04 percent in all of 1988. The booming underground economy remained far from the government's grasp. Of 145 million Brazilians, roughly only three million pay income tax. The so-called "parallel" economy generates an estimated $100 billion, thereby equaling almost one-third of the $330 billion GDP. Brasilia loses both taxes and control as the black market enjoys continued vitality.

Brazil continues to play a game of chicken with its Western creditors. While Western officials demand that Brazil pay $8 billion in arrears before negotiations, Brazil insists that negotiations be held before it will pay back any more money. Until then, Brazil is not entitled to any new money. Still, the Brazilians maintain that this lapse did not constitute a moratorium, because Brazil needed only "temporary delays" in payment to preserve the $5.5 billion held in reserves. On August 9, 1989, da Nobrega announced that foreign creditors had agreed to a delay in debt payments. By that September, the nation's foreign debt totaled $110 billion, the highest of any Third World nation. Brazilian negotiators again emphasized to foreign creditors that the nonpayment of $1.6 billion in interest was not a moratorium but a pragmatic measure to conserve foreign exchange reserves.

Amid mounting worldwide concern over the depletion of the Amazon Jungle, which accounts for over 30 percent of the world's rain forest, several U.S. congressmen toured Brazil on a fact-finding mission in January. 1989. Afterward, the delegation vowed to campaign against U.S. aid for Amazonian projects that lacked "objective" safeguards for peasants, Indians, and the environment.

Brazilian officials responded to U.S. complaints of unfair trade practices by arguing that Brazil's import barriers allowed the nation to build up a surplus to help make payments on the huge foreign debt; the U.S. after all, is Brazil's largest trading partner as well as its largest commercial creditor. The U.S. and Brazil announced the end of the four-year dispute over Brazil's treatment of foreign computer and electronic exports in its protected market. IBM recently announced that it would rescind its normal rule about maintaining 100% of its subsidiaries in order to establish a joint venture in this country's vast market where split ownership is required by law.

Bulgaria

As the exception rather than the rule in Eastern Europe, the Bulgarians freely chose that the Communists stay in power. The Soviet is not regarded as a hostile occupier here, partly because the USSR actually brought economic benefits to Bulgaria in the postwar period. In 1948, 18% of the work force held nonagricultural employment, compared to 80% who do not farm today. Agriculture remains one of the most important components of the economy though, and Bulgaria enjoys one of the highest ratios of arable land to population in Eastern Europe. Currently, this Balkan country strives to modernize its industrial base, to increase efficiency. This means Bulgaria must vitalize its relatively stagnant foreign trade habits, trading predominantly with other COMECON countries.

Bulgaria's change of government in November 1989 amounted to a mere palace coup that toppled Todor Zhivkov. Petur Mladenov replaced him and opened up the political system to other parties. Mladenov emerged from the polls as president, and former Politburo member

Andrei Lukanov, as prime minister. The main opposition party, the Union of Democratic Forces, won heavily in Sofia during the general elections while the Socialists (the former Communists) took the countryside, reflecting a rift in society. Unlike other parts of Eastern Europe, lack of dissent characterized this period. Only recently have protests been made—some because they desire more democracy, others because they believe that there is too much.

In July 1990, over 1,200 dissidents camped out in 165 tents in the "City of Truth" as a protest against the former Communists for continuing to hold power and not pursuing reforms. The poet Kolu Savov organized the protests which successfully demanded Mladenov's resignation. The police did not heed the government's decree to take immediate action against the civil disobedience. The inaction represents the breakdown of the leadership—especially since the camp is strategically located next to the Central Committee building.

Simultaneously, many Bulgarians went on occupational strikes by closing factories and blocking roads to signal their growing fear of the Turkish population. Members of the Fatherland Labor party, shut down Kardzhali, a city of 60,000. Democracy does not appeal to many who live in areas with Turkish majorities, and some remember Zhivkov as a hero since his government persecuted the 1.5 million Turkish minority, for instance, by not permitting the Turkish language to be spoken in public. These nationalists were alarmed that all ten Turkish candidates from the Movement for Rights and Freedoms that ran this region won seats in the 400-member unicameral parliament.

The aging industry presents an immediate danger to the Bulgarians. Spring rains in Kardzhali often kill the flowers. "The centralized way of organizing production still exists in Bulgaria. We don't need filters now. We need a whole new technology. If we had had another technology, we wouldn't have had this pollution," according to Dimiter Raev, the chief environmental engineer at a lead plant. Last year, "Ecology and Management," a government publication, noted that industrial wastes pollute 85% of river water; air polluted beyond the government's "highest acceptable norms" envelopes one-quarter of the country; industrial pollutants have damaged nearly 70 percent of farmland—8 percent of which will not be fit for farm use for up to 50 years.

Colombia

Inaugurated on August 7, 1990, President Cesar Gaviria has continued his predecessor's all-out war with Pablo Escobar and the Medellin cartel. A lack of public support for the anti-dialogue narcotics policy has emerged because conflict generates violence. Colombia's history has been characterized by bouts of bloody conflict, such as the War of a Thousand Days (1899–1902), which took 100,000 lives; *La Violencia* (in the 1940s and 1950s), which cost 200,000–300,000 lives; and the current violence that stems from narcotics activity. Colombia has the highest homicide rate in the world: homicides jumped from 15,672 in 1986, to 23,312 in 1989, to even higher in 1990. That amounts to 68.1 homicides per 100,000 inhabitants.

Of northern South America, Colombia boasts the longest practice of democracy. This tradition revolves around the freedom to vote, the advanced legal system, and the strong educational facilities. These, however, have all been undermined by the flourishing drug trade and the rife corruption. While the absence of a strong military helped democracy to prosper in its early stages without the threat of intervention, the state has become the underdog in the fight against the cartels. Even though the vociferous Medellin group has fallen to tougher times, the Cali clique will quietly pick up its markets. Bogota may triumph if it can remove the outright threat to central authority, but Cali will continue to pull enormous profits and many strings. The emergence of Cali over Medellin in the long run will be due to the fact that Cali did not try to subvert the political system; Cali, quite literally, will have bought into the establishment.

Many differ as to the effects of the drug wars on Colombia. Although most believe that the country has been paralyzed, General Miguel Maza Marquez, the director of the Department of Administrative Security (the equivalent of the FBI) says that phase has passed: "Today, we see a different country. A year ago our institutions, including the presidency, were endangered; now they are recuperating. The cartel had people infiltrated at every level, and that is diminishing. People who once viewed the traffickers with sympathy now give them no political space."

In September 1990, Gaviria offered cocaine traffickers who turn themselves in and confess their crimes the chance to avoid extradition, as well as reduced sentences. After all, members of "The Extraditables" had claimed that they would surrender if they were to be tried in Colombia. Anti-extradition sentiment and nationalism surged after a jury, convicted D.C. Mayor Marion Barry of only one of 14 drug-related charges. Colombians believe that they pay a high personal price to interdict the drug trade, while consumption in the U.S. goes virtually unpunished.

The rest of the Colombian economy has faltered. Some of Colombia's most able citizens have fled the country, placing a heavy burden on those who remain. Inflation rages at annual rates in the 25-30 percent-range. Coffee prices have declined (normally earning about $1.5

billion) as the cost of energy imports has risen. Debt-service payments will strain the government and create a shortfall of funds for social expenditures. If the Medellin group can be brought to justice—and if no other group replaces them and their violent methods—Colombia may get back on track. Coexistence with Cali is possible. The cocaine trade will continue to be a fact and way of life in Colombia—especially since the U.S. has reacted by boycotting other Colombian products. Legalization of drugs within the U.S. would necessarily alter the character of the cartels and further diminish the level of violence.

Costa Rica

Costa Rica remains somewhat of an anomaly in Central America. While many of its neighbors have been torn by ideological differences and civil war, Costa Rica enjoys a stable and developed democracy. The political structure has been enhanced by the fine educational system (94 percent literacy rate), able leadership, comparative prosperity, flexible class lines, and homogeneous society in which an overwhelming 96 percent of the population comes from European descent. Most important, Costa Rica's 1949 constitution abolished the army. The absence of a politically intrusive military has fostered a secure political system conducive to investment in the mixed economy. Unlike many countries in the region, the risk of coups in economically troubled times has become virtually nonexistent.

This is probably just as well, since Costa Rica is recovering from a period of economic crisis and seeks to restructure the economy. Slow growth and soaring annual inflation (24.1 percent for 1980–88) have encouraged efforts to industrialize and shift labor out of the traditional agriculture sector and into more profitable industries. Main exports, such as bananas, coffee, beef, sugar, and cocoa have fallen in value as prices on the international market have fallen.

President Rafael Calderon's government has focused on improving the domestic sphere. His predecessor Oscar Arias won plaudits and a Nobel Peace Prize for his efforts in promoting Central American peace but suffered politically for the lack of prosperity at home.

Investment opportunities exist mainly in tourism, light industries, and agribusiness. Costa Rica seeks to lure more export industries in order to obtain hard currency to help pay back its foreign debt. While San Jose has become highly receptive to foreign investment, program evaluations are often conducted by an inner circle of Costa Ricans. Changes in rules can harm foreign investors if they do not have a contact within this coterie willing to defend their interests.

Czechoslovakia

Many observers have tended to regard Eastern Europe as a single entity—to "lump" it all together. But in 1989, the public outcry for democracy indirectly brought each individual country's history to light. Czechoslovakia gained special attention, perhaps because it has firmer roots in the Western tradition than its neighbors to the east. Even after the Communist coup in 1948 that destroyed the parliamentary democracy, Czechoslovakia's constitution neither made reference to any "dictatorship of the proletariat," nor did it label Czechoslovakia as a socialist republic. Before 1968, Czechoslovakia followed an inclusionary political model. That is, instead of trying to suppress the interests of groups, Prague attempted to forestall frustrated outbursts—trying to rule through reason rather than coercion. But Alexander Dubcek's internal reforms and foreign policy alarmed Moscow to the point of military intervention. After the Warsaw Pact invasion, however, Czechoslovakia became a highly organized society and repressed the unorganized population. The Soviets dismantled the liberalization movement and installed more orthodox elements of the Communist party in Prague.

Ironically, the Soviet Union also provoked the next major change in Czechoslovak politics. Frustrated by the drain the satellite placed on the USSR, Mikhail Gorbachev pressured Milos Jakes to reform his economy, which suffered from shocks resulting from the high energy prices of the 1980s, low investment, and outdated plants and machinery. Czechoslovakia had appeased its citizens with a consumerist strategy that gave them material goods instead of freedom. Now that the living standard declined and mass demonstrations against a similar hard-line government in East Germany proved to be successful, Jakes shielded his regime with police repression. Finally, Jakes resigned on November 24, 1989. Non-Communist dissident playwright Vaclav Havel triumphed in the "gentle revolution" to become the freely elected president.

Havel's main challenge will be that of economic reform. Czechoslovakia must modernize its infrastructure. The industry dates from the 1940s, and energy needs depend on electricity produced by accident-prone, Soviet-planned nuclear power plants. The economy remains a shadow of its former strength. In 1987 GNP measured at an estimated $107 billion, the annual growth rate at 2.6 percent, and per capita income at $6,900. A major shift westward in orientation will benefit trade as well as cut military expenditures.

El Salvador

El Salvador has a remarkably homogeneous population in which nearly 90 percent are *mestizo* (mixed Indian and Spanish). This ethnic similarity has not ensured peace for this nation. Political differences have torn the small state to shreds. The Farabundo Marti National Liberation Front (FMLN), a coalition of a Marxist-Leninist guerilla organization and the political wing of the Democratic Revolutionary Front, has waged a virtual civil war on the government in San Salvador. In the early 1980s, El Salvador reached levels of violence unknown since the 1930s. The Left attacked civilians, and the Right reacted violently in response to sweeping governmental reforms. A new constitution adopted in 1983 strengthened the right of the individual by establishing checks against excessive provisional detention and unreasonable searches. The documents also established a republican form of government with a stronger legislative branch and increased judicial independence. An overriding goal was to guarantee more benefits for labor, including rural workers.

Efforts to end the insurrection have been frustrated. The fourth round of United Nations–mediated peace talks ended in deadlock on August 22, 1990. Although frustrated by the lack of progress, neither side wished to end the monthly contacts, hoping to resolve the 12-year conflict. The U.S. plays an instrumental role in this peace process. Congress has placed increased pressure on the Salvadoran military high command after the November killings of six Jesuit priests and two women. The U.S. has backed San Salvador's 12-year counterinsurgency with $1.5 million a day in military and economic assistance—up to $100 million a year in the mid-1980s, but the budgeted amount for 1991 has been set at less than half of this amount. El Salvador will lose half of this amount if leftist rebels do not negotiate and could forfeit all aid if San Salvador ends the talks or does not adequately investigate murders. Washington has asked the Soviets to assist in talks as well—hoping that this will send a strong signal to the leftist rebels who rely on Cuban aid.

Guerilla sabotage has cost over $2 billion between 1979 and 1987. A 30 percent slice of central government expenditures funds the military's fight. Doubtlessly, the money is sorely needed as the economy remains sickly and will not be reactivated until foreign investment picks up. (It's a vicious circle: no one will seriously consider investing until the insurrection stops.) As the number of guerillas has dropped, they have lost their effectiveness in the countryside and consequently have changed their tactics, resorting to terrorism. Fluctuating world prices for El Salvador's export staples of coffee, cotton, and sugar have also hurt the economy.

The National Union of Workers and Campesinos (UNOC) serves as El Salvador's only democratic union. (The National Union of Salvadoran Workers acts as a front for the FMLN.) The unions still attempt to overcome social injustice left from the days when prior to 1980, 70 percent of all farmers were sharecroppers or laborers on large plantations, or owned fewer than 13 acres of land. El Salvador still has a large lower middle class which hopes for forward-looking agrarian reform. El Salvador has a substantial economy for a small country, which, doubtlessly, would become much more viable without the insurrection. Chemicals, agribusiness, and textiles would all profit.

Businessman Alfredo Cristiani's ARENA (Nationalist Republican Alliance) became the conservative alternative to President Jose Napoleon Duarte Fuentes in 1989. Duarte's Christian Democrats earned a reputation for being excessive in their efforts to halt the civil war. Cristiani maintains that his government favors free market economic growth with limited state involvement to revive the economy's lagging growth rate (an annual -0.4 percent for 1980–88).

Finland

Changes in the Soviet Union will ultimately "de-Finlandize" Finland. The label that political pundits stuck on this Nordic land will lose its meaning in the post–cold war era. States such as Finland will no longer need to be concerned that the Soviet Union could use the fear of imminent invasion to co-opt their political systems and foreign policy. Thus, in this new era of relations, Finland will take a softer stance on its neutrality—making membership in the EC more likely.

A majority of Finns already favor EC membership. Finland, with a population of only 5 million, will find it difficult to compete with larger suppliers—especially the 320 million members of EC. Preparing for 1993 when the EC will allow new members—and the more likely year of 1996—the European Free Trade Association (EFTA) has been carving out a special role for itself. Dubbed the European Economic Space (EES), members will comply with EC laws in exchange for special consultative positions. EES will link EFTA and the EC and should guarantee the free movement of labor, capital, goods, and services.

Based on capital investment and new technology, this industrial economy enjoyed one of the highest growth rates in Western Europe in the first half of the 1980s. Exports today count for one-quarter of GNP; the main industries range from electronics to motor vehicles, with a heavy emphasis on wood and steel. Now the Finns are losing the captive Russian markets which once bought 26 percent of all their exports. Trade, now on a currency rather than barter footing, will turn on oil reserves and prices. On a more positive note, Finland can look forward to taking part in "troika" ventures with the USSR and third countries, drawing on its thorough knowledge of Soviet markets.

Conservative Prime Minister Harri Holkeri suffers from widespread criticism of his handling of the economy, particularly the devaluation of the markka accompanied by the high cost of housing, food, and fuel. Parliamentary elections that must be called by March 1991 could shift the government to a center-led coalition. The economy will continue to decelerate during 1990–1991 in response to the tighter monetary policy and weaker external demand; GDP is predicted to grow by 2 percent in 1990, and then by only 0.5 percent in 1991. Private consumption may decline as well, in response to high interest rates; higher inflation was expected even before the Gulf crisis (6.3 percent this year, 5.5 percent for 1991). The still relatively strong markka will hurt exports, as will the laws that prevent foreign ownership of most Finnish firms. Meanwhile, the deficit climbs rapidly. Speaker of the Parliament Kalevi Sorsa, the man touted to become the next president, has westward leanings and will bring Finland further out of its long Soviet-imposed isolation.

Hungary

Since Stalin's death, Hungary has been Eastern Europe's economic maverick. Khrushchev's "Secret Speech" at the Twentieth Soviet Congress, in February 1956, shook the foundations of power for Stalin's Hungarian appointees. When Matias Rakosi's minor concessions did not appease the populace, Hungarian Prime Minister Imer Nagy embraced the "New Course" which repudiated those policies—until Rakosi engineered Nagy's removal in 1955. The disillusioned, but disorganized Hungarians revolted and temporarily restored basic freedoms such as speech and movement. The sudden widespread opposition accurately reflected the massive, pent-up hatred of the regime and revealed the cracks within the Hungarian Workers party (the Communist party), which broke apart under the stress of the revolt and ceased to function.

Soviet tanks rolled into Budapest at dawn on November 4, 1956. To many, the invasion symbolized the failure of Moscow's policies and promises. As their standard of living decreased, most Hungarians grew increasingly disillusioned with communism's economic policies. Apparently, Khrushchev had paid only lip-service to his plan to permit "separate paths to socialism."

Four decades later, another Soviet leader spoke of economic and political reforms. Gorbachev's foreign policy signaled to then–Prime Minister Miklos Nemeth and Minister of State Imre Pozsgay to accelerate reforms. The economy needs market reforms for the sake of efficiency, especially since one-half of the GNP comes from trade, and Hungary must be able to pay for imports and raw materials. Currently stuck in a strange mixture of market and plan (a "goulash," so to speak), the economy suffers from stagflation—that is, high inflation and low growth. Inflation in 1988 measured approximately 20 percent while the GNP growth rate dwindled to 1.6 percent. More pressing, one-third of the population lives below the poverty line. Hungary must also overcome its dependence on oil. As one of the world's most inefficient users of fossil fuel, Hungary stands to suffer from crises in the Middle East and the Soviet's refusal to continue selling subsidized oil.

The new non-Communist coalition government faces great political challenges as well. The population lacks enthusiasm for democracy. (Not enough people voted in the first election to make it valid.) Entrenched bureaucrats and a disorganized political base will eventually cause problems. And the population is actually declining at a rate of -0.2 percent. Not many have left through the open borders, however, which is a ray of hope for a government that needs it.

Indonesia

President Suharto has led the world's largest archipelago of more then 13,500 islands since 1968. He aided his island nation through economic growth and political stability. Suharto ushered in a "New Order" in Indonesian politics by placing a premium on economic rehabilitation and development. Cementing better relations with the United States has resulted in sizable bilateral trade—$4.9 billion in 1989.

After a difficult economic period in the early 1980s, Indonesia looks to a stronger and more dynamic period in the next decade. Major deregulation has improved business practices, and the devaluation and the convertibility of the rupiah have resulted in important, competitive gains for its exports, notably those of natural gas, oil, tin, plywood, rubber, coffee, tea, and sugar. Unemployment and underemployment still plague the world's fifth most populated country. Indonesia's current five-year plan for 1989–1994 (the Repelita V) stipulates that the country requires real economic growth of at least 5 percent a year to create the 2.3 million–plus new jobs needed annually. In a departure from past policy, the government calls on the private sector to provide 55 percent of this growth. Although Indonesia has a larger unscheduled external debt than any other developing country ($50 billion at the end of 1988), its economic performance has been better than that of most countries in similar positions. GNP for 1988 totaled $75.9 billion.

Fifty-eight prominent Indonesians have signed a petition which asks President Suharto to step down when his fifth term ends in 1993. The military has similarly suggested that the political system should be more open in this country where organized political opposition remains banned. The public has a nagging question concerning 1993: Will the calm and prosperity that Suharto fostered also end? In all likelihood, the next leader will emerge from the military as someone who can reassure this divisive country. Anticipating potential candidates, Jakarta has attempted to cut the civilian role of the military, the country's most powerful institution. In August 1990, the government reshuffled the army senior command, naming Major-General Wismoyo Arismunander (who happens to be Suharto's brother-in-law) as the head of Kostrad, the prestigious Strategic Reserve Command that serves to quench disorder in Indonesia and the capital.

Until recently, the world's largest Muslim country had not suffered from extremism. Insurgents representing the National Liberation Front of Aceh have demanded independence for their province and are thought to be beheading soldiers. Employing anticolonial, pro-Islam language, these radicals have hindered economic development, since workers are afraid to go to Aceh. (Ironically, they complain that Jakarta ignores the economic development of their oil-rich province.) Assuming that this quarrel can be resolved, Indonesia's prospects look bright.

Iran

The fall of the Shah Mohammad Reza Pahlavi during the revolution in 1979 drastically altered Iran's foreign policy to become stridently anti-Western. Crises since then have pitted the U.S. against Shiite hardliners who took 52 American embassy personnel hostage, embarrassed the Reagan administration by trading arms for hostages, and maintain contacts with terrorist groups who continue to hold hostages. In return, the U.S. government has kept frozen billions of dollars worth of Iranian assets, under the International Emergency Economic Powers Act, and has continued a full import embargo.

Despite tortured relations, the U.S. quickly responded to the 7.7 Richter earthquake that killed over 50,000 Iranians. Official U.S. aid totalled about $760,000, and private aid amounted to $1.7 million in supplies and cash. President Ali Akbar Hashemi Rafsanjani, who has led the country since the death of the Ayatollah Ruhollah Khomeini, accepted aid from most nations, snubbing only Israel and South Africa. Thus, he deflated the perceived threat of Iran's foreign enemies—both real and imagined—thereby gaining the high ground politically over extremists who do not tolerate any contact with the West, including assistance or lending agencies.

Rafsanjani has staked his reputation on his ability to repair the war-devastated economy and will need $27.5 billion worth of credits from the West. His five-year recovery plan assaults the radicals' distaste for the West, but Rafsanjani cannot rebuild Iran in isolation. Although the earthquake did not destroy Iran's basic infrastructure, the eight-year struggle with Iraq over the Shatt al Arab waterway damaged many factories, roads, and all the Persian Gulf ports. Rafsanjani needs private or public lenders to revitalize factories with an infusion of cash—on the condition that they would recover their loans later through profits or products regenerated by these factories. Many plants have been shut down for lack of imported materials and spare parts; industry has been reduced to one-fourth of its capacity; and urban unemployment runs at an estimated 25 percent. Consumer goods are in short supply while inflation soars at 50 percent, and the black market flourishes.

Teheran no longer needs to worry that world oil prices will continue to drop; Iraq's incursion in Kuwait has taken care of that—saving his archenemy approximately $3 billion in hard currency. Saddam Hussein's peace overture appeals to Iran since Iraq occupied 1,200 square miles of the Persian Gulf nation's territory. A truce would relieve the tense situation. Hundreds of thousands of troops from each side had remained face-to-face along the 700-mile sealed border, and Iraq held 30,000 Iranian war prisoners. Iran most likely will never receive the $100 billion in war damages that it claims due but desperately needs peace, stability, and the chance to heal.

Iraq

A small group of French-educated Syrian intellectuals originally founded the Arab Socialist Renaissance party (the Baath party) in the 1940s. The group, originally led by a Christian, hoped to unite the Arabs with Pan-Arabism as a secular alternative to Islam. The Baath party took power in Iraq in 1963, and again in 1968. As Ahmad Hasan al-Bakr's chosen successor, Saddam Hussein assumed the offices of president of Iraq and chairman of the Revolutionary Command Council (RCC) in 1979. The nine-member RCC enacts legislation by decree.

Saddam's ambitions do not end in Iraq. He started a war with Iran in 1980 over a small piece of territory. Since his goal remained elusive, rather than give up, he continued to fight for eight years, meanwhile depleting his treasury to build up a formidable army. In 1987, 53 Iraqis out of every 1,000 of the population served in the armed forces—possibly the highest rate in the world. (Seven of every 1,000 Iranians served in the military; 15.5 for the Soviet Union; 9.3 for the United States; 3.3 for Canada.) While claiming that he struggled against the radical Shiism of revolutionary Iran for the benefit of all Arabs, Saddam ran up a debt of over $80 billion, some $30 billion from his Arab neighbors. Much of this money helped to build a terrible arsenal of conventional, chemical, and biological weapons; he also researched the development of nuclear capabilities. (The Israelis temporarily thwarted his nuclear ambitions when they bombed the Osirak plant in 1981.) Violating international law, he tested chemical weapons on the Iranians in battle and on the disaffected Kurdish minority, whom he feared could serve as a fifth column for Iran.

The war took a heavy toll on Saddam's centrally planned economy, reversing the foreign trade balance from surplus to severe deficit. A slump in petroleum prices in 1986 hurt Iraq's heavy dependence on oil exports—petroleum accounts for 32 percent of nominal GNP and for an overwhelming 99 percent of merchandise exports. Baghdad imposed austerity measures and proclaimed that it would not recognize quota restraints—although Iraq's OPEC daily quota at 3.14 million barrels is second only to Saudi Arabia's—and would produce whatever amount best served national interests. Per capita income in 1989 stood at $3,900—a low figure for a country that has 100 billion barrels of oil reserves.

On August 2, 1990, Saddam vented his economic frustrations and imposed his military ambitions on Kuwait. Iraq invaded its tiny neighbor at 2:00 a.m. on a Thursday (the first day of the weekend in the Middle East; the equivalent to a Saturday in the United States) to improve his economic standing. Saddam claimed that Kuwait had profited from his war with Iran. He also alleged that Kuwait needed to be punished for its greediness in exceeding its OPEC quotas—forgetting that Iraq heeded no such limits itself. When the international community turned on him and stationed defensive units in Saudi Arabia, Saddam, oblivious to his own secular background, clamored to have all Arabs rise up to wage a *jihad,* or holy war, to fight the Westerners and those who had sold out to them, compromising Islam's holy city of Mecca.

Saddam failed to grasp the full folly of his miscalculations. The U.S.-led coalition stayed intact—thanks, no doubt, to Israel's admirable restraint even after Scud attacks on its main cities. Iraq left Kuwait an economic and environmental disaster. Iraq's overwhelming defeat did not allow Saddam to claim even a marginal victory, but he has quashed the factions that immediately sprung up to challenge the Baathist leadership. It will take years to reconstruct Iraq's bomb-damaged physical infrastructure. It will take longer to repair the damage to Iraq's international standing. And it may be impossible to placate Iraq's nationalities. The Iraqi Kurds capitalized on the confusion of the moment to push for their goal in the northern oil-rich third of Iraq. The Shiite majority has also rebelled against Saddam's ruthless regime. The U.S. warned Teheran not to support the insurrection in southern Iraq near Basra and Iraq's only access to the Gulf. The ruling Sunis have been put in a difficult situation: they must somehow remove their entrenched leader, support him despite his ignominy, or risk losing their precarious hold on power.

Jamaica

Elected in April 1989, Prime Minister Michael Manley enjoys continued popularity as the political system has swung to a more moderate shade of the spectrum. The ruling People's National party (PNP) promises to improve social and educational services and to expand the private sector with the help of private investment. The two main political parties interact closely with the two major trade unions. The PNP acts with the National Workers Union (NWU) as a social democratic party. The Jamaica Labor party (JLP), associated with the Bustamante Industrial Trade Union, emphasizes the private sector with the need to restructure the economy and reform the government to entice foreign investment.

Although the political system remains stable, severe economic conditions continue to exacerbate social conditions, even though Jamaica's diversified, multiracial society has suffered little ethnic strife, adhering to the ambitious national motto, "Out of many, one people." High unemployment—18.2 percent in 1988—and the lack of foreign exchange top the list of grievances. The shantytowns built around urban areas such as Kingston suffer from high crime rates. These will have to be cleaned up since they could eventually damage tourism—an important source of both income and hard currency. Jamaica's lopsided trade balance depends on this infusion; in 1988 the island-state spent $1,673.2 million on imports while exporting goods worth only $944.8 million. A declining growth rate of -0.7 percent for 1988 and inflation climbing to over 18 percent make matters worse.

Jamaica will be affected by problems abroad, such as high oil prices and recessions in the economies of its major trading partners—the U.S. takes 37 percent of its imports, the U.K. 18 percent, and Canada 14 percent. Difficult times, a sharp devaluation, and soaring interest rates loom on the balmy horizon. Until then, Jamaica can take some solace in its profitable free-trade zones that have spurred investment by foreign firms in garment manufacturing, light manufacturing, and data entry. More than 150 U.S. firms operate in Jamaica with investments exceeding $1 billion. Other important industries include fishing, the extraction of high-grade bauxite with new technologies, and guano, which is used for fertilizer and chemicals.

New Zealand

During its 16 years in office, the Labour party implemented comprehensive social security, large-scale public works, a maximum 40-hour workweek, a minimum wage, and compulsory unionism. Although the party enjoyed its successes and a popular mandate in 1987 when it was voted back to office with an increased majority, it has been forced to raise taxes to cut budget deficit and to scrap subsidies and many regulations. Inflation has been brought down from 10 percent to an annualized rate of 5.3 percent, unemployment will likely continue to fall from 7.3 percent and the economy has finally started to grow again—the budget predicts a 2.5 percent growth rate in real GDP for 1990–91. But most voters were not impressed. Polls showed that Geoffrey Palmer would receive only 28 percent of the vote against National party candidate, Jim Bolger, in elections scheduled for October 27, 1990. Seven weeks before the elections, Palmer resigned as prime minister to spare his party—a device becoming common to Labour leaders. With Labour likely to lose up to two-thirds of its seats, External Relations and Trade Minister Mike Moore replaced Palmer. Even his new policy initiatives may not appease voters who have grown tired of the Labour party.

Palmer's predecessor, David Lange, sacked his finance minister, Roger Douglas, during his second term as prime minister—immediately before resigning. "Rogernomics" had enjoyed great popular support as it brought double-digit inflation down, halved taxes, spared the labor market, and reduced one of the highest per capita deficits in the industrialized world. But after a 1987 stock market plunge and the implementation of a flat tax, the economy began to contract severely. Unemployment jumped by more than 50 percent in 1988 and businesses collapsed, but Douglas would not sacrifice long-term goals to ease the situation—a stubbornness that infuriated the public.

New Zealand can look forward to the fulmination of its 1983 "Closer Economic Relationship" agreement with Australia, which will create a single market of 19 million consumers in 1990. This pact will increase the importance of trade and lessen the effects of numbing protectionist legislation, which has encouraged inefficiency and slowed economic growth. New Zealand's leading manufacturing sectors in food processing, metal fabrication, wool and paper products will either benefit directly or indirectly from this new trade relationship.

Nicaragua

U.S. foreign policy toward Nicaragua has been problematic since the 1979 revolution which overthrew the U.S.-supported Somoza regime. Although then-president Jimmy Carter recognized Daniel Ortega as leader of his country, candidate Ronald Reagan's campaign platform rejected Sandinista rule in Nicaragua. The Reagan administration feared that socialism would spread throughout the hemisphere to bolster insurgencies in places such as El Salvador. To combat this threat, the Reagan administration used both legal and illegal means to support the contras, many of whom had been members of Somoza's National

Guard. After a decade of rule, Ortega agreed to stand for popular election. Although polls predicted that the referendum would send him back to office, Violeta Chamorro beat him by a margin of 55-41. The window of the martyr whose murder touched off the 1979 revolution, Chamorro headed a fourteen party coalition known by the acronym UNO (National Opposition Union), which is also Spanish for *one*.

By Chamorro's inauguration on April 25, 1990, Nicaragua had become not the showcase of socialism but rather the basket case. The badly managed economy relied on Soviet subsidization. Chamorro inherited such economic woes as hyperinflation, which soared at an annual rate of more than 900 percent. Plans to stabilize the currency have lagged, and in July 1990, inflation ran at 185 percent (or at 200 percent, according to the opposition). The government wants to put the economy back on track via privatization in order to end the subsidies for public transportation, telephones, and water.

The deep social divisions afflicting Nicaraguan society will be even more difficult to repair. Chamorro encounters strong opposition, compounded by the fact that Sandinistas still control the army and police. After 8,000 contras had laid down their weapons—virtually disintegrating as a political force—the National Workers' Front declared a strike in July 1990. A first strike in May had been resolved without violence, but this one erupted in the bloodiest situation since the revolution, leaving five dead and over 90 injured within ten days. The dispute over government wages recalled Ortega's vow to "govern from below," and the Sandinista promise to take "not one step back" in their defense of the "conquests of the revolution." Nine-tenths of the 100,000 government workers walked off their jobs, suspending almost all government and commercial business. Gunplay, five-foot barricades on every major thoroughfare, burning tires, and Molotov cocktails led UNO to concede to increase salaries, suspend the program to rent confiscated land to previous owners, compensate fired bureaucrats, and guarantee job protection for the strikers. The fledgling democracy will have a difficult time trying to attain prosperity, let alone unity.

Pakistan

In early August 1990, President Ghulam Ishaq Khan dismissed Prime Minister Benazir Bhutto on charges of corruption and nepotism, focused primarily on Bhutto's husband Asif Ali Zardari and his father Hakim Ali Zardari. Her ouster followed months of ethnic violence in the southern Sind Province and widespread disaffection with Bhutto. General Mirza Aslam Beg, who challenged Bhutto's authority and leads the 450,000-member armed forces, holds considerable prestige in a nation which spends a quarter of central government expenditures on its military. Pakistan's generals have ruled their country for 24 of the 43 years of independence. In the 1976 coup that interrupted the democratic process, General Zia ul-Haqin executed Bhutto's father, former prime minister Zulfiqar Ali Bhutto. Ghulam Mustafa Jatoi, who has led the combined opposition parties in parliament, will serve as the interim prime minister.

Benazir Bhutto attempted to maintain a government of compromises, trying to balance opposing factions in this socially conservative country, where most Pakistanis live in poverty in the countryside—GNP per capita amounted to a scant $350 in 1988. The Westernized urban elites, especially feminists and liberals, criticized the Pakistan People's party for not promoting secularism. Radical clerics influenced by the Iranian revolution, on the other hand, were frustrated with their inability to assert themselves on the government. Bhutto's scarf symbolized her willingness to make concessions—or her inability to take a stand, as her opponents alleged: she would wear the cloth wrapped loosely around her head, sometimes allowing it to fall down to her shoulders. That she would continue to wear it, outraged the liberals; that she would do so carelessly, infuriated the religious reactionaries.

On the day after Bhutto's dismissal, senior government bureaucrats came to work in the traditional loose *shalwar kameez* clothing—not the suits and ties that they had worn during her tenure, feeding fears that the shift would revert habits to those of the Zia days—meaning the curtailment of liberal, Western images and ideas. On August 10, intelligence agents arrested five Pakistani journalists after they left the home of an Indian diplomat; the next day a court in Islamabad charged them with violating the Islamic ordinance banning the drinking of alcohol. The abrupt change in government may affect U.S. relations, which partly consist of close military ties and $700 million in annual aid.

Few issues unite the Pakistanis, and the most pressing one has strong military overtones. The conflict with India over the Kashmir region has rankled both sides since Britain granted the two counties their independence in 1947. Hostility has festered since then and worries the international community—especially since India's arsenal contains nuclear weapons, and Pakistan has secretively worked on their development. The eight-month insurgency flared in August 1990 when a battle between militants and troops left at least 28 dead. India has opened talks on decreasing border tensions, as it fears that Pakistan's new caretaker government will increase aid to the valley's Moslem Separatists.

Panama

Long known as *puente del mundo*—"the crossroads of the world"—Panama has achieved international importance due to its canal.

The Panama Canal aided the country by contributing to its yearly growth rate of 5 percent through 1982. In 1983, however, this pace slowed, and in 1984 the economy even shrank. Having recovered over the next few years, the economy again contracted amidst political chaos in 1987. By 1988 Panama had fallen into a severe economic recession with a 20 percent decline of GDP. Economic mismanagement and severe repression led to declines in almost all major sectors.

After both the OAS and an internal coup attempt failed to dislodge strongman, Manuel Antonio Noriega, the head of the Panamanian Defense Forces who had stolen a democratic election from Guillermo Endara, the U.S. invaded Panama in December 1989 to remove the dictator wanted on drug charges in Florida. "Operation Just Cause" destroyed 1,800 family homes in the El Chorrillo district and hurt much of the local economy. Although most Panamanians welcomed Noriega's ouster, they bitterly resented the American destruction; the tent cities and Red Cross refugee camps operating in two airplane hangars did little to win the affections of the displaced persons. The $32.6 million emergency aid package and the extra $420 million in economic aid approved in July 1990 from the U.S. have helped repair the economy. Bank deposits have started to rise again, but unemployment has climbed from 10% in 1987 to 30% since the end of 1989, and 44% of the population lives in poverty. The fact that the establishment of a democratic government does not guarantee security or economic turnaround has been a rough lesson; meanwhile, President Guillermo Endara's approval rating has fallen to 30%. To make matters worse, American troops failed to meet a summer deadline to return to their bases outside Panama City.

The future of the Canal remains an important and nagging question for this small country whose future has been fused to the locks that carry 5 percent of the world's oceangoing trade. The 1979 treaty that will turn the Canal over to Panama on noon of December 31, 1999 weighs heavily on the more than half of the population, that lives in the Panama-Colon metropolitan corridor around the Canal, as well as the rest of the world. Although the 51.2-mile waterway no longer functions as a vital strategic and military asset, it remains an important link for international commerce to both coasts of the United States, Japan, Europe, and Latin America. The uncertainty has been compounded by increased international competition and flat revenue and tonnage figures for the last several years—after decades of dramatic growth—accounted for by declining U.S. imports of Japanese cars, sluggish grain sales, and slower economic growth in the U.S. and Japan. Mounting competition from an oil pipeline across Panama and the increased use of trains double-stacked with containers have also whittled away at the use of the

Canal. In 1989, toll revenues came to $329 million, a figure little changed since 1986, and the number of ships using the canal remained steady at about 12,000. The increasing costs for labor, maintenance, and equipment may even have rendered the Canal something of a white elephant. Panama City has not yet resolved the fundamental question of whether to run the Canal as a government agency, an autonomous entity, or as a partnership. Worries about Panama's ability to run the Canal efficiently have been fueled by the country's experience with the Canal's two ports, Balboa and Cristobal. Endara would like to complete the privatization of state assets, including these ports.

Peru

Alberto Fujimori, the "Change 90" candidate, triumphed at the polls on June 10, 1990 to succeed President Alan Garcia Perez. The elections renewed hope in Peru's democratic process. Dr. Garcia, after all, had participated in the first exchange of power from one democratically elected leader to another in 40 years. Despite having run on a vague platform, the so-called "Stealth Candidate" defeated the more widely known author, Mario Vargas Llohsa. Fujimori appealed to the voter's desire to avoid radical change—such as "shocks" to the economy—and proposed only moderate reform akin to Lima's current policies. Fujimori portrayed himself as a political outsider and one of the common people. Fujimori also assured voters that he would use his Japanese ancestry to advantage in obtaining aid—much needed by the faltering Peruvian economy in which the inflation rate then jumped by about one percent a day.

Fujimori visited Japan at the end of June 1990, a month before his inauguration. Peru has received development assistance from Japan since the early 1960s; Japan allotted Peru the most in all of Latin America until Lima stopped paying back official government yen loans. For fiscal 1988, Japanese Overseas Development Assistance (ODA) amounted to $27 million, half in grants and half in technical assistance. "If Peru meets the international obligations concerning its arrears in debt payments to such organizations as the International Monetary Fund (IMF) and the World Bank, Japan will be ready to make drastic commitments to other categories of assistance," Kabun Muto, minister for international trade and industry, commented. An estimated $17.5 billion in foreign debt threatens substantial aid.

Nonetheless, Tokyo granted Fujimori $4.6 million for an irrigation project to boost food production, and will explore approaches to economic cooperation, and the Ministry of International Trade and Industry will send experts to help the country plan economic and social reforms. The local government of Fujimori's parents' home, the Kumamoto Prefectural, agreed to provide funding for education, extend medical cooperation, and receive agricultural trainees; Governor Morihiro Hosokawa plans to establish a group that will seek donations for health, welfare, and education in Peru. The Japanese private sector also opened its pocketbook: Kokusai Shotokan karate school pledged to build a $650,000 martial arts hall in Lima, and one citizen gave $65,000 to aid Peruvian children.

Fujimori will need all the aid he can find. Peru suffers from desperate financial straights. In the third largest country in Latin America, real income has fallen by more than 20 percent; the overall economy has shrunk by 12 percent; only 15 percent of the workforce enjoys full employment (10 percent have no work, and 75 percent have marginal work, according to Fujimori); the government's cash reserves are essentially exhausted as the central bank holds only $150 million in reserves.

On August 9, 1990, Fujimori's government announced emergency measures to curb the runaway inflation—which had reached 90% in July—and to cut Peru's huge national debt. Prime Minister Juan Carlos Hurtado Miller proclaimed measures such as the immediate removal of all government consumer subsidies and an increase in the prices of staple foods and utilities (gasoline prices increased by 30 times, and the prices of bread and milk nearly tripled). The government ordered employers to provide bonuses of at least $23 to employees within five days, to partially compensate for the sudden upsurges. The government also imposed a 10 percent tax on exports and ended the currency exchange system to allow the *inti* to float to its free-market value. Lima hopes that such action will win international approval and reopen the flow of development funds.

Peru's bleak economic situation has worldwide implications since it leads many Peruvian farmers to grow lucrative coca leaves; Peru provides 60 percent of the world's supply of the basis for cocaine, worth an estimated $1 billion per year. Fujimori favors an approach to the drug problem based on economic development so that coca-growers can find another means of making a living. A major shake-up in the national police force's anti-narcotics unit in August 1990 will give more power to the military for an integrated effort to combat drugs and guerilla violence. Half of this Andean state is currently under military rule to combat the Maoist Sendero Luminoso (Shining Path), which has terrorized the country for the last decade by killing over 17,000 people.

Peru drastically needs the very "shock" measures that Fujimori campaigned against. Much hope rides on Fujimori's ability to deliver development aid, to save the faltering economy, and to curb the coca problem.

Philippines

Corazon Aquino continues to weather the many disasters facing her presidency. While her people respect her for promoting democracy and ousting dictator Ferdinand Marcos, she is regarded as a weak leader. Widespread disillusionment with the "people power" revolution stems from the fact that the poor measure success in terms of their standard of living. The populace also decries the lack of roads, schools, and basic services. Resentment over the centralization of power in Manila and cynicism over government initiatives feed the sense that things are only getting worse. Aquino has warded off two major coup attempts—one in August 1987 and one in December 1989. Meanwhile, trying to forestall discontent, the government plans to increase foreign exchange reserves to make more money available for oil imports. Subsidies should keep the price of oil low enough for consumers; but continuing escalations in prices will land the government in the red. The best that Manila can hope for will be lower inflation and a milder recession.

The Iraqi invasion of Kuwait will have repercussions beyond that of the price of oil. The Philippines' profitable banana industry will suffer from reduced exports to the Middle East. Sixty-thousand Filipinos overseas have lost their jobs. And 250,000 Filipino contract workers will not easily be able to send home an estimated $250 million to $1 billion in hard currency this year. With this crisis, in addition to the earthquake that devastated cental Luzon, the drought, typhoons, and floods in the past 10 months, the country may achieve economic growth of 3.8 percent now, compared to the targeted 6.5 percent considered essential to pull the population out of poverty.

Defying economic sense, then, in September 1990 Aquino called for the "orderly withdrawal" of American forces from the country within a year. The U.S. favors a more steady pullout over a period of about 10 years. Clark Air Base, Subic Bay Naval Base, and four smaller facilities, after all, are no longer vital to the projection of American military might needed in the Pacific to counter a Soviet threat. Aquino asked for the U.S. to end its 92-year-long military presence in the Philippines shortly after the Philippine riot police battled anti-American protesters near the U.S. Embassy. The 1987 constitution bars any extension of the current military bases agreement which expires in September 1991 unless the accord is ratified as a treaty by the Philippine Senate or approved in a national referendum. Ironically, surveys show that most Filipinos do not oppose the bases; in a 1989 poll, only 13 percent of respondents wanted the bases removed by 1991; 40 percent favored keeping them indefinitely, and 35 percent were unaware that they existed.

Now, however, public debate in the Philippines has shifted from whether the bases should be removed to how long the transition period should be. Most agree that a sudden U.S. pullout would hurt the Philippines. Bases generate 80,000 jobs—a payroll second only to that of Aquino's government—and generate approximately $1 billion a year in U.S. aid and expenditures. Each year the American armed forces (15,000 soldiers and 20,000 civilian workers and their families) spend $530 million in the country. Foreign trade with the U.S. holds a critical place in the Philippine economy. The U.S. traditionally has been the Philippines' largest trading partner, accounting for 35 percent of its exports and over one-fifth of its imports. Total trade with the U.S. in 1988 came to more than $4 billion.

Aquino's government cannot last much longer. She staved off the second coup attempt only with the assistance of the U.S. By biting the hand that has helped feed her people, she will be making the economic situation precarious and ripe for another coup. Anti-American attitudes and violence will make the Philippines an unfriendly place to do business and will ultimately hurt foreign investment and tourism. Remember, the Peace Corps cannot protect its volunteers here, and since 1987, 10 Americans have been killed by suspected Communist guerilla assassination squads.

Poland

Solidarity, the first non-Communist organization to break the Communist monopoly on power in Eastern Europe, has begun to see strains in the alliance between intellectuals and workers. Victory over the common enemy of communism has the different sides at odds about how to govern. While former Prime Minister Tadeusz Mazowiecki argues that there are no painless cures for decades of mismanagement, his challenger Lech Walesa, the former leader of the movement, demands that the government act more sympathetically toward the workers. Warsaw has eclipsed Gdansk as the center of political activity, and Walesa clearly desired to exert more control over the process. In April 1990, Walesa announced that he would like to replace General Wojciech Jaruzelski in the fall, even though the leftover Communist's presidential term did not officially expire until 1995.

In mid-July of 1990 the main chamber of parliament passed a bill to sell state-owned industry to private investors—a step that the other reform governments in Eastern Europe have not yet taken. The bill passed the Sejm by a margin of 328 to 2, with 39 abstentions. The wide-ranging legislation will affect 7,600 state enterprises which constitute 80 percent of the national economy. To reassure those who fear that restructuring the centrally planned economy along Western lines will sell the country to bargain-hunting foreigners, special incentives will encourage domestic investment. For instance, Polish workers may buy up to 20 percent of the shares at half of the market price and will also be able to take out low interest loans.

Austerity measures in the first six months of 1990 have ended hyperinflation. The recession, however, has reduced economic activity by 30 percent. At the end of June, 570,000 people, or 4.2 percent of a work force accustomed to full employment, lacked jobs. Wage controls have decreased the average Pole's buying power by 40 percent. The small farmers who make up 12.5 percent of the population stand to lose the most in the coming months. Reforms will necessarily result in the bankruptcy of thousands of farmers, most of whom tend small and inefficent plots. A strike in July revealed their anger, as they demanded guaranteed prices for their crops, to cover the costs of fuel, farm machinery, and fertilizer.

Poland's success will rely on convincing the population to continue with reforms for their long-term benefit, even though the short term will be bitter. Free markets will have to appeal to the Polish people in more than theory. The local elections may already reflect disenchantment with the new government—although Solidarity won, only 42 percent of the eligible voters came to the polls.

Portugal

On June 1, 1989, the Portuguese Parliament approved reforms that removed the Marxist phraseology imbedded in the 1976 constitution. Prime Minister Anibal Cavaco Silva's Social Democratic party (PSD) and the Socialist party spearheaded modifications that altered the textual goal of creating "a classless society" to "trying to construct a free, just and united society." Portugal then embarked upon the denationalization of industries and the sale of majority stakes in state-owned enterprises in preparation for EC '92 program.

The state previously could sell only minority shares, as it did when it offered 49 percent of the Unicer brewery for sale in April 1989, and then the Banco Totta e Acores in July. Alianca Seguradora and Tranquilidade, two insurance companies, were targeted next for privatization. The government announced its aim to create a strong core of native shareholders to ensure that important companies, especially financial institutions, remain under Portuguese control. Robust foreign demand has spurred fears about "the country being up for sale." Cavaco Silva maintains that his reprivatization program is vital for the economy's competitiveness and efficiency. Eighty percent of the capital generated by privatizations will be used to reduce the public debt. The deficit—which represents 75% of the gross domestic product (GDP)—not only absorbs money that otherwise would be available for investment but also fuels inflation by requiring great levels of liquid assets for government spending.

Yet this Portuguese *perestroika* could become a victim of its own success: while privatization reforms may ultimately reduce the public debt, they also drive an overheated economy. Private consumption rose two percentage points above growth in industrial output, swelling the deficit to $5.7 billion in 1988, a record high. By April 1989, the annualized inflation rate reached a three-year high of 13.2 percent. The high rate of investment in industry has stimulated capital goods purchases from abroad. This fact, combined with the strong influx of imported consumer goods, has had a negative effect on the trade balance.

The government estimated the 1989 growth rate at between 3.5 and 4 percent (GDP growth in 1988 reached 4.1 percent) and the 1989 budget deficit to be just under 8 percent of GDP. Strong growth cut unemployment from 6.7 percent in the last quarter of 1988 to 4.9 percent in October 1989. This relatively low level, however, may not be maintained as companies rationalize production, yet cannot retrain their employees. About 90 percent of the Portuguese manufacturing industry is either small or medium-sized and find it difficult to compete with larger foreign firms.

U.S. Secretary of State James A. Baker III visited Portugal during his tour of NATO capitals in February 1989. Baker pledged expanded economic aid—from $117 million in fiscal 1988 to $150 million for fiscal 1989—resulting from Cavaco Silva's consultations on compensation for U.S. use of the military base in the Azores. Washington also agreed to supply Portugal with twenty F16 fighter bombers, Hawk missiles and other military equipment. The aid package strengthens Portugal's role as a strategic ally in the mid-Atlantic.

Romania

The Red Army invaded Romania at the end of World War II and installed a coalition government with the Communists in dominant positions. The Romanian Communists sorely lacked popular support and were regarded as antinationalist and overly dependent on the USSR—epitomized by their desire to give Bessarabia to the Soviet Union.

Elected as the country's first president in March 1974, Nicolae Ceausescu, however, rejected Soviet control over the domestic economy and foreign policy. In the parlance of the day, he claimed his "own road to socialism." Ceausescu spurned Marxist-Leninism as well as the USSR. He adopted a neo-Stalinist personality cult—just about the only aspect of Soviet society that he would emulate. He amassed so much personal power that he came close to destroying the Party. Soviet leaders acquiesced to his plans mainly because Romania was not considered militarily significant, and the Romanian deviation did not entail decentralization. In fact, Ceausescu took centralization to an extreme, creating a merging of party and state within his person.

Ceausescu's stated government policy blatantly contrasted with reality. While local governments were supposed to be given independence and responsibility, they actually were given responsibility without autonomy—they were given guidelines on what to produce but no money to do so. Bucharest's extremely exploitive system squeezed resources out of local governments.

Ceausescu's personalized power could be seen in his ubiquitous portraits, the mandatory rallies, and the strong nepotism ("socialism in one family") with 40 members in top Communist party, ministry, and military posts. The cult of personality ultimately resulted in the destruction of the norms of politicalization. The system lacked any form of collective leadership as bureaucrats were rotated constantly in their governmental jobs to prevent potential rivals from creating power bases. But this extreme measure also prevented these technocrats from building expertise or competence. All rivals were purged, and there was no debate over policies. Laws were simply decreed. Ceausescu's tunnel vision led to a misguided, destructive, and unchecked policy. The Communist party only nominally held power; Ceausescu's government lacked an independent ideology.

Ceausescu's refusal to share power strengthened Romania's nationalistic foreign policy. He clashed often with the Soviet Union, notably maintaining relations with China, establishing relations with Israel in 1967, allowing Jews to emigrate, denouncing the 1968 Warsaw Pact invasion of Czechoslovakia, and courting the West. He also refused to accept the USSR's demand that Romania serve as an agricultural producer in COMECON, and instead decided to build heavy industry. Such disputes served as a legitimization tactic for many years; Ceausescu could not employ consumerism as did several other East European leaders, especially since Romania could not afford to do so in the midst of its quest to rapidly build heavy industry.

Eventually, Romania became more centralized and skewed toward heavy industry than any of the other countries of Eastern Europe. Romania suffered from the characteristic problems of central planning with the added twist that Ceausescu demanded an unrealistic annual growth rate of 10–15 percent and imposed punitive measures on those who did not fulfill their quotas. This harsh strategy seemed to pay off in the 1970s, riding on its annual growth rate of about 8% a year between 1965 and 1974—the highest in postwar Europe. This approach become unglued in the 1980s as managers felt forced to lie about figures of production and to achieve bottom line results by resisting investment in research or infrastructure. Other economic headaches included an agricultural crisis, the effects of the worldwide recession, high energy costs, an unfavorable debt maturity structure, and the decision to build a huge petrochemical industry—creating a total economic disaster during the oil crisis in the early 1980s. The incipient economic collapse was worse than anywhere else in Europe, with near zero growth in the late 1980s.

Ceausescu blamed Western exploitation for his economic woes. He decided that he wanted Romania to be self-sufficient and so inflicted domestic austerity to pay off foreign debts, repudiated most favored nation status with the U.S., and undertook other irrational and xenophobic measures that cut Romania off from foreign technology and credits.

While the economy broke down without investment or improvements, Budapest spurned reforms suggested by Moscow. The most adamant of all the East European leaders, Ceausescu delivered a three-hour tirade against reform in 1987 while Gorbachev waited on the platform. Eventually, Gorbachev basically cut ties with Ceausescu. Soviet influence did not have much impact on the Romanians; rather, Bulgarian television inspired the dispirited populace.

The Romanians' economic despondency matched their social plight. Ceausescu persecuted and resettled minorities; he also wanted to increase population despite basic problems of malnutrition—weekly monitoring attempted to force each woman to bear five children. The politically deactivated population lived in fear and spent much of its free time searching for food for survival. One out of three people worked as secret police informants. Finally, in December 1989 the citizens voiced their discontent, perhaps believing that they no longer had anything to lose. What began as a protest over the arrest of a popular Protestant minister in Timisoara escalated into civil war between the army and many factions in Bucharest. The Romanian army deserted to side with the people in a bloody and violent upheaval to overthrow Ceausescu's police state. Ceausescu's rule was destroyed in a week, proving again that absolute systems are strong only as long as they are absolute.

The National Salvation Front's (NSF) Ion Iliescu emerged victorious from the controversial election on May 20, 1990. The first multiparty presidential and legislative elections in 53 years were held too soon for political groups to consolidate and organize. As a result, an overwhelming 7,000-plus candidates sought seats in the 387-member Assembly of Deputies and in the 119-member Senate. In turn, only the organized political entity, the NSF, a coalition of former Communist officials and workers, could capture a majority of the votes. Many intellectuals and anti-Communists believe this victory to have been stolen, claiming the 85 percent margin of victory to be suspicious and reminiscent of past "victories." In the summer of 1990, Iliescu bused in vigilante miners to break up antigovernment protestors.

Whether or not Iliescu's government is legitimate it confronts a stark legacy. The population, so long repressed, will not easily overcome their terror and divisiveness. Already, one of society's most stable elements, the German population, has begun to head home in droves. Before 1989, 200,000 ethnic Germans resided in Romania. A year later, fewer than 100,000 remain; by December 1991, only 20,000 will likely be left. Ethnic squabbles have become deadly—especially for Hungarians and Jews in Transylvania. The economy will not be readily healed; the lack of modern infrastructure will hamper reform. Ceausescu made a destructive mark which will not be easy to erase.

Singapore

In August 1990, Prime Minister Lee Kuan Yew announced his plans to step down as prime minister in November, after more than 25 years of ruling the prosperous city-state with an iron hand. Goh Chok Tong, then first deputy prime minister and defense minister, promises less domineering leadership: "The people are better off today, well-educated. There is a larger pool at the top who can contribute very much to policy-making, formulation [and] analysis. So one of the changes I have in mind is to get this group to play a bigger role in building the next stage for Singapore. Hence I have chosen to have a more decentralized style of government."

Singapore appears to be bending to the same democratic pressures felt throughout the world, reflected in the growing desire of young, affluent professionals to move away from authoritarianism. Yet, there remains the question of how the new leader can succeed when Lee intends to stay active as a senior cabinet minister without portfolio. Insiders fear that Lee's son, Brig. Gen. Lee Hsien Loong, will also unduly influence the political system.

Singapore became self-governing in 1953; a decade later, it joined the Federation of Malaya, Sabah, and Sarawak to form the Federation of Malaysia. Indonesia, the island's second largest trading partner, however, charged that the new grouping represented a "British colonial creation" and adopted a policy of a "confrontation." Indonesia resumed trade with Singapore only after it separated from Malaysia on August 9, 1965 to become an independent republic. Lee and his People's Action party (PAP) promulgated the Internal Security Act to purge suspected leaders of a Communist insurgency and to smooth racial and religious divisions. Opposition parties are legal but not encouraged; the PAP holds 80 of 81 seats in the unicameral parliament.

Singapore overcame its geographic vulnerability and lack of natural resources by first serving as an *entrepôt* center for the area. After independence, the city-state industrialized its infrastructure and placed an increasing emphasis on high-technology, high-value-added goods and services. As Singapore became an electronics and banking center, it shifted toward importing capital goods and raw materials for industry, and exporting locally manufactured products. Its strategic location and people (the population density ranks as one of the world's highest, with 4,231 people per square kilometer, or 10,961 per square mile) have given Singapore the third highest per capita income in Asia ($9,100 in 1988), an impressive GNP growth rate (7 percent in 1980–88), and strong foreign reserves holdings ($16.6 billion, at the end of 1988).

South Korea

The South Korean economy has grown spectacularly for the past 25 years. In a single generation the Republic of Korea (ROK) has progressed from one of the world's poorest countries to nearly full industrialization. This growth seems near miraculous in light of the scarcity of natural resources and the drain the large military places on the budget, accounting for just over one quarter of all central government expenditures. The division of the peninsula led to both handicaps. With the partition, North Korea inherited most of the mineral and hydroelectric resources as well as the industrial base built by the Japanese. South Korea lacks oil, and energy problems plague government planners. The Democratic People's Republic of Korea (DPRK) still poses a security threat. Furthermore, the influx of refugees to South Korea has resulted in one of the highest poulation densities in the world—even higher than those of India and Japan.

The German model for reunification may have given the two Koreas inspiration, but not success. Progress on unification fizzled again on August 13, 1990 when both governments were supposed to begin a week of "open borders." Not a single person crossed the open space on the southern bank of the Injim River. The week highlighted August 15—Korean Independence Day, commemorating the day the Allies defeated Japan in World War II, ending its half-century of colonial rule on the peninsula. After all, resentment of Tokyo's ruthless efforts to replace the Korean language and culture does not stop at the 38th parallel. Many hope that Panmunjom will successfully serve as a site for reunification; if it does, it will supplant its reputation as the site where the DPRK signed armistice negotiations with the U.N. to end the Korean War.

In 1988 mass demonstrations forced the ROK military dictatorship to allow free elections. After two years of watching basic legislation die in the legislature, President Roh Tae-woo merged his Democratic Justice party with two conservative opposition parties in early 1990. The booming economy has slumped since the bickering government could not effectively deal with labor demands. Kim Young-sam—who may be pegged to replace Roh—and his Reunification Democratic party as well as Kim Jong-pil's New Democratic Republican party, will join Roh to form the Democratic Liberal party which hopes to rule by consensus. Most important, they will attempt to repair the economy which, after three years of double digit growth, witnessed widespread labor unrest, exorbitant annual wage increases (20–25 percent for three years running), record trade dificit, and unprecedented inflation. The remaining opposition leader, Kim Dae-jung, of the Party for Peace and Democracy, warns that the government now could easily slip back to authoritarianism.

Spain

In the 1989 Spanish elections the Socialist Workers' party (PSOE) won an absolute majority in the parliament by the slimmest possible margin. On October 29, the Socialist Workers' party lost 14 seats in the national election called well ahead of the June 1990 deadline. By capturing 176 seats in the 350-member lower house of parliament, the Socialists retain a scant one-seat majority. The major Madrid daily, *El Pais* concluded that "Spaniards have decided with clarity that they want to continue being governed by the Socialists, but with no less clarity they demand changes in the way things are done." Such demands include calls to reevaluate economic priorities and fight corruption in government. Cries of corruption followed the contested results.

For the third year in a row, overall growth has remained above 5 percent—faster than that registered by any other European state. At the same time, however, unemployment stood at 16.6 percent in August, down 3.2 percent from a year before. Although the lowest rate during González's tenure, this figure, which means that more than two million Spaniards are jobless, is the highest in Western Europe. The expanding economy shows signs of overheating. By the first quarter of 1989, Spain's trade deficit widened to $6.04 billion, up from $4.08 billion for all of 1988. Inflation rose to a 6.8 percent annual rate in October, well above the 5.8 percent for 1988.

Despite the expulsion of 72 U.S. F-16 fighters from the Torrejón Air Base in 1988, González expressed the belief that Madrid and Washington are now entering a "stage of normality in relations." When González and President George Bush met in Washington in October 1989, Bush praised Spain's transition from dictatorship to democracy as a possible model for Eastern European countries attempting similar transformations.

González chaired the semiannual summit meeting of heads of EC nations held in Madrid on June 27, 1989. In his role as the EC president for the first six months of 1989, González gave impetus to an economic and monetary union scheduled to take effect at the end of 1992. Under his supervision the Spanish *peseta* fully entered the European Monetary System with its inclusion in the exchange rate mechanism.

Sweden

As Eastern Europe seeks a model for transforming itself to capitalism, the long touted "Swedish model" may no longer be appropriate. Although the cradle-to-grave welfare system may be appealing, the stellar 64 percent income taxes seem overbearing and the high inflation rate, stifling.

The Social Democrats hold their lowest level of support since the 1920s. They may even have to team up with the Liberals in the September 1991 election, to retain power. Many Swedes are dissatisfied with Prime Minister Ingvar Carlsson's drive toward a market-oriented economy which includes tax reform and deregulation. Sweden also struggles with the dilemma of joining EC; this contentious issue becomes increasingly important as 1992 approaches. Sweden's small work force cannot compete against the monolithic organization; but neutrality is a highly prized commodity in this country which has not fought in a war in over 170 years.

Nonetheless, the economic forecasts look bleak and sluggish overall. The GDP growth rate will decelerate sharply from 2.1 percent in 1989 to an estimated 0.5 percent in 1990 and 0.2 percent in 1991. Meanwhile, inflation will continue to rise to 11.8 percent by 1991. The oil shock will only exacerbate inflation. Business confidence will decline as a result of the high interest rates, weaker private consumption, and a low rate of investment growth.

Severe problems also plague the famous social-welfare system. Public consensus demands that taxes must be reduced but without cutting the universal benefits. Nearly one-fifth of the population draws some form of old-age, disability, or survivor's pensions that strain the health care system as well as the tax base. Demographic data further irritate this problem: Sweden boasts one of the world's highest life expectancy's and a low birthrate. Immigration continues to rise—placing more pressures on the burdened system. Government spending is estimated to slow down from 1990's 1.8 percent to 1.0 percent in 1991.

Venezuela

Venezuela's great hydroelectric and oil resources make this country worthy of consideration for investment. Caracas has noted its willingness to modify its Central Bank in order to seek loans from the World Bank. President Carlos Andres Perez has decided to proceed with tariff reform to make his country more friendly to foreign investment. The U.S. already accounts for the majority—55 percent of new investment in 1985—in Venezuela. A new foreign investment code provides unlimited openings to investors and ends ceilings on the repatriation of capital and profits. Private investors may also be attracted to the debt-for-equity swap system.

Domestic progress may become more difficulty for the ruling Accion Democratica (AD). Attempts to change the public administration will meet many challenges and much resistance. Labor law reform will raise private-sector costs to 5–7 percent in the short-to-medium term. Companies anticipate work force cuts to help recover from the higher cost of labor and the recession.

Venezuela enjoys relative political stability, since the central government cultivates good relations with both the military and the labor unions. Since 1959 the armed forces have rejected playing a direct role in national politics. An intermingling of political and trade union life allows labor to work within the framework of government. It is not uncommon for trade union members to serve as representatives and even as senators. Despite a lack of technically trained personnel, the disciplined multiparty labor movement has achieved relatively high industrial wages, benefits, and conditions for its workers.

GDP growth will be a sluggish 1 percent for a year or so—especially when compared to 1989's spectacular 8.1 percent—but will inevitably turn upwards. The stagnant manufacturing sector likely will grow 2–3 percent, after having shrunk 12.4 percent in 1989 when suffering from tougher competition and high financing costs. Inflation should fall, down to around 40 percent, and the balance-of-payments will improve. The oil industry and growing export sector continue to provide glowing bright spots in the forecast. Even before the Iraq-Kuwait crisis, the Petroleosde Venezuela (PDVSA, the state oil company) expected export sales of $10.3 billion in 1990, up $200 million from 1989. Escalating oil prices as well as a surge in nontraditional exports clearly will benefit the trade surplus.

One of the Western Hemisphere's least densely populated countries, most Venezuelans reside in the Andes and along the coast. Only 4 percent of the population dwells in the half of the country south and east of the Orinoco River. One of five Venezuelans lives in Caracas. Of demographic significance: the population doubles every 20 years, meaning that 40 percent currently are under the age of 15, 70 percent under age 30. An unequal distribution of wealth exists between those who live in the capital and those who live on its outskirts in terrible slums called *barrios*. A significant percentage of Venezuelans have poor nutrition, housing, clothing, and education.

A word of warning: While Venezuela remains a fairly safe place to invest, it must be realized that corruption runs rampant, and it can be difficult to deal in a country where it seems that everybody has a price.

Yugoslavia

Prime Minister Ante Markovic's economic reforms have made him his divisive country's most popular politician—for the moment. In 1989, inflation soared at 2,500 percent. A wage freeze became instrumental in throttling inflation in this decentralized country where workers can vote themselves raises. The reform package that Markovic implemented in January 1990 has stablized the dinar by pegging it to the German mark. Both exports and imports have risen, foreign investment climbs now with fewer restrictions, and hard currency reserves expanded to $10 billion. The second stage of the reform program will call for the wholesale privatization of state-owned industry, a dramatic increase in governmental control over banks, and a radical change in the federal tax structure. With Belgrade demanding systemic changes in business operations, the six republics will be asked to bend to the will of the federal government.

Despite the upward direction of the economy under these plans, the republics will be loath to relinquish their cherished autonomy. Yugoslavia, after all, has the greatest ethnic and religious diversity in Eastern Europe, with more than a dozen nationalities, six languages, three religions, and even two different alphabets. Serbia, Coratia, Slovenia, Bosnia–Herzegovina, Montenegro, Macedonia, and the two self-governing provinces Kosovo and Vojvodina all tenaciously push their own agendas. For instance, Slovenia and Croatia, the two richest republics, have declared their intentions to secede unless Belgrade will guarantee them status in a Yugoslavian "confederation" (similar to France's involvement in the EC). These two republics also have asserted sovereignty over economic and military affairs—resenting the central government's tax plan and authority. Serbia, the largest province, has indicated that it has little interest in democracy or privatization. Serbia itself suffers from a secessionist movement. The 1.7 million ethnic Albanians within the Kosovo region of Serbia claim that they are maltreated and demand full autonomy as a new republic within Yugoslavia. In mid-August, Serbia voted for political autonomy in defiance of a ban Belgrade had placed on the poll.

Heated disputes in this fractured country ultimately may lead to civil war. Despite improving economic prospects, the state of political flux and social change threaten stability. Belgrade faces dire challenges to its authority in the coming months; how it resolves these questions will determine whether or not the country will fracture permanently.

The fragile unity and the vacuum of central authority will make the management of a transformation to democracy extremely difficult. A policy stalemate will be much more likely. And as with the other countries of Eastern Europe, the chain of irresponsibility, bankruptcy, and chaos will be hard to overcome. Even if the country can hold together, it will want to join the EC to hope for survival. The chance of this seems remote in light of Yugoslavia's poor human rights record, especially after the arrest and expulsion of the delegation sent to investigate alleged abuses in the summer of 1990.

Index